PICASSO THE PRINTMAKER: GRAPHICS FROM THE MARINA PICASSO COLLECTION

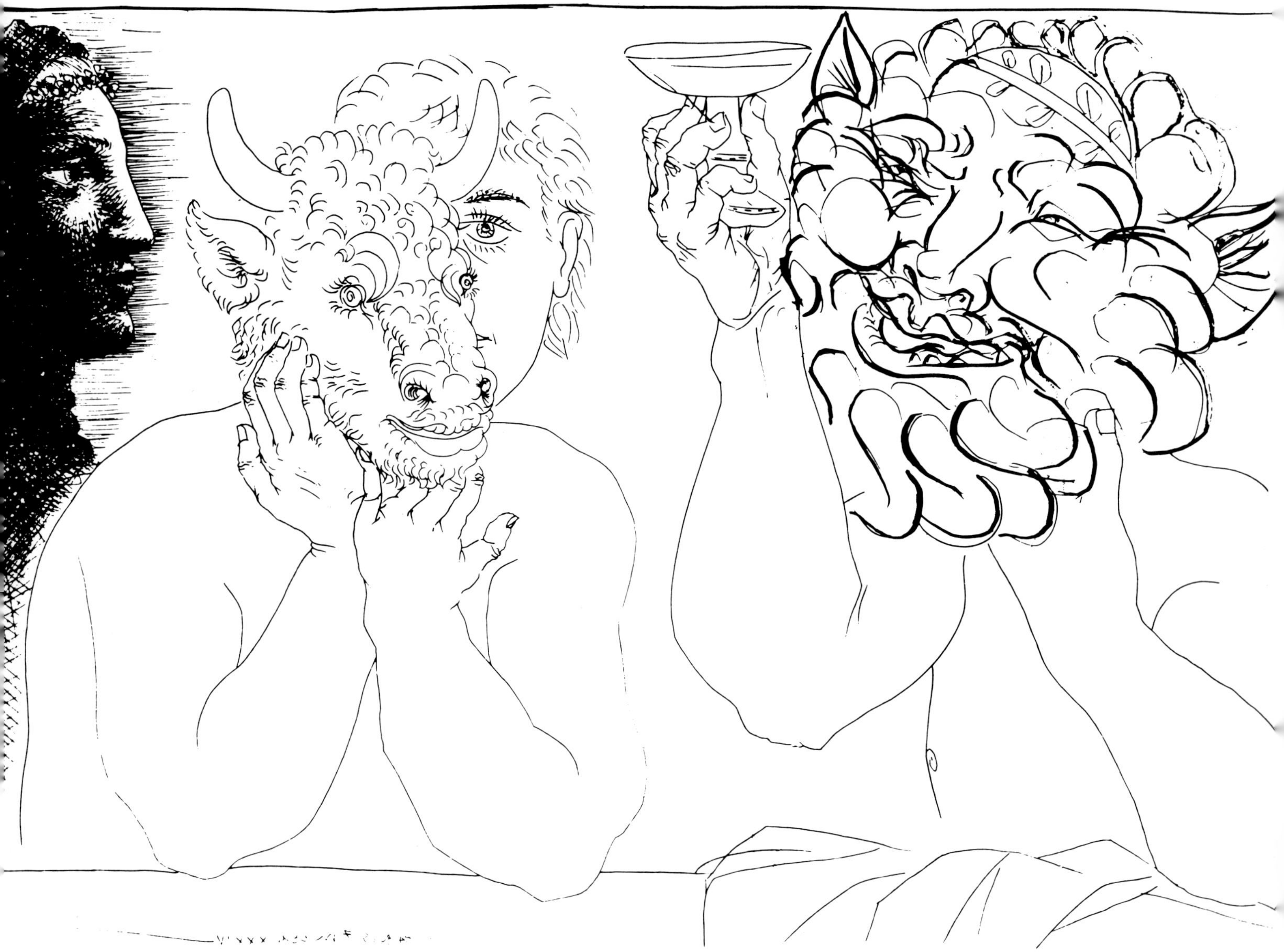

PICASSO THE PRINTMAKER: GRAPHICS FROM THE MARINA PICASSO COLLECTION

CATALOGUE BY:
BRIGITTE BAER

ORGANIZED BY:
STEVEN A. NASH

DALLAS MUSEUM OF ART

This exhibition was organized in cooperation with
Marina Picasso and the Galerie Jan Krugier, Geneva.

Exhibition dates:

Dallas Museum of Art	September 11 - October 30, 1983
The Brooklyn Museum	November 23, 1983 - January 8, 1984
The Detroit Institute of Arts	January 31 - March 25, 1984
The Denver Art Museum	April 7 - May 20, 1984

ISBN 0-9609622-4-7
Library of Congress Catalogue Card Number 83-072427
Printed in U.S.A. Brodnax Printing Company
Color separations: Harper House
Univers type: Typography Plus

Publisher: Robert V. Rozelle
Design: James A. Ledbetter
Editor: Dr. Steven A. Nash
Copy Editor: Allen T. Rozelle

Cover:
Tête de faune, cat. no. 169.

Frontispiece:
Jeune homme au masque de taureau, faune et profil de femme, cat. no. 45.

Table of Contents

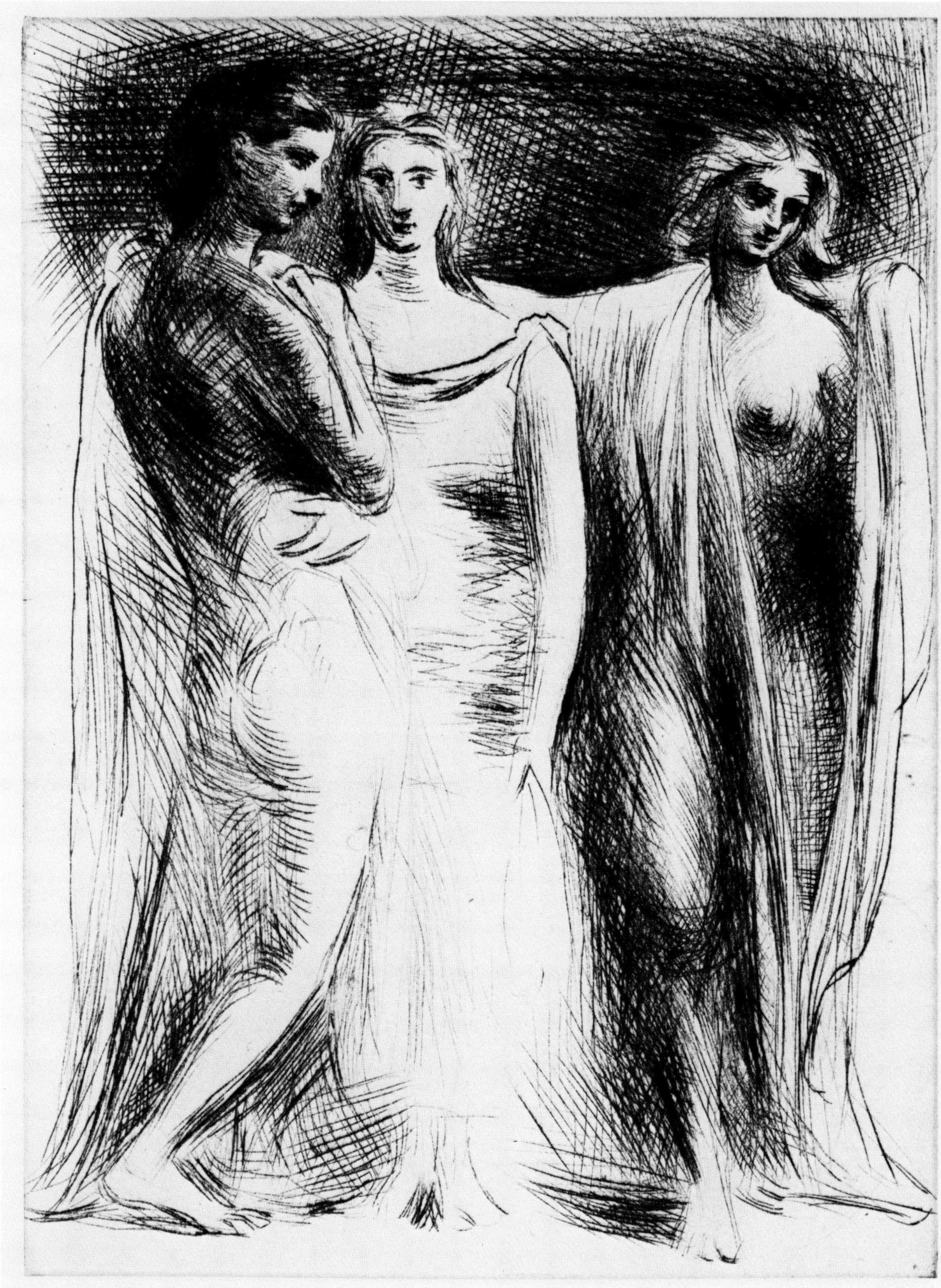

18d. Les Trois femmes

Preface

Of the great masters of the 20th century, none matched Picasso in commitment to the art of printmaking. Picasso's lifetime graphic achievement embraced a spectrum of technical means, from aquatint to lithography to linoleum cut, and he was capable of invention in each medium. The basic subject matter and themes of his painting oeuvre are often explored in great depth in his printmaking, where the numerous states of individual prints testify to his searching imagination. Not infrequently, he first experimented with an idea through printmaking before incorporating it in a painting. Picasso's lifelong interest in printmaking helps explain why he retained ownership of the vast collection of prints inherited by his granddaughter, Marina Picasso.

We are very proud that the Dallas Museum is the source of *Picasso the Printmaker: Graphics from the Marina Picasso Collection,* the first public exhibition of prints from this remarkable collection. We are grateful to Marina Picasso for sharing her collection with the American public. Following its opening in Dallas, the exhibition will travel to The Brooklyn Museum, The Detroit Institute of Arts, and The Denver Art Museum.

Jan Krugier, of the Galerie Krugier, Geneva, first suggested the idea for the exhibition and was instrumental in helping to coordinate the exportation of the art works. Brigitte Baer, who has spent the past three years completing the catalogue raisonné of Picasso's graphics begun by Bernhard Geiser, is the author of this catalogue and selected the works displayed in the exhibition. Her insightful and original observations will certainly stimulate additional interest in the artist's uniquely comprehensive oeuvre.

Dr. Steven A. Nash, Assistant Director/Chief Curator, organized *Picasso the Printmaker* and coordinated the demanding international effort necessary for its realization. His scholarly contribution to the catalogue is also considerable. Robert V. Rozelle, DMA Publisher, supervised the production of the exhibition catalogue.

We are confident that this exhibition portends an ambitious program of creative exhibition development, origination and circulation in the new Dallas Museum of Art, opening in 1984.

Harry S. Parker III
Director

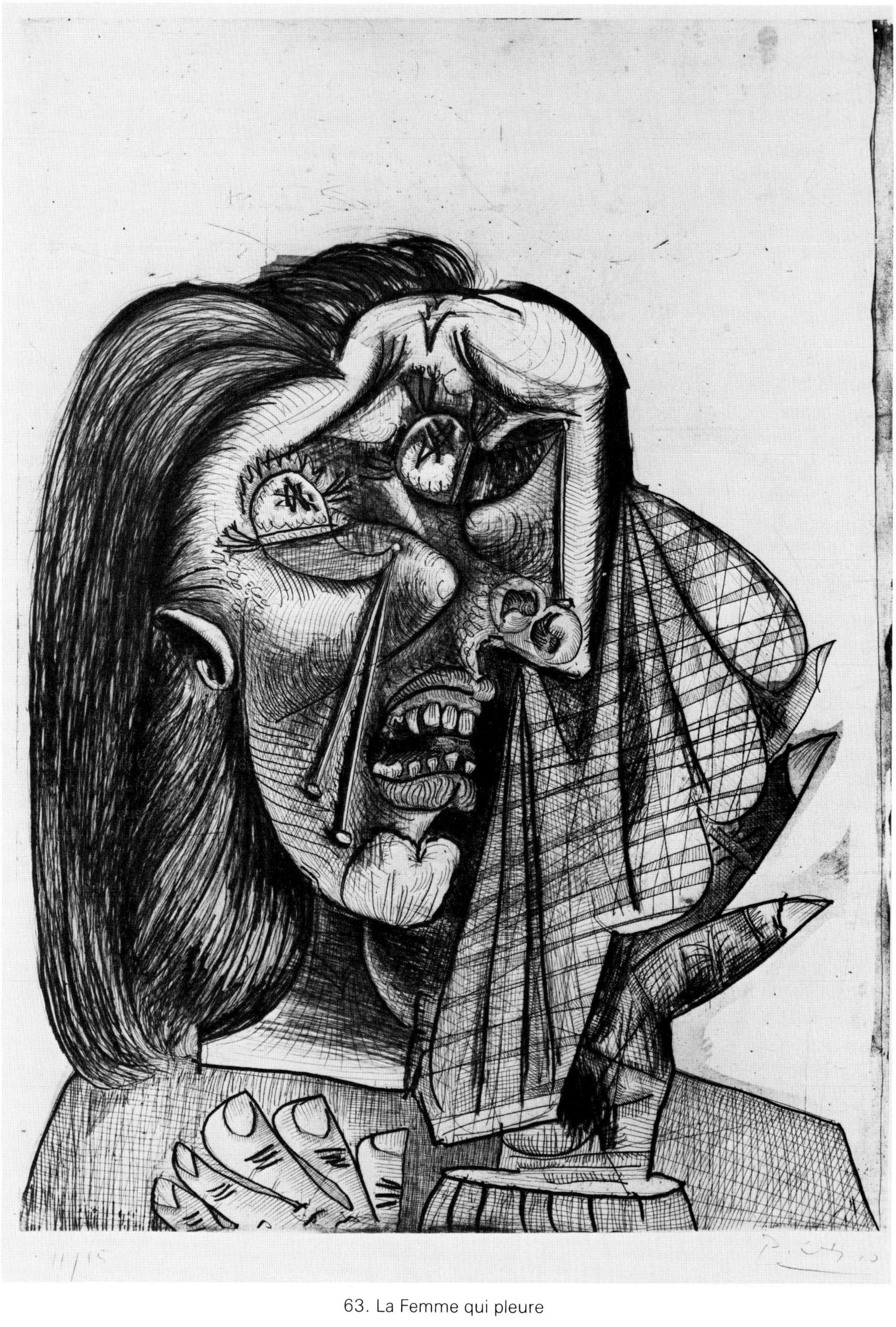

63. La Femme qui pleure

Foreword

Picasso . . . this magician with pen, brush and etching needle, this civilized shaman, this tragedian and humorist. So much has been written about him, yet so much remains to be learned and comprehended. One particularly fertile territory for further study is found in his prints, which to date have been only partially catalogued and which form an immense body of formal and thematic explorations produced in counterpoint to his work in other media. As Brigitte Baer explains in her catalogue text, they are perhaps the most consistently autobiographical aspect of Picasso's *oeuvre,* forming a visual diary of the artist's thoughts and experiences.

We are therefore particularly pleased to be able to present so large and distinguished a selection of Picasso's graphic work, ranging in date throughout virtually his entire career and in media and style over the full scope of his output. The last exhibitions devoted exclusively to Picasso's graphics appeared in this country many years ago. This is the first since the artist's death, and the first one, therefore, in which his total achievement as a printmaker can be assessed. Futhermore, the catalogue accompanying the present show, while containing a great deal of new technical and factual information about the works exhibited, also represents the first time that many of these works have received a thorough-going iconographical analysis.

The person making all of this possible, and to whom we owe a great debt of thanks, is, of course, Marina Picasso, who has generously agreed to lend 253 prints and 25 printing plates from her personal collection of her grandfather's work. Other segments of Marina Picasso's collection have been exhibited in Europe and Japan, but this is the first occassion on which her prints have been allowed a public audience. Particularly exciting is the fact that the exhibited selection contains so many rare states and complete runs of states. We are convinced that the exhibition will provide a fascinating and moving experience for its visitors, and for this opportunity we are extremely grateful to Marina Picasso.

The first idea for this show arose in conversations with Jan Krugier, and throughout the organizational process we have been aided by the kind assistance of the staff of the Galerie Krugier in Geneva, particularly Jeannine Stepczynski. We are especially indebted to M. Krugier for one brilliant suggestion, his nomination of Brigitte Baer as our guest curator. The exhibition, quite simply, could not have been accomplished without Brigitte Baer's intelligent and dedicated guidance. Under the most stringent of deadlines, she made the selection of works, catalogued them, arranged for photography, arranged for inking of the exhibited printing plates and wrote an extensive essay. Her efforts can only be described as Herculean.

To organize so major an exhibition in so short a period of time (we began only in April 1983) places a great burden on all involved. It therefore is a special pleasure to be able to thank those staff members of the Dallas Museum of Art who participated so helpfully and energetically. Anne Umland, Curatorial Administrative Assistant, and Elizabeth Simon, Curatorial Intern, put long and hard hours into research and manuscript preparation, and Melissa Berry, Educational Administrative Assistant, also assisted with the manuscript. Robert Rozelle, Editor and Publicity Director, managed under a great deal of pressure the production of the catalogue; Debra Richards, Registrar, handled insurance and shipping arrangements; Anna McFarland, Assistant Curator for Exhibitions, worked with Fine Arts Express of Boston on matting and framing; Donna Rhein, Librarian, helped with research; Thomas Livesay, Assistant Director for Administration, worked out contractual details; and Harry Parker, Director, provided general support from the outset of the project. I would also like to thank Allen Rozelle, of Geneva and Paris, for assistance in editing, and Jim Ledbetter, of Dallas, for his sensitive catalogue design.

Steven A. Nash
Assistant Director/Chief Curator

Dedicated to Dr. Bernhard Geiser

Introduction and Acknowledgments

Given the fact that it is now some eight years or more that I have been exclusively buried in the work of Picasso, often actually handling his paintings, sculptures, drawings, prints, manuscripts, etc., I am particularly grateful to Marina Picasso, Jan Krugier and Steven Nash for having given me the opportunity to show in Dallas some of the prints I especially like. In addition, it is three years now since I began work on completing the catalogue raisonné of Picasso graphics begun by Dr. Bernhard Geiser but left unfinished, as his death intervened when he had reached the year 1934. The volumes continuing this *magnum opus* will be published shortly.

This exhibition is made up of a selection of prints drawn exclusively from the personal collection of Marina Ruiz Picasso. In addition to the limitations imposed by the scale of our exhibition, certain prints and proofs which I would have liked to include were beyond our boundaries since they do not form part of Marina Picasso's collection. The visitor should realize that, after the death of the artist, his estate was divided into several parts which were then allotted to the various heirs.

Furthermore, I should point out, without discharging any of my personal responsibility for the inevitable errors in the text, that the final arrangements to hold the exhibition were only agreed upon in April of this year, with a deadline for catalogue text in July. This obviously necessitated certain rapid choices both in the selection of prints, which is a highly personal process, and in the approach to Picasso in the text. Hence, the actual writing and translation of the catalogue was done in less than seven weeks.

Whenever possible, I have attempted to include results of my research into Picasso's iconography. In fact, an enormous amount of work needs to be done on this aspect of the artist, especially regarding his prints. Given the short period for producing this catalogue, what I propose here are tentative analyses and in no way should be considered definitive judgements. Hopefully, this exhibition will stimulate further research into this fascinating and complex subject.

It is thanks to the familiarity which I have acquired during my eight years of daily contact with Picasso's work that I have made some rather daring attempts at unravelling his mysterious and hard-to-penetrate iconography. Picasso made about 2,500 intaglio prints, lithographs and linocuts. As is well-known, his inventiveness, his sense of humor, his skill and the boldness of his genius were expressed in a free way owing to his daily use of the tools of his trade. Hardly a day ever passed in 75 years without Picasso being found hard at work. This is one of the reasons why I have chosen to show so many states of prints as well as the copperplates, linoblocks and other working materials, so that the visitor may perceive the day to day progression both of the development of his ideas and of the purely technical changes in his work.

Picasso's graphic work constitutes a personal daily diary even more, if this is conceivable, than the other varied aspects of his creativity. With the exception of *Guernica*, the artist never gave a single title to any of his works. All the titles by which we know them now have more or less haphazard origins. This hatred for labels does not make our task any easier when we try to understand or to enter into his world. Everything should be self-explanatory, if explanation there is. We should never forget simply to look, just as Picasso always wanted his public to do.

Finally, I hope that I have been able to communicate to the visitor the personal love which Picasso felt for ''his'' plates. If so, both he and I will be more than satisfied.

I would like to thank for their kindness and help during my research into Picasso's graphic work: Irina Antonova,

Martin de Alzaga, Marie-Laure Barnadac, Pierre-André Benoit, Georges and Jenny Bloch, Hans Bolliger, Dominique Bozo, Anselmo Carini, François Chapon, Victor Carlson, Riva Castleman, Alfonso Ciranna, Patrick Cramer, George A. Embericos, Jean Fournier, Eleanore Garvey, Gustav Gili, Patrick Goetelen, Sebastian and Herman Goeppert, Jean Hughes, Colta Ives, Harold Joachim, André Koti, Jan Krugier, Marcel Lecomte, Louise Leiris, Bernard Lirman, Florence Loewy, Laurence Marceillac, Mr. Mazo, Stephen Mazoh, Paule Mazouet, Sarah McNear, Jean-François Méjanès, Manuela Mena, P. Michel, Ted Mosher, Fernand Mourlot, Maïte Ocaña, Priscilla Owens, Jean Parisel, Bernard Picasso, Claude Picasso, Jacqueline Picasso, Marina Picasso, Paloma Picasso-Lopez, Christine Picasso, Pierre Rosenberg, Bill Rubin, Yves Sangiovanni, Larry Sapphire, Hélène Seckel, Christine Stauffer and all the staff of the Galerie Kornfeld, Barbara Stern-Shapiro, Denise Sugar, Erwin Treu, Javier Vilato, Mr. Walker, Françoise Woimant, Susumu Yamamoto.

I would like to thank especially Daniella Benedetti who drew the map and the instruments reproduced in the glossary, selected the list of exhibitions and was of great help in establishing Picasso's biography, and Judith Schub who translated the chapters dealing with Dora Maar and Françoise Gilot and helped in compiling the glossary and the biography; also Anne Worms who typed them, David and Caroline Leclerc who verified all the numerical references in Zervos, etc., Martine Jolibois whose devotion to Picasso's prints helped a great deal in the practical work of selection, Darryl Isley who helped with the selection and the translation, Josep Paulau i Fabre whose oral communications were precious, as well as Antoine Coron who kindly lent me the result of his work on *Le Sagittaire*'s archives; Aldo and Piero Crommelynck who inked the copperplates when it was necessary and gave me invaluable information concerning Picasso's technique in the very last series of prints.

I am especially indebted to André Green, Yves de Fontbrune, who gave the authorization to reproduce Picasso's photograph of Dora Maar, Maya Picasso, who lent me the photographs of her mother and her drawings and gave me continuous moral support during this long, and too short, period of intensive work, and Michele Richet who allowed me to disturb the Musée Picasso's daily routine in order to verify the dates and techniques of the early prints.

I am also extremely grateful to Hélène Iliazd, who with patient resignation allowed me to burrow like a mole through her extensive documentation of her late husband's work. Without Ebi Kornfeld and Georges Bloch, I would never have embarked on the continuation of Geiser's catalogue raisonné. With his quiet understanding, Ebi Kornfeld has allowed me to anticipate the forthcoming publication of our catalogue so as to give the visitors to this exhibition the opportunity to share in some of the results of my research.

Finally, I must say that without Madeleine Lacourière and Jacques Frélaut, I would never have been able to write this catalogue. Both of them were infinitely patient with my never-ending questions during the last three years; patient, helpful and supportive in the kind of isolation in which one finds oneself when doing such minute research. It is thanks to Jacques Frélaut, who patiently explained to me all the nuances of a printer's technique and who showed me how Picasso's hand would work on the plates, that I have acquired the little knowledge which I possess on the subject. Lastly I must thank I. W. whose desire is to remain anonymous but who translated most of this catalogue and helped me to put directly into English the last chapter.

Paris, the 7th of July, 1983
Brigitte Baer

List of abbreviations

B.	Georges Bloch, *Pablo Picasso, Catalogue de l'oeuvre gravé et lithographié;* I, Berne, 1968; II, Berne, 1971; IV, Berne, 1979.
Bloch, Livre	*Ibid.,* I, chapter on books, p. 305 ff.
Bartsch	Adam, Bartsch, *Catalogue raisonné de toutes les estampes qui forment l'oeuvre de Rembrandt, et ceux de ses principaux imitateurs,* Vienne, 1797.
D.B.	Pierre Daix and Georges Boudaille, *Picasso 1900-1906,* Neuchâtel, 1966.
D. R.	Pierre Daix and Joan Rosselet, *Le Cubisme de Picasso: 1907-1916,* Neuchâtel, 1979.
Engelberts	Edwin Engelberts, *Georges Braque. Oeuvre Graphique,* Genève, 1958.
Friedländer-Rosenberg	M. J. Friedländer and J. Rosenberg, *Die Gemälde von Lucas Cranach,* Berlin, 1932.
G.	Bernhard Geiser, *Picasso peintre-graveur,* 2 volumes, Berne, 1933 and 1968.
G.W.	Pierre Gassier and Juliet Wilson, *Vie et oeuvre de Francisco de Goya,* Fribourg, 1970.
L.	Galerie Louise Leiris, *Picasso, 156 gravures récentes,* Paris, 1973.
Lemoisne	Paul André Lemoisne, *Degas et son oeuvre,* Paris, 1946-1949.
M.	Fernand Mourlot, *Picasso lithographe,* Monte-Carlo, 1970.
Matarasso	H. Matarasso, *Bibliographie des livres illustrés par Pablo Picasso, 1905-1956,* Nice, 1956.
Palau	Josep Palau i Fabre, *Picasso vivent: 1881-1907,* Barcelona, 1980 (English ed.: *Picasso: the Early Years 1881-1907,* New York, 1981).
S.V.	Hans Bolliger, *Pablo Picasso, Suite Vollard,* Stuttgart, 1956 (English ed.: New York, 1956).
Spies	Werner Spies, *Les Sculptures de Picasso,* Lausanne, 1971.
Z.	Christian Zervos, *Pablo Picasso,* Paris, 1932-1978, 34 volumes, I-XXXIII.

Catalogue Notes

1. The measurements given in this catalogue (height precedes width) refer to the size of the plate mark on the proof and not to the size of the plate itself. A discrepancy therefore exists with measurements given by Bloch in volumes II and IV of his catalogue raisonné, as he relied in these volumes on the size of the copperplates communicated to him by the Crommelynck brothers. On the contrary, in his volume I, Bloch, just as Geiser, gives the size of the plate mark. One must also be aware of the fact that, while Japan paper hardly shrinks at all in the drying process, Arches wove paper shrinks somewhat more and Rives wove paper shrinks even more. The papers which shrink the most are Auvergne handmade paper and, to a lesser degree, Montval laid paper. Trial proofs can shrink more than numbered impressions as they sometimes dry in rather haphazard circumstances.

As for the lithographs, the measurements are those of the image; lithographic stones and zincplates are usually larger than the ''imaged'' part of them. The measurements of the linocuts refer to the size of the image although this size usually corresponds also to the size of the linoblock.

2. When we write that a proof is annotated without mentioning by whom, it means that it was annotated by the artist himself. The same applies to the copperplates and linoblocks.

3. As the visitor will see, there are very few signed proofs in our exhibition. Picasso never signed his state and trial proofs unless he was about to give one to a friend, which was very rare (Paul Eluard received a few). As a matter of fact, he never signed his work before it was either put on sale or given away. When he received, as a kind of payment, a large number of copies of a book illustrated with his prints, he often did not bother to sign his own copies (e.g. *Gongora* or *La Tauromaquia*). After 1961, he never took the time to sign his own artist's proofs of the linocuts. He found signing proofs to be a bore, especially when done in large quantities, and felt his time was better spent in other ways. Furthermore, it was a type of security for him. He knew that unsigned works would be less likely to be ''borrowed'' by souvenir hunters visiting his home.

Printers' proofs are also rarely signed, which does not mean they are not often of very high quality, being usually trial proofs pulled before the definitive printing of the commissioned impressions. Occasionally someone bought one or two from one of the printers and took them to Picasso to have them signed.

Clearly in Picasso's case the fact that a work is unsigned has no influence whatsoever on its authenticity nor has it any bearing on its value. For the reasons cited above, practically all Picasso's works in his estate had never been signed.

4. From 1929 to 1936, Picasso used to date his works with the year in Roman numerals. In 1929 he used both Arabic and Roman numbers. From 1930 to the end of 1936 he used exclusively Roman. In 1937, he returned to a system of Arabic numeration. Although there is no known explanation for this fact, the period of exclusively Roman numeration coincides almost exactly with the appearance of Marie-Thérèse in his work and was terminated at the moment Dora Maar settled into his life. It is somewhat ironical when we think of Picasso's attitude in general towards art history, that he took such pains from 1926-1928 onwards to date with extreme precision all aspects of his work. It is almost as if, despite everything, he became more and more conscious, as time went on, of the future of his place in the history of modern art. Even a series of works executed on the same day is correctly annotated in its exact chronological order, indicated by a number in Roman numerals.

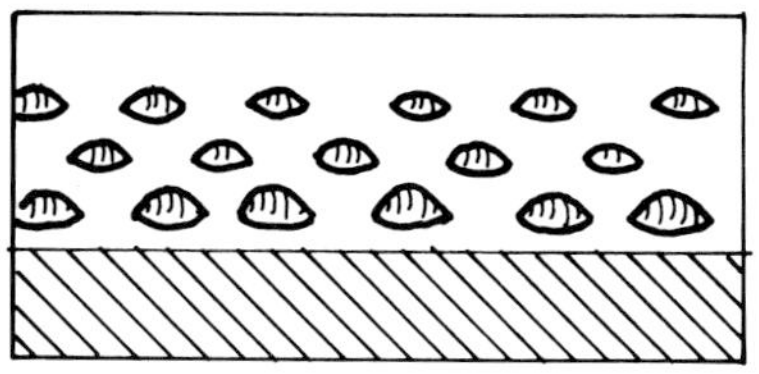

Aquatint resin grains on the plate.

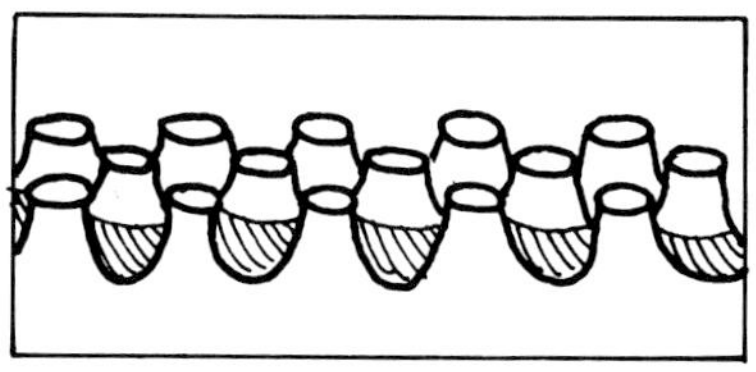

Aquatint grained plate after biting.

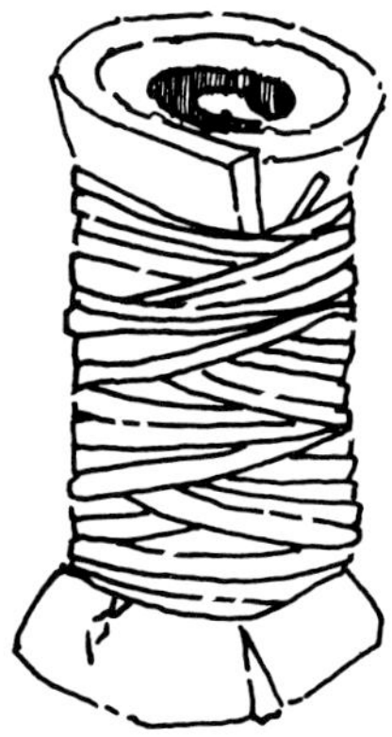

The dabber

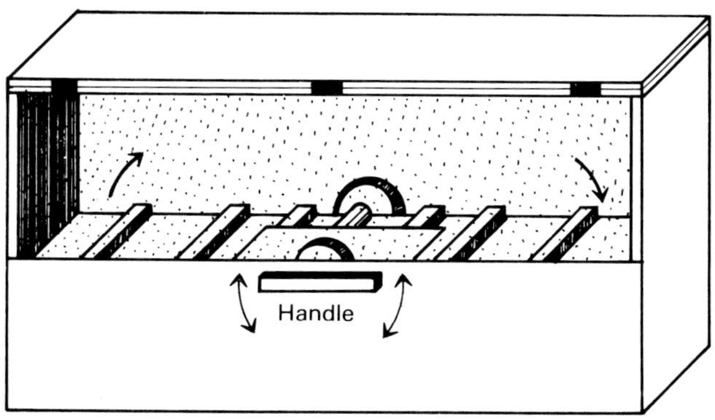

The dusting box

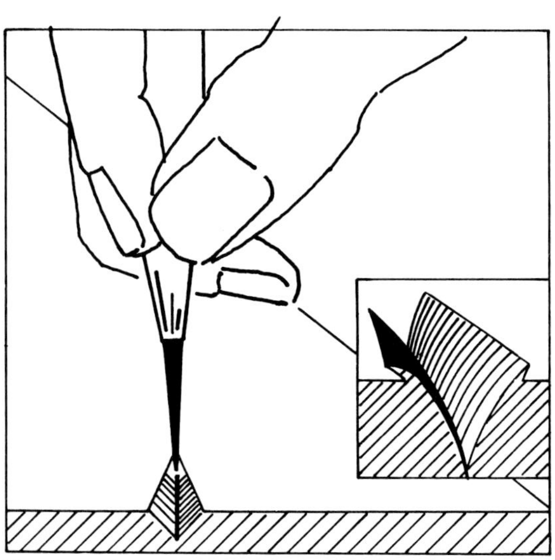

The dry point

Glossary

A brief list of terms related to Picasso's printmaking techniques

Aquatint

An etching process used to produce continuous areas of tone on the copperplate through the controlled application of small particles of resin. These particles are uniformly distributed on the plate by using a dusting box. Then they are fused to the plate by heating. When the plate is put into an acid bath in order to be bitten, the resin particles protect the small surfaces they cover from the biting, and the result is , on the proof, a dark surface with small roundish white spots. Aquatint can be used on all the surface of a plate, and then worked with a scraper. It can be used also on a plate where the areas which should remain white on the proof are protected with varnish from either graining and biting, or only from biting. It can also be employed with the sugar-lift technique: see chapter 7.

Burin

Sharp, square-headed tool used to incise lines into a copperplate. *Pushing* this tool through the metal requires a great deal of force. The beginning of a burin stroke is always pointed; the end tapers to a point in most professional engravings. Picasso usually did not taper the end of his lines.

Dabber

A small roll of cloth used to ink the copperplate with inks of different colors. A brush can also be used. The word dabber is a general term for anything used in putting several colors of ink onto the plate.

Drypoint

A sharp unwieldy needle which scratches into the plate without removing any substance: the metal is simply deflected up out of the grooves into flanking ridges. These ragged ridges catch the ink and produce a velvety burr around the printed line. After a few proofs are pulled, the burr wears out and the ridge of metal prints white. Drypoint is usually *pulled* into the metal of the plate.

Etching

A technique in which the surface of the plate is covered with a ground, usually varnish, that is then scratched into by the artist using a needle or scraper. The plate is immersed in acid which eats away those parts of the plate no longer protected by the varnish ground. Aquatint is based in the same technique.

Intaglio
Category of printmaking in which the lines to be printed are below the surface of the plate. The plate is inked and wiped. The paper is dampened, and plate and paper are put through a press which forces the paper into the inked grooves. Since the paper is usually larger than the plate, a mark, called a plate mark or plate line is left on the paper.

Linocut
See chapter 11. As in the production of woodcuts, a gouge is generally used to make a linocut. Both are means of making relief prints, in which everything is cut away from the block except the lines to be printed. Picasso used all sorts of tools to excavate his linoblocks.

Lithography
Printmaking process using fine limestone or chemically treated zincplates. The image is drawn onto the stone or plate with greasy ink or crayon, then the stone is wet down. When the greasy printing ink is applied, the wet areas repel the ink, while the drawn areas retain the ink. Printing is made on slightly dampened paper (see chapter 10). There are usually no plate lines in lithography. The stone or zincplate is usually much bigger than the "imaged" parts of them. The artist can draw with lithographic crayons, or with greasy lithographic ink. He can also scrape and engrave the stone or zincplate, to create clean open areas.

Mezzotint
Engraving technique used to produce areas of full black and white. The engraver textures the entire plate with a rocker, producing an allover black. Then he scrapes and burnishes the metal to lighten different parts of the plate in order to produce his image. Picasso never used this technique. He preferred making his black background through the use of very fine resin aquatint.

Scraper
Engraving tool with sharp triangular edges. The scraper blade is usually bent to facilitate using one of these triangular edges. Picasso used this instrument extensively. He used it in a traditional manner to scrape lines or aquatinted areas, obtaining wide, white lines or whitish surfaces. Sometimes he used the sharp edge to produce wide, grey strokes which were short and parallel, since the scraper slid on the copperplate, digging in only at intervals. He also used the sharp end pulling it like a drypoint needle.

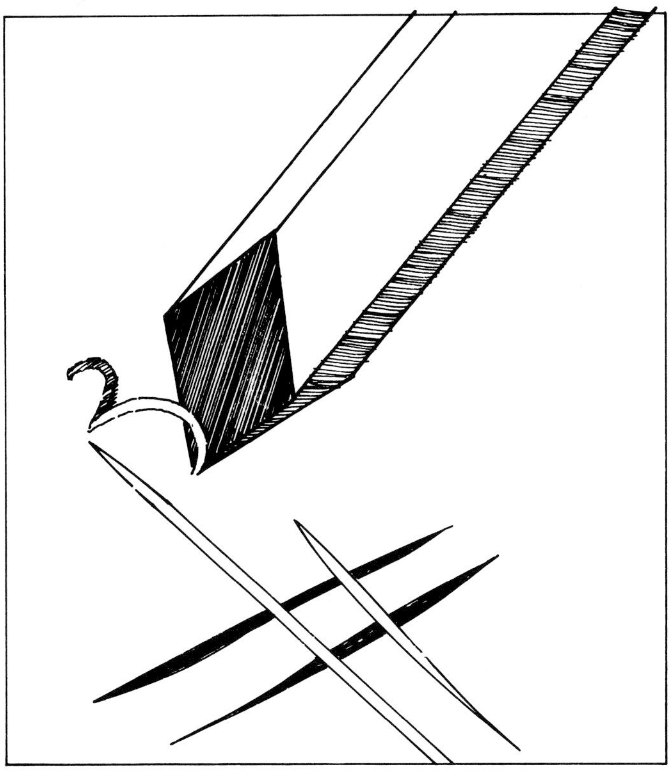

The burin

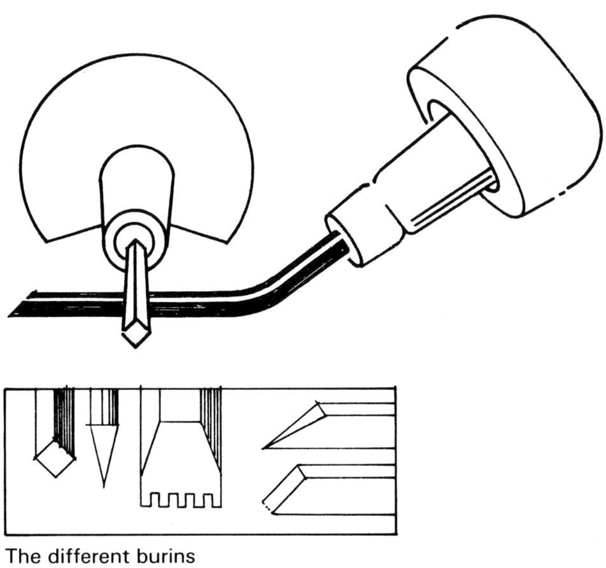

The different burins

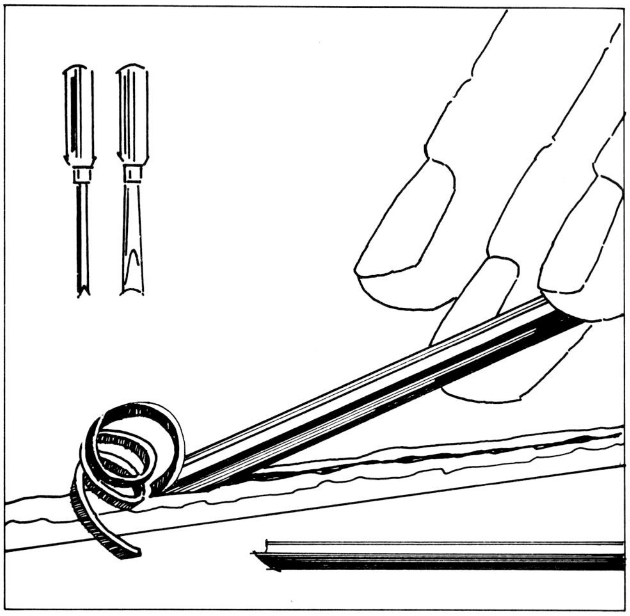

The woodcut / The lino-cut

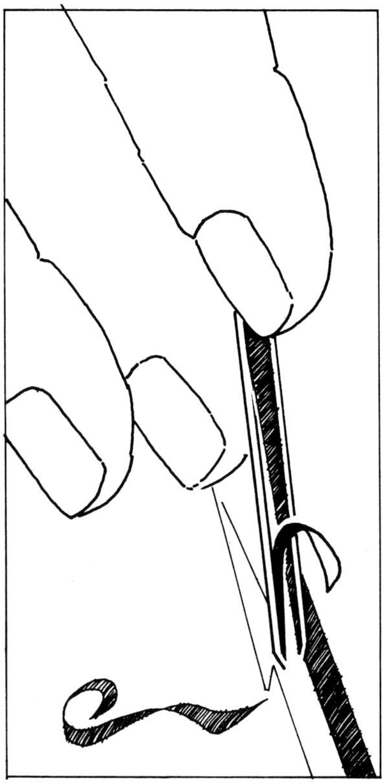

The woodcut / The lino-cut

State
When a plate or stone is printed and then changed, each step for which prints exist is called a state.

Steelfacing
Copper is a soft metal, which gradually wears out as numerous impressions are pulled from a plate. By means of a catalytic process, a very thin layer of steel can be applied to the printing surface of a copperplate. Before the plate is steelfaced, its edges are usually bevelled so that the plate does not tear the paper when both are put through the press under pressure. Sometimes the plate is already bevelled before the artist begins work on it. Some of Picasso's plates had to be steelfaced without being bevelled, since he had worked the plate all the way to its edges. The copperplate for the *Minotauromachie*, however, was already bevelled before Picasso worked on it. Picasso always hated steelfacing, and only after 1963, when he began to work with the Crommelynck brothers, were all of his copperplates automatically bevelled and steelfaced. Vollard, too, steelfaced his plates as a matter of rule, since he made very large editions. Lacourière only steelfaced a plate if it was too fragile to print more than a few impressions. When Frélaut pulled the prints in the group called *La Caisse à remords*, he sometimes could only produce four, twelve or eighteen impressions, since the copperplates were not steelfaced. As Iliazd only made small editions, he never steelfaced his plates.

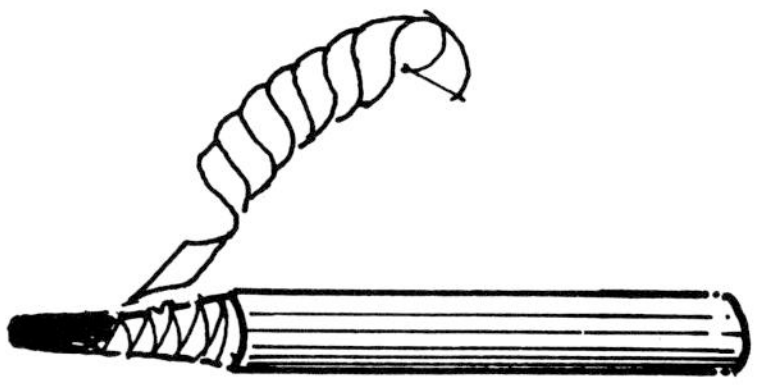

Litho-crayon in pencil form

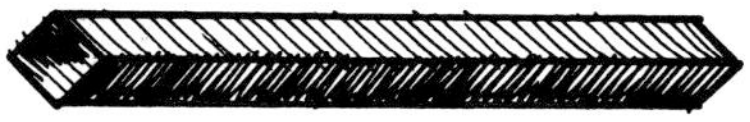

Litho-crayon in sticks

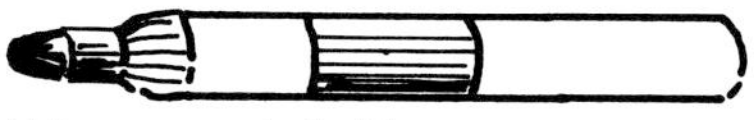

Litho-crayon in holder

Instruments used for lithographic drawings.

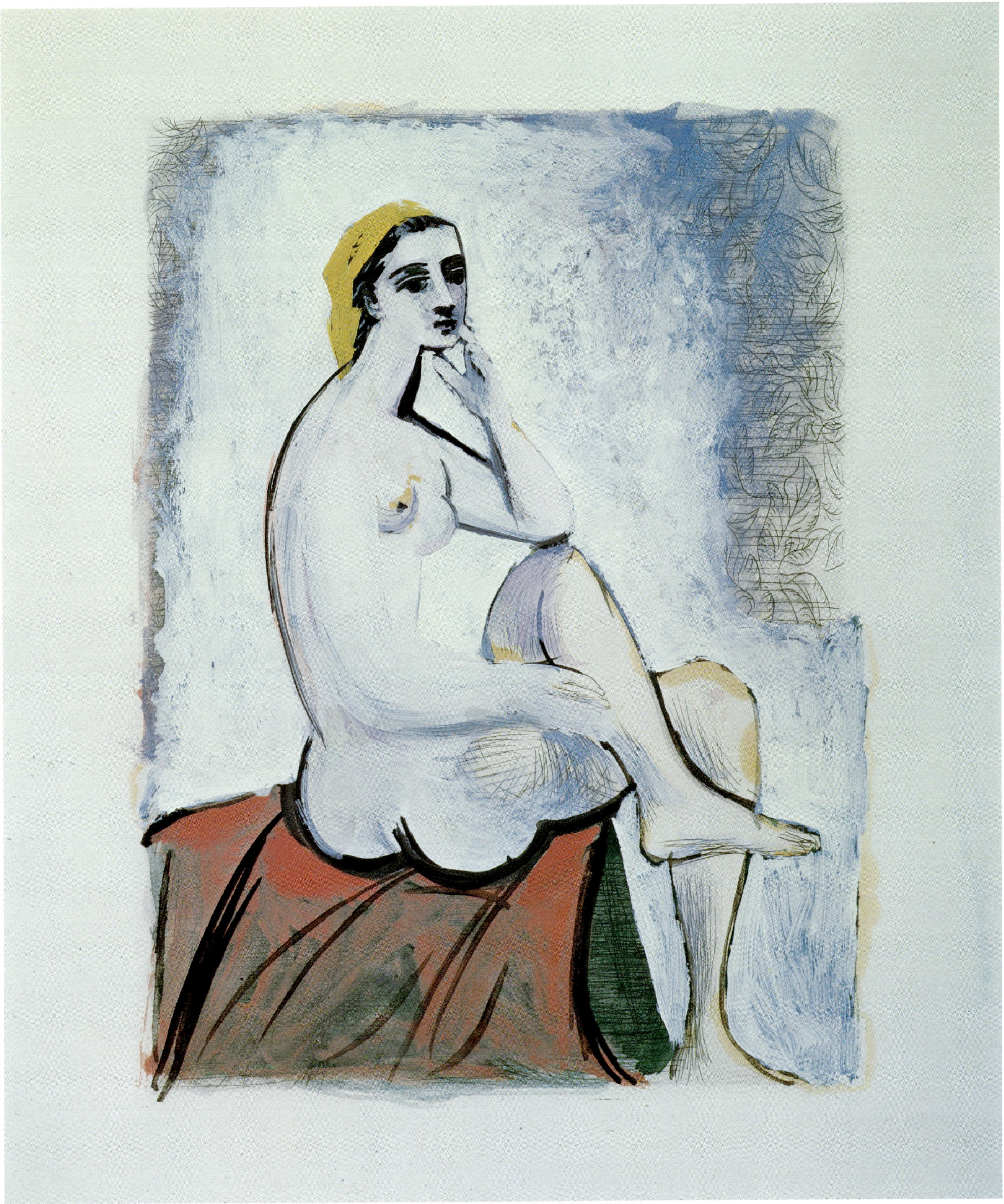

20. Baigneuse au pouf rouge

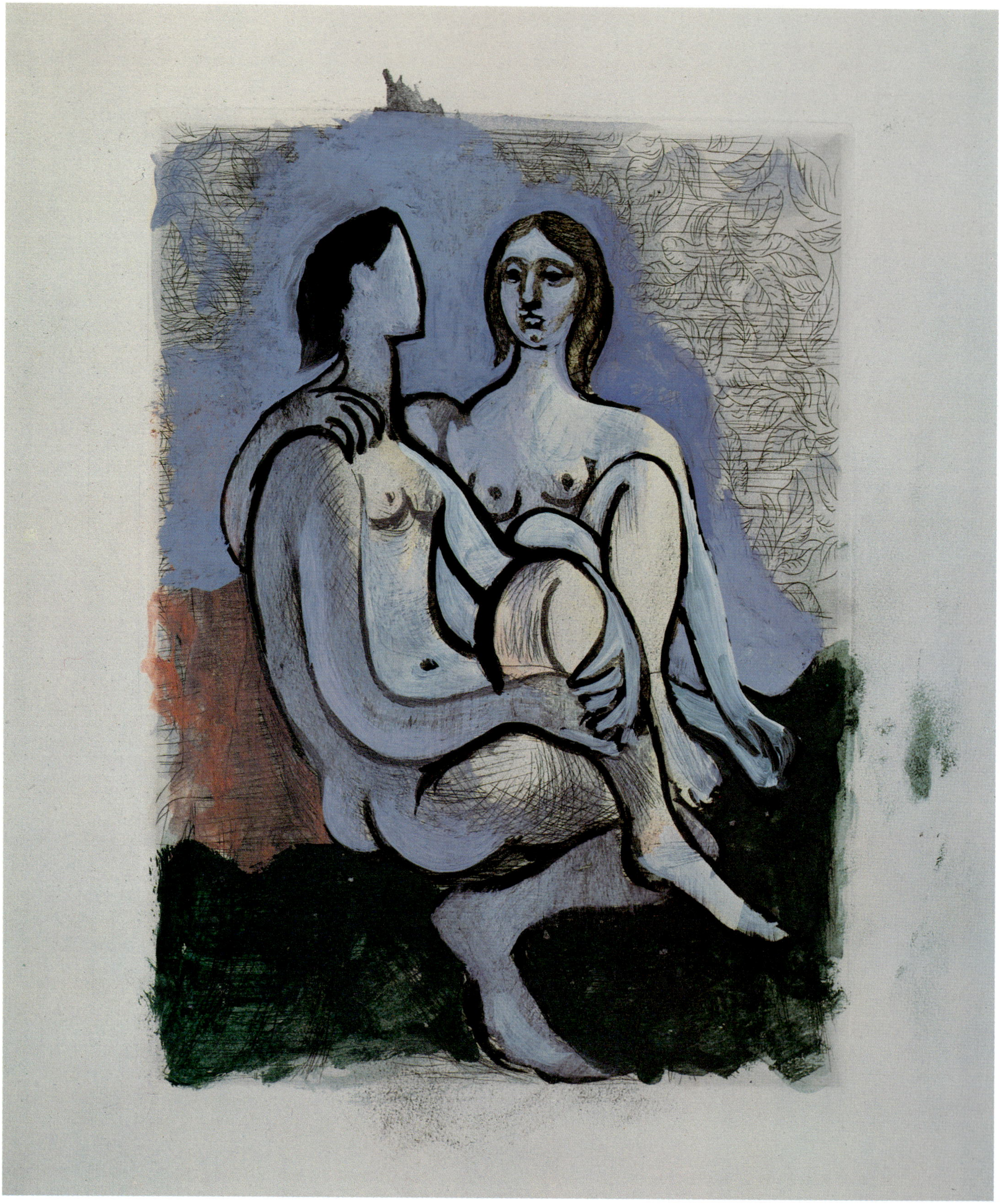

21. Deux Femmes

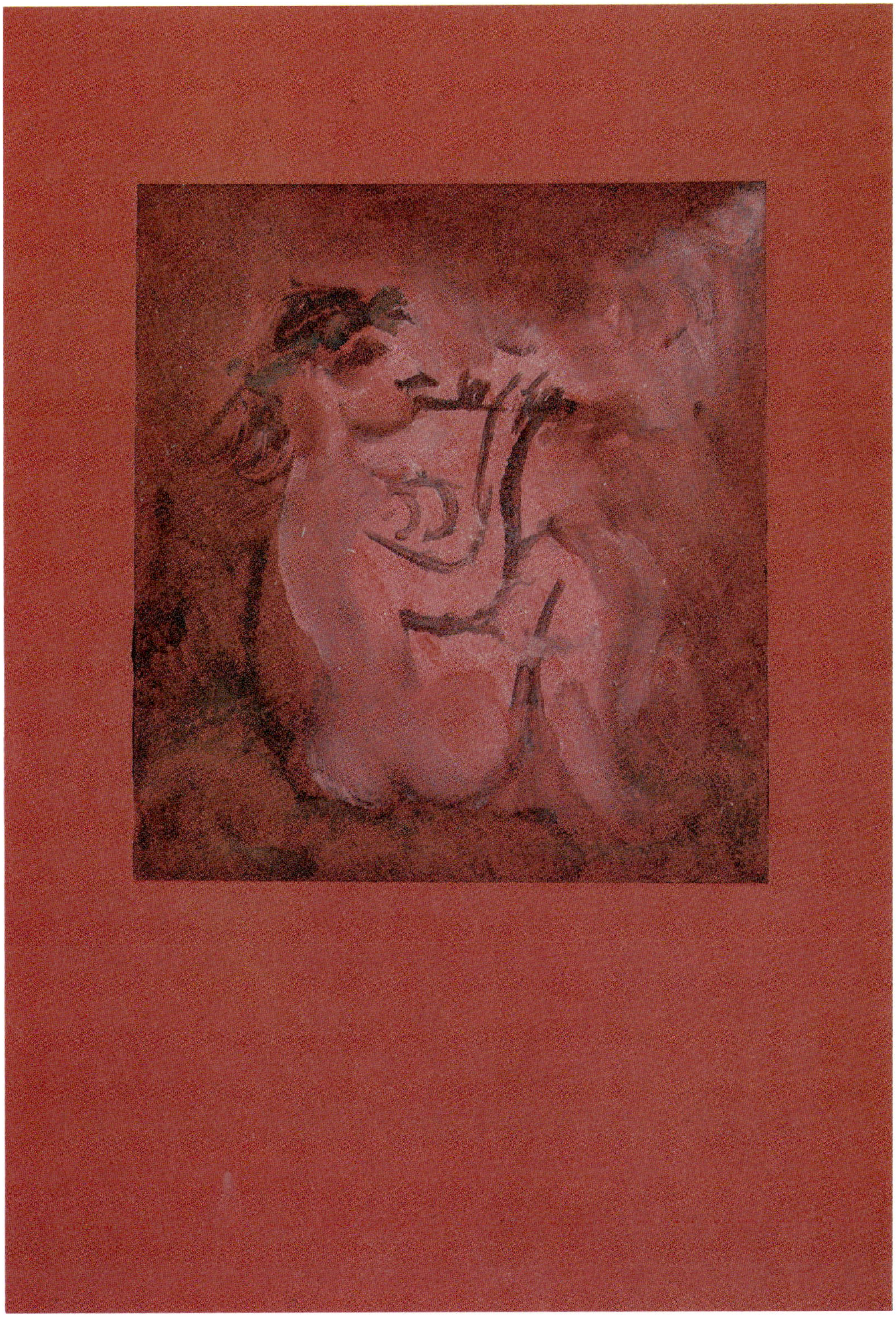

32a. Flûtiste; Musicienne et dormeuse

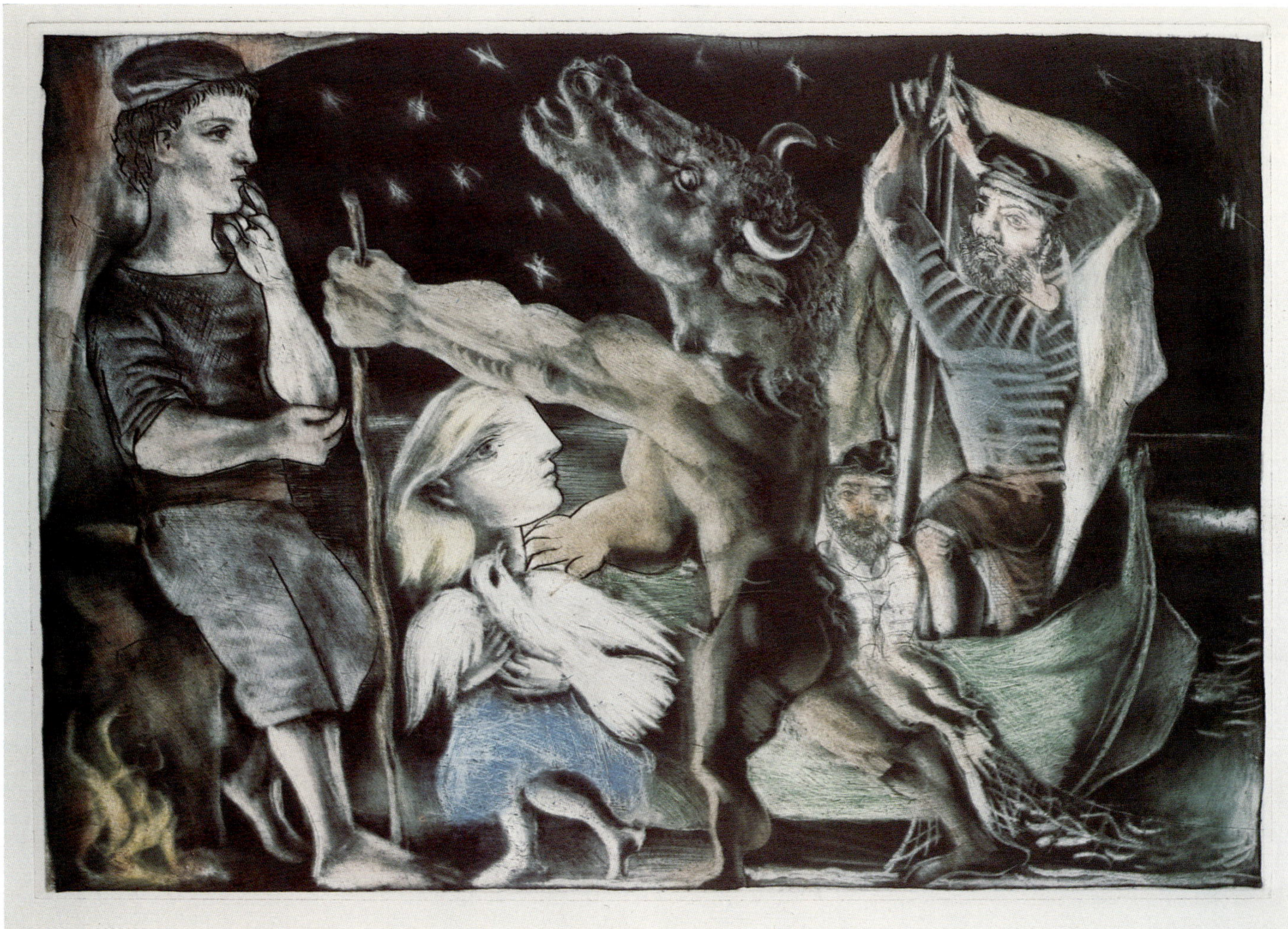

50. Minotaur aveugle guidé par une fillette dans la nuit

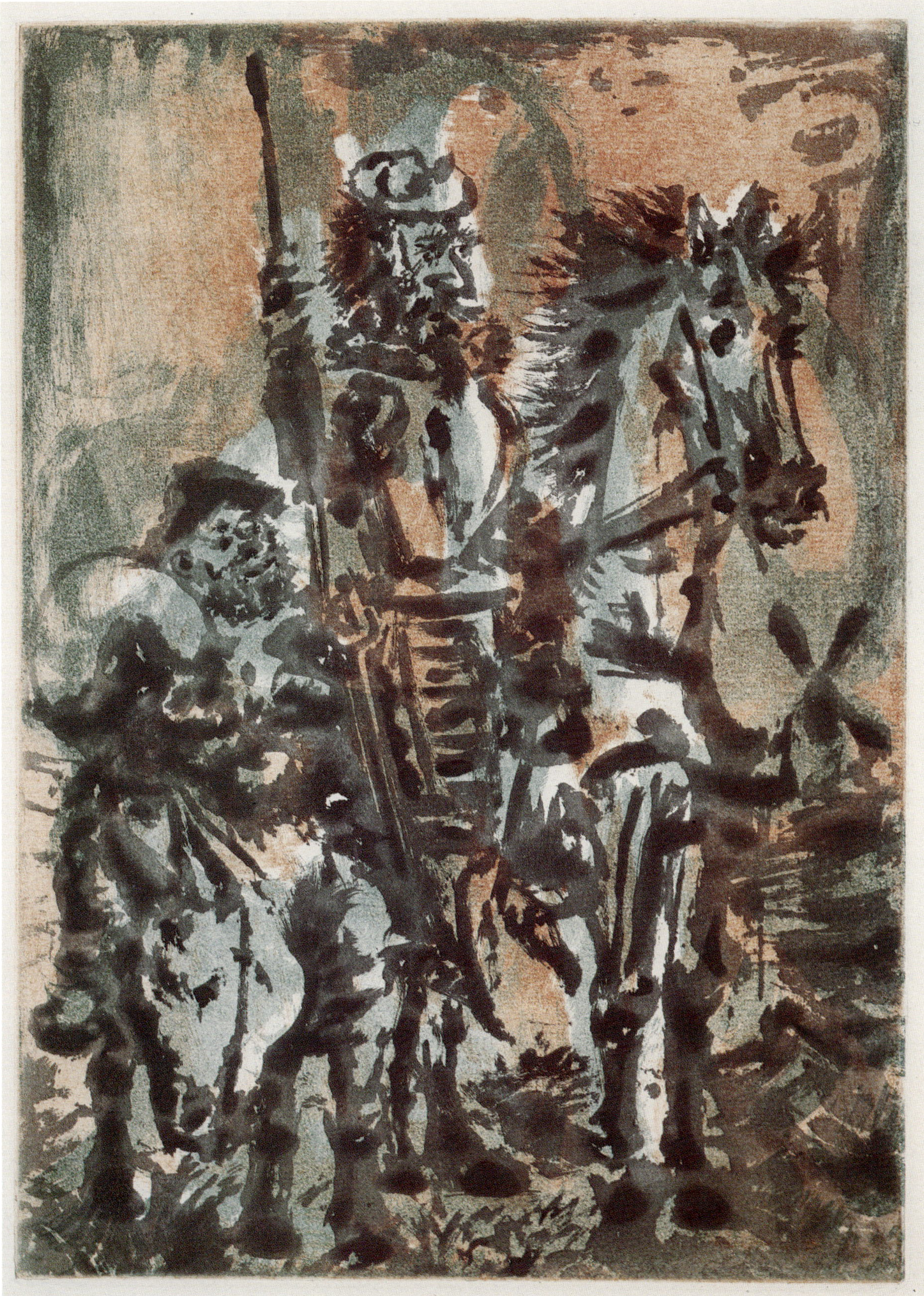

65b. Don Quijote y Sancho Panza

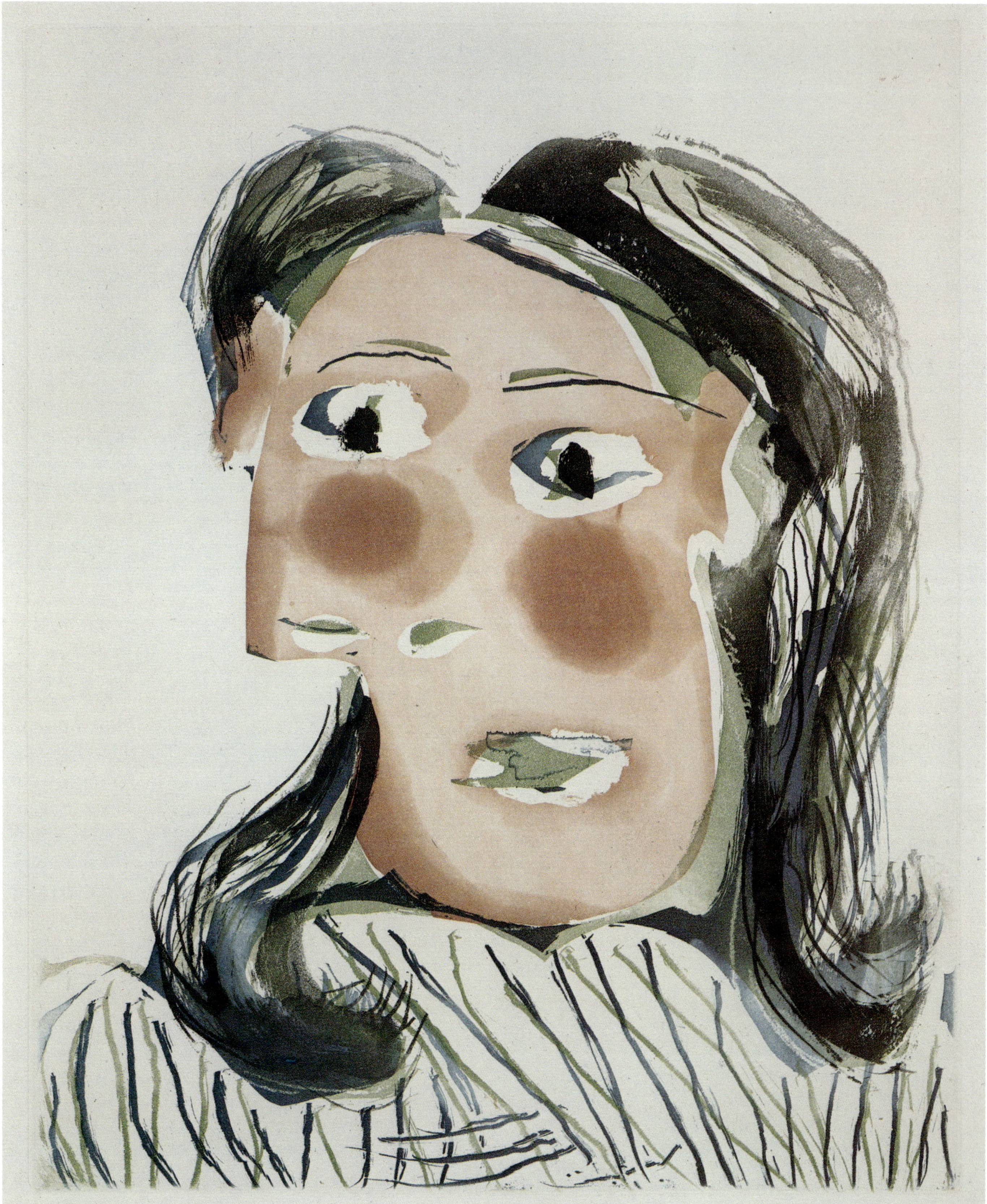

72. Tête de femme no. 6 - Portrait de Dora Maar

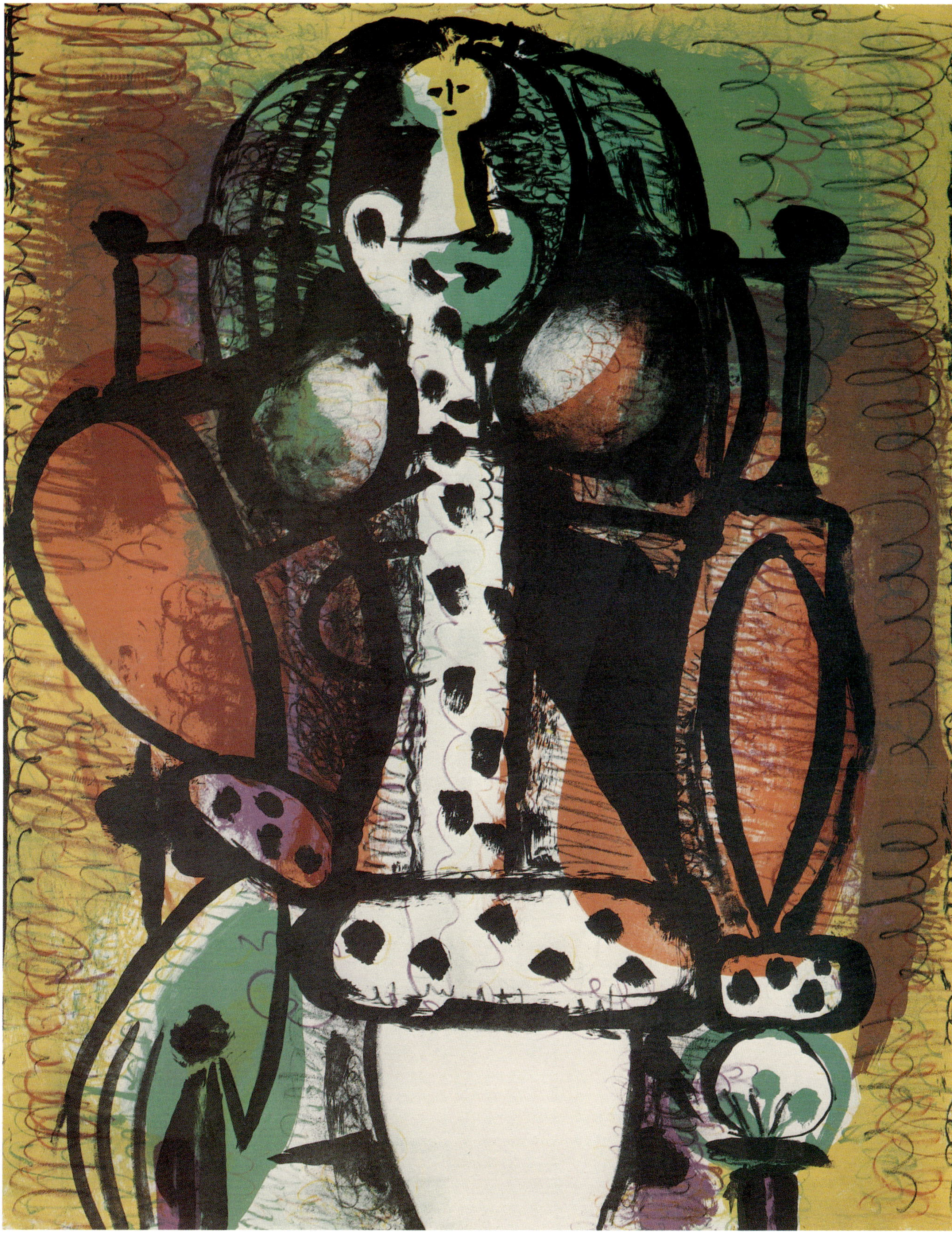

101. La Femme au fauteuil

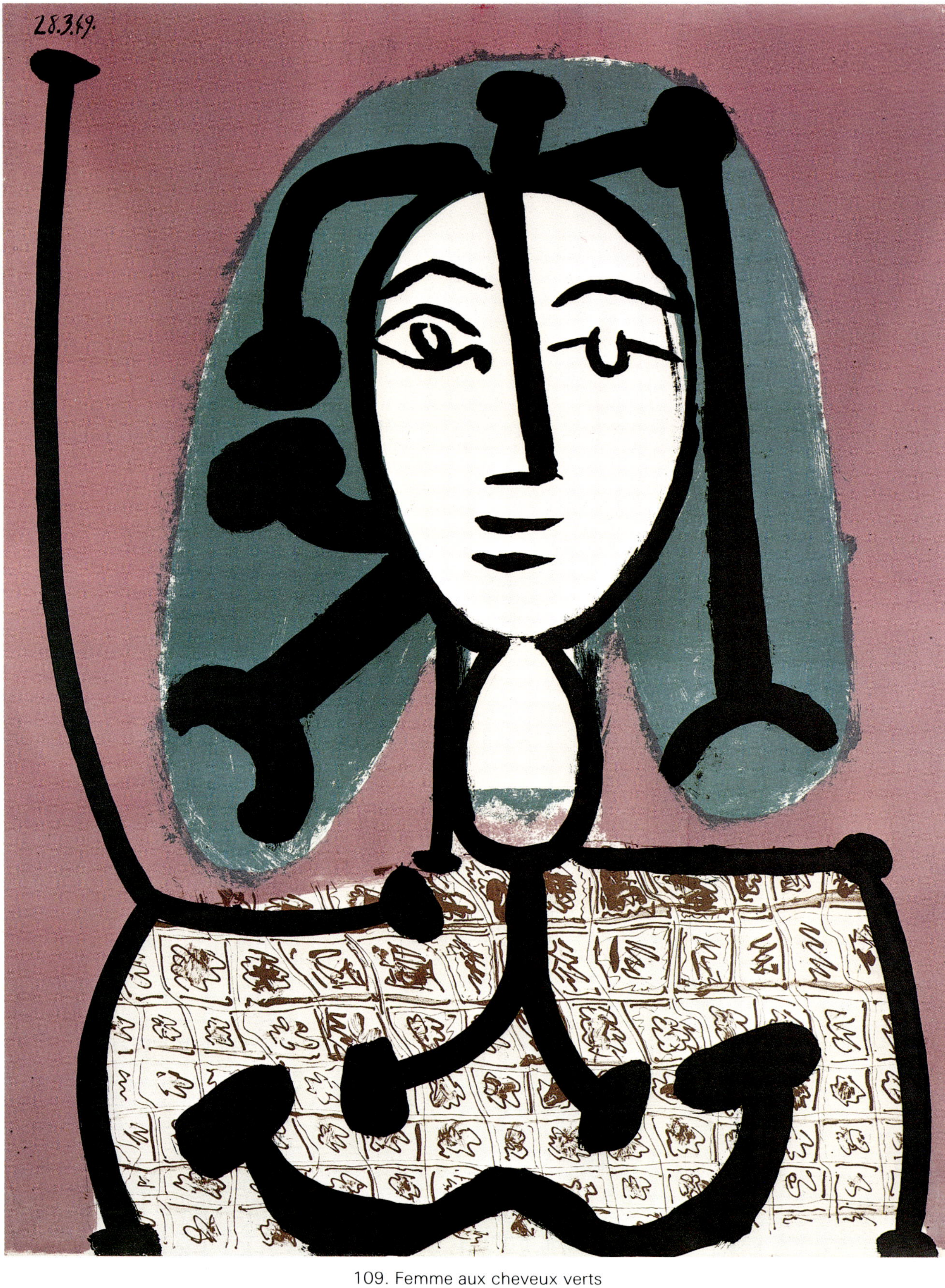

109. Femme aux cheveux verts

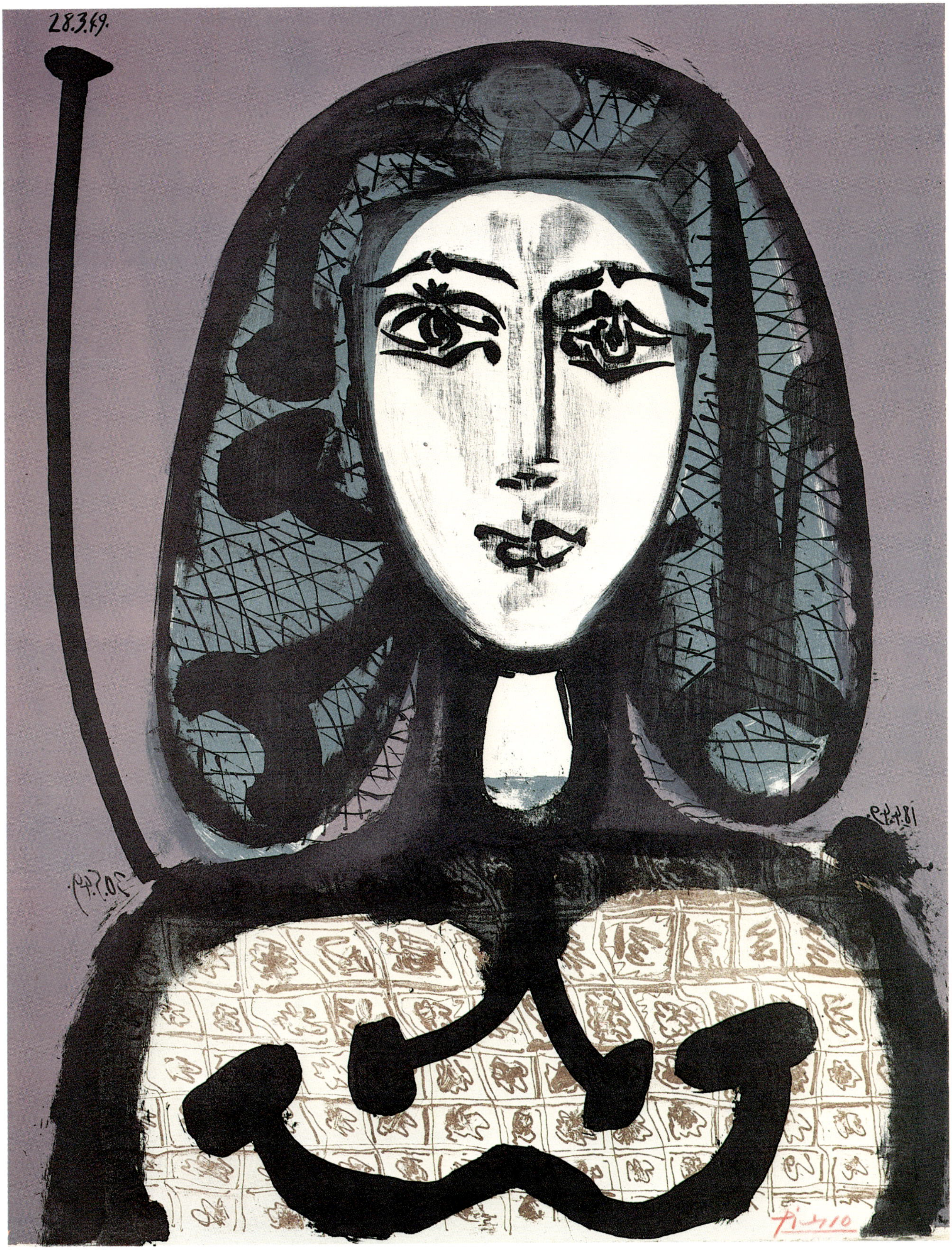

111. Femme aux cheveux verts or Femme à la résille

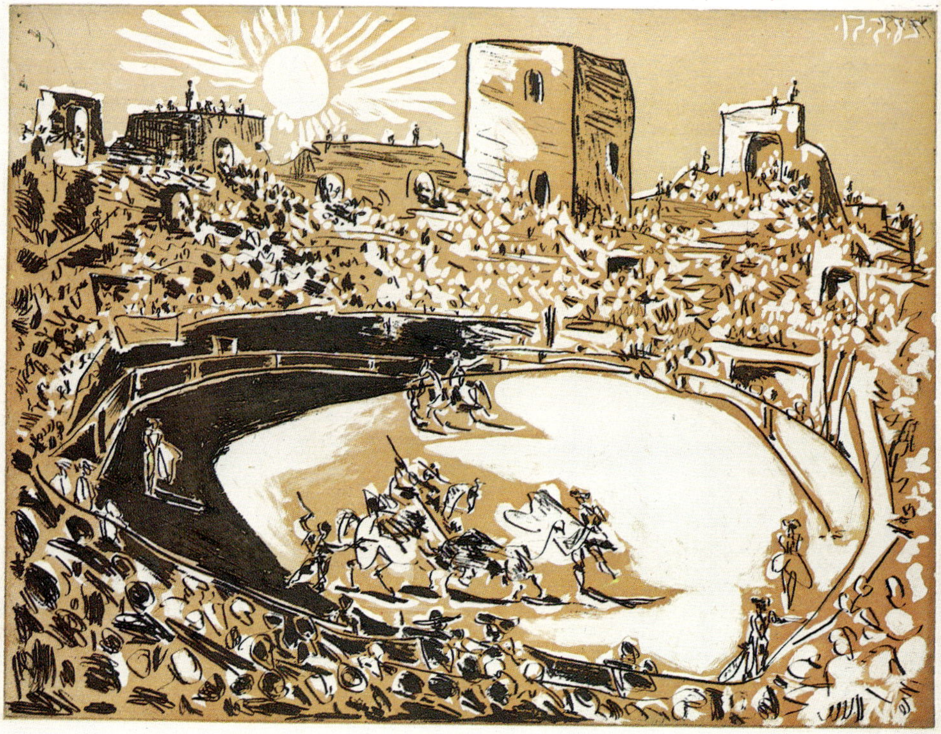

115. Corrida en Arles

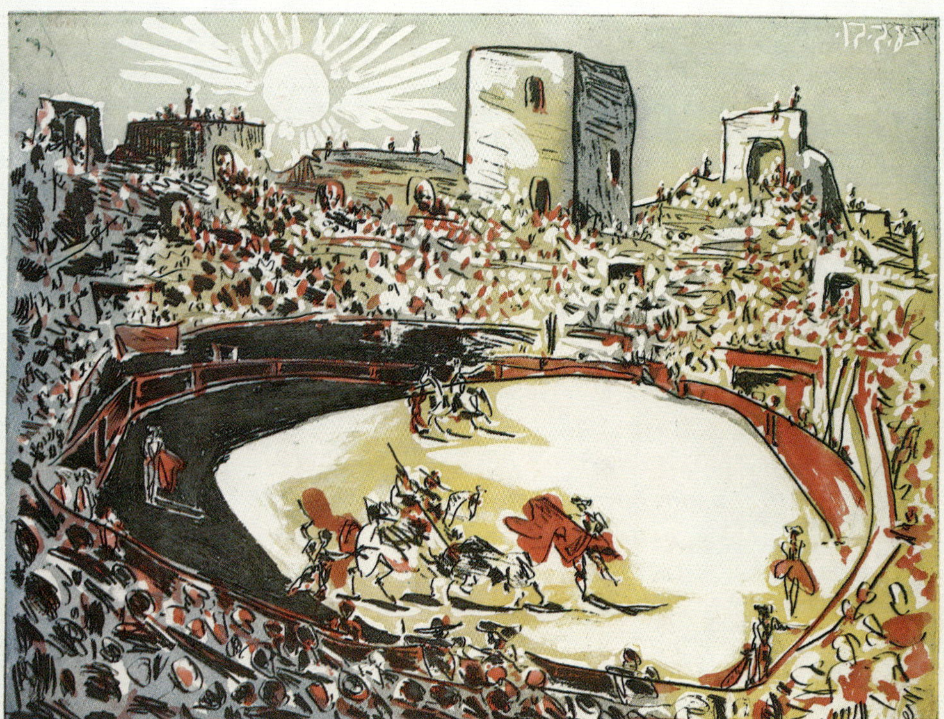

116. Corrida en Arles

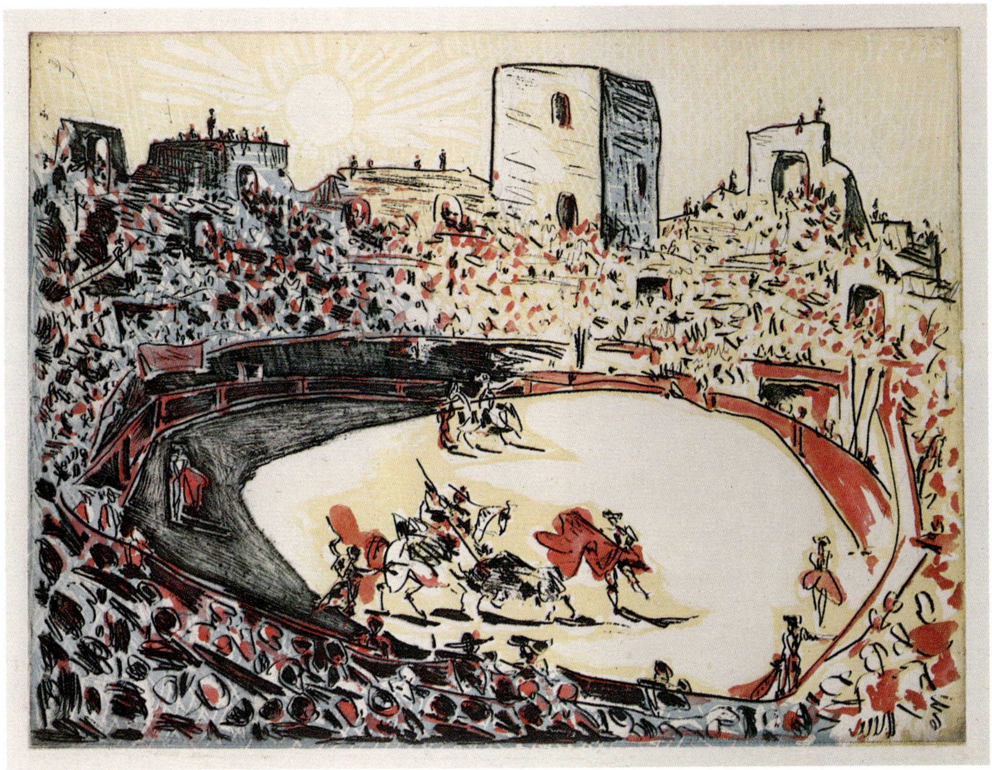

119. Corrida en Arles

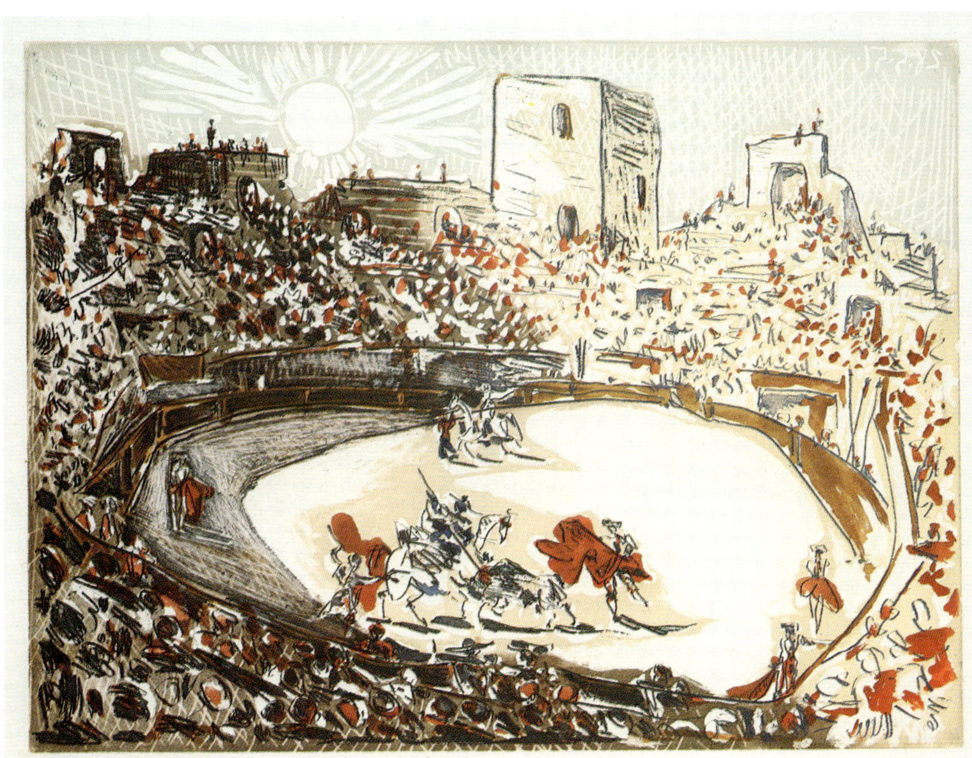

120. Corrida en Arles

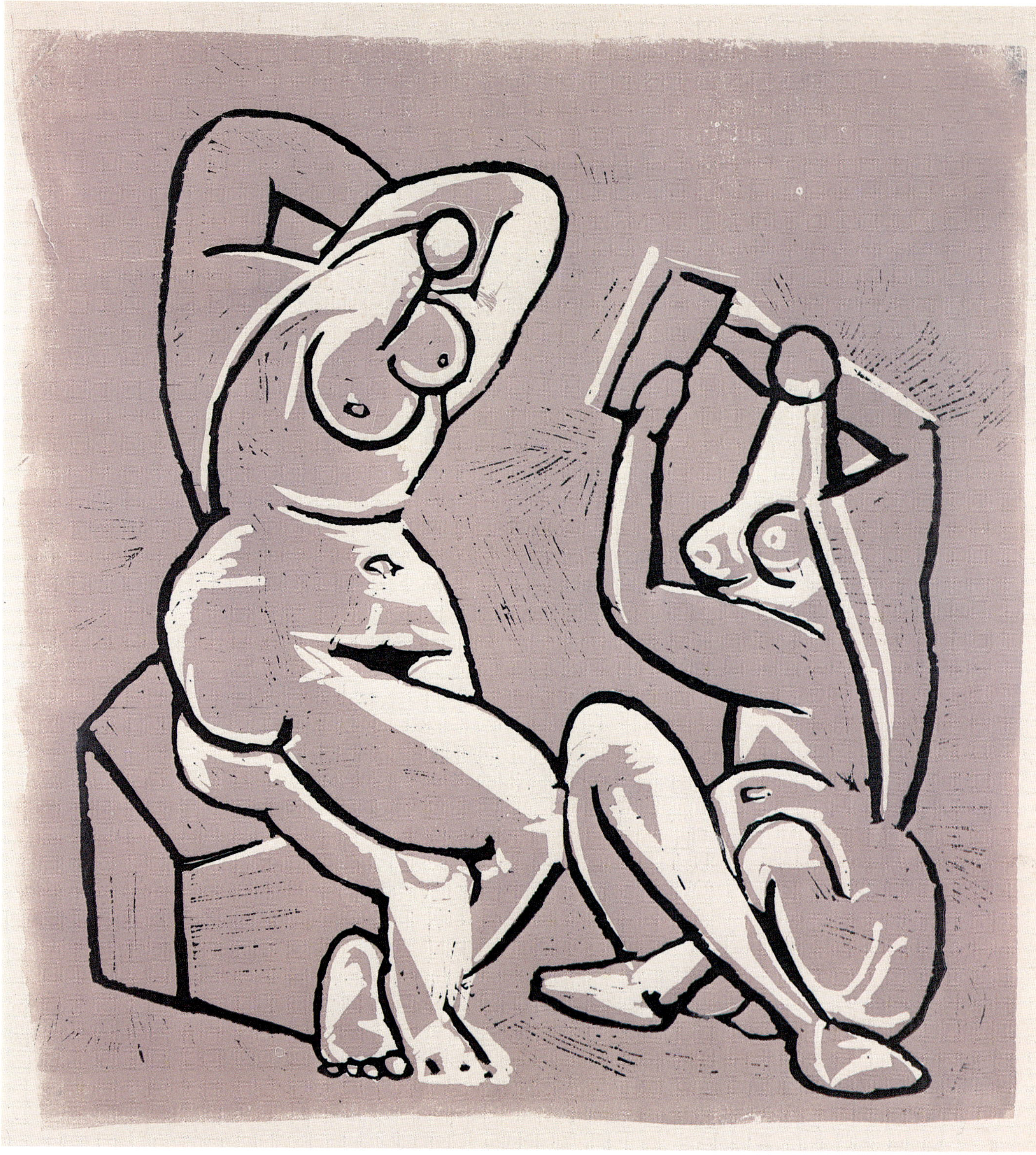

133. Femmes à leur toilette

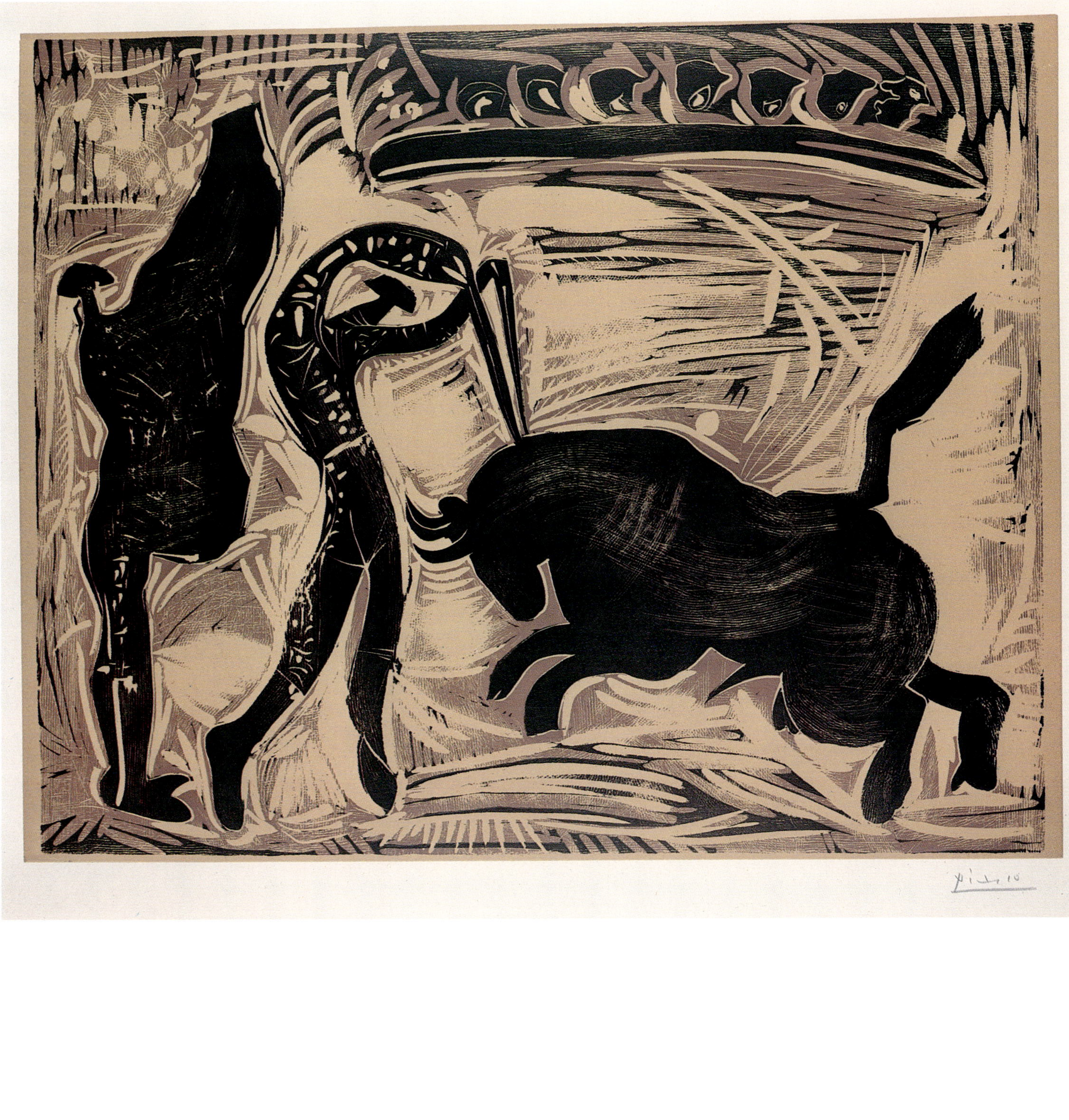

141. Les Banderilles

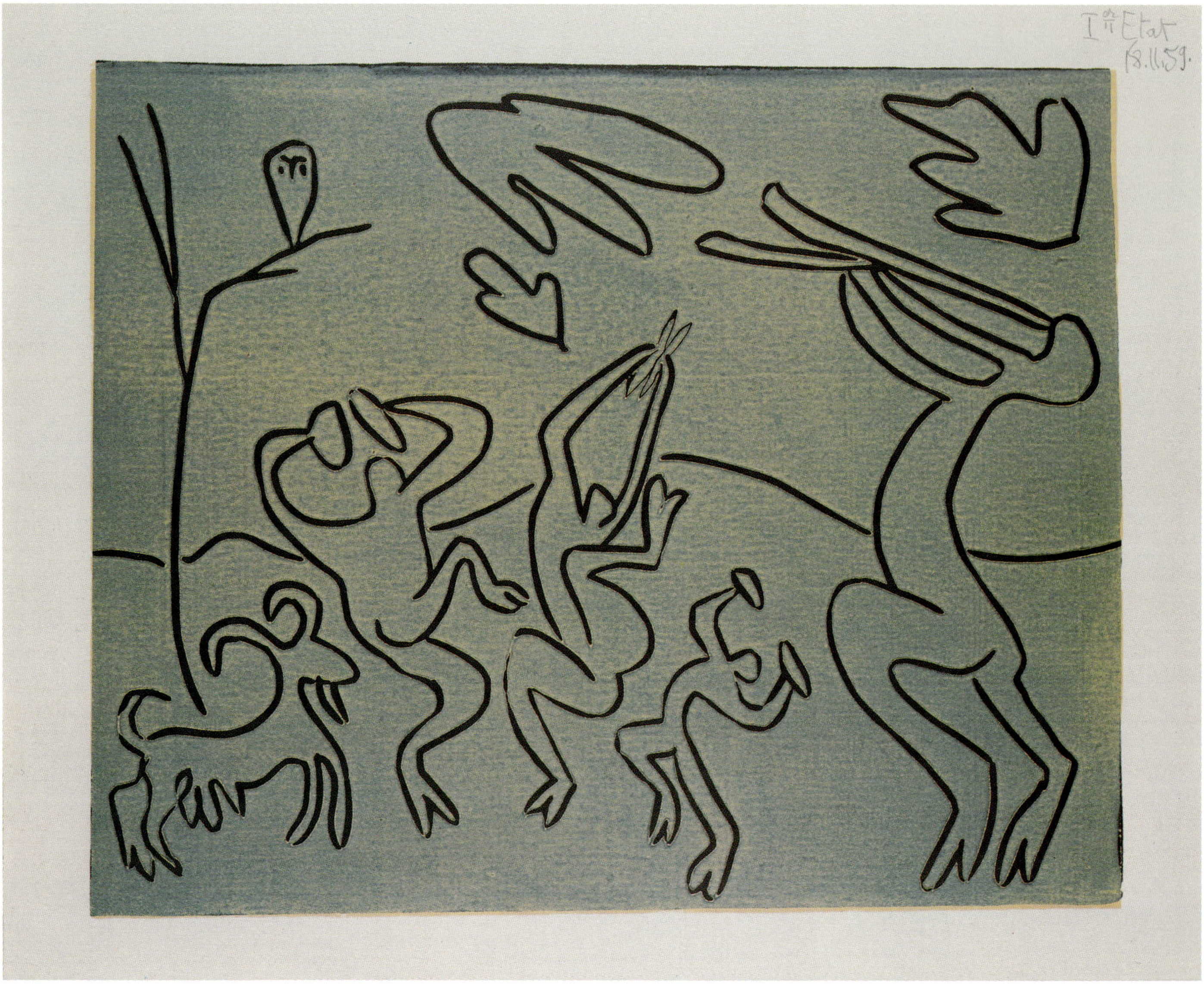

142. Les Danseurs au hibou

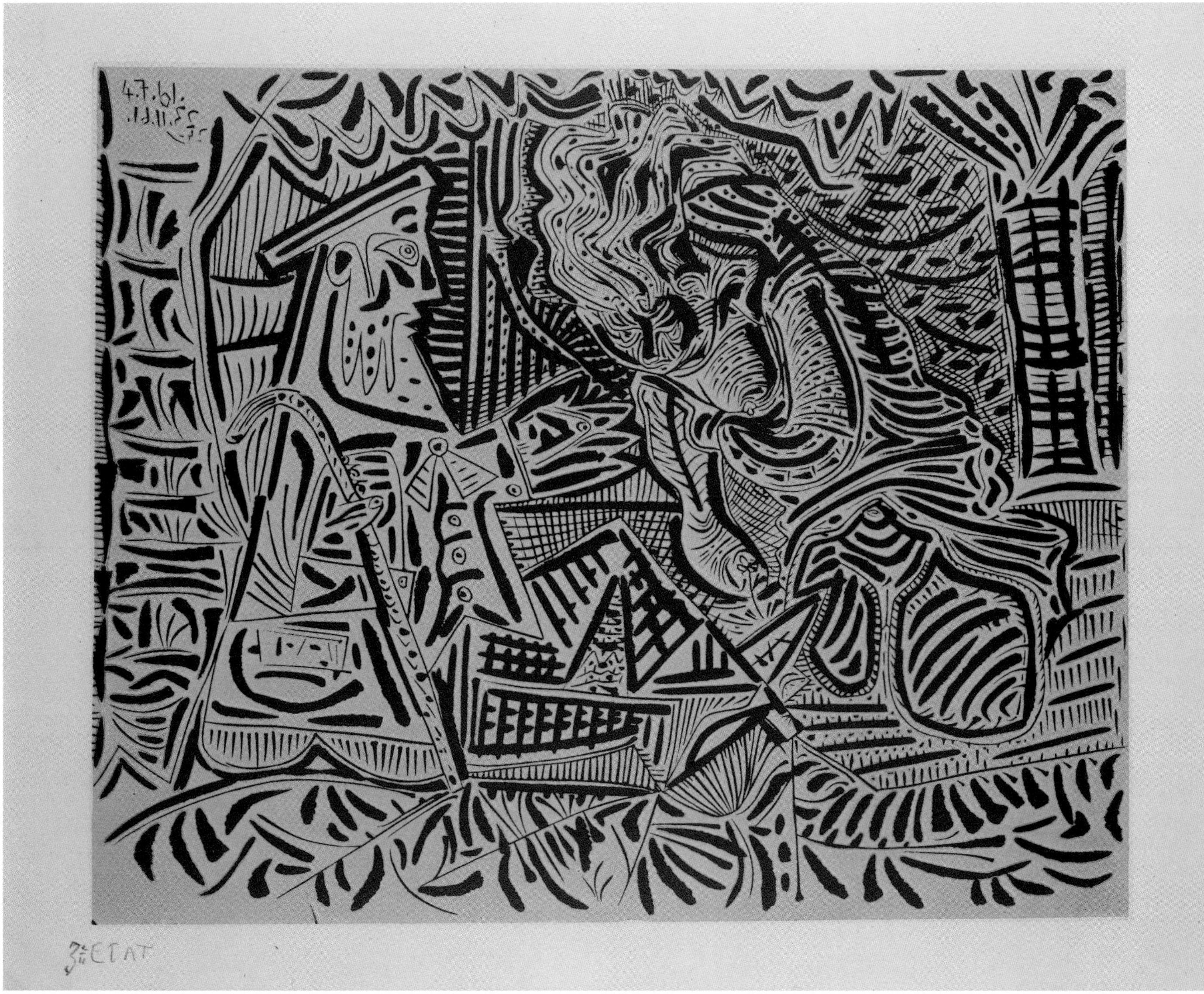

163. Le Déjeuner sur l'herbe, d'après Manet

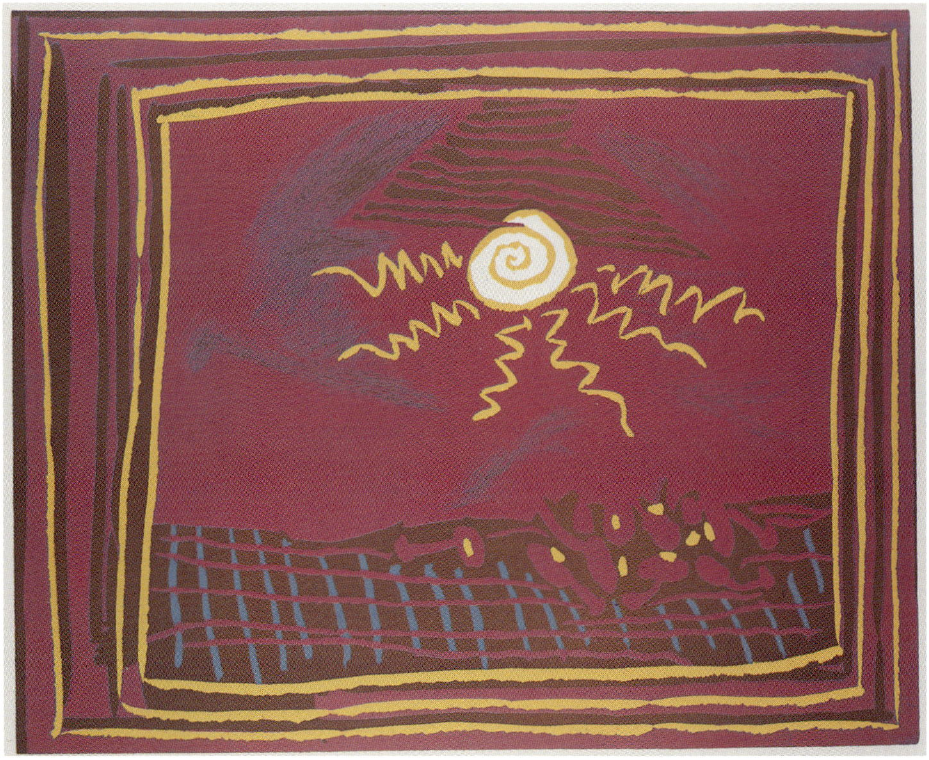

173. Nature morte à la pastèque

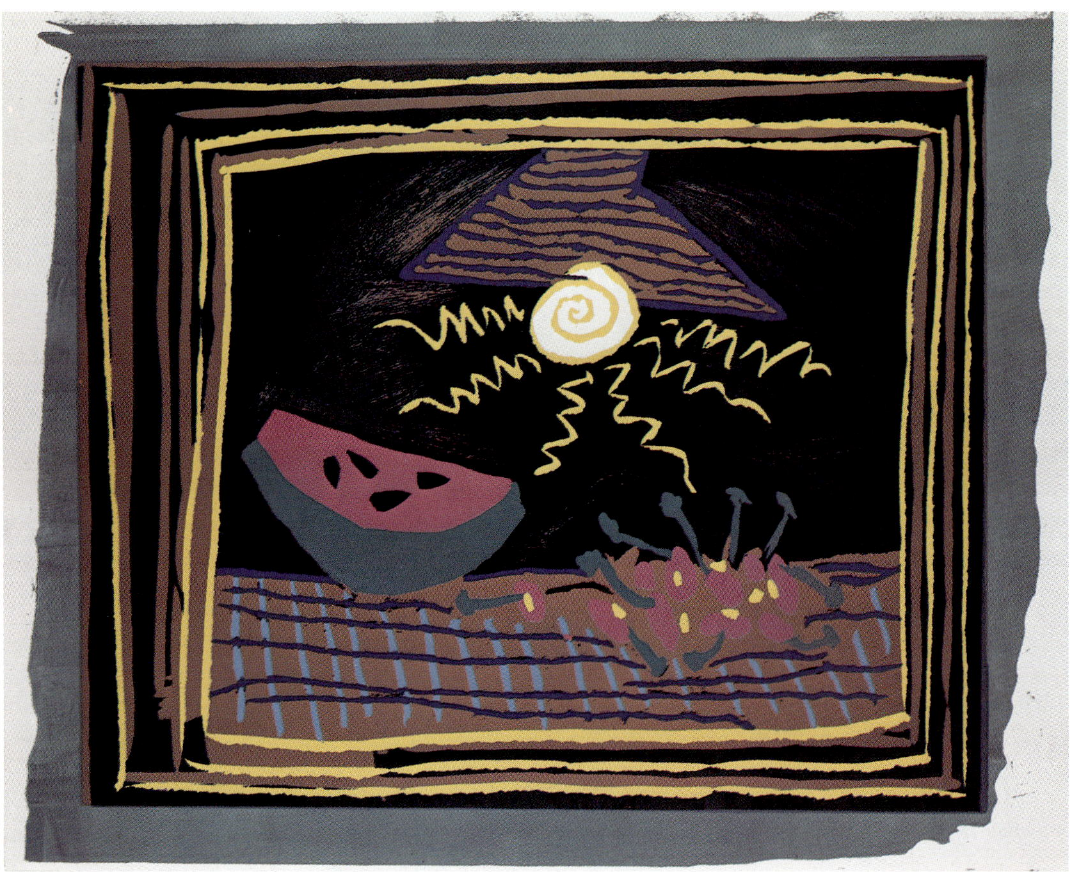

176. Nature morte à la pastèque

Catalogue of the Exhibition

Mes pareils à deux fois ne se font pas connaitre,
Et pour leurs coups d'essai veulent des coups de maitre.

[Men like me don't need a second chance to prove themselves,
They are determined to make their trial efforts master-strokes.]

Corneille, *Le Cid*, Act II, sc.2

I.

Le Repas frugal and the Saltimbanques

Could such an etching as *Le Repas frugal*, universally recognized as a great work of art, suddenly be produced by Picasso, just as Athena sprang fully armed from Zeus's head? It seems impossible without any formal training or preliminary trials, and yet . . . .

Picasso never received art-school training in the techniques of engraving. During 1899, in his studio in the Calle de Escudillers blancs, Barcelona, he executed a small etching which shows a picador inside a room, somewhat surprisingly accompanied by a tame owl (Palau, p. 163). Only one proof of this etching seems to have survived, with watercolor added by hand and annotated by the artist ''*El Zurdo*'' (The Left-Hander). Clearly Picasso had not realized that the image would be reversed when printed, and that the picador would then hold his lance in his left hand. Picasso juggled his way out of it, like an acrobat, by inventing his title.

About 1900, he playfully attempted another graphic work, which was published by Zervos as a monotype (Z.VI.282): a torero, with his cape, is drawn in ''negative'' on a prepared surface washed with gouache. The ''drawing'' was made on a round object, approximately 155 mm. in diameter. It is difficult to decide whether this is a real monotype or not. Given the hesitant quality of the handling, it could be either a trial for a woodcut or a woodburning or ''poker work.'' Two proofs exist: one in the Museo Picasso, Barcelona, and one in the Musée Picasso, Paris.

Furthermore, there is another engraving in existence which represents a bust-length portrait of an old woman wearing a scarf, seen in profile (185 × 130 mm.). A very damaged and weak proof on laid paper was found in the artist's collection. However, it is difficult to establish if this proof is by Picasso himself, or by one of his Catalan friends. We must, nonetheless, add that the old lady is quite like other old ladies who appear in some of Picasso's drawings of this period, e.g.

Z.XXI.256 and Palau.520 (dated 1901); see also D.B. IX.28 (Daix dates this last drawing 1903). The old witch's features reappear later in the character of "La Celestine" from 1955 until 1971.

Apparently, it was only in the autumn of 1904 that Picasso's friend, Ricardo Canals, who was living, as was Picasso, in the Bateau-Lavoir, showed him the techniques used by a professional engraver and especially the technique of etching. With his, or more probably Auguste Delâtre's assistance, he executed in September 1904 in only two states *Le Repas frugal*.

Between the end of 1904 and the beginning of 1906, Picasso made 16 other etchings and 13 drypoints. Whereas 30 proofs of *Le Repas frugal* were pulled, without steelfacing, by Delâtre and put on sale by Clovis Sagot or "Le Père Soulier," only a few trial proofs of the other plates exist. We know that *Le Repas frugal* was exhibited, with two other "etchings" (?), at the Serrurier Gallery between February 25 and March 5, 1905. They do not appear to have provoked any special interest or attention.

In 1913, Vollard acquired the 15 plates and decided to have them printed by Fort after steelfacing. He left aside the compositions engraved on the verso of one copperplate (G.7) and one zincplate (G.15), and published an edition which, from then on, was known as the *Suite des Saltimbanques*. One of the plates was damaged in the steelfacing process and Vollard destroyed almost all the proofs. Hence the suite is usually reduced to 14 engravings.

Vollard's large edition (29 proofs on old Japan and 250 on Van Gelder wove paper) allowed the series to be sold relatively cheaply. From then on and up until the present day, the wide distribution of the *Suite des Saltimbanques* has guaranteed its huge international audience.

Picasso had met Fernande Olivier in the autumn of 1904, but he does not seem to have used her as a model for any engravings of the series. Even so, we must not overlook the small portrait of Fernande, an etching and drypoint, which she had reproduced as a frontispiece to her book *Picasso et ses amis* (as if it were a drawing), and which can be dated circa 1905. Only four proofs are known to exist and the copperplate is lost.

1.
Le Repas frugal
The Frugal Repast

1904 (September, Paris)

Etching on zinc

463 × 377 mm.

2nd state before steelfacing.

One of the thirty proofs pulled by Delâtre on Arches laid paper, signed and numbered "no. 1" in pencil.

G.2.II.a.

One or two proofs were printed in blue ink (one in the Art Institute, Chicago). Prussia blue ink is often found in an engraver's or printer's studio as it is commonly used to transfer a print onto another plate. Therefore, it seems prudent to ascribe the choice of blue ink for this proof(s) to experimental or playful reasons rather than to infer any symbolic significance.

2.
Le Repas frugal
The Frugal Repast

1913 (Vollard edition)

2nd state after steelfacing.

One of the 250 impressions on Van Gelder wove paper.

Edition: 29 on old Japan paper.
250 on Van Gelder wove paper.

G.2.II.b; B.1.

This second proof has been included in the exhibition as a visual example to show clearly the difference of quality between the two.

We know that the plate was worked by Picasso in Delâtre's studio sometime in September 1904: a proof dedicated to Sebastian Junyent is dated by the artist "Paris, septiembre 1904." The zincplate had already been used to depict a landscape. J. Palau i Fabre orally confirmed to the writer of this catalogue that Picasso told him that the landscape was by Joan Gonzalez, the elder brother of Julio Gonzalez, the sculptor. Picasso scraped the plate clean before starting work. However, traces of the previous landscape (a stream, reeds and pebbles) are still visible on the right side of the proofs, especially after steelfacing. Between the 1st state (one proof in the Musée Picasso, Paris) and the 2nd, there are no second thoughts or corrections. Picasso only worked on the lighting, adding hatching to the background and some redefinition to the man's arm.

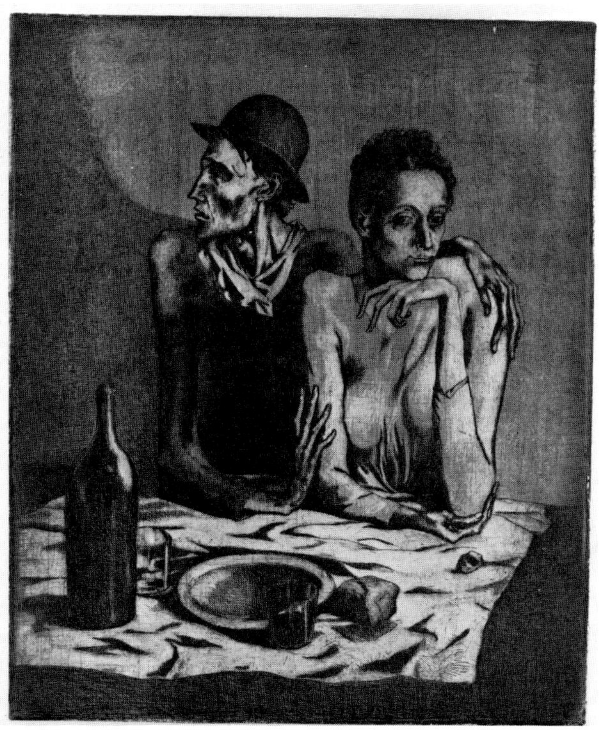

1.

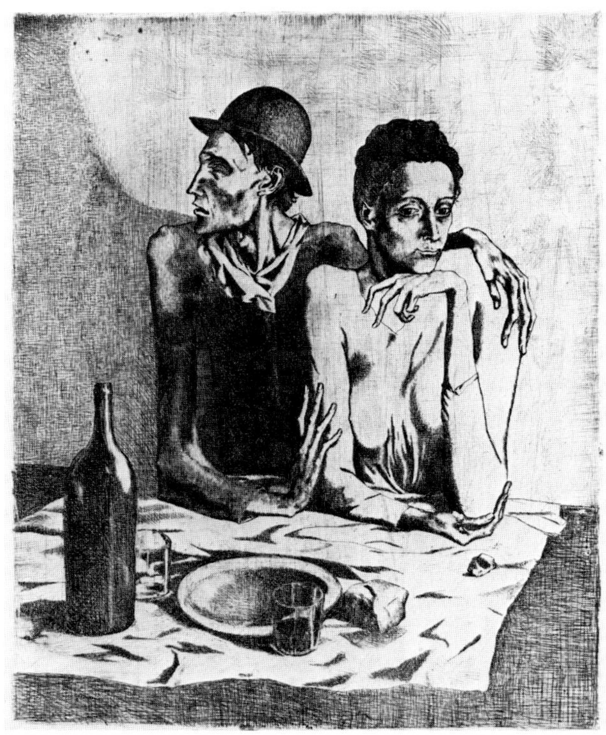

2.

It is obvious that the purely plastic beauty of the composition cannot explain completely its enormous public success. We have to look for some other explanation. The strength of its impact is surely due to the universal and timeless submeanings of the subject: the mutual loneliness of two people, even though they share everyday life, no matter how attached they may be to one another. There is no one who has not experienced this feeling of being far more lonely with the person with whom they are supposed to be closest, than when in fact alone. Extremely sensitive and demanding children experience this feeling of loneliness when babies in their mothers' arms, and even the less sentient among us catch at least glimpses of it more often than we realize during our lifetimes.

In spite of the somewhat tender but clutching quality of the man's gesture, the two personages are, at that particular moment, completely estranged from one another, both mentally and emotionally. This mutual solitude is underlined not only by the way their heads are turned away (forming an angle of more than 135 degrees), but also by the noncommittal, cramped position of the woman's hands and, above all, by their respective gazes: the man stares outward with half-closed, empty, almost blind eyes, entirely withdrawn into himself; the woman's gaze is lost in the distance.

The print was entitled by André Level *L'Aveugle* (*Picasso*, Paris, 1928, Grès et Cie.). The writer of this catalogue has not been able to establish the authorship of the title by which it is now universally known, *Le Repas frugal*. It is difficult to be sure whether the man is blind or not and, in any case, it is of no great consequence for our understanding of the subject. Whether blind, wishing to be blind, or self-absorbed, it all amounts to the same thing in this case. Whoever gave the print the title it now bears was accurate, when one realizes that it does not refer to the lack of food on the table. Picasso had a very strong Judeo-Christian background and, with this in mind, we can assume that the bread and wine are there as the perfect symbols of what can and should be shared. The ''frugality'' is elsewhere. Between the two of them, nothing is shared, no interaction takes place. They just sit numbly like two passengers in a railway carriage side by side, touching but never truly in contact.

The subject is far from novel. If one is irresistibly reminded of Degas' *L'Absinthe* (1876), however, and if Picasso himself seems to allude to this painting by his use of a similar man's hat, we should not forget that Picasso explored this subject over and over again, although his treatment of it continued to change throughout his life. To cite only those examples dating from the early period: 1901, *Les Deux saltimbanques* in the Pushkin Museum, Moscow (Z.I.92); 1903, *Le Ménage de pauvres* (Z.I.167) and *Sebastian Junyer Vidal et une femme au café* (Z.I.174); 1905, *Au Lapin Agile* (Z.I.275). In general, artists adhered to the late 19th century convention of using the café as a backdrop, whereas, in our print, the total absence of any decor emphasizes the parable-like quality of the scene, situating it outside space and time.

No known drawing can be directly related to this composition. From the outset, Picasso seems consciously or unconsciously to have made a choice, that engraving is a distinct art in itself which necessitates a loving and direct contact and struggle with the metal plate. With a few minor exceptions, he kept to this choice until the end of his life.

The mannerist treatment of anatomy, gestures and particularly hands is commonplace in Picasso's work of this period. The man here clearly shares much with ''the blind man'' who reappears so often in the early years of the century. Picasso's obsession with blindness is well documented, if variously interpreted. Of particular relevance is *The Blindman's Meal* in the Metropolitan Museum of Art, New York (Z.I.168) and its related drawings. It is interesting to note, for example, that the still life on the table with the crumpled tablecloth is nearly the same in the 1903 painting and in the print of 1904. One may note too that, in one of the preparatory drawings for the still life, the bottle of wine in our print replaces the jug of the painting. The woman, with her bizarre features, resembles another model who appears in two small drawings of 1903 (see D.B.D.IX.6 and Z.VI.451). In the first of these, the comparison is particularly close with the woman's empty, blind gaze.

Blindness is somehow the subject of the scene, but what sort of blindness? We do not think that it can be physical blindness, although it should be noted that Penrose interpreted the blind man as looking at the world through the woman's eyes (bringing to mind the later blindness of the Minotaur). The subject seems to be the blindness of the mind and heart of the two characters. Both are wrapped up in themselves, each incapable of seeing the other. The retrospective character of the print (all the drawings and paintings close to it are dated 1903) might remind us of Picasso's obsession with the drama of his friend Casagemas with Germaine, but the meaning is of a wider order: blindness to one another and, as already pointed out, loneliness.

Ambiguities abound in the image and add to the powerful feeling of solitude and misery. The woman knows she is missing something and searches, therefore, through the emptiness of a world we do not see, a dream-image, somewhat imprecise perhaps, but all the more vital because of its lack of clarity. The man realizes that she is pursuing the phantom of her desire, but he turns away, refuses to see, and seems to be or wants to be blind. He is only interested in his *own* fantasies.

To study the print is to take part in unbearable anguish. Whatever personal nightmares this may evoke in us, the great beauty of *Le Repas frugal* allows us to accept the brutal reality of its meaning.

3.
L'Abreuvoir
The Watering Place

1906 (spring or early autumn)

Drypoint on copper

122 x 188 mm.

One of the rare proofs pulled by Delâtre, before steelfacing, on Arches laid paper.

G.10.a.

There is a later edition by Vollard in 1913: after steelfacing; see no. 2. (B.8).

Although Geiser and Zervos dated 1905 both this drypoint and the works on paper (D.B.XIV.3-16) leading up to the important gouache in the Worcester Art Museum (the composition of which is almost exactly a reversed version of our drypoint), more recent research has established that the *L'Abreuvoir*, as well as the *Chevaux au bain*, can be redated to the spring of 1906, if not slightly later in the same year (see D.B., chapter XIV). Although one might think that the series of fully worked-up and precise drawings, sometimes highlighted with gouache or watercolor, is nothing but preliminary study in order to arrive at the incredible surety of line in the drypoint, such is not the case. We know now that the artist was in the process of preparing an extremely large canvas which was never completed and that the drawings under discussion were all related to this abandoned project. Hence the large gouache referred to above, together with our drypoint, must in fact be the end of Picasso's work on this theme.

Gauguin's *Cavaliers sur la plage* of 1902, certainly known to Picasso, must have been the direct inspiration for the *L'Abreuvoir*. Both give a feeling of space, freedom, youthful beauty and joy. The fact cannot be ignored that Picasso deliberately omitted the feminine characters present in Gauguin's canvas, leaving only young boys. This perhaps is the reason that Palau advances the theory that the composition represents a vision of Arcadia. The taut quality of the drypoint, the purity of line (only the back of the rider on the right is shadowed by hatchings) reinforces, in comparison with the gouache, the feeling of romantic pastoralism.

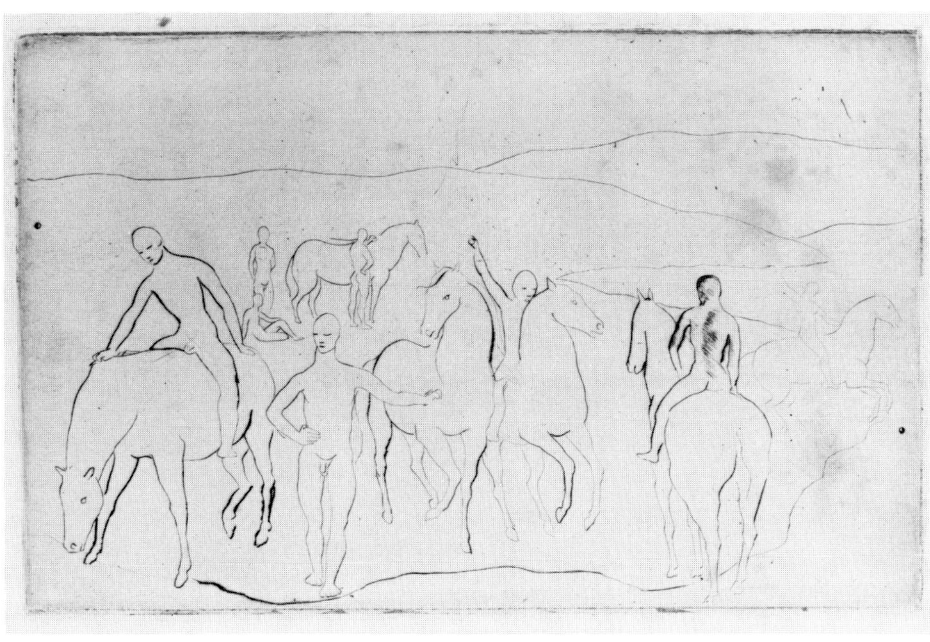

3.

II.

Cubism

In the context of our exhibition, which is limited to a selection of Picasso's printed work, it would be foolhardy to attempt either to explain fully the history of Cubism or to summarize the enormous mass of theoretical literature on the subject. What we have done is to select a small number of rare proofs which illustrate as far as possible the development of this visual and intellectual adventure.

Picasso and Braque met in October 1907. This was the beginning of a friendship based on a type of loneliness different from that outlined above. It was a shared investigation, contrary to all accepted artistic canons, which was totally incomprehensible to the outside world. It was scandalous, as not only did it break away from the accepted ''look'' of things, but, most of all, it attacked violently and directly the human body. Braque's and Picasso's iconoclasm went much further than any previous ''mannerist'' movement in the history of art and was far more revolutionary than, for example, the Nabis' attempt to change natural color values. One must remember that the idea that Man is God's creation, made in his image and likeness, is continually preached to children from birth. To reconstruct the human body in one's own way, to break it apart in order to piece it together differently carries strong overtones of sacrilege, especially if one is Spanish.

Until the end of his life (see no. 193), Picasso never rid himself of his obsession with his father, who was a painter and an art-school teacher. The father died in April 1913 without having ever understood the work of his son on whom he had lavished so much hope. It is possible to interpret this break with realistic images, God's work, as a battle against Tradition and the Law, hence, as an attempted rupture with a father figure. Further, even if all this anguish was no doubt channeled into experimental creativity, the battle had still to be paid for. The price was high: incomprehension of the public and solitude. Not being alone certainly made it easier to face this opposition: Picasso and Braque could share their hopes and disappointments, their ideas, their insights. The one could, if only by competition, stimulate the other to fresh efforts. They could not ignore a heroic flavor in the idea of fighting, and the two of them soldiered together until the declaration of World War I.

To return to the graphic work, in the first months of 1907, before he had met Braque, Picasso, who was inordinately impatient by nature, bought a small hand-operated printing press so as to be able to control the development of his prints, state by state, without being dependent on Delâtre. The famous old man was now 85 years old. He died on the 26th of July, 1907, and his son, Eugène, took over the family workshop. Always in a hurry, Picasso pulled his proofs without taking much trouble. He was interested not in obtaining professionally perfect results but in seeing immediately how his work was progressing on the plate. His plates were often badly inked (too much or too little), and the paper sometimes crumpled in the press. In addition, he would pick up and use whatever piece of paper was nearest to hand. Hence the rough but touching quality of several of the proofs in the exhibition.

His first attempt, in the beginning of 1907, was *Le Nu debout* (G.19.I). The only extant proofs (Musée Picasso, Paris) were exhibited in *The Cubist Print* at the University Art Museum, University of California at Santa Barbara in 1981-1982. A partial explanation for Picasso's choice of celluloid as a medium is that probably it was easier to handle than a metal plate. The period of the *Demoiselles d'Avignon* and of the *Three Women* in the Hermitage Museum has no parallels in the artist's graphic work. It is only in 1909, and then only twice, that Picasso took up again his engraver's tools: at the beginning of the year with *Deux figures nues* (G.21) and in the autumn with the *Nature morte au compotier* (G.22). In both cases, the influence of Cézanne, who had died in October of 1906, is clearly visible. Since the period of the Saltimbanques, Picasso's use of drypoint had completely altered. Short broken strokes and shadow-hatching replaced his pure outlines. The compositions became pyramidal in form and, in the second print, there is an effort to fragment the surface, to restructure the lighting and to find a new formal rhythm.

In 1910, Picasso stayed in Cadaqués from the end of June to the beginning of September, first alone with Fernande, later with her and the Derains. It was there that he began to work on the six etchings that were to illustrate *Saint Matorel*, a book written by his friend Max Jacob. As is well-known, the summer in Cadaqués was of paramount importance in Picasso's development. He was struggling with new ideas which were already nascent in the work of spring 1910 (see D.R. 349-352), and, to quote Kahnweiler, began "to blow up the coherent form." It seems likely that the etchings for *Saint Matorel* were the catalysts for the birth of what is now called Analytical Cubism. Picasso's discontinuity of line and spatial values allowed a radical breaking-up of the surface but also called for a complete and coherent reconstitution of structure. Daix (chapter 6, p. 81) made a pertinent remark when he wrote that Picasso did not have to worry about the horrific problem of color in his engravings when he was "extruding" his subject. (Picasso himself always spoke of "extruding" a portrait). "Pictorial unity creates the obligation that all sense data have to have the same values." Hence, the severe and monochromatic paintings.

The proofs of the first states of the etchings for *Saint Matorel* (G.23-28) were pulled in Paris by Delâtre and, therefore, not before the autumn of 1910. However, it is conceivable that the first state of *Mademoiselle Léonie dans une chaise longue* (G.25 - at this stage, there is no easy chair and the girl is standing) was done in Paris, before the journey to Cadaqués. The two extant proofs having been printed by Picasso, one cannot be dogmatic about the exact date as it is equally possible that the first state was pulled in Paris in the autumn. At any rate, the question is not of great importance as the second state (not in Geiser; some shading with small strokes, especially on the legs), of which one unique proof was pulled by Delâtre in the autumn, does not show any radical changes. It was only later that the plate was transformed and so constitutes an important landmark in the history of Analytical Cubism. In the 3rd state, the face was scraped and reworked. An elaborate system of cross-strokes and hatchings delineates the volumes and "frames" the discontinuity of the contour lines and the explosion of the forms. The girl is seated and the top of the easy chair is defined, in the top right corner, by two right-angled oblique lines which are unchanged in the final state. It is only in the 4th state that, in the bottom left, the easy chair is completed and that the curved stroke appears (on top of Léonie's foot) which equilibrates the whole composition. Thus the etching reaches its termination.

We have included in the exhibition the first states of *Mademoiselle Léonie* (cat. no. 4) and of *Mademoiselle Léonie dans une chaise longue* (cat. no. 5). Thus we can see that the main lines of the body and the limbs of the female nude, although treated in a geometric manner, remained perfectly legible.

It was in the autumn of 1911 that Picasso met Eva, the extremely pretty mistress of the painter and engraver, Marcoussis. After a rather murky period, characterized by the scandal of the Iberian bronzes stolen from the Louvre, both the artist and Cubism once again found their happiness. A new love affair and new ideas helped give him a new lease on life. This produced *La Nature morte à la bouteille* (G.33). Kahnweiler had commissioned this work from Picasso while, at the same time, commissioning from Braque the large composition entitled *Fox*. Apart from the prints illustrating Max Jacob's books, this is the only one published without delay (1912).

The importance of *La Nature morte à la bouteille* in Picasso's career cannot be overestimated, as it marks a shift of approach. The volumetric concordance of parts, the way objects are separated one from the other and integrated into the surrounding space, the assertion of certain naturalistic details, and the strictly triangular composition: all help once again to give objects a real presence.

The next two prints to be considered are very dissimilar. On the one hand, we have the *Femme* of 1913 (cat. no. 8) from Max Jacob's *Le Siège de Jérusalem*, which is a particularly good illustration of Synthetic Cubism. The radiant woman, with her body in the form of a guitar, her small head leaning to one side and her crossed legs, is detached from the background where each plane, shadowed by strokes in drypoint, is divided into areas, each of which is delineated and cross-hatched in a different way. This is one of the most disturbingly dehumanized of Picasso's print images. On the other hand, the small etching *Femme nue dans un fauteuil* (cat. no. 9) suddenly seems to be almost naturalistic in treatment. This work is a first thought for the large painting *Femme en chemise* (D.R.642), also known as *Femme aux seins dorés*, which André Breton baptized as "proto-surrealistic," and it should be dated together with all the preliminary variant studies for the painting, that is (according to Daix) the autumn of 1913 (see D.R.635-641 and Z.VI.1260, for a drawing which is even closer to our etching). Even if the woman, still nude and without her chemise, has been reconstructed conceptually, the low stuffed armchair with its Napoleon III arms and fringe is treated completely realistically.

Perhaps not yet in our etching, but certainly in the large painting, Picasso has succeeded in placing an object lyrically created, his woman, in an entirely real and naturalistic setting.

From 1914 we exhibit two works rather different in both style and conception. If *L'Homme au chien* (cat. no. 10) seems quite familiar and is no longer "hermetic" in treatment, despite the staggered planes superimposed on one another supposedly reminding us of the collages, this print is still cubist in spirit. But when we come to the *Pommes* (cat. no. 11) with the telling detail of the curling peel, we are abruptly brought down to earth with an apparent return to traditional still life, hardly influenced at all by cubist severity. The former should be dated to the beginning of 1914, the latter to the autumn of the same year, when Picasso returned to Paris from Avignon after the declaration of war.

The *Homme au chien*, even with the duplication of his nose and hat, evokes more forcibly than the *Femme nue dans un fauteuil* a feeling of intimate domesticity, something like the atmosphere in *L'Interieur d'une salle à manger* by Martin Drolling (1815, Musée du Louvre). This early 19th century painting depicts a man in his bedroom slippers, with a dog in front of him quietly sipping his coffee in the midst of the morning's disorder in a bourgeois apartment, which is heated by a stove. The man in our print, comfortably installed in an armchair with his back to the chimney, is absorbed in the morning newspaper in a setting which, while the perspective of the room has been altered, still gives the impression not only of a comfortable interior, but also of a quiet, happy life. All the elements for this are present: an attic with its pitched roof, the window through which we see a bridge, a tree and some houses, a well-fed dog asleep on the carpet. The setting, the objects and the room are real. The dog (perhaps Sentinelle, the Derain family dog) reappears in the *Guitar Player* (Z.XXIX.91), sprawled on the floor, or, sitting quietly and well-behaved, in the *Femme au chapeau* (Z.XXIX.107 and 109) and the *Femme au renard* (Z.XXIX.122).

A very good example of Picasso's tentative return to naturalistic forms, at a later date in Avignon, is the canvas entitled *Peintre et son modèle* in the Musée Picasso, Paris (D.R. 763). Our still life print of apples either dates from this period, or, more probably, from the time of the artist's return to Paris in the autumn. Given the small size of the plate, it could have been etched in Avignon and then later put in an acid bath in Paris, before Picasso pulled himself the few existing proofs.

To use an understatement, 1915 was not the brightest of years in Picasso's life. The majority of his friends were fighting in the trenches (Braque, Apollinaire, Derain), Kahnweiler was abroad, and Eva, her condition worsening day by day, was to die in December. Turning his back on the temptations of a return to naturalistic form, Picasso again invoked Cubism, in a mode known as "Black Cubism." At this time, or a little later, there was an attempt to blend the two approaches, and this ambiguity or hesitancy is mirrored in his graphic work. But, to quote Daix again (D.R., p. 172): "Picasso does not possess the necessary mental equipment which would enable him to make a valid combination of two distinct figurative systems."

The *Nature morte, guitare et clarinette* (cat. no. 12) should be dated in the context of a group of drawings which Joan Rosselet places in 1915 (D.R.818-828). Certain details have been changed: the fruit bowl has been discarded in favor of a bottle of wine wrapped in a piece of paper and the musical score has been replaced by a newspaper. But the most striking alteration is a new tautness in the composition. The background, still dark in the 1st state, gradually becomes lighter and lighter, and finally, in the 5th state, is completely empty on the left side. Little by little, the print, despite its small size, takes on a poetic, balanced quality (the neck of the guitar in equilibrium with the neck of the bottle) and it simultaneously acquires a certain ambiguity because of the displacement of the composition toward the right, with the resulting emptiness on the left. In the final state, the reversed letters ''JOU'' seem to metamorphose into a café glass, called in café slang ''un ballon''. Here, there is a play on words which is not easy to translate: the letters JOU can be the beginning of the word JOUr (day), of the word JOUrnal (newspaper) and also of JOUer (to play). Further, in French, the same word (ballon) is used for a childrens' ball and for a small glass of wine. We are given a still life, to be sure, but also a *vanitas*: in Picasso's work Eva is inextricably linked with café life and music, and Eva is dangerously ill.

From this year also came the two engravings *L'Homme à la pipe* (cat. no. 13) and *L'Homme attablé, IV* (cat. no. 14). They should be dated in reference to a drawing of 1915 (D.R.840), rather than classed with a group of drawings of the same subject dating form 1914 (Z.VI.1194-1216). Apart from any other considerations, these two prints are interesting as they represent Picasso's first attempt to use the technique of aquatint. Both times, in the 1st states, the plates were uniformally grained and bitten by the acid so that, on the proofs, only a rectangular surface is visible: almost black for the former (no. 13), much lighter for the latter (no. 14). If, in the *L'Homme attablé, IV*, which probably antedates the *Homme à la pipe*, Picasso, ignoring the light aquatint which remains on the proof like a mere tone, was satisfied with the solution of using etching to ''draw'' the composition, he radically changed his approach when he came to no. 13 . Using the burnisher (a tool which he rarely used later, preferring the cleaner effect of the scraper), he gradually freed from the background, as if he were employing mezzotint, the face, the hand, the crumpled sleeve, and then the hat, the waistcoat and the shirt. Even though the etching lines, added from the 3rd state onward, are important to complete the structure and add features like the pipe, they are only employed, when necessary, for details. It is the clearing of the aquatint which defines the shapes and the volumes. Picasso never wanted to employ mezzotint, as the manipulation of the rocker seemed to him both laborious and nonproductive. ''Why give yourself all the bother,'' he would say to Lacourière, ''when aquatint can give the same result?'' As we shall see, he used the same technique, this time without the addition of the etching needle, for the *Minotaure aveugle* of 1934 (cat. no. 50).

Finally, *La Lessive* from 1915 (cat. no. 15) presents a puzzling case. Whereas Geiser's date of 1912 seems persuasive on technical grounds, certain details such as the small broken strokes, the crescent shape of the arm, the reappearance of realism with the house on the left, the bucket, the twisted floor-cloth, and the scarf blowing in the wind all point to a later date. A drawing, exactly reversed, on a wooden panel (Z.XXIX.143, now in the Musée Picasso, Paris) shows in addition a tree plus a door and a window on the facade of the little house. All these realistic details argue for a date of 1915. The shape of the arm (cf. the series of ''Drinkers,'' e.g. D.R. 884; Z.VI.1320) is very typical of Picasso's work from the end of 1915 and even the beginning of 1916.

4.
Mademoiselle Léonie
Saint Matorel, illustration I

1910 (summer, Cadaqués)

Etching on bevelled copper

199 x 141 mm.

Unique proof of the 1st state, pulled by Delâtre on old Japan.

G.23.I.

In the 2nd state, thin, parallel broken strokes have been added on the right of the vertical line which divides the body: Paris, autumn 1910.

5.
Mademoiselle Léonie dans une chaise longue
Mademoiselle Léonie in a Chaise Lounge
Saint Matorel, illustration III

1910 (summer, Cadaqués or Paris)

Etching on copper

198 x 142 mm.

One of the two proofs pulled by the artist on wove Canson et Montgolfier paper.

G.25.I.

During the three subsequent states, further work in drypoint and etching: Cadaqués (?) and Paris, autumn, 1910.

Saint Matorel, by Max Jacob:

Edition of the book: Kahnweiler, Paris, 1911.

The four plates were pulled by Delâtre (G.23.II.b; G.24.b; G.25.III.b; G.26.b; B.19-22.).

106 copies: 19 on old Japan (nos. 1 to 15 and I to IV); 87 on Van Gelder laid paper (nos. 16 to 100, and 0 and 00 for the *Dépot légal*.[1]

The two copies in the Bibliothèque Nationale, Paris, do not have a complete text, but they do have two series of illustrations: before and after cancelling of the plates. The cancelled plates have been lost.

Matarasso, 2; Bloch, Livre, 2.

In June 1901, Picasso met Max Jacob at Vollard's exhibition and the two men became fast friends. Max Jacob's triology, *Saint Matorel, Le Siège de Jérusalem* and *Les Oeuvres burlesques et mystiques de frère Matorel*, of which Picasso illustrated two volumes (see cat. no. 8) and Derain in 1912 the third, tells the story of a minor employee in the Paris subway who converts to catholicism, becomes a monk and ends as a saint. Several critics have used the adjective "cubist" to describe the style. Certainly the story line, if one exists, is broken up and discontinuous.

The gods of Olympus, devils and Christian saints, for example, are on the best of terms. This parody and allegory, the exact significance of which is by no means clear, is a sort of mixture of Flaubert's *La Tentation de Saint Antoine* and Joyce's *Ulysses* in the brothel chapter. Mademoiselle Léonie is Victor Matorel's mistress before he becomes Brother Manasse; starting life as a washerwoman, she later becomes an oriental dancer at the Eldorado.

6.
Nature morte, bouteille
Still Life with a Bottle of Marc

1911 (autumn, Paris)

Drypoint on copper

500 x 306 mm.

Unique proof before steelfacing, pulled by Delâtre on Arches laid paper, annotated in pencil bottom left: "I."

G.33.a.

7.
Nature morte, bouteille
Still Life with a Bottle of Marc

1912 (Kahnweiler edition)

After steelfacing.

One of the 100 impressions on Arches laid paper, signed and numbered "no. 39."

G.33.b; B.24.

Edition: 100 on Arches laid paper, signed and numbered.
A few artist's proofs, signed and numbered "O."

The cancelled copperplate has been lost.

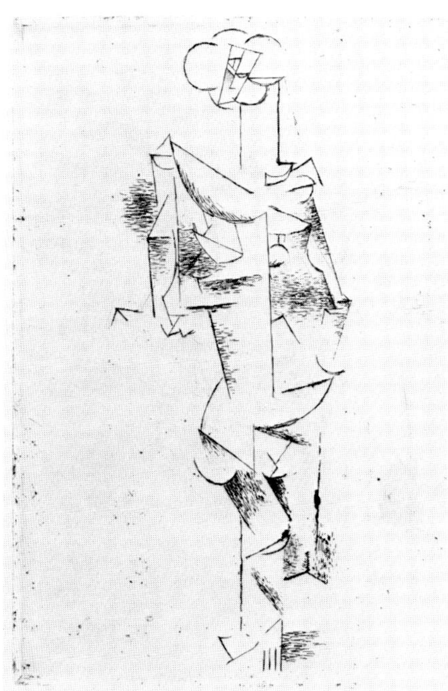

4.

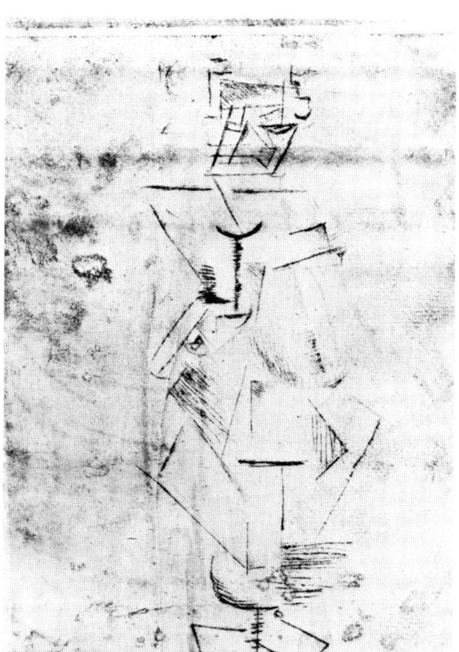

5.

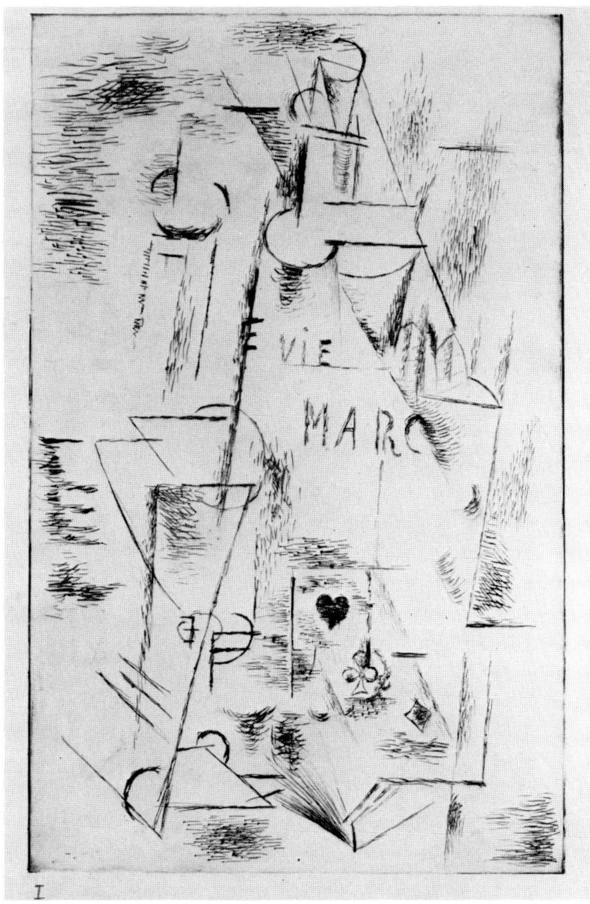

6.

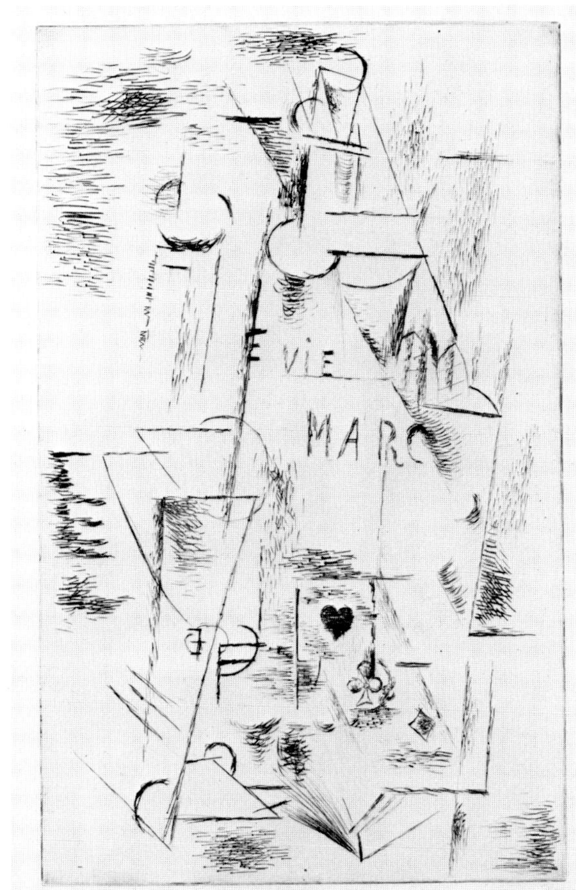

7.

Even though the components of this still life seem to have been chosen merely as a function of their place in the underlying structure of the composition, a still life often carries *vanitas* overtones. Picasso at this time was in the process of breaking off his relationship with Fernande and beginning a new love affair with Eva. With this in mind, the ace of hearts is sometimes interpreted as an allusion to Eva, his "ma Jolie," who never figures directly in Picasso's work (for a possible exception, see D.R. 763). What is certain is that the artist always uses in his work the ace of clubs, which signifies money and also good luck because of its association with the four leaf clover (in French, the ace of clubs is called the ace of clovers). Also, it is not without interest to note that the third card is the ace of diamonds which signifies change, new direction, news, etc. (The absence of the ace of spades is normal because of its sinister connotation with death.). The type of brandy *(eau de vie)* called *marc* is produced by the fermentation of what is left over in the wine press (a mixture of grape skins, pulp and pips) after the juice has been extracted in the wine-making process. Hence *marc* is the product of a fruit that has already been squeezed dry. Should we see an allusion here to the end of the relationship with Fernande? There is also an optimistic note in the word *vie* (life), with possibly erotic connotation (*vie*/life and *vit*/penis). But this could refer simply to a new feeling of well-being provoked by a new love affair.

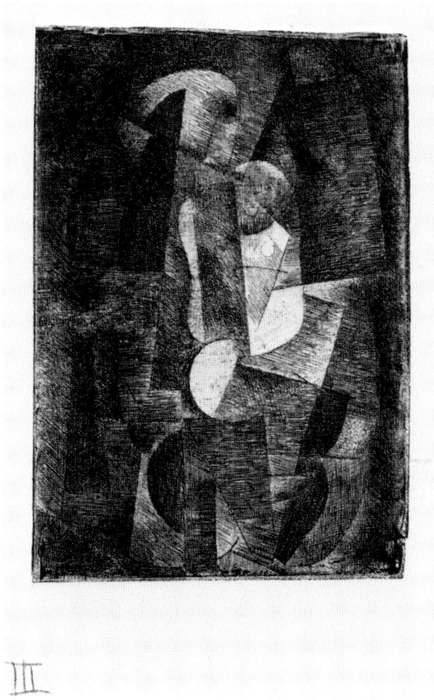

8.

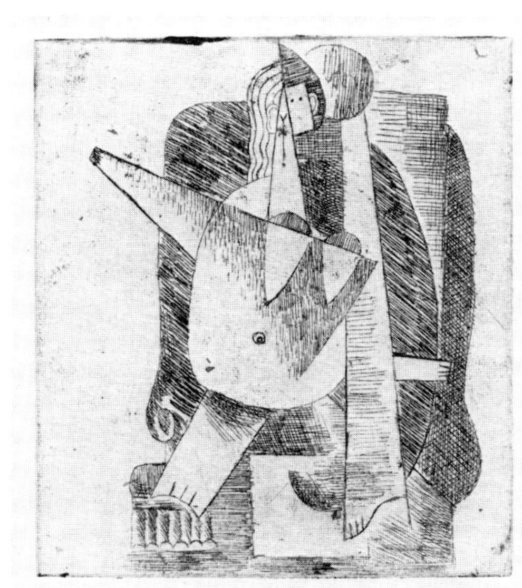

9b.

8.
Femme
Woman
Le Siège de Jérusalem, illustration III

1913

Drypoint on copper

160 x 109 mm.

Proof of the 3rd state on Rives laid paper with the watermark "Eug. Delâtre," annotated bottom left in pencil "III."

G.37.III.

Practically no differences from the 4th state: quite simply, the plate has not been bevelled yet. There are three proofs of the 3rd state in existence: one which was pulled by the artist himself (Musée Picasso, Paris) and another which was in the Kahnweiler Collection.

Le Siège de Jérusalem, by Max Jacob:

Edition of the book: Kahnweiler, Paris, 1914.

Three illustrations for the book were pulled by Delâtre: G.35.VI.b; G.36.II.b; G.37.IV.b; B.25-27.

A similar edition to that of *Saint Matorel*.

The Bibliothèque Nationale, Paris, has a copy numbered "O" which contains only the proofs of the cancelled plates. The cancelled plates themselves have been lost.

Matarasso, 3; Bloch, Livre, 3.

9a&b.
Femme nue dans un fauteuil
Nude Sitting in an Armchair

1913 (autumn)

Etching on copper

78 x 69 mm.

G.41.

a. One proof on old laid paper, pulled by the artist.
[not illustrated]

b. One proof on old laid paper, pulled by Fort in 1930.

The artist first pulled three proofs of this small plate (which still exists) and, later in 1930, Fort pulled two more. In 1929, when Marcel Guiot published G.51, and in 1930, when Vollard acquired the plate of *L'Homme au chien* (cat. no. 10), Picasso had Louis Fort pull some trial proofs of plates which had been made at various times in the past. Sometimes, as in our case, the plates dated as far back as fifteen years. Just as he did in 1960, he approved some and refused others. As far as the trial proofs of the years 1929-1930 are concerned, it is possible that Vollard or Guiot had some say in the selection. However, the *Femme nue dans un fauteuil* was never published and the plate was never steelfaced.

10.
L'Homme au chien
The Man with a Dog

1914 (early)

Etching on copper

278 x 218 mm.

Proof of the 1st state, pulled by Fort, in 1930, on Arches wove paper.

G.39.I.

The artist himself pulled two trial proofs in 1914. Afterward, the plate remained as we see it here (1st state) until 1930, when our proof was pulled. Then Picasso began to burnish some areas: under the letter r of *journal*, in the funnel-shaped area (2nd and 3rd states), and then on the reader's nose which is in the shape of a T (3rd state).

The plate was then steelfaced and pulled by Fort: several trial proofs on Arches wove paper (signed), then 60 impressions also on Arches wove paper of which 54 are signed in red pencil, two more on glossy Japan paper (signed also in red pencil), and, finally, 40 more on old Japan paper, also signed in red pencil. Vollard's edition dates toward 1930-1931: G.39.III with the forthcoming addendum; B.28.

A few proofs were pulled from the cancelled plate which is in the possession of M. Marcel Lecomte; on the verso of the plate, also cancelled, is the *Nature morte au trousseau de clefs*, G.30.

11.
Pommes
Apples

1914 (autumn)

Etching on copper

152 x 190 mm.

Proof pulled by the artist on wove paper without watermark.

G.38; B.1307.

First, nine proofs were pulled by the artist on different papers in 1914, then, at the same time, Delâtre pulled one further proof. The history of the plate is identical with that of no. 9; four trial proofs were pulled by Fort in 1930, but there was no edition. The plate exists.

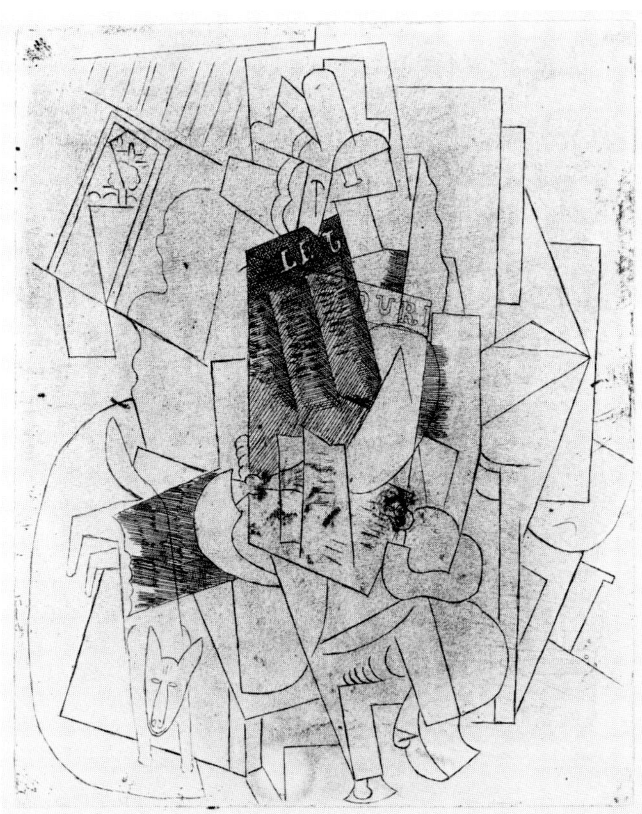

10.

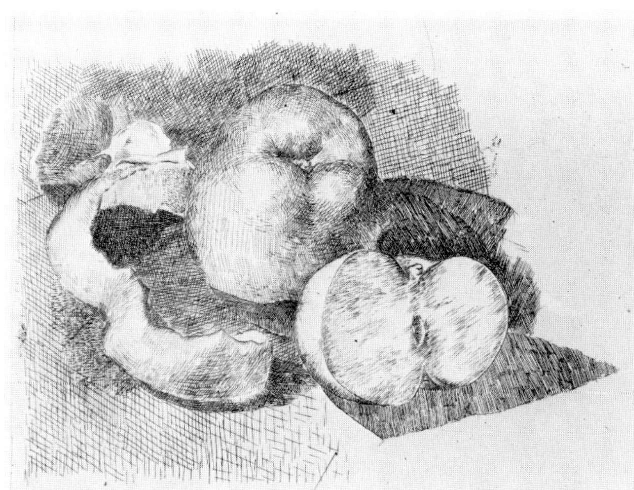

11.

12a,b,c.
Nature morte, guitare et clarinette
Still Life with a Guitar and Clarinet

1915

Etching on zinc

69 x 68 mm.

a. 1st state, on Ingres paper, annotated bottom left ''I.''

b. 3rd state, on Ingres paper, annotated bottom left ''I'' and, next to it, ''III.''

c. 5th and final state, on Ingres paper.

All three proofs pulled by the artist.

G.43.I,III,V.

All five states of this small plate were in the exhibition *The Cubist Print*, held at the University Art Museum, University of California at Santa Barbara, 1981-1982. In the 1st state, the bell of the clarinet and the reversed letters ''JOU'' do not yet appear. The 3rd state shows the evolution of the gradual lightening of the plate. In the 5th state, the neck of the guitar which, up until this state, was indicated by the strings, parallel to the neck of the bottle, is taken up again and reworked on a slant towards the left to balance the entire composition. The surface of the guitar, up until now rectangular in shape, takes on the shape of a guitar, whereas the perspective angle of the sound box, formerly distinctly outlined, becomes less defined. ''JOU'' seems to take on the form of a glass.

Just as in the case of cat. nos. 9 and 11, the zinc, which is still extant, was left on one side after Fort had pulled one (or two) trial proof(s) in 1930.

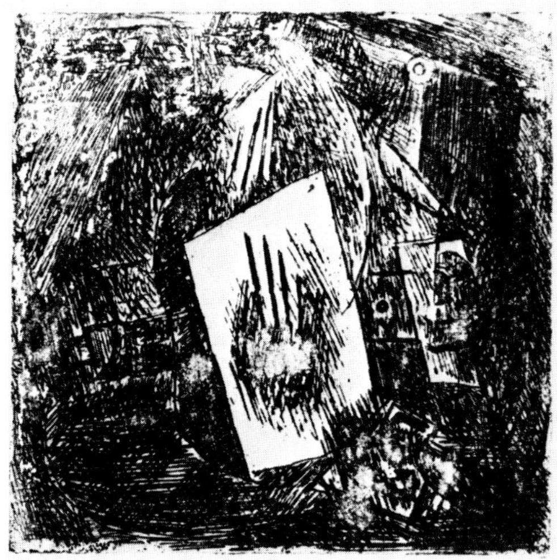

12a.

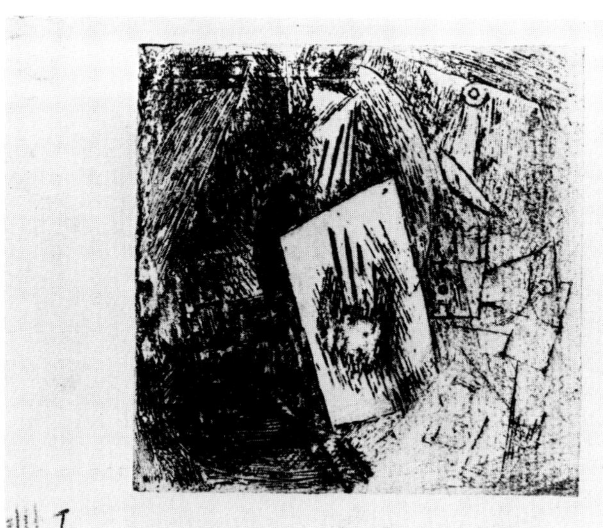

12b.

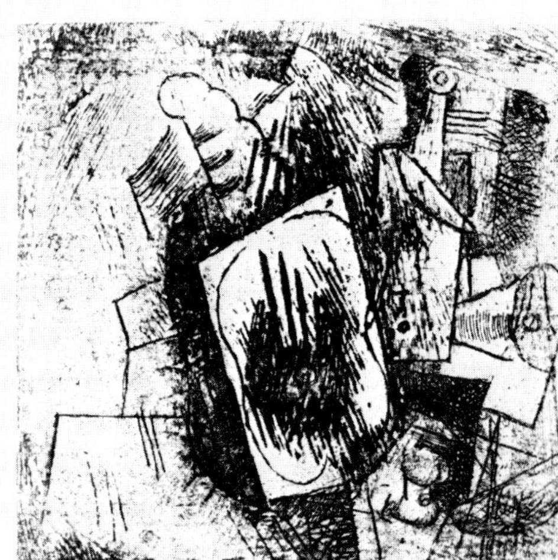

12c.

13a&b.
L'Homme à la pipe
Man with a Pipe

1915

Aquatint used like mezzotint and etching on zinc

75 x 53 mm.

a. 5th state: one of the six proofs pulled by the artist on Ingres paper.

b. 8th and last state: one of the two or three proofs pulled by Fort on laid old Japan paper, in 1930.

G.45.V and VIII.

Apart from five proofs of the 5th state, five proofs of the 6th state, and the proof, pulled by Fort, which we exhibit here (it is possible that Fort kept a proof for himself), all the other proofs of this small plate are in the Musée Picasso, Paris. The zinc exists. As for the proofs pulled by Fort, see cat. nos. 9, 11 and 12.

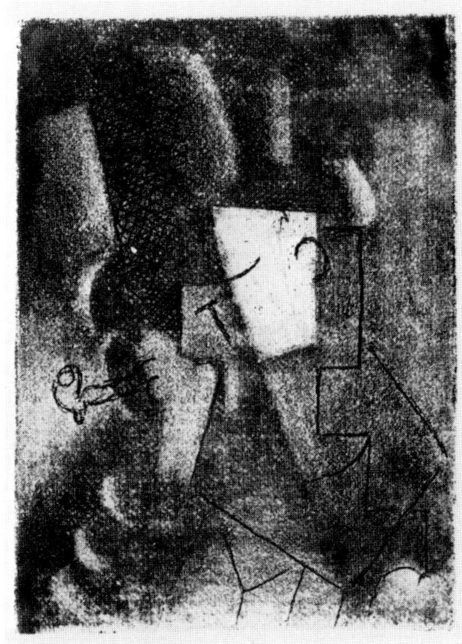

13a.

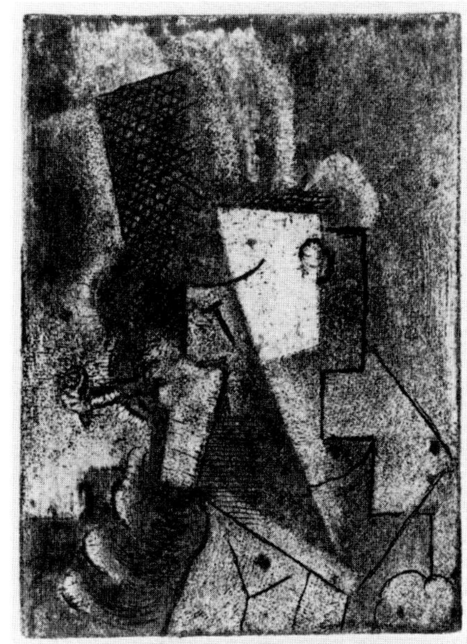

13b.

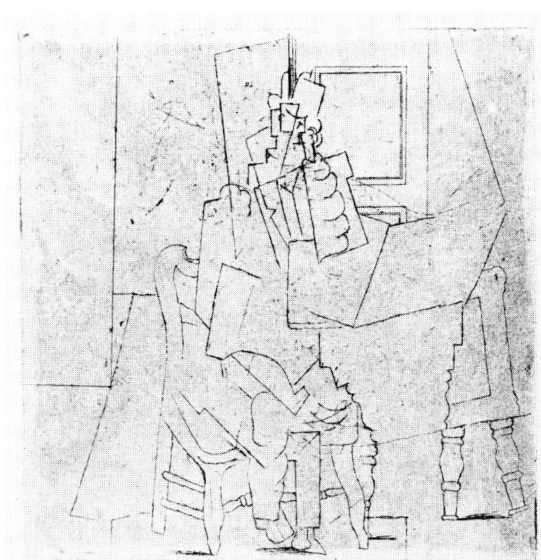

14.

14.
Homme attablé, IV
Man Seated at a Table, IV

1915

Aquatint and etching on copper

120 x 114 mm.

2nd state. Proof pulled by Fort in 1930 on laid old Japan paper.

G.50.II.

As we have seen above, in the 1st state the plate was uniformly bitten with aquatint. It is more than likely that the artist considered this a failed experiment and left it at that. In the 2nd state, he restricted himself to the use of the etching technique as if the plate had not yet been worked on. He pulled four proofs himself and then gave up, leaving the plate in the condition we see here.

The copperplate exists. As for the Fort proofs, see cat. nos. 9, 11, 12, 13.

15.
La Lessive
Woman Wringing her Floor-Cloth

1915

Etching on copper

94 x 48 mm.

Proof pulled by Fort in 1930 on laid old Japan paper.

G.34.

Only four other proofs exist, pulled by the artist in 1915. The copperplate which existed when Geiser published his first volume in 1933 has since been lost. As for the Fort proofs, see cat. nos. 9, 11, 12, 13, 14.

Note

[1]*Dépot légal* is the French term for the obligation of every publisher to give at least one copy of any printed matter he publishes to the Bibliothèque Nationale, Paris. In principle, this obligation also extends to the printer who should send a further copy to the Bibliothèque de l'Arsenal, Paris. However, in the case of an extremely small and limited edition, the printer's obligation is often overlooked and the Bibliothèque Nationale accepts a single copy.

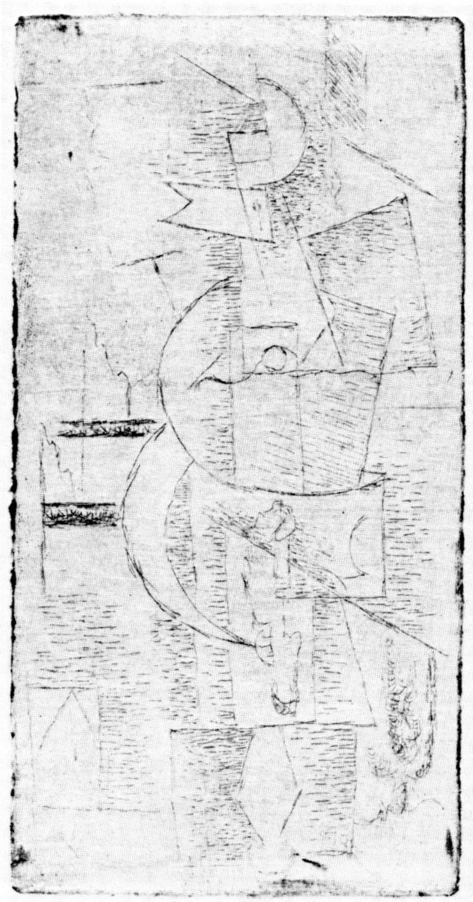

15.

III.

Naturalism, Classicism, and Olga

Picasso's graphic work, apart from a few plates such as the post-cubist *Arlequin* in the *Cornet à dés* (G.54) or the *Guitare sur la table* of 1922 (G.72) or the curvilinear cubist *Femme* (G.99, which should be redated to 1924-25), or those more troubling works such as the *Figures* of 1927 and, later on, the ''surrealist'' images like the small *Baigneuses* of 1932 (see cat. nos. 23, 24, 25), progressively detached itself from the mainstream of his work in other media. It would remain classical in inspiration and handling for many years to come.

Obviously, the same themes and obsessions are shared with other aspects of his *oeuvre*, but in practically every case the approach is different. Picasso's contact with the metal plate seems to have forced him to stand back from himself, even to question, somewhat anxiously at times, the rest of his work. If it has often been said that his work is autobiographical, never is this statement more valid than in reference to his prints. The illustrations of 1927 for Balzac's *Le Chef-d'oeuvre inconnu* provide further confirmation: the engravings remain highly naturalistic, classical and traditional (one could almost say ''Poussinesque'' with the text in mind), whereas it is the drawings depicted in the illustrations such as the one represented on the canvas in G.126, which remind us more typically of the *oeuvres* of Picasso and Frenhofer, Balzac's protagonist. Let us add that it is only after his intimate collaboration with Lacourière, that is to say post-1934, that Picasso became technically a great modern engraver. Until then, he was merely a traditional practitioner who did not really strive to tap all the possibilities latent in a clean, virginal copperplate, which can be said to invite ill-treatment in a free and perhaps even ''erotic'' way.

In 1917, Picasso traveled to Rome, Naples, and Pompeii and met Olga, whom he would marry in 1918. At this time, Olga was truly Ingresque, her classical features combining those of *Mademoiselle Riviere* (1805, Musée du Louvre) and those of *Madame Devaucay* (1807,

Musée Conde, Chantilly). The mixture of Olga and Rome sent him back to classicism and naturalism, the direction in which he had been tempted since 1914. It seems, nevertheless, that he neglected his engraved work during this entire period.

Up until 1923, Eugène Delâtre pulled the plates by Picasso that were to serve as frontispieces or illustrations for books: Max Jacob's *Le Cornet à dés, 1917, Le Phanérogame*, 1918, *La Défense de Tartufe*, 1919; the album *Tricorne*, 1920; Reverdy's *Cravates de chanvre*, 1922; André Breton's *Clair de terre*, 1923. Then, until 1927, Picasso does not appear to have had a printer. In any case, it is likely that he was no longer a regular visitor to Delâtre's workshop. He would work at home, alone, pulling his trial proofs himself. It was only around 1929-30 that Louis Fort, who had worked for Picasso in 1927 at the time of the *Chef- d'oeuvre inconnu*, pulled the trial proofs of numerous older plates. Sometimes Picasso had not pulled a single proof, and other times the plate had not even been bitten, as, for example, with G.88.

If we discount these rather limited editions destined to illustrate books, no other engraved work was published between 1917 and 1927. It was after 1927 that Vollard, for whom Fort had been working for a long time, started to publish the plates from previous years: G.60, G.68 (see cat. no. 18), G.117 (which Geiser dated 1927 but which in fact dates from 1923). Guiot, who employed Leblanc and Trautmann, at this time also began to publish plates from previous years: G.61, G.102, G.105, G.108.

In the meantime, however, Picasso was working. He produced a whole series of small experimental plates which should probably be dated 1923-1924 and encompass research into movement, experiments with the superimposition of a profile on a frontal view, and examination of subjects related to the preliminary studies for the backdrop of *Mercure*. Normally, he would pull a single proof, then abandon the idea. He also produced the series on the Three Graces and the Three Women as well as several portraits. One might ask, nevertheless, why his output was so relatively low. Was he preoccupied by his painting and his public and private lives? Did he lack the necessary equipment in his apartment in the Rue la Boétie? In his prints, one finds little trace of the mannerism of his ''Giant Women'' where, drawing upon Poussin, he dared to blow apart the relatively timid ''lesson'' taken from Ingres' *Bain turc*. He may have been handicapped by the monochromatic nature of engraving, since color was so vitally important in his painted work of the period. Perhaps too he was vaguely tempted by the process of lithography, although his work in this medium lacks any passion or originality, remaining very close to drawing.

Even though no proofs from it have been included in the exhibition, since they have become widely known in the last two years, it is perhaps opportune to mention here the saga of the *Caisse à remords*.[1]

The story is typical of Picasso's way of life. Just as Fort, between 1929-1932, had pulled trial proofs from old plates so that the artist and his potential publishers could choose what was to be published, so when Picasso's boxes were moved from Rue la Boétie to La Californie at Cannes, he and Frélaut made a sort of progressive selection. They went through not only the old plates but also more recent plates which had not yet been pulled. Frélaut has related how Picasso used to look at the copperplates and then discard some of them without a word of explanation or discussion. Then he would choose some plates from which Frélaut would pull a trial proof. These proofs were then perforated and made into an album in a ring-binder. Among these were such widely known plates as the *Sueño y Mentira* series. Then came a second thinning out: some plates were passed over by the artist, others were given to

Frélaut who would then pull three proofs on different kinds of paper (normally laid Auvergne paper, Richard de Bas, colored laid Arches, old paper, or various exotic papers made by Lafuma). On the 30th of October, 1960, Picasso gave the *bons à tirer*[2] for 66 of the plates, without bothering at all about the fact that 12 of them had already been pulled by Lacourière in 1942 on the ''Vollard-Picasso'' paper left over in his workshop. It should be remembered that not infrequently these *bons à tirer* are pulled on a paper which is not that of the ''edition'': for some plates, Frélaut was obliged to hunt all over Paris in order to find a sufficient quantity of rare paper to pull the required quantity of impressions. It is for that reason, too, that some of the plates were printed on three or even four different kinds of paper.

The packets of impressions pulled by Frélaut in Lacourière's workshop in 1961 for Kahnweiler ought to have been signed. Ten of them were in fact signed and put on the market by the Leiris Gallery in 1961. All the rest became the *Caisse à remords*. Frélaut had suggested to Kahnweiler that he bring them to Notre Dame de Vie little by little, wrapped up in a number of small parcels, so that Picasso would not be faced with the daunting prospect of a mountain of signatures. Kahnweiler completely ignored his advice and arrived one day with Frélaut and Jardot and the *caisse*. Picasso took one look at it and asked for it to be put in a corner. He never plucked up the courage to sign them, preferring to get on with his actual work. Kahnweiler felt guilty because of his clumsy psychological approach. Picasso felt guilty for, although he had given the *bons à tirer* and promised the edition to Kahnweiler, he never did sign them.

Finally, it was only in the last months of 1981 that these impressions were put on sale by the Leiris Gallery, after marking each one with a stamp reproducing Picasso's signature. Frélaut pulled the plates as he found them: a few which had been pulled in 1942 had already been steelfaced but the majority had not. Picasso did not approve of the process of steelfacing, thinking it to be a useless and dangerous habit. Among the plates which had not been faced, several did not stand up well to the printing process. Hence, for example, only four proofs could be pulled from G.383, while in the case of G.381 Frélaut only made 15 impressions, being obliged to stop before reaching the edition of 65.

16a&b.

a. Joie maternelle
Maternal Happiness

1922

Etching on zinc

100 x 149 mm.

One of the three proofs pulled by the artist on old laid paper.

G.66; B.49.

The plate, which was pulled later by Frélaut, has vanished.

b. Mère et fils
Mother and Child

1923

Etching on zinc

138 x 128 mm.

Only proof pulled by the artist on a kind of yellowish wove paper.

G.67; B.50.

The plate, cancelled in 1979, exists.

In 1930, Fort pulled two trial proofs from each plate, after which they were left untouched until 1960. In 1961, Frélaut pulled 68 impressions of no. 16a and 72 of no. 16b (Edition Leiris Gallery; *Caisse à remords).*

In 1919-20, Picasso had done a harsh drypoint portrait of Olga, which she probably did not like (one could be forgiven for imagining that the masterful drawing of 1920 [Z.IV.90] could have been transformed into a superb etching). Be that as it may, Olga's Ingresque physique, perhaps because of the very perfection of its soft sculptural form, never seems to have stimulated the artist to take up his etcher's needle. A needle, whether used directly on the metal plate or less brutally on the varnish covering the plate, is by its nature more aggressive than the lead point of a pencil.

Paulo was born in February 1921, and the ensuing familial warmth became the subject of these two prints, nos. 16a & b. It is fascinating to compare the different handling in the two plates. The former, entitled by Geiser *Joie maternelle* (Picasso detested titles) received the mannerist treatment of the *femmes géantes*. And Picasso, as if extracting the rudimentary cross-hatching technique from an old master print, constructed his image from quiet, strong, crossed strokes.

The pose of the child seems directly inspired by the posture of the Cupid wrestling with a baby satyr in Poussin's painting of *Venus and Mercury* (Alleyn College, Dulwich, England), which Picasso could only have known from a reproduction.

The second plate, *Mère et fils* (dated by Geiser 1922 but, because of Paulo's age, more likely to date from 1923), is an intimate and conventional family portrait, full of hesitations and second thoughts and composed in a loose style reminiscent of Bonnard. The artist wanted to see himself as a faithful husband and good father and so tried to pin down the reality of an everyday domestic occurence. It is no longer a ''symbol'' of motherhood, but a live sketch of a real scene. The same theme reappeared circa 1924 in a large etching (B.70), of which the zincplate, rediscovered around 1955 covered with automobile paint, was then pulled by Lacourière and published by the Leiris Gallery.

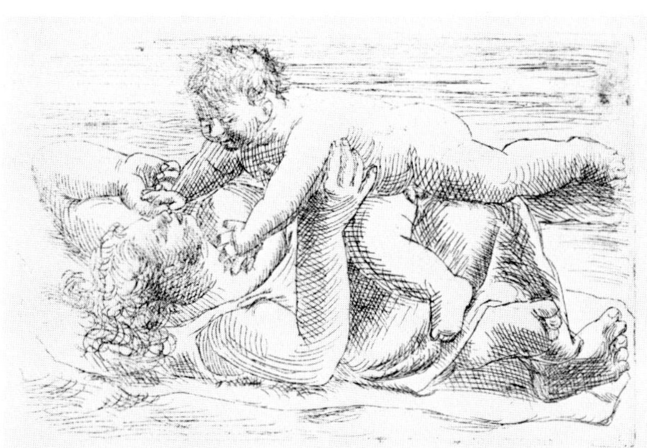

16a.

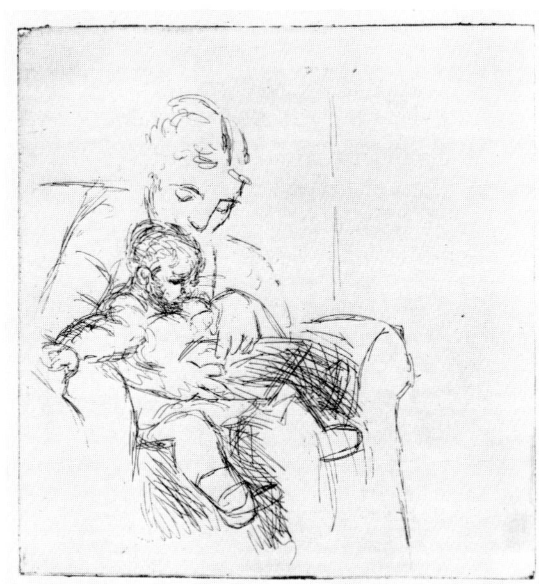

16b.

17.
Portrait de Mme. Picasso, II
Portrait of Madame Picasso, II

1923

Drypoint on zinc

495 x 492 mm.

One of the three proofs pulled by Fort in 1930 on wove Arches-Perrigot paper.

G.109.

This plate was only pulled in 1930. A further six proofs exist, with tone, which were pulled later, after the plate had been bevelled. Perhaps they were trial proofs pulled by Lacourière at the same time as he was pulling B.70, referred to above. The zincplate exists.

Olga had been ill during the last months of 1922, a fact which seems to register in the sadness and resignation of her expression and posture. The Ingresque qualities are now submerged and the drypoint treatment is arid and harsh. Her right eye is thinly veiled, inevitably reminding us of the *Celestine* of 1903. Is it possible that already in Picasso's mind Olga had been placed in that highly Spanish category of ''married women and mothers''?

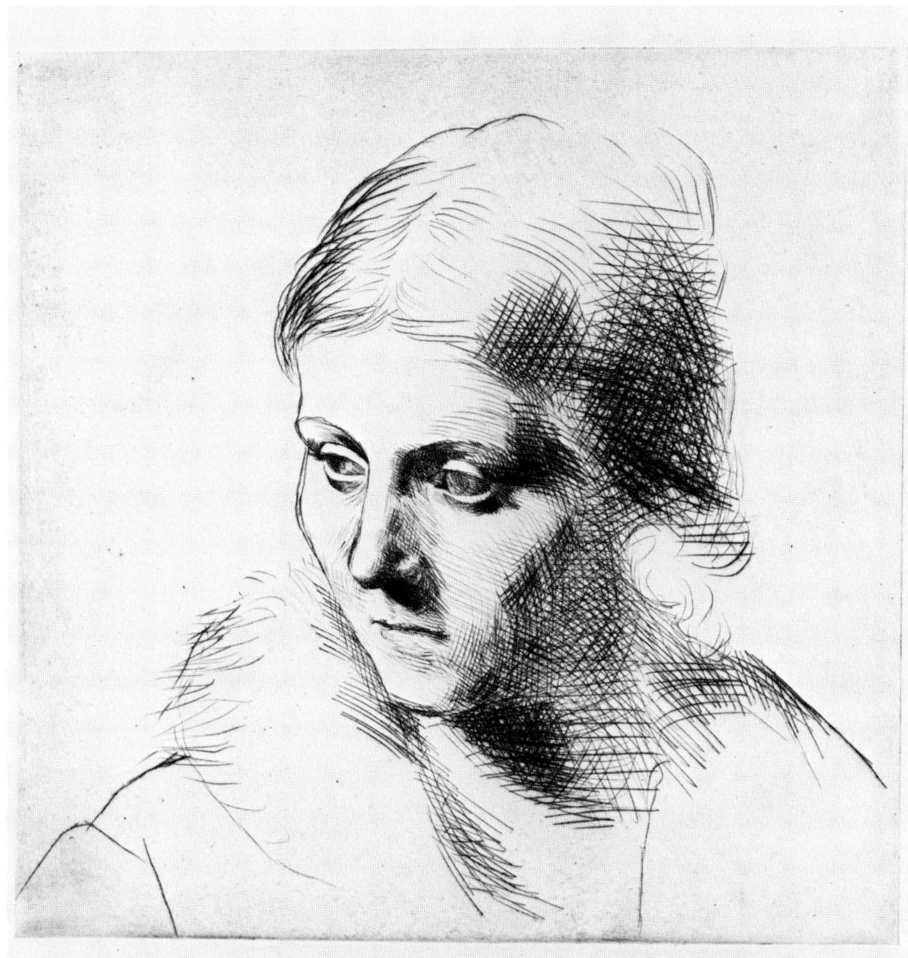

17.

18a-d.
Les Trois femmes
The Three Women

1924

Etching on zinc

175 x 130 mm.

a. 1st state: one of two proofs pulled by the artist on old paper.

b. 2nd state: one of two proofs pulled by the artist on old paper.

c&d. 3rd state: I) one of six proofs pulled by the artist on old paper. II) one of the few proofs pulled by Fort before steelfacing in 1930 on wove Arches paper.

The plate, steelfaced circa 1930, was then published by Vollard (a few trial proofs on wove Arches paper, signed; 60 impressions, wove Arches paper, signed; three on glossy Japan, signed; 40 on Japan, signed). There exist a few proofs pulled from the cancelled plate which belonged to Vollard: B.51; G.68.III.B in the unpublished forthcoming supplement of Geiser's first volume.

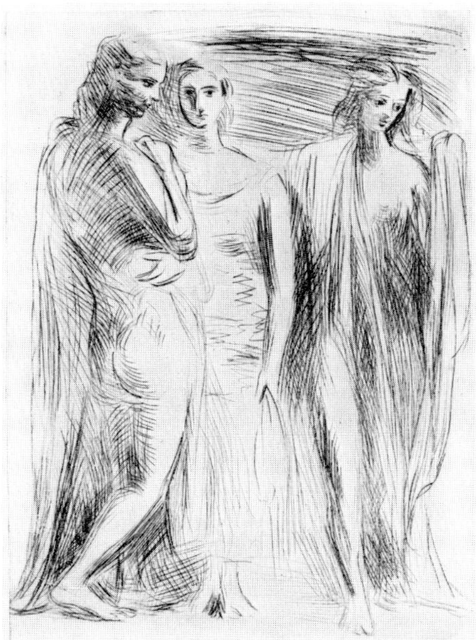

18a.

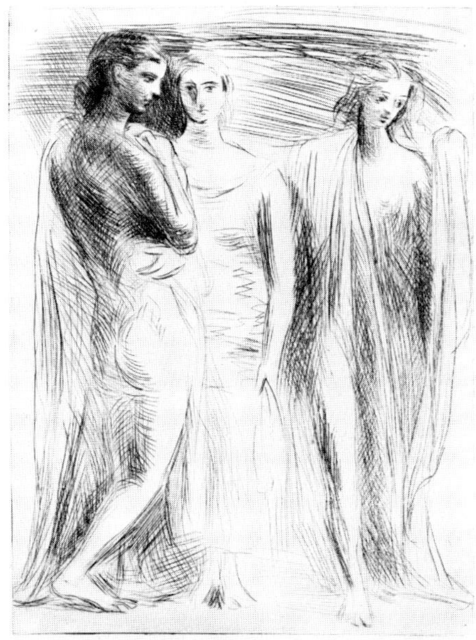

18b.

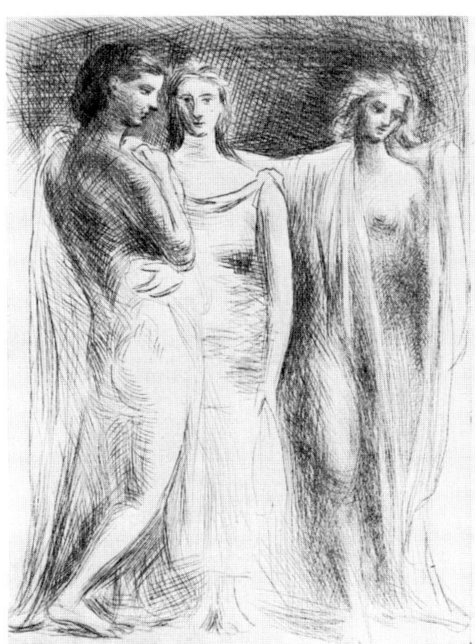

18c.

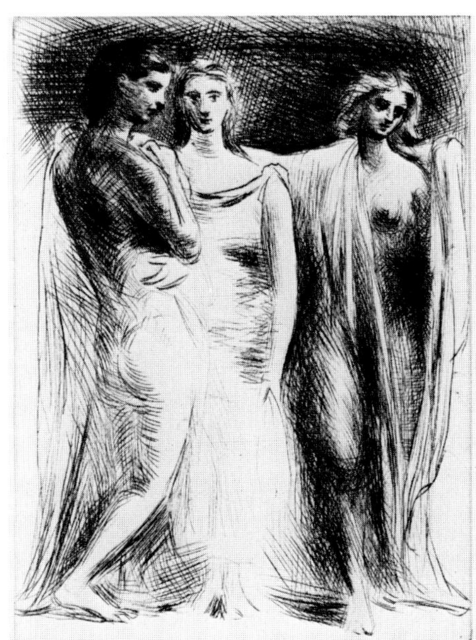

18d.

Three points need to be stressed here:

1. Picasso painted in *grisaille* an almost identical composition, reversed, on an extremely large canvas (*Les Trois graces*, Z.V.250; 2.50 x 1.50 m.), which is generally dated 1924; hence, our dating of the engraving to the same year (Geiser's date is 1922). It was one of the last times in Picasso's life that an identical subject was repeated in a painting and in an engraving. It is impossible to establish whether the engraving antedates the painting, or vice-versa, or whether they were executed simultaneously. The woman on the left, when reworked in the 2nd and 3rd states of our engraving, seems to be an actual portrait, more beautiful and alive than her ''sister'' on the canvas, whereas the woman on the right in the engraving, on the contrary, takes on far more grace and nobility on the canvas.

2. It is well-known that Picasso once said to Zervos (see *Cahiers d'Art*, vol. X, no. 7-10, Paris, 1936, p.37): ''In the old days, paintings were developing progressively. A painting was an amalgam of additions. My paintings are an amalgam of destructions.'' As far as his prints are concerned, this statement becomes more and more true: the visitor to this exhibition can follow the process state by state as in, for example, cat. nos. 144 to 161. But at this early date it is not yet entirely accurate: the states of no. 17 ''develop progressively'' in a traditional manner.

3. Another question springs to mind: why in the 1920s does the theme of the Three Women and the Three Graces occur again and again? In general, this theme symbolizes feminine friendship. Later on, Picasso treated, under various guises, the theme of ''two women'' in a way which is at one and the same time more precise and more suggestive. All his life, he was disturbed by the theme of ''women together.''

We must not forget to say a word or two about the artist's passion for old paper. As we saw above, in 1961 Frélaut was obliged to rush around Paris looking for a sufficient quantity of paper to pull the *Caisse à remords*, and, for example, the majority of the seven states of the *Minotauromachie* are printed on old paper. Picasso bought up every single old sketchbook he could find to draw or to write in. It is not unlikely that this mania became even more compulsive during his Italian trip, where it was still possible to obtain marvelous, bound, old but clean sketchbooks.

Notes

[1] *Caisse à remords*: the original French is kept here as, on the one hand, this is now the ''official ''title of this group of engravings and, on the other hand, it is not possible to translate it well or concisely. Literally, it means packing-case of remorse. The reasons why this title was originally adopted are explained in the text.

[2] *Bon à tirer*: a technical term used throughout the world nearly always in French. The words can be roughly translated as ''O.K. for printing.'' That is, the artist has chosen, after various trial proofs, one which seems to him to correspond best to his intentions. No further corrections are necessary, the inking suits him, etc., so he gives his go-ahead to the printer who, during the printing, uses the annotated and signed proof as a guide.

IV.

Marie-Thérèse

1927 is a crucial date in the life and work of Picasso. Early in the year, the 45 year old artist, in full creative prime of life, met Marie-Thérèse Walter, 17, blond, athletic and beautiful. She was to become not only his great love but also his inspiration, his ever-present muse.

A new love, and a new creative impulse meant that his work could not help but change. His day-to-day existence still revolved around his wife, Olga, and their young son, Paolo, but Marie-Thérèse became the center of his work whether in paintings, drawings, sculpture or engravings. Not only did Picasso paint her portrait over and over again, not only is she present through the cypher MT or MTP, which baffled the public of the period, or in the enormous *Still-life on a Pedestal Table* of March 1931 (Z.VII.317), not only does the whole of the Boisgeloup sculpture series spring from this obsession, but further, one cannot escape the impression that for years, even after meeting Dora Maar, Marie-Thérèse haunted his pencil, his pen, his brush, during every creative movement.

As far as the subject of engraving is concerned, Marie-Thérèse is omnipresent: asleep, awake, bathing on her favorite beaches, his friend, his love, his model for sculpture, the Minotaur's eternal companion, torero, spectator, child, doubled, tripled, infinitely multiplied. Just by casually leafing through Geiser's catalogue, her face and features become so familiar that we greet her like an old friend. Thus, Picasso's entire graphic output from 1927 to 1937, highly autobiographical, is nothing but a never-ending lyrical poem to Marie-Thérèse. Already in 1927 she appeared, as she looked then, in cat. no. 19, and as an unformed adolescent in *Le Modèle nu* (G.119) and in the *Chef-d'oeuvre inconnu* (G.130 and 135). In fact, the artist inscribed every single page of one of the 99 suites: ''For you and for me,'' with also the cypher ''WT'' (W being the inverted M of Marie and standing for Walter).

In Picasso's illustrations of Ovid, her face appears again in the marginal drawings or *remarques* (e.g. G.163), and particularly in the margins of the unpublished plates (G.179 and 180). From 1931 until 1937, Marie-Thérèse was a constant theme. Although sometimes disguised, as in certain rape scenes, Marie-Thérèse never underwent that ''process of destruction'' which Picasso mentioned in his conversation with Zervos and which seems so obvious to those who look closely at his paintings.

At this time Picasso also managed to find a printer again, Louis Fort. As we have mentioned, Fort used to work for Vollard and had pulled Vollard's edition of the *Saltimbanques* in 1913. Between 1927 and the summer of 1932, it was Fort and not Picasso who pulled all the trial proofs. This alone proves that Picasso was often in Fort's workshop. In the summer of 1932, the artist installed Fort's printing press at Boisgeloup and once more began to pull the trial proofs of his engravings, probably because Fort was on the verge of retiring for good to Golfe-Juan. He seems to have pulled one more edition of G.206 for Vollard about 1933, although at that time he was, for all intents and purposes, in complete retirement.

There can be no doubt that a strong bond of friendship existed between the artist and his printer until the latter's death. However, despite the plates worked on in Antibes from the end of September to the beginnning of October 1945, from which Fort pulled a few trial proofs (cat. no. 78 and a group of engravings to be described in the forthcoming supplement to Geiser's catalogue), and despite *Les Pipeaux* (B.1347-1349), which no doubt were produced during Picasso's stay with Fort together with Françoise Gilot at the end of the summer of 1946, there is no sign of a true collaboration between the two men. Fort was merely an intaglio printer; artists used to bring him engravings to be pulled and his intervention stopped there. Unlike Lacourière, he did not have a workshop where Picasso could work on the copperplates themselves, and, unlike Lacourière, Fort was not and never became an engraver himself. After the masterpieces of technical boldness which Picasso created with Lacourière, it is not without interest to note that the Antibes and Golfe-Juan etchings of 1945-46, possibly put in the acid bath and certainly pulled by Fort, mark a short return of the artist to a more conventional and classic technique.

19.
Portrait de Marie-Thérèse
Portrait of Marie-Thérèse

1928

Lithograph: lithographic pencil and wash (?) on stone

220 x 172 mm. approximately

3rd and 4th states pulled head to tail on the same sheet of ordinary coated paper, annotated "1e" and "2e" by Duchâtel, the printer.

G.224 ("*Tête de jeune fille*"); M.XXIV.

This is a classical portrait, life-like and conventional, of the 18 year old Marie-Thérèse with a hairstyle typical of the period. In contrast with the other portrait of Marie-Thérèse from 1928 (G.243; M.XXIII; B.95), which is a transfer of a drawing of the same dimensions simply "corrected "with a lithographic crayon on the stone (heavier shadowing, especially on the brow), our lithograph must have been directly executed on the stone. In the 1st to the 4th states, the only work done is with the scraper, which results in a lightening of the face and the brow. Only 11 proofs of this lithograph were pulled and numbered, as on our example, from "1" to "11" including seven proofs of the 2nd state. Proof no. 10 is missing at the present time.

20. (see color plate)
Baigneuse au pouf rouge
Bather on a Red Cushion

c. 1930-1931

Oil paint on etching

Size of the proof: 260 x 186 mm.

Size of the paper: 385 x 300 mm.

Inventory No. of the Picasso Estate: 12549.

G.200.III.

Oil paint on a trial proof, pulled on Rives wove paper by Vernant or Fort, of the 3rd state of G.200 (*Deux nus assis*, etching on copperplate). The copperplate had already been cut, bevelled and steelfaced. An edition of 100, printed by Vernant and Fort, was published by the "Nouvel Essor": B.133.

21. (see color plate)
Deux Femmes
Two Women

c. 1930-1931

See no. 20.

Inventory No. of the Picasso Estate: 12550.

Oil paint on a second trial proof of G.200, 3rd state.

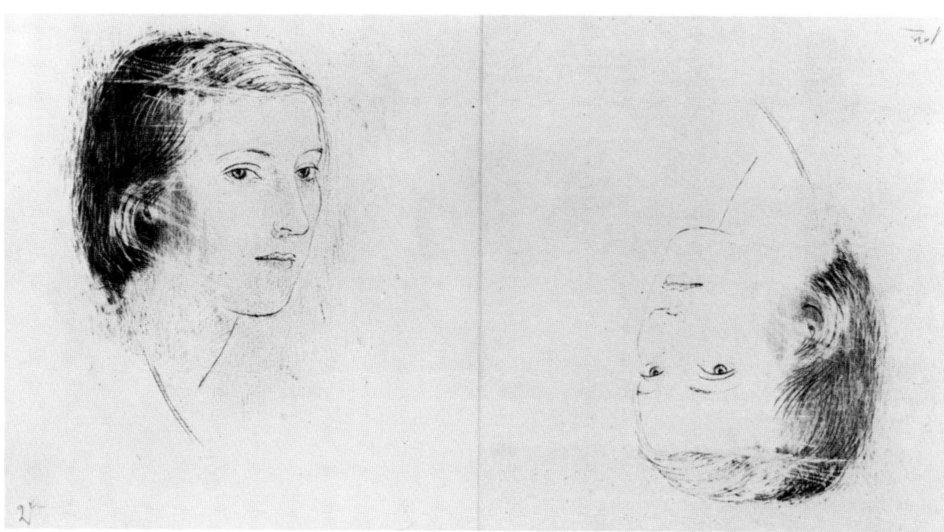

19.

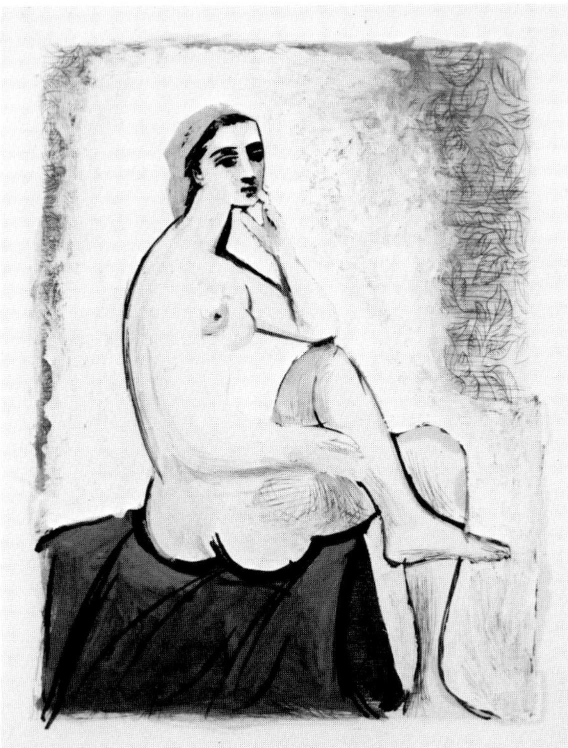

20.

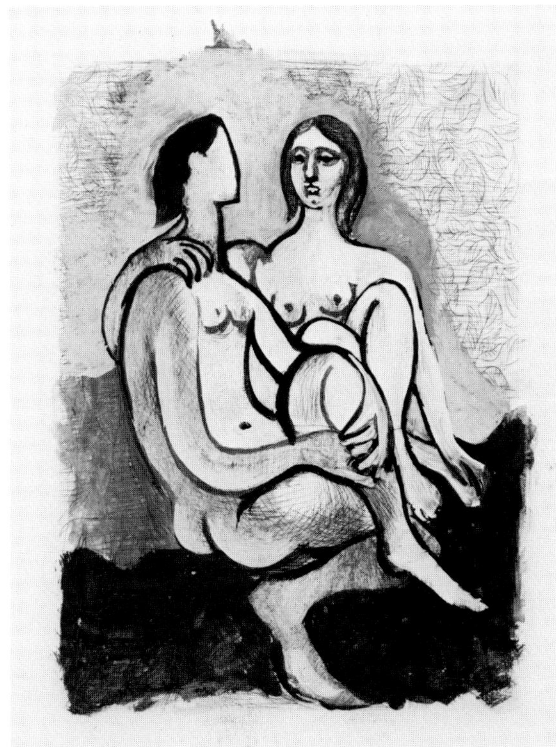

21.

The two "sister" etchings (G.199 and 200) cannot be separated from one another. G.199 is dated 30 September 1930 and our etching should probably be given the same date although this is difficult to establish as the copperplate has never left the editor's possession so it is impossible to determine if any date is scratched on the back of the plate. In G.199 and 200, the woman on the left bears a strong resemblance to Marie-Thérèse. In her counterpart in cat. nos. 20 and 21, however, her features, having been worked over in paint, are no longer recognizable.

Cat. no. 21 follows the etching (G.200) faithfully, the oil wash serving only to emphasize the twin-like quality of the two original etchings, creating a sort of intermediate state between the two poses. Once again we are faced with the theme of "two women," which, for a long time to come, would displace the Three Graces. Picasso concentrated here on the relationship between two women and their intimacy as they bathe or wash themselves, far from prurient masculine eyes. Marie-Thérèse had a sister, Jeanne, who had an almost incestuous passion for her. It was platonic but Picasso sensed it and it bothered him. His resulting jealousy prevented him from ever liking her. The fact is, however, that this theme is a recurring motif in Picasso's work from 1904 onward (see Z.XXII.63).

Cat. no. 20, in a more detached way, is also linked to this theme. Our *Baigneuse* is a reinterpretation of the *Baigneuse de Valpinçon* painted by Ingres in 1908 (Musée du Louvre), which itself was reused by the artist in his *Petite baigneuse. Intérieur de harem* of 1828 (Musée du Louvre), a painting that clearly stresses the theme of "women together." Furthermore, Picasso seems also to refer to an Ingresque technique or process. We know that Ingres had no compunction about reusing the pose of one of his models by "flipping it over." For example, the naked woman playing the rebec who is seen from the back in the foreground of the *Bain turc* (1859-62, Musée du Louvre) has the same pose as the woman playing the rebec, fully dressed and seen frontally in the *Odalisque à l'esclave* (1842, Walters Art Gallery, Baltimore). In a similar fashion, Picasso takes the *Baigneuse de Valpinçon* and "flips her over "in order to show her frontally. The 1828 *Baigneuse* then enters the process, lending the red of its drapery to the cushion in the Picasso and the yellow stripes of the turban to Picasso's yellow scarf.

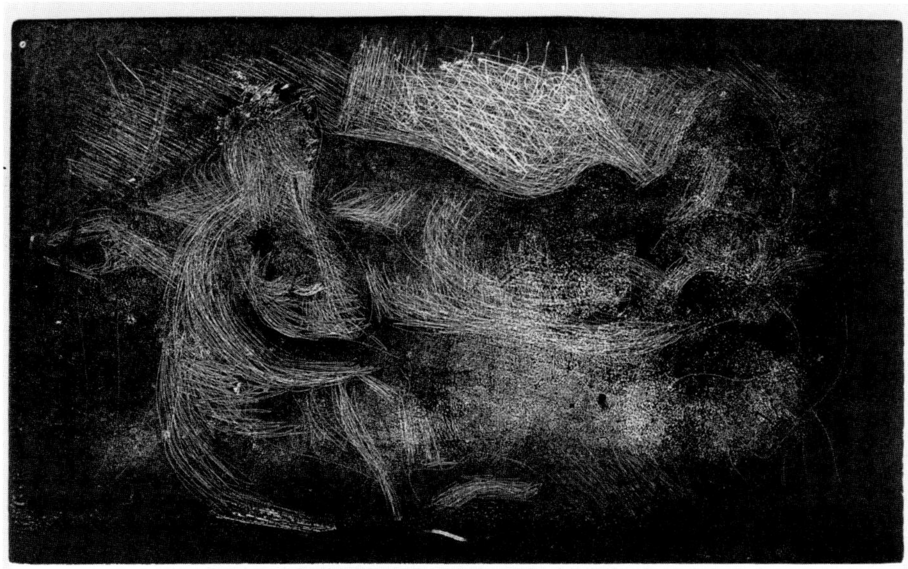

22a.

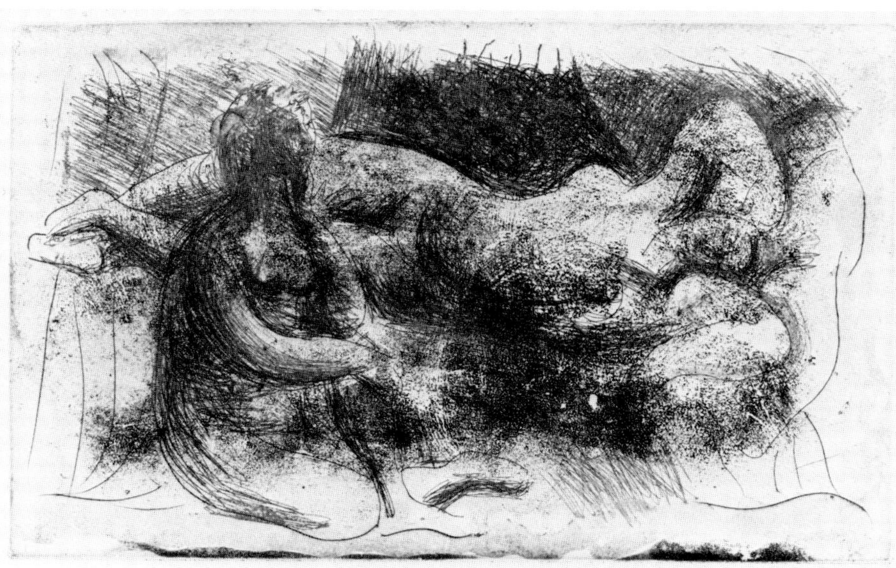

22b.

22a&b.
Dormeuse veillée par une femme assise
A Sleeping Woman Watched Over by a Seated Woman

1932 (probably July)

Etching, with a few drypoint strokes, on copper (something happened to the varnish when the plate was bitten by acid; hence, the black spotting on the positive proof. Picasso was fond of this type of "accident.")

184 x 296 mm.

a. One proof pulled in negative on ordinary wove paper, either by the artist, or later on by Lacourière, or even later on a lithographic press for a possible transfer.

b. One trial proof pulled by Lacourière in 1942 on wove Montval paper with Picasso watermark, before the contemporary edition of 55 proofs (B.238). The edition was pulled from the plate after steelfacing. The plate, cancelled in 1979, exists.

G.261 (*"Femme assise et Femme étendue"*); B.238.

The subject, which is evidently related to the *Odalisque à l'esclave* (see no. 20), is the second appearance in Picasso's engraved work of one of his favorite themes, following the superb *Femmes se reposant* (G.210) of nine months earlier. It takes different forms: a woman gazing at a sleeping man or Minotaur, or a man gazing at a sleeping woman. In this case, the gazing man is replaced by a second woman. We know that Marie-Thérèse loved sleeping, that she went to bed very early and got up early too, while Picasso much preferred going to bed and getting up late. But once again, it would be a mistake to read too much importance into such a factual detail. A handsome 1904 drawing, with highlights in watercolor, (Z.I.235) already shows the importance of this idea, depicting Picasso himself as he watches a woman sleeping. We have here another variant of the motif of a couple's mutual loneliness. The sleeper, lost in her dreams, escapes the watcher; the watcher, even though the object of his desire is at his mercy, remains aloof, revelling perhaps in his freedom but, from time to time, painfully lonely.

Relevant to this print are the facts behind the 42 plates pulled by Lacourière on laid Montval paper with the Picasso or Vollard watermark in 1942. In 1940, during the "Exodus," the Lacourières fled from Paris, like many others, but they rapidly decided to return and they settled in their country house at Chessy on the outskirts of the city. The workshop was closed as there were no workers and the artists had mostly left Paris. At least at Chessy one could find food and there were always the vegetables and fruits from the garden. Nevertheless, Lacourière, bored with the country, used to go to Paris to visit his workshop and to walk around in the city streets. One day in 1941 he met Picasso there and they started talking. There was one worker left, Le Père Molinier, too old to have been a soldier during "the phony war" and to have been captured, like Frélaut, too old to be called to work in Germany. Some of the paper from the *Suite Vollard* still remained, and paper was scarce. Picasso, wishing to help Lacourière, decided to let him pull the 42 plates we have mentioned. 55 or 56 impressions were made of these plates if their condition allowed (for example, G.382 only withstood 28). These editions were never put into circulation except the *Combat* (B.301), which went on sale at the Galerie Leiris in 1943. The remaining impressions stayed piled up in Picasso's apartment. It should be pointed out that the copperplate of our etching, from which Picasso pulled one proof at Boisgeloup, is the last in date from which Louis Fort, at that moment, pulled two trial proofs inked in red.

V.

Women on the Beach

In May 1931, Picasso moved into the Château de Boisgeloup, the proximity to Paris of which was highly convenient for him. He turned the stables into a workshop, where he set up Louis Fort's printing press a bit later. This marked the start of a whole series of experiments in engraving which he pursued without any outside help. As we have seen, after a year without touching a copperplate, he began in July 1932 to pull trial proofs (cat. no. 22).

In the summer of 1932, Olga and Paulo left for Juan-les-Pins, but it would seem that Picasso himself stayed on at Boisgeloup. Many paintings and drawings dated June, July, August, September and October 1932 bear the annotation: Boisgeloup. Where was Marie-Thérèse? She may have paid a few brief visits to Boisgeloup, although this is not known for sure. She certainly was spending time on beaches.

In August and September, the artist produced a series of canvases representing women bathing at the beach. At the end of August, he executed two extremely large canvases (146 x 114 cm.) in both of which the women wear the same odd mauve swimming costumes with triangles: white triangles for the sitting woman with Marie-Thérèse's head (August 24), and yellow triangles for the famous *Baigneuse à la balle* in the Ganz Collection (August 30, Z.VIII.147). One remarks that the landscape of this second canvas cannot possibly be that of Juan-les-Pins. The cliff, the flag and the bathing hut are much more evocative of the Normandy beaches. Then, between the 4th and 15th of September, Picasso executed a series of about 20 very small paintings (19 x 23 cm., 22 x 33 cm., etc.), all of which represent women frolicking on the beach. Some are naked, some wear highly colored bathing costumes, all of them are playing like children. The paintings are gay, burlesque and ''cartoon-like.'' The women disport, feature amoeba-like anatomy pushing and pulling in different directions, and sometimes bend their bodies with the professional movements of Picasso's circus acrobats of February 1933 (see e.g. Z.VIII.231). The meaning of this series may be gleaned from a small canvas, dated September 30, where a satyr is chasing a similar group of naked young virgins. It is well-known that Picasso was exceedingly jealous, and Marie-Thérèse had great success on the beaches.

Picasso made no prints during the summer, but at the end of November and the beginning of December in Paris he reused the theme of bathing women, this time on zinc and copperplates. The result, once again, is some twenty small images (roughly 15 x 10 cm.) oriented vertically rather than horizontally like the paintings (G.262, to be dated the 29th of November, and G.265-284). The series ended with three somewhat larger compositions of a rectangular horizontal format, the *sauvetages* (life-savings). Here there is a difference with the women in the canvases: surrounded by curious, even monstrous shapes, Marie-Thérèse is always there, always beautiful. In G.270 (B.242), we can count up to six Marie-Thérèses, stretched out on the sand, diving and swimming. In the *sauvetages* she again has multiple embodiments, one of them as an unconscious, perhaps drowned swimmer. Is this rescue scene an allusion to a real story which Marie-Thérèse had told Picasso, and/or the imaginary fantasy of revenge/anxiety felt by the artist? One can only hypothesize. Although some of the women at the beach remind us of those individuals obsessed by the sea in summer, these beach scenes could also be a response to the austerity of winter, to Picasso's renewed conjugal existence, to a desire for freedom, nature and fresh air.

Was the choice of small formats for the canvases (in 1928, he did a series on the same subject with a similar format) and for the plates a conscious one? Picasso may have had in mind Seurat's *petites poseuses*, which would not enter the Louvre until the Fénéon sale in 1947 but which he had certainly seen at least in reproduction. On the other hand, it may be just a coincidence. These images all give the impression of an amusement or a distraction. After his gigantic canvases and monumental sculptures, they could have served as a relaxation, although he went back to monumental works between the two series with the drawings inspired by the *Crucifixion* of Grunewald.

These little plates were pulled by the artist, who seems to have been enjoying the process of experiment. Some are done with granular outlines simply produced by leaving, without pricking them with a goose feather, large bubbles in the acid which bites the lines. Different types of inking are found (proofs pulled in negative, or proofs pulled without any inking at all). In some cases, several plates are printed on the same sheet of paper. Picasso was working hard, but since he was also having fun he managed to impart to these small proofs a kind of ripeness which makes them both touching and extraordinary objects. They are all different and they chronical a merger of whim, obsession, art and craftsmanship.

Individual plates met different fates. A few were given by Picasso to surrealist writer friends as frontispieces for their books: *L'Antitête* by Tzara (1933, G.280); *Petite anthologie poétique du surrealisme* by Hugnet (1934, G.278); the *Album Jakovski* (1934, G.268). *La Plongeuse* (G.277) was pulled in 1936 by Le Père Molinier in Lacourière's workshop with different cut-outs used as collages which Picasso added one by one as the 30 proofs were pulled. The remainder either were never published or else only in 1961 as in the case of seven of them in the *Caisse à remords*.

23a,b,c.
Trois femmes sur la plage
Three Women on the Beach

1932 (November 23, Paris)

Etching on copper

125 x 92 mm.

a. One proof on wove Whatman paper, annotated on the bottom in pencil ''planche I, du 23 novembre XXXII.''

b. One proof on wove paper without watermark (Whatman?) pulled with tone.

c. One proof on laid Italian paper with the watermark ''L I,'' pulled in negative.

All three proofs pulled by the artist.

The copperplate (on exhibition), annotated on the verso ''PARIS/23 novembre XXXII,'' was cancelled in 1979.

G.268.A,a,b (''*Trois figures sur la plage*'').

After steelfacing, edition of 30 pulled on wove paper by Tanneur: *Album Jakovski* (ed. Orobitz, 1935): 23 engravings by Arp, Gonzalez, de Chirico, Miro, etc. (B.241). The humoristic quality of this plate made it eminently suitable for inclusion in an album of this type.

24a,b,c.
Jeux au bord de la mer, II
Beach Games, II

1932 (November 29, Paris)

Etching on copper

140 x 112 mm.

a. One proof on heavy Japan paper.

b. One proof on heavy Japan paper pulled in negative (grey background).

c. One proof on heavy Japan paper pulled in negative (black background).

G.281.a,b,c.

The plate, not steelfaced, exists with the scratched annotation on the verso: ''PARIS/29 novembre/XXXII/III.'' The number ''III'' following the date indicates that it was the third plate engraved by the artist on that day.

All the 12 proofs were pulled by Picasso. Note the grainy strokes obtained by allowing the acid bubbles to bite around the lines drawn in the varnish. Note also the profiles of Marie-Thérèse on each side of the proof.

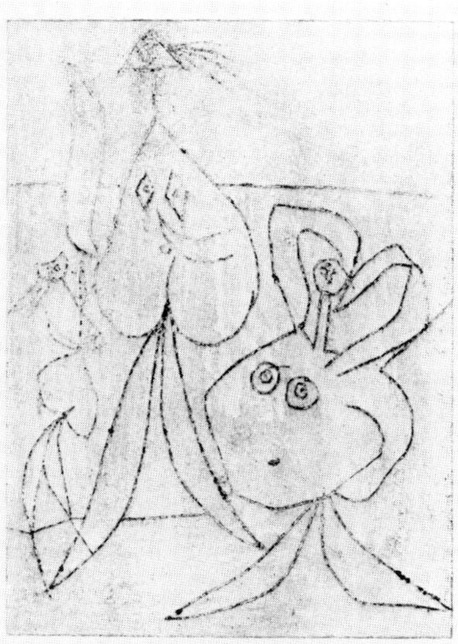

23a.

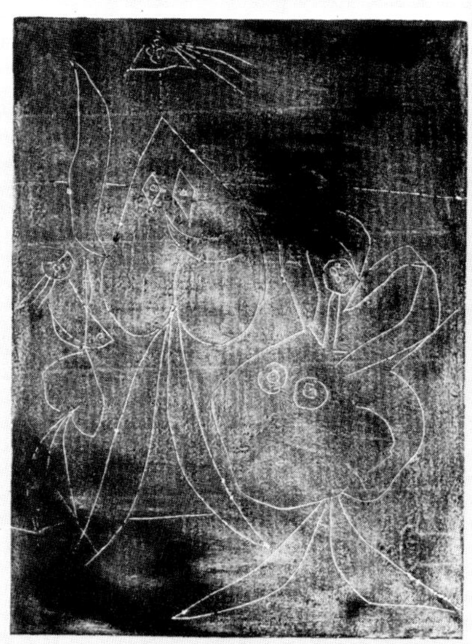

23b.

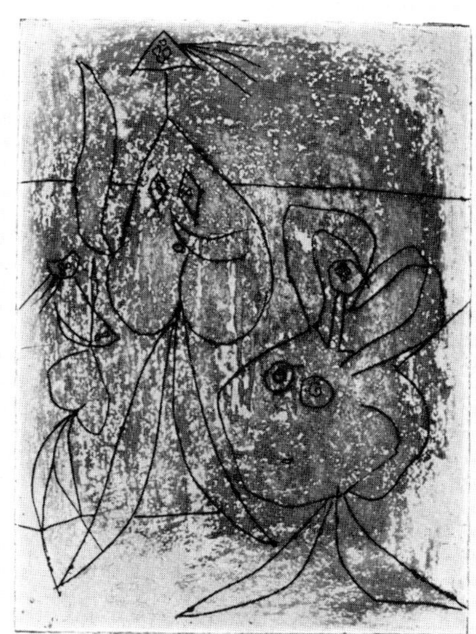

23c.

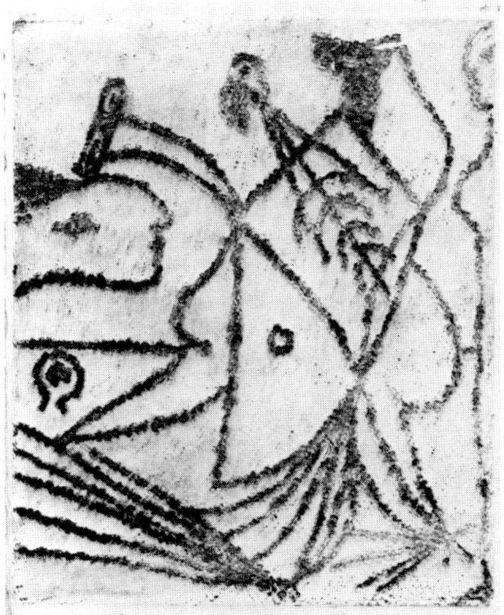

24a.

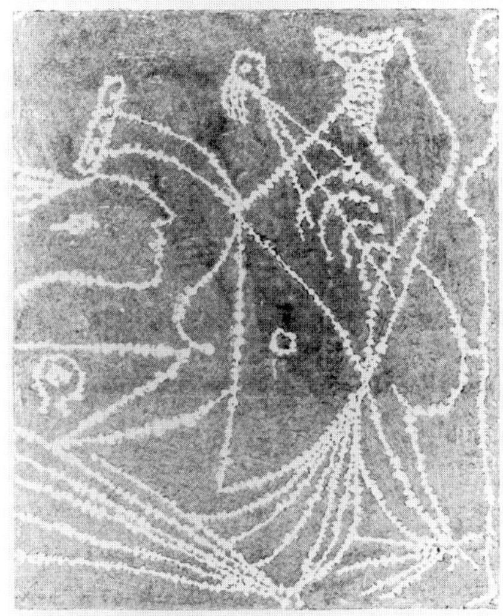

24b.

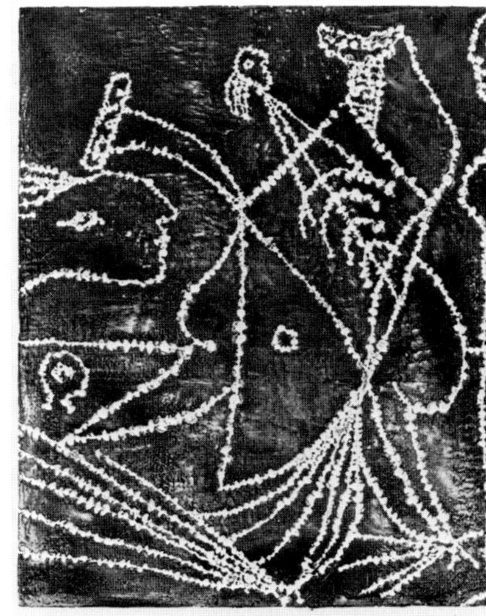

24c.

25a&b.
Trois baigneuses
Three Bathers

1932 (December 7)

Etching on copper

140 x 113 mm.

Two proofs with different inkings pulled by the artist on heavy Japan paper.

G.283.A.

The copperplate exists, not steelfaced, and with the scratched annotation on the verso "7 décembre XXXII.II."

In addition to the four proofs pulled by the artist, there is a further proof in negative pulled by Lacourière in 1933 or later. Note here also the effect of the acid bubbles and the profiles of Marie-Thérèse. We reproduce here a small painting, dated 4 September 1932, which shows exactly the same scene (fig. 1).

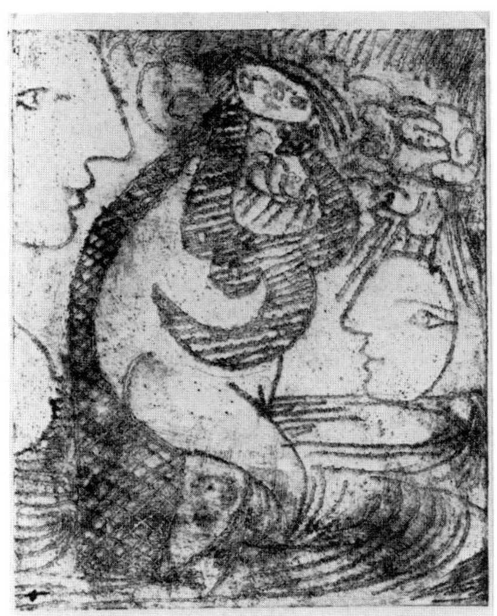

25a.

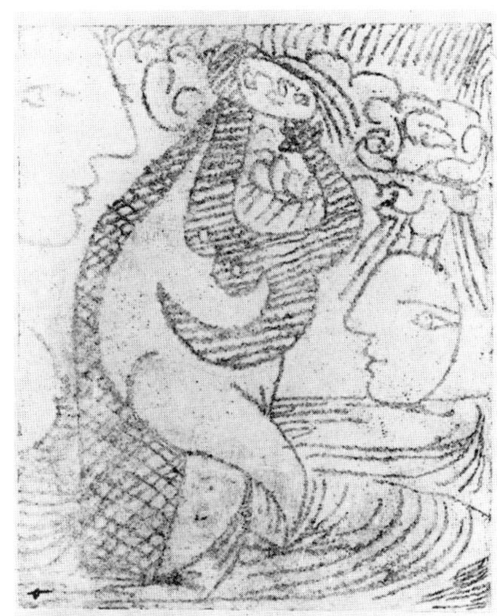

25b.

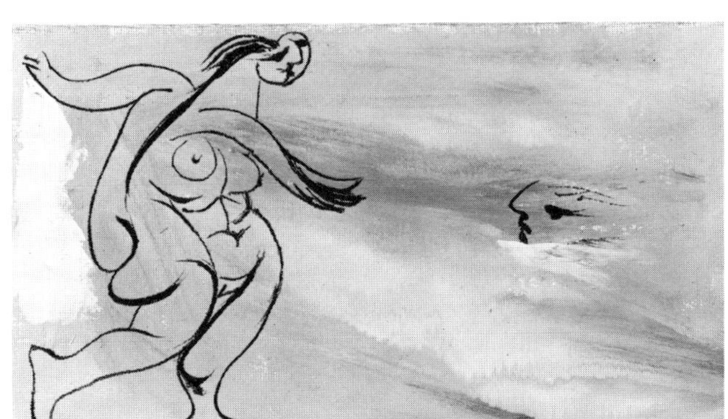

Fig. 1. Picasso, *Bathers*, Sept. 4, 1932, oil on canvas, 19 × 23 cm., Marina Picasso Collection, Picasso Estate Inv. No. 12627.

VI.

Erwinography and Monotypes

We now have to retreat a few months in order to describe the Erwinographies on exhibition which probably date from June - July 1932 and which can be compared with the monotypes of early 1933. Even though, as we shall see, Erwinography is in principle a type of reproduction process, Picasso in his usual way manipulated it to such an extent that the results of his experiments can be linked with his monotypes.

On the 26th of May, 1932, Picasso employed Erwinography in the normal way: that is to say, he drew on tracing paper and then ''printed'' on paper with various inkings using the process described below. It probably was Julio Gonzalez who introduced his ever curious countryman to this technique, as there are a group of other Erwinographies where it is difficult on purely stylistic grounds to distinguish the hand of one from the other.

Dr. Geiser spent a long time studying this process and our technical explanations are based on his unpublished research, which in turn was based in part on explanations by the inventor of the process. Geiser decided not to include the Erwinographies in his catalogue raisonné of Picasso's engravings. One can well understand this decision when one looks at the work of the 26th of May cited above: a bearded man's head for which a drawing on tracing paper was found in the artist's portfolios. However, the modifications Picasso made to the basic process (cat. nos. 26-30) justify in our eyes their inclusion here.

Erwinography was invented and perfected between 1914-1924 by Erwin Quedenfelt first in Vienna and then later on in The Hague. It never had an enormous success, especially since the inventor would only reveal the special formula of his gelatin to clients who paid for an individual license. The patent was granted at The Hague around 1924. It is not known how Picasso, or Gonzalez, obtained the vital chemical formula.

Gelatin expands in water. When it is ''tanned'', for instance by exposure to sunlight, it dries up and can no longer expand. The matrix of an Erwinograph is a glass plate covered with a special gelatin which is sensitized with ammonium bichromate. In principle, the artist draws on tracing paper and then applies this drawing to the glass plate before exposing it to varying intensities of daylight according to the degree of tanning desired. Those areas of gelatin protected by the drawing stay tender and capable of expansion in water, whereas the rest is ''cooked'' by its exposure to the light. Then one has only to plunge the glass plate in cold water for the untanned gelatin to expand so that the raised areas can be inked (Erwinography is a relief-printing process). Then, by manual pressure on the back of the glass plate, the inked portions are pressed onto a sheet of paper. Each time the matrix is reused, the gelatin must be cooled again in water so that it can expand again. The inking is usually done with printers' ink thinned with turpentine, or with watercolor mixed with gum arabic. The artist must ink the plate himself with a brush and thus there can never be two identical proofs.

Picasso, of course, chose to modify the technique. In our example, he applied directly onto the glass plate pieces of tarlatan, a feather and a cut-out of a head. Then in the six ''states'' he altered the gelatin, whether by scraping or by using alum as a tanning agent, in order to transform his subject. In one example he even pulled the plate in negative so as to obtain a positive small portrait of Marie-Thérèse, engraved with the needle on the tanned gelatin of the background, as we can see on the left of cat no. 30. In the Musée Picasso, Paris, there is a subsequent 6th state (the central head has long hair and Marie-Thérèse's features in negative) as well as some proofs of the 2nd state printed in color.

Between the end of December 1932 and March 1933, Picasso produced about 20 monotypes, of which he usually pulled one, more often two, or sometimes even three or four proofs. The technique of the monotype is well-known: the artist paints on a flat clean support (in our case, copperplate) with printers' ink, gouache or oil paint. The plate then passes through the press like an engraving. Generally, it is impossible to pull more than two proofs and the second one is always weaker.

On the 19th of January, Picasso began a series of 47 monotypes, all different, on the same copperplate which he would later use for a related etching *Flûtiste et dormeuse I* (G.287), and which he would literally plough into during the execution of the 31 states. Curiously enough, when dealing with an analogous subject, *Les Deux femmes* of January 1946, once again Picasso would rework the composition, this time on the lithographic stone, through 21 states (see cat. nos. 79-84). As we have seen, he was fascinated by the motif of ''women together'' and also by that of a sleeper being watched over by another person whose sex varies. In the monotypes exhibited here (nos. 31 and 32), he was more precise in meaning: the watching woman is playing a flute, thus giving a clear erotic connotation to the subject.

Cat. nos. 33 and 34 carry on the theme of Marie-Thérèse in monotype but pose a problem. As we know, the monumental Boisgeloup sculptures representing the head of Marie-Thérèse date from 1931-1932 and it was from February 1933 onwards that Picasso returned to this composition in his engravings and monotypes. Perhaps he was looking back over his shoulder at his sculpted work, or was attempting to compress three dimensions onto a single plane, or was beset by doubts about his earlier work. At any rate, in numerous plates of the *Suite Vollard* we are going to find these same heads resurrected again, next to the sculptor and his model.

26.
Tête avec plume et tarlatane
Head with a Feather and a Fragment of Tarlatan

1932 (probably June-July)

Erwinography on glass

305 × 258 mm. approximately

1st state: unique proof on imperial Japan paper pulled with printers' ink.

It seems logical to date this proof after the 26th of May, the date when Picasso used this technique following word for word, as it were, the instruction manual. This 1st state clearly illustrates the results of "collages" by themselves. The mark on the top left is most likely the result of applying a substance such as sand, but it could simply be an accident. Tarlatan is a stiff, loosely woven cloth in everyday usage in an intaglio printer's workshop. It is also employed for draining soft white cheeses.

27.
Tête avec plume et tarlatane

See no. 26.

2nd state: one of the four proofs pulled on imperial Japan paper with printers' ink (the others in the Musée Picasso, Paris).

Additional strokes in the gelatin covering the head; an eye has been added. In order to make the stroke visible it suffices to lower the level of the swollen gelatin. It is nearly impossible to reconstruct the exact method the artist used.

28.
Tête avec plume et tarlatane

See no. 26.

2nd state: proof pulled with white oil paint on a prepared brown canvas.

29.
Tête avec plume et tarlatane

See no. 26.

4th state: one of the two proofs on imperial Japan paper, with printers' ink.

Most of the gelatin on the head has disappeared; there remains only the outline of the profile and the eye, produced either by scraping or by tanning with alum, more likely by the former.

30.
Tête avec plume et tarlatane

See no. 26.

5th state: unique proof pulled in negative on imperial Japan paper, with printers' ink.

The gelatin was beginning to dry out, hence the possibility of pulling the proof in negative. In relief-printing, a negative proof gives approximately the same impression as a positive proof pulled by the intaglio printing process; the engraved parts show up, when inked, on the paper. We must not forget that the artist inks with a brush in whatever way he likes; the background, which is by necessity lower than the head, has not been consistently inked. On the left, there is a profile of Marie-Thérèse, traced with the needle. As previously stated, all the proofs were pulled by the artist.

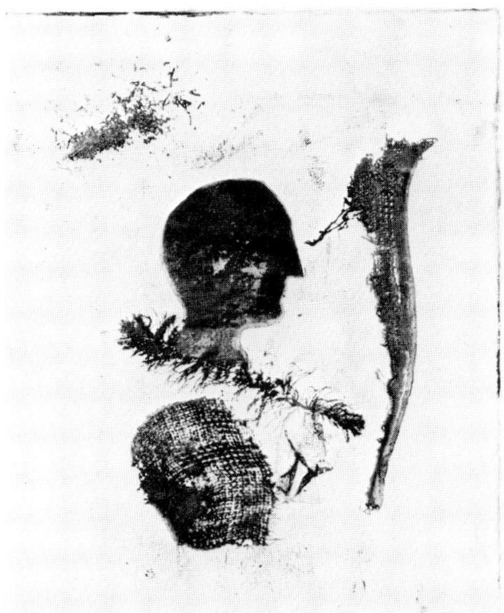
26.

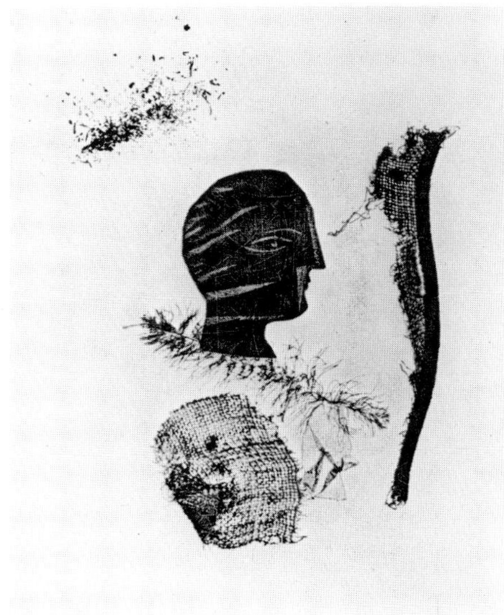
27.

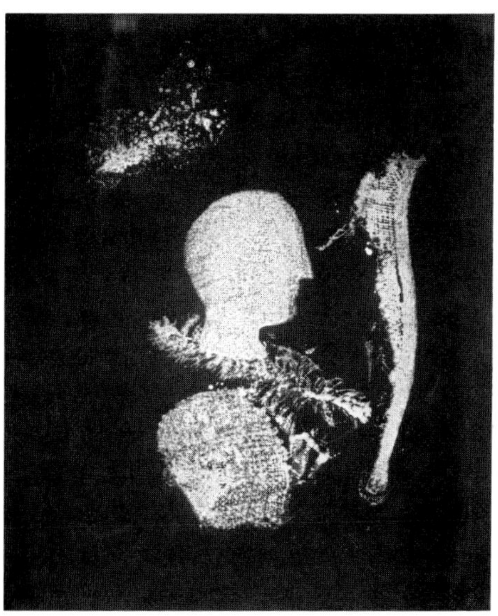
28.

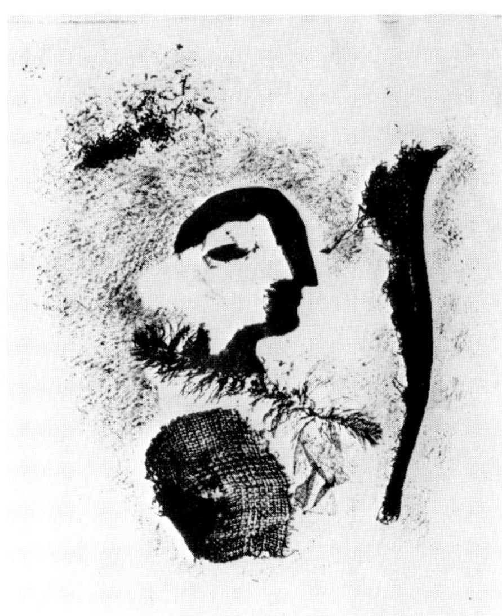
29.

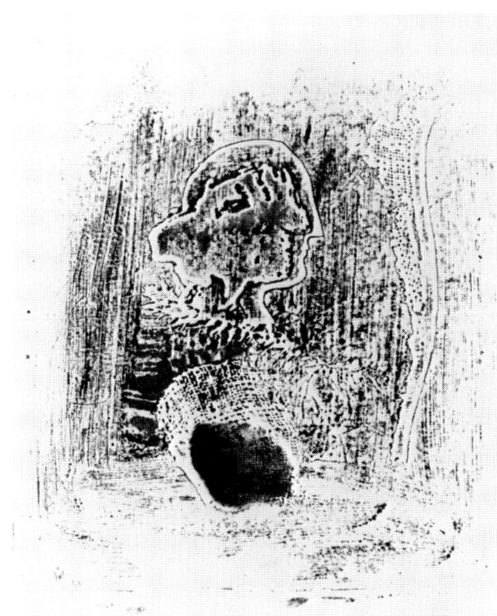
30.

31a-e.
Flûtiste assise et dormeuse
Seated Woman Playing a Flute and a Sleeping Woman

1933 (second half of January)

Monotypes on copper

150 x 188 mm.

a. Monotype VII: first of two proofs pulled by the artist with printers' ink on handmade laid Arches (G.470).

b. Monotype XI: first of two proofs pulled by the artist with *encre de Chine* on handmade laid Arches (G.474).

c. Monotype XII: unique proof pulled by the artist with printers' ink on handmade laid Arches (G.475).

d. Monotype XVI: first of two proofs pulled by the artist with printers' ink on handmade laid Arches (G.479).

e. Monotype XXVII: unique proof pulled by the artist with printers' ink on handmade laid Arches (G.490).

These monotypes are all pulled from the copperplate of G.287: *Flûtiste et dormeuse, I.* The Roman numerals indicate the chronological development, the "states." As we can see, the sleeping woman and, sometimes, the woman playing the flute have Marie-Thérèse's features.

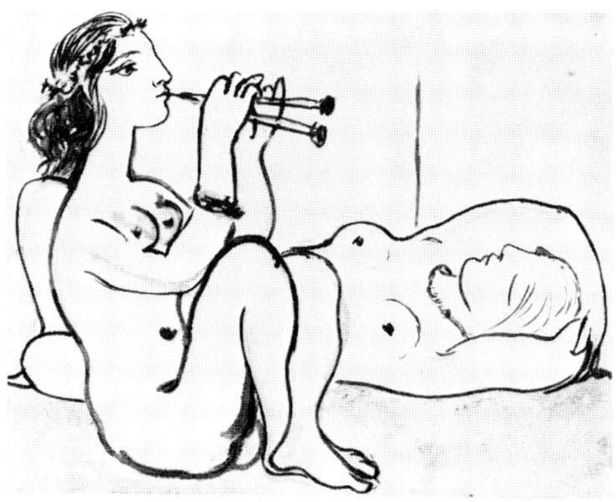

31a.

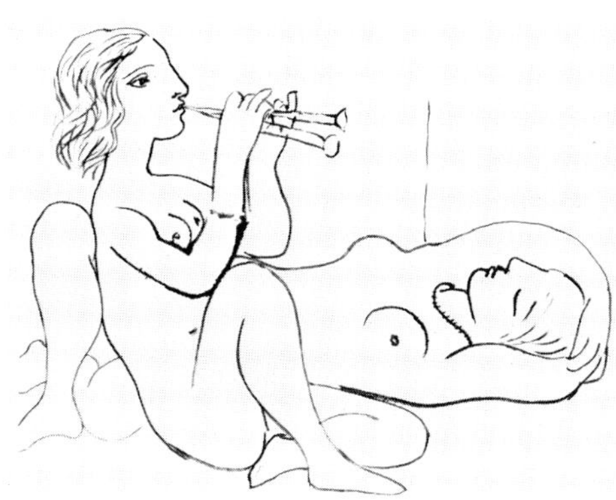

31b.

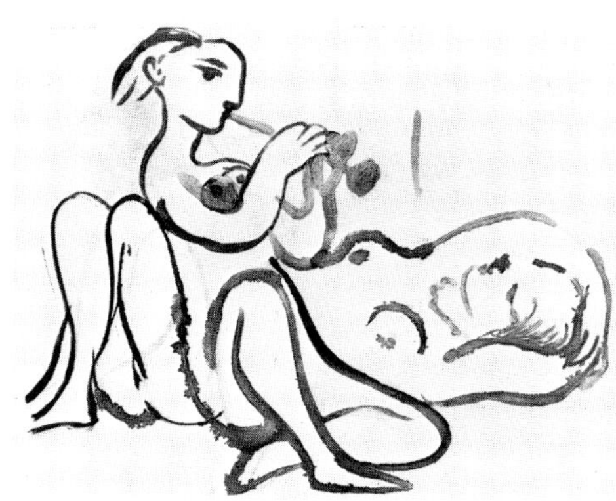

31c.

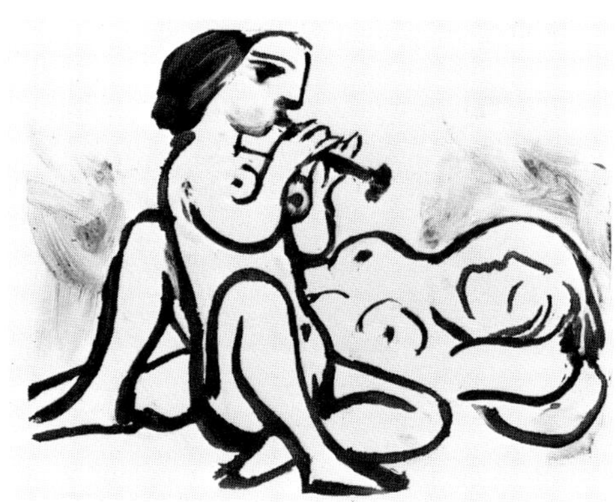

31d.

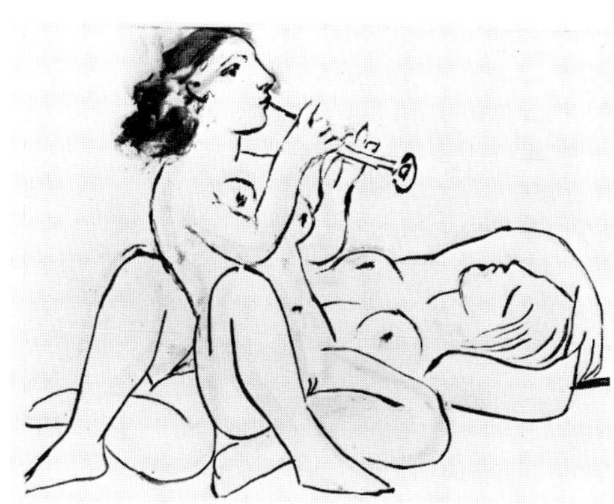

31e.

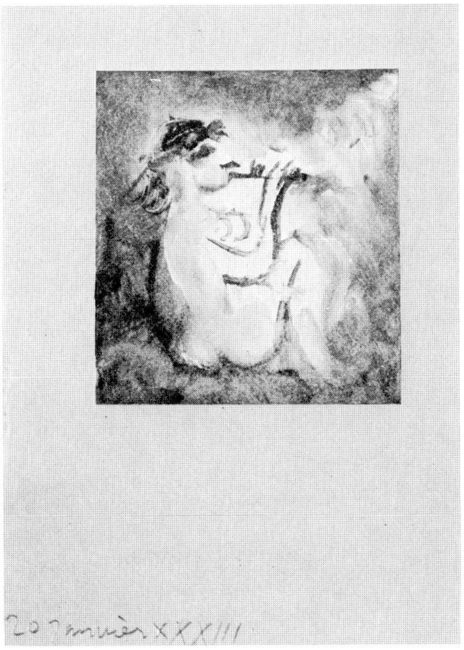

32a.

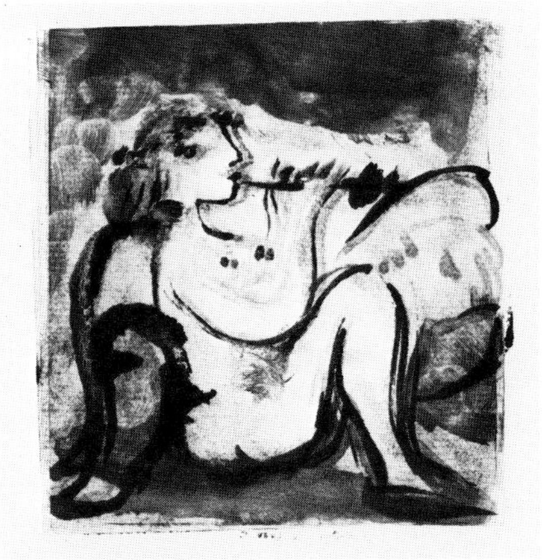

32b.

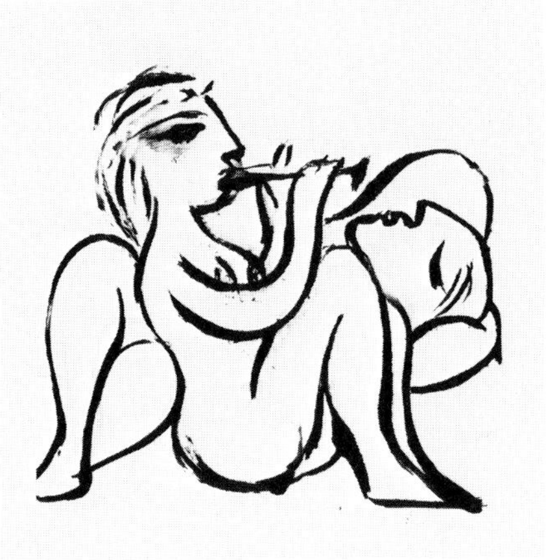

32c.

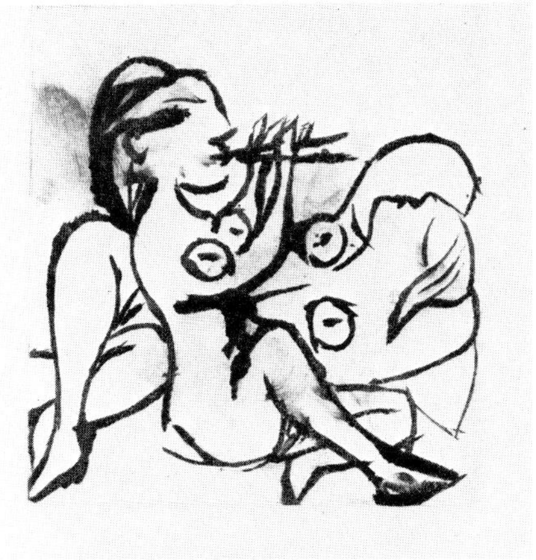

32d.

32a-d. (see color plate)
Flûtiste; Musicienne et dormeuse
Woman Playing a Flute; Woman Playing a Flute and Sleeping Woman

1933 (January 20 onwards)

Monotypes on copper

88 x 80 mm.

a. *Flûtiste*: second proof pulled by the artist on card paper, colored cinnabar (dark red), with printers' ink and gouache; annotated in pencil bottom left: ''20 janvier XXXIII'' (G.511 (I).).

b. *Musicienne et dormeuse, I*: unique proof pulled by the artist with printers' ink and gouache on handmade laid Arches; annotated in pencil bottom left: ''20 janvier XXXIII'' (G.512 (II).).

c. *Musicienne et dormeuse, V*: first of the two proofs pulled by the artist with printers' ink (G.516 (VI).).

d. *Musicienne et dormeuse, XI*: first of the two proofs pulled by the artist with printers' ink on imitation thick colored Japan paper (G.522 (XII).).

It seems probable that all the exhibited monotypes under no. 32 were pulled on the copperplate of the etching *Flûtiste et dormeuse, II*, even though the latter is only dated March 6. The composition is identical with that of the last three monotypes in the exhibition, which are part of a ''series'' of 15, and the copperplate has exactly the same measurements. *La Flûtiste* (G.511), even granted that the composition has only one figure, is obviously part of this series (cf. the proof with that of G.512). Hence, in fact, the series comprises 16 monotypes. Both the sleeping woman and the one playing the flute have Marie-Thérèse's features. For the Roman numerals in brackets, see above. We have simply advanced Geiser's numeration by one number as the *Flûtiste* is the beginning of the series.

33.
Marie-Thérèse de profil
Marie-Thérèse in Profile

1933 (February)

Monotype on copper

317 x 227 mm.

Second proof, pulled by the artist using a brush and inkwash on handmade laid Arches; annotated in pencil top right "IV E," and on the verso top left "V."

G.554 ("*Tête de femme*, IV").

The first proof of this monotype, annotated on the verso "V (16 fevrier XXXIII)" is in the Musée Picasso, Paris. Although the engraving (G.294) is dated on the back of the copperplate "March 7," and although Geiser gives the dimensions of the plate mark as 318 x 228 mm., it is probable that the monotype, together with the series of the three previous ones, annotated 1st, 2nd and 3rd state, was executed on the copperplate used to engrave G.294. In fact, Geiser measured the plate mark of this engraving on a proof pulled on wove Arches paper and not on laid Arches paper. As we know, apart from Japan paper, wove Arches paper is the paper which shrinks the least during the drying process. Hence, a difference of one millimeter in the dimensions is easily explained. Further, in his notes, Geiser gives the following dimensions for the proofs on laid Arches: 316 x 227 mm. Clearly a comparison should be made with the monumental sculptures depicting the head of Marie-Thérèse, in particular with that of 1932 (Spies, 133).

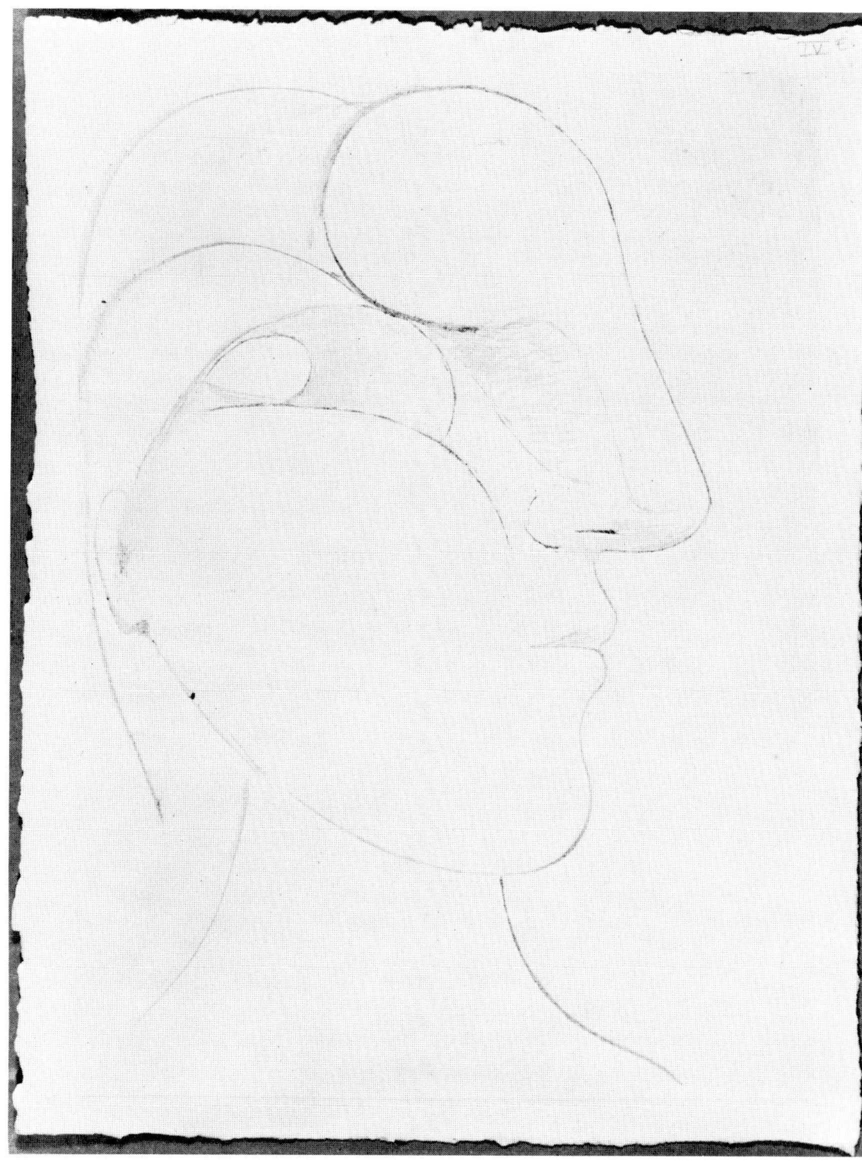

33.

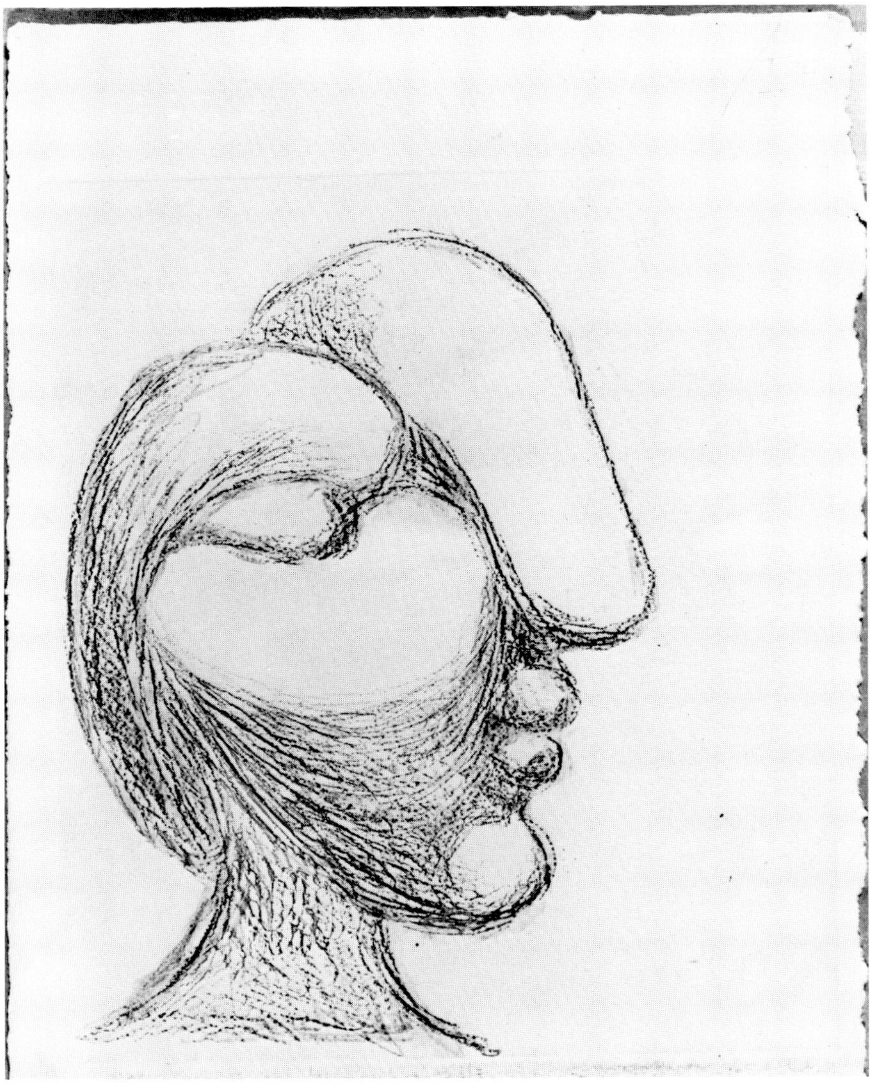

34.

34.
Tête de Marie-Thérèse
Head of Marie-Thérèse

1933 (March 12)

Monotype on copper

176 x 155 mm.

Second proof, not in Geiser, pulled by the artist using a lithographic crayon on hand-made laid Arches, annotated top right "I E." Date scratched on the back of the plate.

G.295 ("*Tête*")

In 1961, the plate was pulled by Frélaut and published by the Leiris Gallery in an edition of fifty proofs (B.256).

Here we have a technical problem as the "drawing" on the copperplate instead of being sunken, as usual, is in relief. The trial proofs, pulled by Picasso, are all inked in very different ways: sometimes in positive, as our monotype, sometimes practically in negative as in the Leiris 1961 edition. The procedure was probably as follows: first, the artist drew the head with a lithographic crayon (which is extremely greasy) and then pulled the monotype, the first proof of which is in the Musée Picasso, Paris; then he plunged the plate in an acid bath, which lowered the area not protected by the lithographic crayon. As the lines drawn with crayon were grainy, this left in the completed etching a positive rendering on the proof: as we know, the acid bites deeper along the outline of the *réserves* (here the *réserves* are made with greasy crayon). One of the trial proofs, pulled by Picasso, has been reworked with the lithographic crayon, which could substantiate our theory. In any case, no other technical explanation is convincing. Among the sculptures, cf. Spies, 132 and 133.

VII.

Lacourière

Picasso's meeting with Lacourière was just as vital for his engravings as his meeting with Marie-Thérèse was for the whole of his work. Marie-Thérèse inspired him for at least ten years and Lacourière stimulated him to leave behind the classical and traditional engraver he still was to seek new inventive horizons. In this way Picasso would eventually surpass himself and become the most important engraver of this century and one of the four greatest engravers of all time.

We do not wish, of course, to denigrate Picasso's earlier work. The artist always had a special affinity for the metal plate. What would change particularly after 1934 is the audacious way he attacked the plates. On the one hand, his discovery of the sugar-lift aquatint, which he went on to use with the brio and mastery we now acknowledge, provided him with an exceptional tool. On the other hand, his way of employing drypoint, burin and etching would show a freedom, a distancing from the traditional manipulation of these techniques and a wholly new personal aggressiveness that are truly astonishing. For instance, cat. nos. 24, 25 and 34 allow us a glimpse of a new and freer technique in germination, but it was after 1934 that he succeeded fully in throwing off all the accepted rules.

In 1939, when Picasso started the Dora Maar portraits using four or five colors, he monopolized Lacourière himself and every available craftsman in his shop for more than three months. When Madeleine Lacourière asked him if there was going to be a published edition, for only a published edition would bring money to the workshop, he lost his temper and replied that he and only he had worked during the three months. This was capricious exaggeration, of course: in reality he worked hand in hand with Lacourière who prepared, bit and painted the plates and who was the sensitive, inventive technical assistant, the indispensable helper with whom Picasso could communicate without words. As in the case of Marie-Thérèse, Picasso's meeting with Lacourière was pure chance. The artist was ambling down the steps of the Rue Foyatier, just below the basilica of the Sacré Coeur, when he suddenly caught sight of some printing presses through a window. He went in, spoke to the workmen and then asked for the boss, who happened to be Lacourière. It was Picasso who sent Vollard to Lacourière. These events took place at the beginning of 1933, possibly in March. Just as the Marie-Thérèse we know as transformed by Picasso only fully took form in his work after several years, the fruits of the artist's collaboration with Lacourière only become apparent around November 1934. Up until then, notwithstanding a bit of ''flirtation'' with the printer (see nos. 37 and 38), Picasso continued to work alone and to pull the trial proofs of the various states of his plates at home.

At Lacourière's workshop in the Rue Foyatier, there was a studio where Picasso could work with everything he needed at hand: tools, baths, a dusting-box, acids, presses and workmen who could pull his proofs when he needed them. What is more, Lacourière was not only an intaglio printer, like Fort or Leblanc, he was also an engraver himself, son and nephew of engravers, and he could establish an atmosphere of collaboration with the artist. He would show him new techniques. He could discuss or even suggest new ideas, probably not from the artistic point of view (he was proud of being an artisan and would not have allowed himself to do so), but from the technical angle. He knew every trick of the trade, was always on the lookout for novel ideas, and, being an engraver, was capable of imparting the desire to work hard on processes to artists. The copperplates were blackened with smoke so as to get a better appreciation of what had been done and the sugar was dyed with *encre de Chine* so as to get a better idea of what one was doing. It was indeed Lacourière who had perfected the technique of sugar-lift, the invention of which is attributed to his father.

Moreover, it is interesting to note that between the small aquatint of 1915 (no. 13) and the sugar aquatint which Geiser dates January 1934, even though there is no date on the back of the plate, Picasso had abandoned this process. The 1934 sugar-lift aquatint (G.416, cat. no. 37) was started, at least as far as the sugar process is concerned, at Lacourière's workshop. It is Lacourière who pulled the two trial proofs of the 1st state. So between 1915 and 1934, there is not a single aquatint. If one carefully examines, state by state, proofs of plates such as G.340, 342, 378, 379, one notices that they are not aquatints at all, but only the results of direct biting with acid and a brush: the resulting ''wash'' shows no sign of graining. When one becomes aware of how often Picasso employed the technique of aquatint in every conceivable form from then on, one can only be filled with emotion and admiration when standing in front of the small engraving we exhibit here as no. 37.

A few words about the technique of sugar-lift aquatint are necessary. An aquatint is obtained by depositing grains of resin on a copperplate where they are fixed by heating. Next, the plate is dipped into an acid bath. The areas which are protected by the grains prevent the acid from biting and will form miniscule white spots which, according to the size of the grains, are visible or not to the naked eye. The area around the grains is bitten by the acid, producing when eventually printed the velvety surface that we know. To obtain a light image, one can either scrape the plate (e.g. cat. no. 13) or create with varnish, before graining and the acid treatment, *réserves* which will remain untouched (see no. 52). It is equally possible to bite the grained copperplate directly by using a brush loaded with acid and thus, as Picasso often did later on, use the acid as a sort of wash, although this method is difficult to control and to manipulate (see. no. 181). Sugar allows the artist to ''paint,'' as it were, on the copperplate. He executes his composition with a mixture of sugary syrup and ink, the latter being used to permit a visual control. The entire plate is then varnished and dipped into water. On the areas where the sugar melts the varnish is stripped off. Finally, the plate has only to be grained and then bitten to reveal the original composition in aquatint. The sugar-lift aquatint technique can, of course, also be used in conjunction with *réserves* in varnish, scraping, etc.

With this technical information in hand, we can turn now to a consideration of the *Suite Vollard*. The title given this series of 100 engravings could lead one to suppose that it was commissioned by Vollard, which would then lead to surprise at the incoherent nature of the series. The plates are of every conceivable size, and the subjects vary constantly. In fact, this is due to the deal Picasso made with Vollard when he wished to buy some pictures in Vollard's stock. In exchange, the artist selected, from a large number of copperplates, 97 which had been made between September 16, 1930, and June 12, 1936, and gave them to Vollard. He completed the number with three portraits of the dealer which he made on March 4, 1937. There was another portrait which Vollard rejected (B.1332), and which was the fourth Picasso had done as we know from the annotations on the backs of the plates.

The plates were pulled before Vollard's death: three suites on parchment; 50 suites on laid Montval paper with large margins (76 × 50 cm.); 250 suites on laid Montval paper with the ''Picasso'' or ''Vollard'' watermark. The three suites on parchment were signed and numbered in red ink (but only one is still complete). Ten out of the 100 engravings of the suite were signed and numbered from 1/15 to 15/15, and were probably put on sale by Vollard at that time (large sheets; B.165, 174, 175, 176, 192, 200, 213, 217, 220, 221; Una E. Johnson in her catalogue *Ambroise Vollard, éditeur*, 1977, includes among these 10 numbers the B.144 and omits B.217).

The rest of the edition stayed piled up in Vollard's shop until his accidental death in 1939. Petiet, the print dealer, then bought the proofs of the 97 plates, either directly from the Vollard Estate or through the intermediary, Fabiani. Marcel Lecomte bought the three portraits of Vollard. After 1956, 99% of the latter were signed by Picasso. Petiet also had some of his prints signed. It appears that most of the 50 suites on large sheets of Montval were signed as were those prints on small paper which Petiet considered the most valuable.

We should point out that there must have been some hesitation about the inclusion of the large plate *Femme Torero, I* (G.425; B.1329). The Museum of Modern Art, New York, has one proof of this on parchment, signed and numbered 1/3 in red ink as in the case of the three suites on parchment. Picasso possessed two other proofs on parchment of which one was signed and numbered 2/3 in the same way, but the number and the signature have been crossed out in the same ink. However, the dimensions of the plate made it impossible for it to be pulled on the laid Montval paper used for the big suites, and obviously would not suit the small ones. The 100 plates, which were cancelled in 1956, were given to the Musée Picasso, Paris, in 1980 by Madame Lacourière.

It was out of the question to include in this exhibition all 100 prints of the *Suite Vollard*. In any case, they are well-known and, also, it is perhaps preferable to extract a few major themes from this heterogeneous collection: the sculptor's studio (work, rest, fantasies), rape, Rembrandt, and finally, the saga of the Minotaur. We have chosen to exhibit here one example from the *Sculptor and Model* series, one example of a rape (which does not actually belong to the *Suite*), the first sugar-lift aquatint attempted by the artist, and all the states of a plate from 1934. Then we shall focus our attention on the Minotaur.

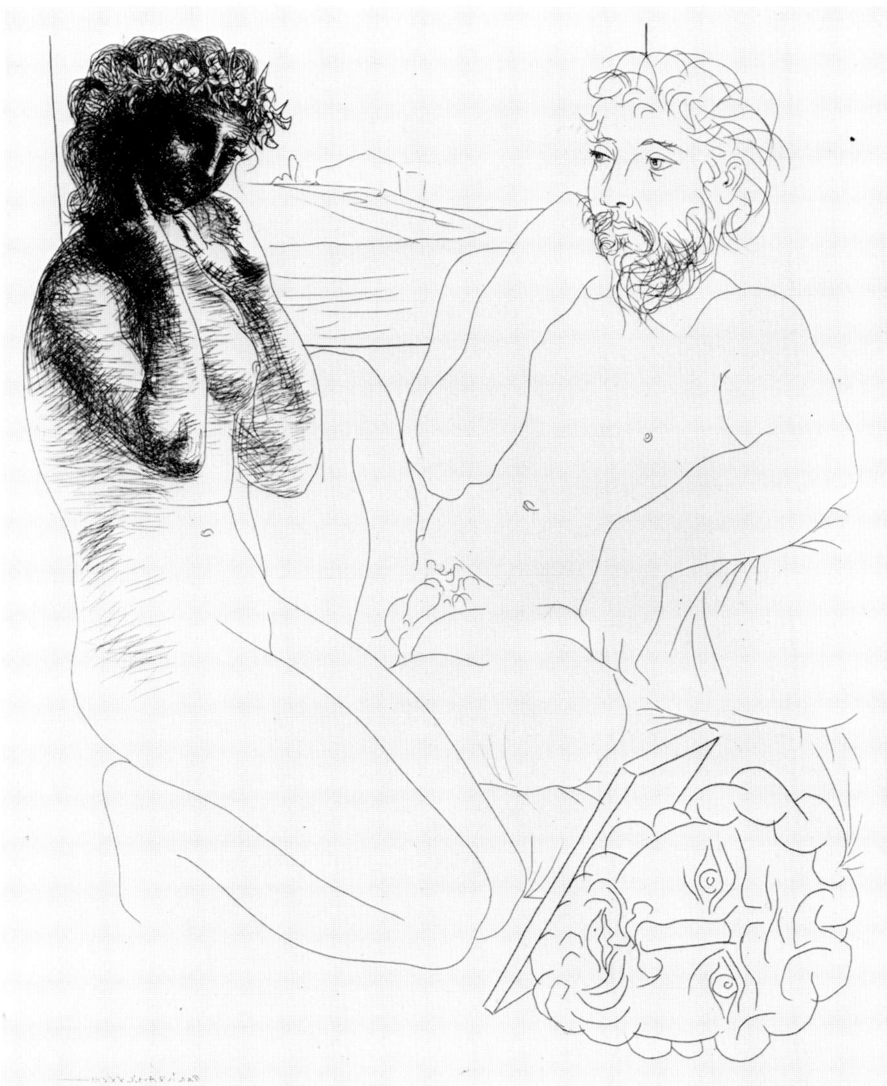

35.

35.

Sculpteur et modèle agenouillé
Sculptor with Kneeling Model

1933 (April 8, Paris)

Etching on copper

367 × 298 mm.

Proof on Montval laid paper with ''Vollard'' watermark.

G.331.II.c; B.178; S.V.69.

There is nothing rare about the proofs included as cat. nos. 35, 43, 44, 45, 48, 49, 51, 53 and 55. They all came from a series of trial proofs after steelfacing; that is, from one of the 250 suites in the dealer's possession. Interestingly enough, apart from the suite to which he was legally entitled, Picasso only had this suite on paper with small margins. He did not possess a suite on the big sheets of Montval. These proofs have been included in the exhibition because of their iconographical interest.

Picasso's treatment of the theme of the Sculptor and his Model often involved an iconographical duplication: Marie-Thérèse the loved one and Marie-Thérèse the model, as embodied in sculpture (in general, one of the so-called Boisgeloup heads). Here the splitting of the two characters is more mysterious and more striking: Marie-Thérèse, for once with frizzy hair, crowned with a wreath of flowers, is looking at her image in a mirror. Neither we nor the sculptor can see the reflected image. Does she see in the mirror the reflection of one of those sculpted heads that she has become in the artist's work, or is she holding onto her true identity? It seems most likely that she sees both at once and that this puzzles her. The sculptor is also split in two: on the one hand, a man tenderly and thoughtfully looking at the woman who is, at one and the same time, both his love and his model, and on the other hand, a sculpted head, wrinkled by worry, which supports the mirror. Thus, this work asks multiple questions about the identities of the two figures, their ''mirrored'' identities, and those complex dualities of model/love and love/creativity.

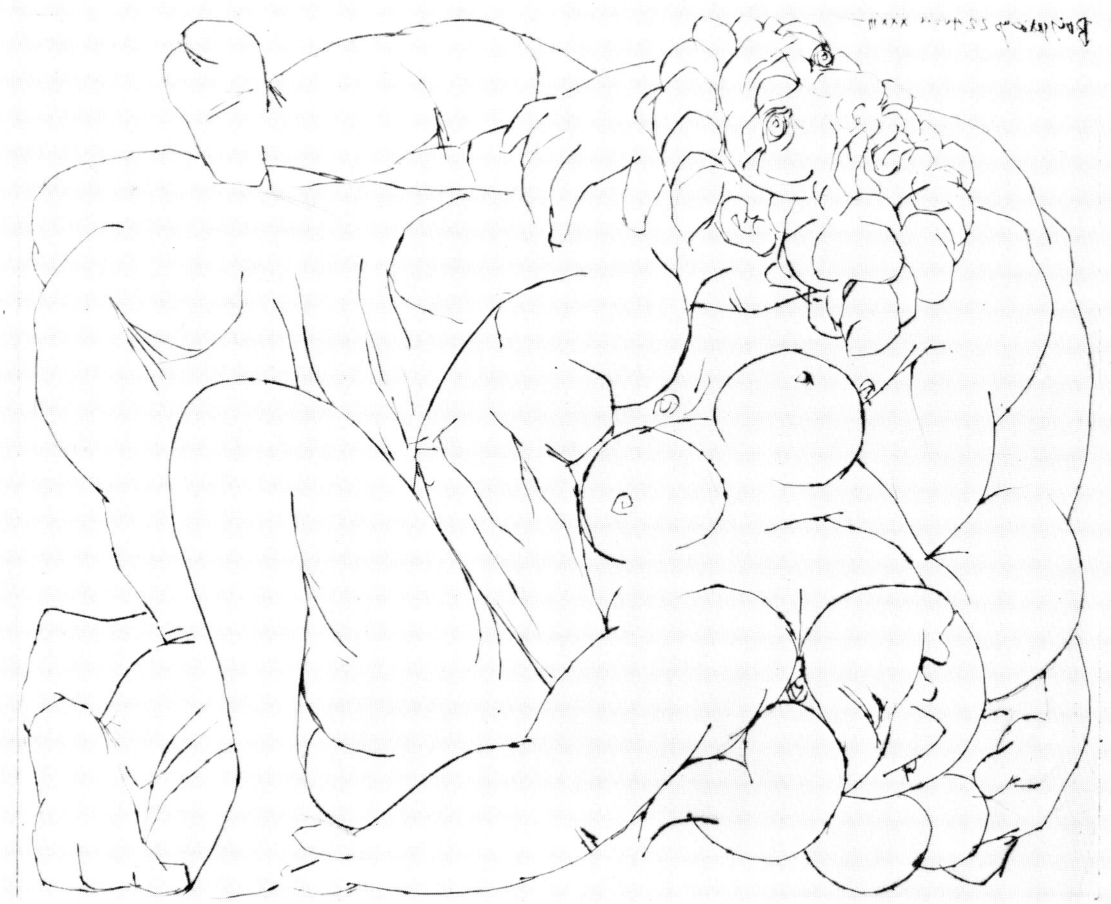

36.

36.
Le Viol, I
The Rape

1933 (April 22, Boisgeloup)

Drypoint on copper

300 × 369 mm.

One of the three proofs pulled by the artist, before steelfacing, on wove Arches paper. The copperplate is annotated on the back "I."

The copperplate (on exhibition) was cancelled in 1983.

G.339.A ("*Le viol*, III").

After steelfacing, 56 impressions were made by Lacourière in 1942, on the "Vollard-Picasso" Montval laid paper, which had been used for the *Suite Vollard*. In 1960, Frélaut pulled the trial proof on Rives wove paper, destined for the ring-binder, but he never pulled the usual three trial proofs on different papers, which Geiser refers to.

This rape scene, which does not belong to the *Suite Vollard*, is close to two others (G.338 and 340), which were made the same day, but is more anguished and tense. In fact, it is the first of the three, as the copperplate is annotated on the back "I." It is less tender, with sharper lines, then G.338 (B.180) which depicts the lover gazing at his companion's face, and it is certainly more anguished and disturbing than G.340, where the man is also lifting his head to the sky but where the woman, with wide-open eyes, seems to dominate the situation. Here, the despair is underlined by the jerky lines and the harsh use of the drypoint.

What does the man in this "embrace," artist and lover, see in the stars he is gazing at like a caged tiger (big cats when they are caged up fall victim to what is called "star sickness" because they are continually staring at the heavens)? Is it his art? An impossible love everyone dreams about? The projected image he has of the nearly faceless woman he holds in his arms, or his angst over the duality of man and beast? We struggle to understand but are reminded of what Picasso once said to Zervos (*Cahiers d'Art*, vol. X, No. 7/10, 1936, p. 42): "All the world wants to understand painting. Why don't they try to understand bird song?"

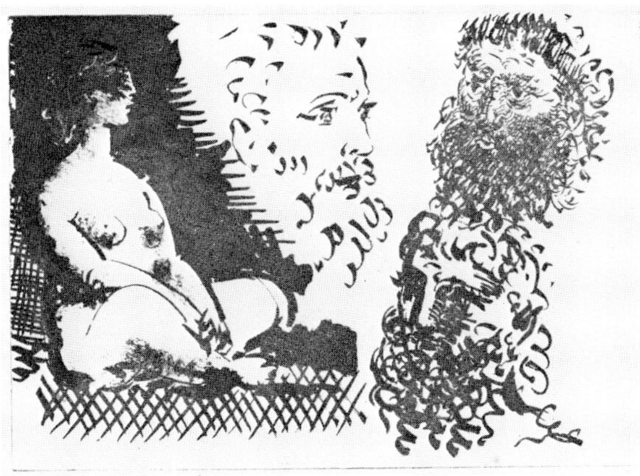

37a.

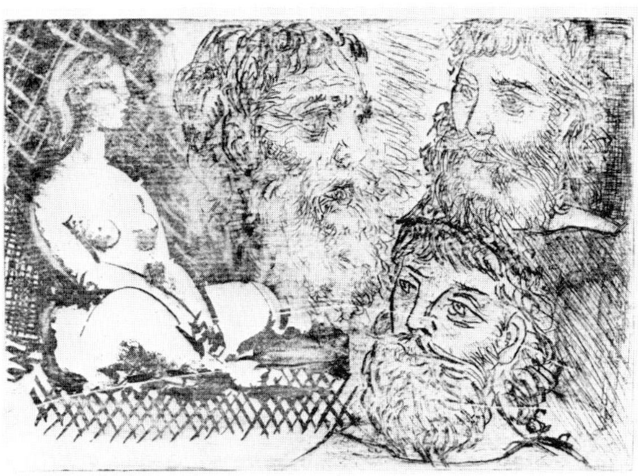

37b.

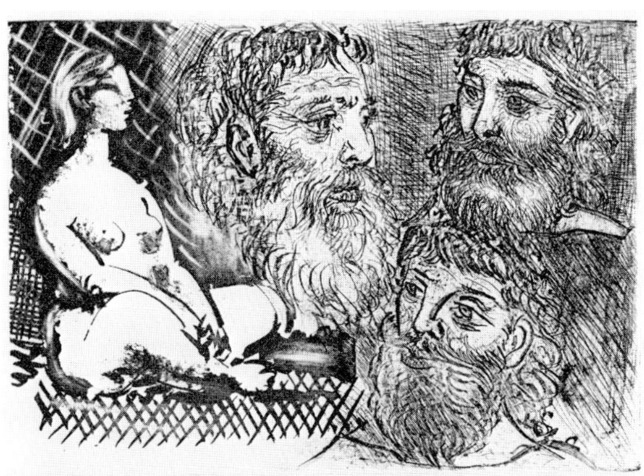

37c.

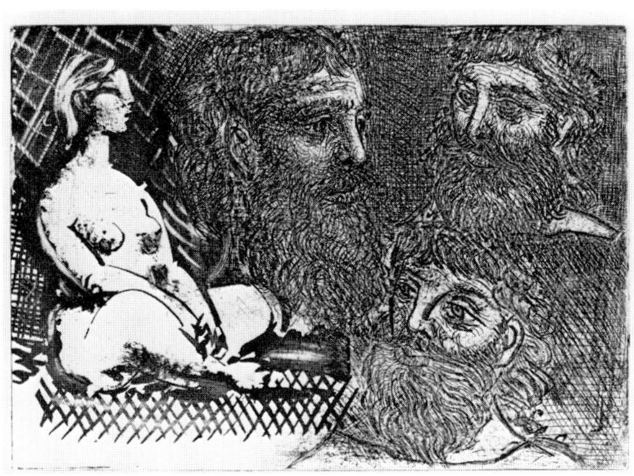

37d.

37a-d.

Femme nue assise et trois têtes barbues
Seated Naked Woman and Three Bearded Heads

1934 (January ?)

Sugar-lift aquatint, scraper, drypoint, etching and burin on copper

130 × 179 mm.

a. 1st state: one of the two proofs on Arches wove paper, printed by Lacourière.

b. 4th state: one of the two proofs on Japan paper, pulled by Picasso, and annotated top right "IV E."

c. 5th state: one of the two proofs printed by Lacourière on Arches wove paper, annotated top right "V E."

d. 6th state: one of the three proofs pulled by Lacourière on Arches wove paper.

G.416.I,IV,V.b,VI.

At the 7th state, i.e. after steelfacing and bevelling, the plate was printed as part of the *Suite Vollard* (G.416.VII; B.216; S.V.25).

After the 1st state, executed simply with sugar-lift aquatint (some slight reworking with drypoint in Marie-Thérèse's hair), Picasso either took the plate home (it is he who pulled the proofs of the 2nd state), or, more probably used one of Lacourière's presses. Lacourière pulled the 3rd state, Picasso the 4th; then it was Picasso, followed by Lacourière, who pulled the 5th state (one proof pulled by the artist). Finally, Lacourière pulled the trial proofs of the 6th and definitive state.

In the 2nd state, we can see some reworkings with the scraper and drypoint on the three heads of the bearded sculptor, and it is this left side of the plate (on the right in the proof) that Picasso worked over and over again: with etching (3rd and 5th states), with the scraper (4th state where, as we see, the background behind Marie-Thérèse is filled with wide white cross-hatching), then with the burin (6th state). During the whole of this reworking, the ravishing silhouette of Marie-Thérèse, sitting cross-legged, was left untouched. She may be dreaming of these three images of the same man, each one with a different expression, or, more likely, since she remains intact, she is the dream image of these three bearded sculptors.

38.
Quatre femmes nues et tête sculptée
Four Naked Women and a Sculpted Head

1934 (March 10, Paris)

Etching, scraper and burin on copper

223 × 316 mm.

1st state: etching. One of the six proofs pulled by Lacourière on Arches wove paper.

G.424.I.

A 2nd state probably exists in which the body of the woman lying on the bed has been clarified with the scraper. Geiser thought that it was simply the inking that was different. As we have not had access to the proof for some time, we shall assume it is a 2nd state (one proof).

39.
Quatre femmes nues et tête sculptée

See no. 38.

3rd state: scraper and burin. One of the four proofs pulled by Lacourière on Arches wove paper. Geiser's 2nd state.

G.424.II.

40.
Quatre femmes nues et tête sculptée

See no. 38.

4th state: scraper and burin. One of the three proofs pulled by Lacourière on Arches wove paper.

One proof exists, pulled by the artist, on Arches laid paper. It is so badly inked that Geiser, who photographed that particular proof, became confused. In reality, Geiser's 3rd state should include this proof, plus the three pulled by Lacourière. At any rate, Geiser's description is not accurate, confusing what he thought to be the 3rd and 4th states - our 4th and 5th states. We should not forget that Geiser's second volume was published posthumously with an edited text. To summarize: the proof, erroneously catalogued by Geiser in his 2nd state, belongs to *his 3rd* state.

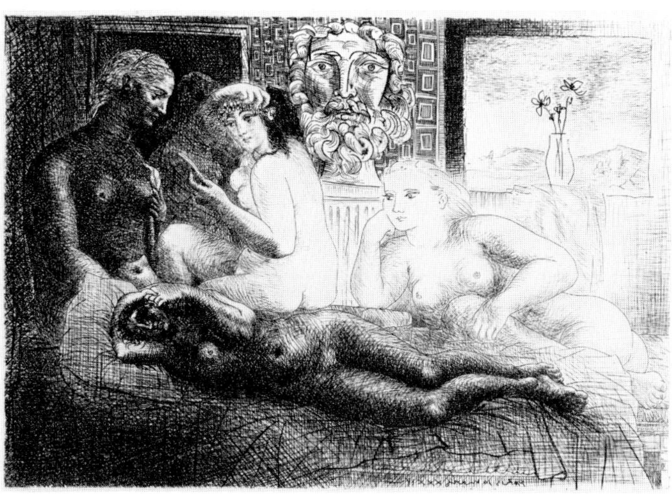

38.

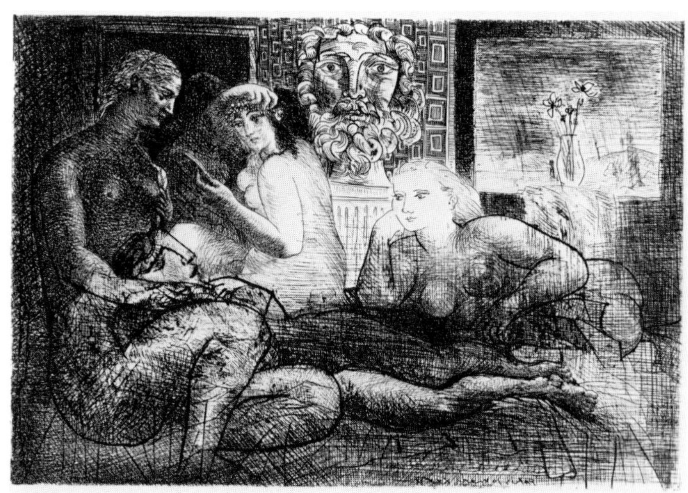

39.

41.
Quatre femmes nues et tête sculptée

See no. 38.

5th state: burin. One of the four proofs pulled by Lacourière on Arches wove paper.

G.424.IV (erroneously described).

The plate was afterwards steelfaced and printed like the rest of the *Suite Vollard.* B.219; S.V.82.

It is interesting to follow the gradual transformation of this plate "by destruction," as Picasso would have said. As he once told Zervos (*Cahiers d'Art*, vol. X, No. 7/10, 1936, p. 37): "It would be very amusing to freeze photographically not the stages in the evolution of a painting, but its metamorphoses." Beyond all doubt, the states of a proof, much more than any other part of the artist's work, allow us a glimpse of "the likely road which the brain takes in making real its dream." (*Ibid.*)

The inspiration here is clearly Ingresque. In the 1st state, the woman lying on the bed has both the position and the pillow of *L'Odalisque à l'esclave*. The bunch of flowers which evokes Marie-Thérèse has replaced the top of the fountain and the bearded head of the sculptor "stands in for" the eunuch in the middle distance of the painting. Then the same woman more or less takes up, on the knees of the large nude on the left, a position reminiscent of that of Octavia, lying against her brother's knees, in Ingres' *Virgil Reading the Aeneid to Livia, Octavia and Augustus* (1812). The raised shoulders of the woman on the right, leaning on her elbow, remind us of those of the young girl in the pool of *La Petite baigneuse*. Finally, the big nude on the left of our engraving has the same posture as the rebec player in *L'Odalisque à l'esclave*, and so, reversed, as the rebec player in the *Bain turc*. As for the young girl with a mirror doing her hair, the position of her arm and her back are a somewhat fainter echo of the young slave girl with a turban who is dressing the hair of the blond girl in the top right of the *Bain turc*.

Here once again is the theme of "women together" (three of whom resemble Marie-Thérèse), and of their intimacy in a harem-like context. The statue, although made of stone and therefore impotent like the eunuch of *L'Odalisque à l'esclave*, and which one sees again later in an etching of 1970 (L.3; B.1858), looks on with eyes glaring with curiosity, so taking us forward to the numerous "peeping-toms" in the graphic work of 1968-1972.

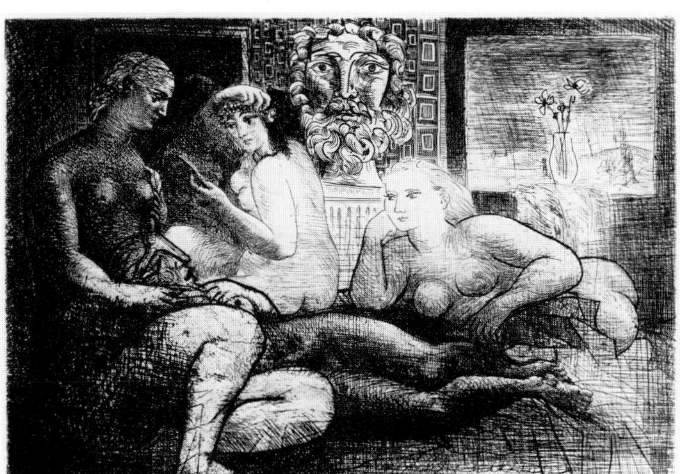

40.

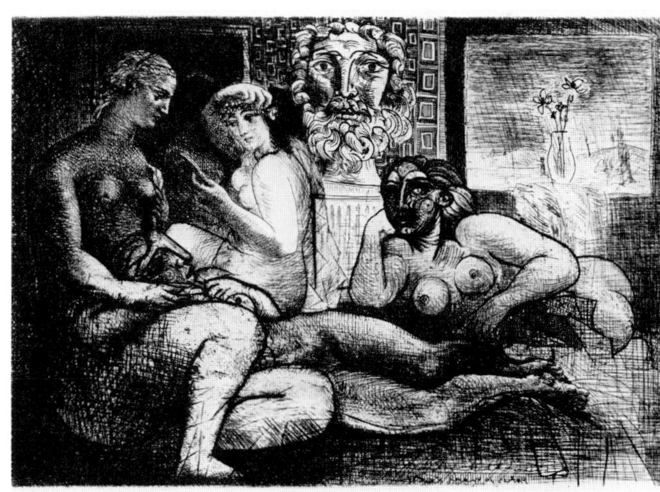

41.

VIII.

The Minotaur

Although the very first appearance of the Minotaur in Picasso's work occured in the painting belonging to the Museum of Modern Art, Paris (Z.VII.135), dated June 1, 1928, he did not take final form until 1933. It was on April 11, 1933, that the Minotaur embarked into the prints. In an engraving of that date (cat. no. 42) he holds an upright sword which is not only an obvious symbol of masculinity, but also is an echo of the infancy of Theseus, who was obliged to hunt for and to ''conquer'' the sword, the unique proof that he was his father's son.

The series of five sword-bearing Minotaurs (four of which were reproduced in the first number of the eponymous revue *Le Minotaure*) were made the same day as G.332 (B.179; S.V.70), where the swordbearer is a creation of the sculptor, a young man whom Marie-Thérèse is watching. This series of six prints follows our no. 35 by three days.

It is said that the only surrealist influence that Picasso would admit to was this creation: the Minotaur. Thus it is necessary to situate this symbol in the context of the period. According to the ideological currents of those years, the Minotaur was the symbol of unconscious impulsions. Half-man, half-beast, living in a labyrinth which is also part of himself, he is a creature from the depths of the sea where gods live side by side with monsters. He is also the symbol of artistic ''vision,'' the extralucid eye which sees what others cannot: the Minotaur ''sees'' in the darkness of the Labyrinth, but is blinded by natural light in which the rest of the world sees without difficulty. Finally, he is the symbol of passion. He is the son of a bull, which Minos with his grasping nature refused to sacrifice, and of Pasiphaë, who had succumbed to unnatural lust.

As we can see, this symbolism is relatively straightforward. There is no denying that Picasso flirted with the surrealists and was often in the company of the group of writers who wrote for *Le Minotaure*. However, in prints such as cat. no. 42, there is no point in looking for more recondite meanings, despite the symbolism of the sword and the ambiguities of G.332, the first work in the series. Picasso was primarily interested in the *story* of his Minotaur. In any case, we can only consider the ideology of the period as a backdrop: the iconography of an artist as both direct and impenetrable as Picasso cannot be simply inserted in any group's ideology, but must instead be considered in its own terms. A few final words of explanation will help to understand the complexities of the subject at hand. As we shall see, there is not only a conflation of imageries, but also a conflation of mythologies. On the one hand, Picasso uses the theme of the *corrida* or bullfight, which has long been present in his work. On the other, he extracts what he needs from the story of Theseus. In a sense, it is a meeting between the reality of Picasso's Spanish heritage and the mind-world of our inherent Graeco-Roman background, which suddenly took on a particular significance for him.

42.
Minotaure marchant avec un poignard
Walking Minotaur with a Sword

1933 (April 11)

Etching on copper

266 × 194 mm.

One of only three proofs pulled by Lacourière: on thick wove paper. Plate is annotated on back "I."

G.337. [Note: Geiser's numeration is not exact. Our etching is the first in the group; the second is G.334; the fifth is G.335.]

The copperplate exists.

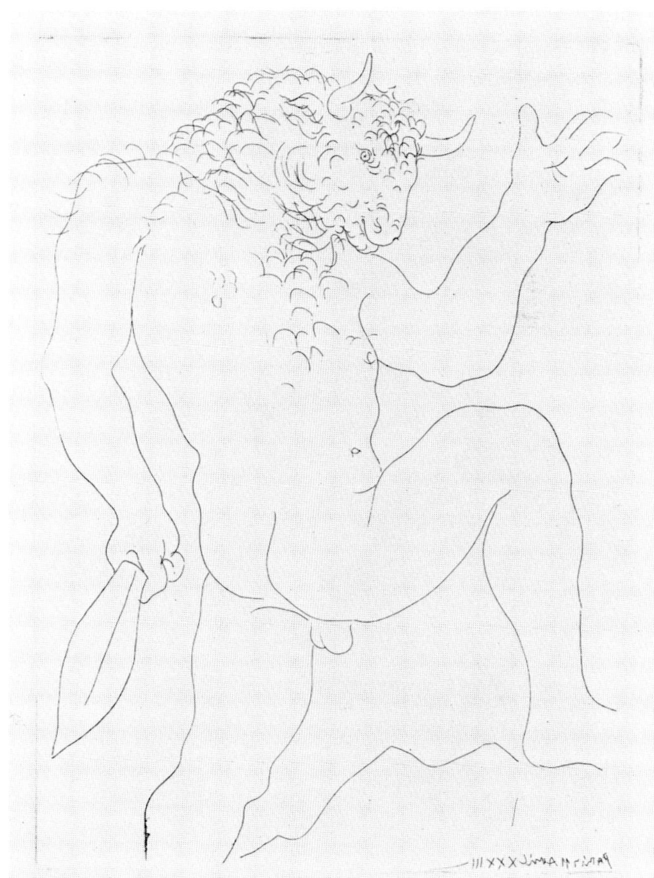

42.

We have chosen to exhibit this etching from among the five Minotaurs of April 11 because of its special significance. The artist chose another of the three proofs of this print and began to highlight with gouache: three triangles of various colors divide the proof along the right side of the Minotaur, and a fourth triangle fills the bottom left corner. Then he stuck a label with the word ''Minotaure'' in printers' type on the upper margin. Doubtless, this was a first idea for the cover of the magazine. Moreover, it was the first plate etched that day and so the first appearance of the series' famous personage. He will only acquire a tail in the later versions of the same day. At this stage he closely resembled the Minotaur of Antoine-Louis Barye's bronze *Theseus Fighting the Minotaur* of c. 1840, and his appearance will not change much.

The Minotaur put in a second appearance on May 17 (G.349; B.190;S.V.83), this time to enter into the iconography linked with Marie-Thérèse. His actions and roles are complex: he is seen as lover and drinker, both sleeping and raping, as wounded and dying, as sculptor's companion, but always haunted by and haunting Marie-Thérèse. This iconography is still not very personalized and remains close to the traditional interpretations mentioned above, although the violence of certain rape scenes already hints at a transformation in the erotic symbolism with undercurrents of the theme of destruction and avidity, hence that of primary femininity. If Eros is present, Thanatos is already starting to surface.

Although transposed, this theme is still linked with that of the relationship of the couple (cf. above no. 35). As the fires of passion grow stronger, the splitting or duplication process becomes more and more clear. We have chosen from the artist's ''small'' *Suite Vollard* two etchings, dated June 18, 1933, which in our opinion summarize, at least in the mirroring of identities (here Marie-Thérèse), the renewed ambiguity in the relationship of sculptor and model, and, in a wider sense, the ambiguity in a relationship of love.

43.
Minotaure, buveur et femmes
Minotaur, Man Drinking and Women

1933 (June 18, Boisgeloup)

Etching on copper

298 × 365 mm.

One proof on Montval laid paper with the ''Vollard'' watermark. Plate is annotated on the back ''I.''

G.368.IV.c; B.200; S.V.92.

Marie-Thérèse is dreaming in her bed. What is she dreaming about? Is it the duplication of the sculptor/ Minotaur, here in perfect harmony drinking and joking together? Is it about her own duplication in the love of the sculptor/Minotaur? On the right, we see one image of her as she was, with her fair hair (this only appears in the 2nd state), and on the left, another image of her with classical features and hairstyle *à la Grecque*. In the 1st state, her features correspond more closely to her real face. Who is who? Who loves who? Whom does she prefer? And, inversely, which Marie-Thérèse do the sculptor and the Minotaur love? Is the ''other'' only a creation, a reflected image?

A drawing, dated July 29, 1933, makes the image more precise. It shows Marie-Thérèse's silhouette as she pensively rests her elbow on a table. On the table, a sculpted arm supports the sculptor's head. He is young, worried and thoughtful. Beside this, the head of the Minotaur is curling out of a vase like a genie from the Arabian Nights. How can she reconcile both loves? Whom should she choose? Can she choose? The broken table is supported by a sphere, possibly the totality of the universe. Is she trying to make sense of all this, trying to know at last who is who, to reconcile, even at this early stage, the duality of masculine/ feminine?

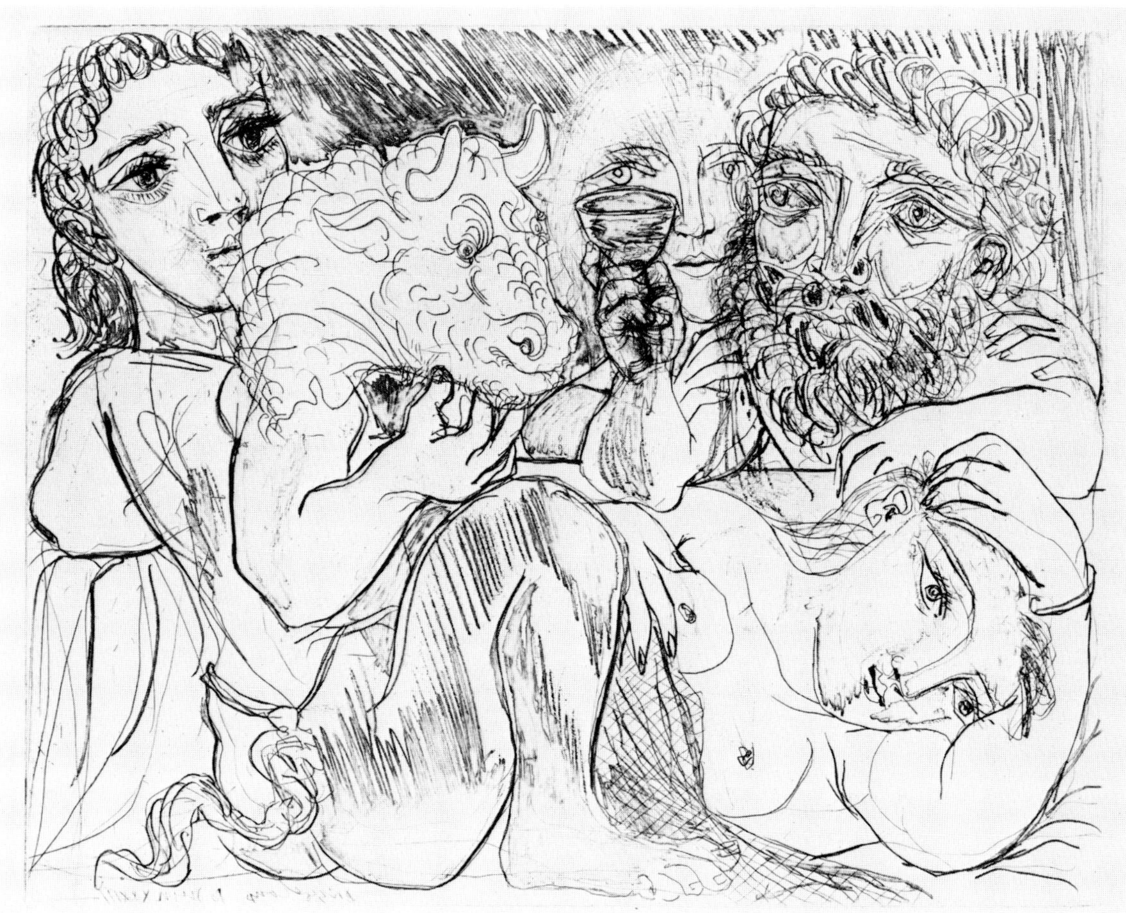

43.

44.
Minotaure caressant une dormeuse
Minotaur Caressing a Sleeping Woman

1933 (June 18, Boisgeloup)

Drypoint on copper

300 × 370 mm.

One proof on Montval laid paper with "Vollard" watermark. Plate is annotated on the back "III."

G.369.III.c; B.201; S.V.93.

Marie-Thérèse is asleep. In her dream, she has made her choice: it is in reality the Minotaur that she is waiting for, but a human and tender Minotaur, not the avid and destructive beast that he can be. It is worthy of note that this Minotaur already wears the kind of mane which he will have in the *Minotauromachie*. The other two plates of the same day repeat both themes.

Even though the Minotaur goes on loving Marie-Thérèse in the drawings, he will only appear in the engraved work again after the *Lysistrata*, where the theme is that of women trying to prevent men from indulging in typical mens' work and their favorite pleasure — war. This, of course, is not unrelated to the woman's choice of sculptor or Minotaur that we have followed above.

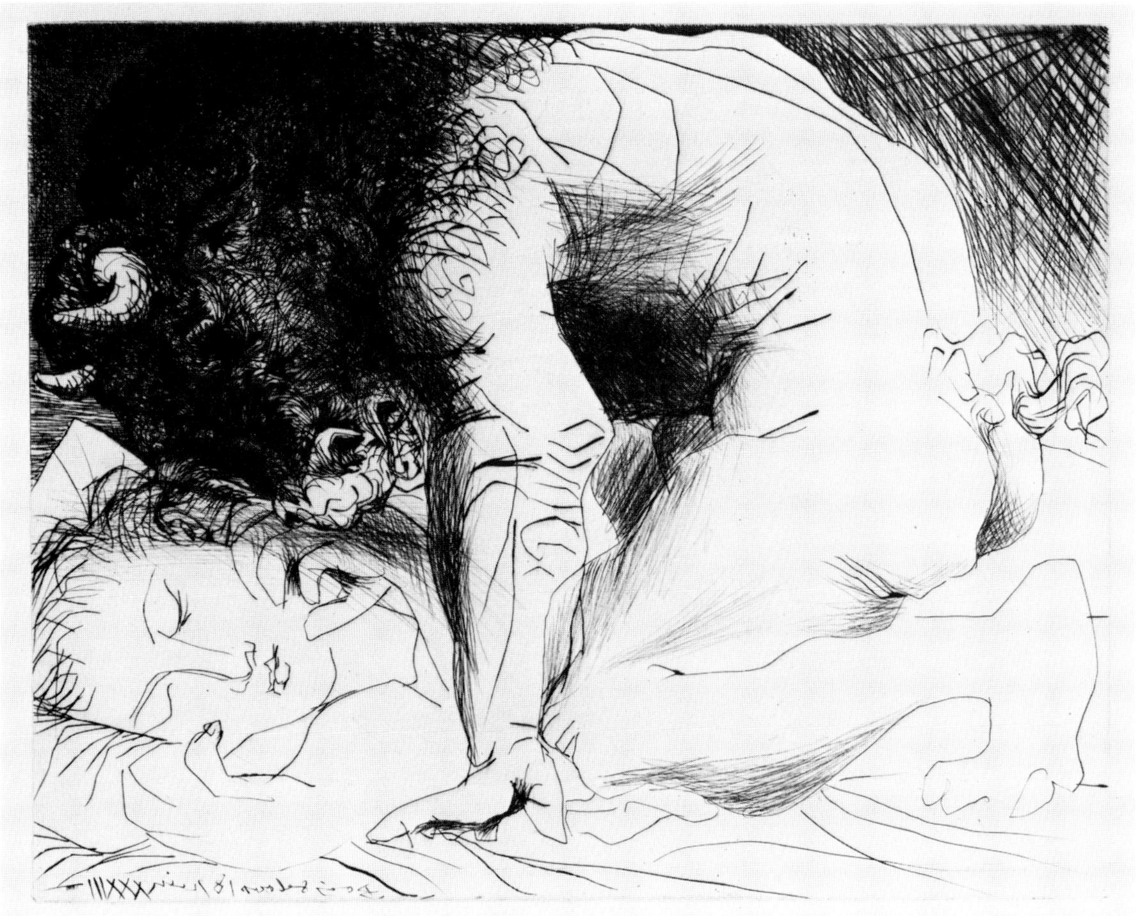

44.

45. (see frontispiece)
Jeune homme au masque de taureau, faune et profil de femme
Young Man with Mask of a Bull, Faun and Profile of a Woman

1934 (March 7, Paris)

Etching on copper

223 × 313 mm.

One proof on Montval laid paper with "Picasso" watermark.

G.422.B.b; B.279.

Our proof is one of 54 pulled by Lacourière on the remaining paper with the "Picasso" or "Vollard" watermark. The plate was pulled again in 1961 and put on sale by the Leiris Gallery in 1981.

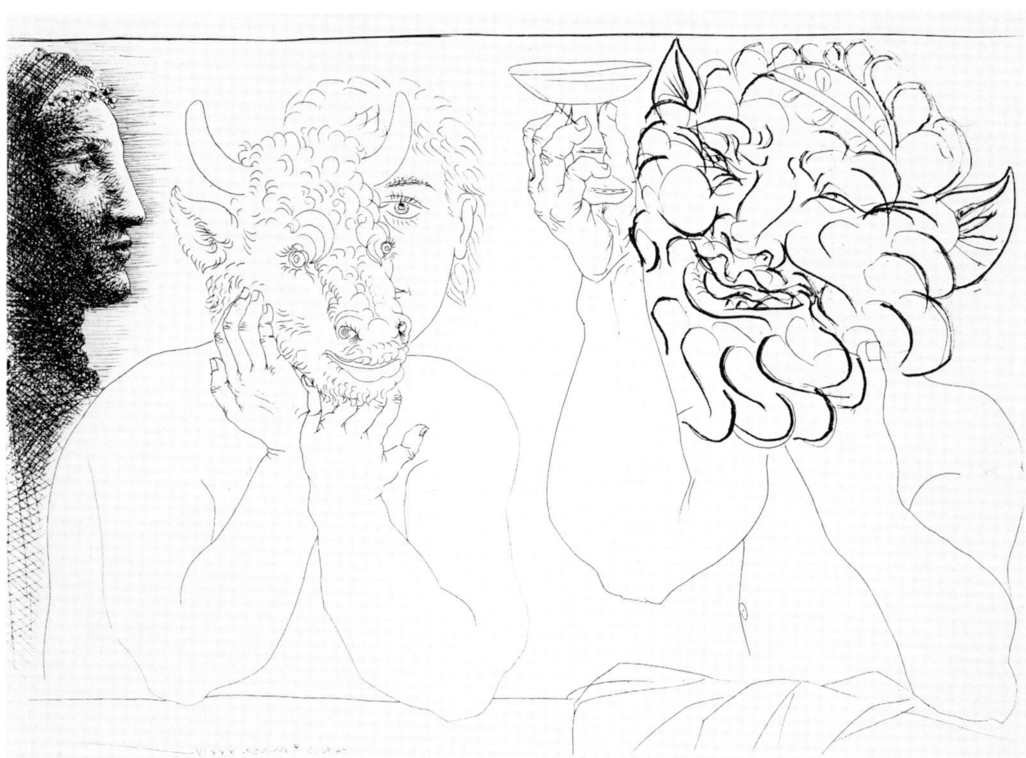

45.

From March 7, 1934, we have a puzzling and somewhat ironical composition (cat. no. 45). Picasso is not taken in by his projected identifications and his creature, the Minotaur, is seen as only a Halloween mask. Under the distant gaze of a superb Marie-Thérèse, tranformed into a Greek goddess, two strange guests toast one another, as elsewhere do the Minotaur and the sculptor. The young and beardless sculptor is partially hiding behind a shoddy mask, but who is hiding behind a laughing satyr's mask, which has a vague resemblance to Bacchus? Perhaps the old and bearded sculptor? Are we back again to the theme of masculinity, with potency (youth has the potency of the Minotaur) contrasted with impotency (the old sculptor, hidden under the form of a slightly ridiculous faun, drowning his sorrows in drink)? Marie-Thérèse is a hieratic female sphinx. The young man is approximately her real age, not even 24 years yet.

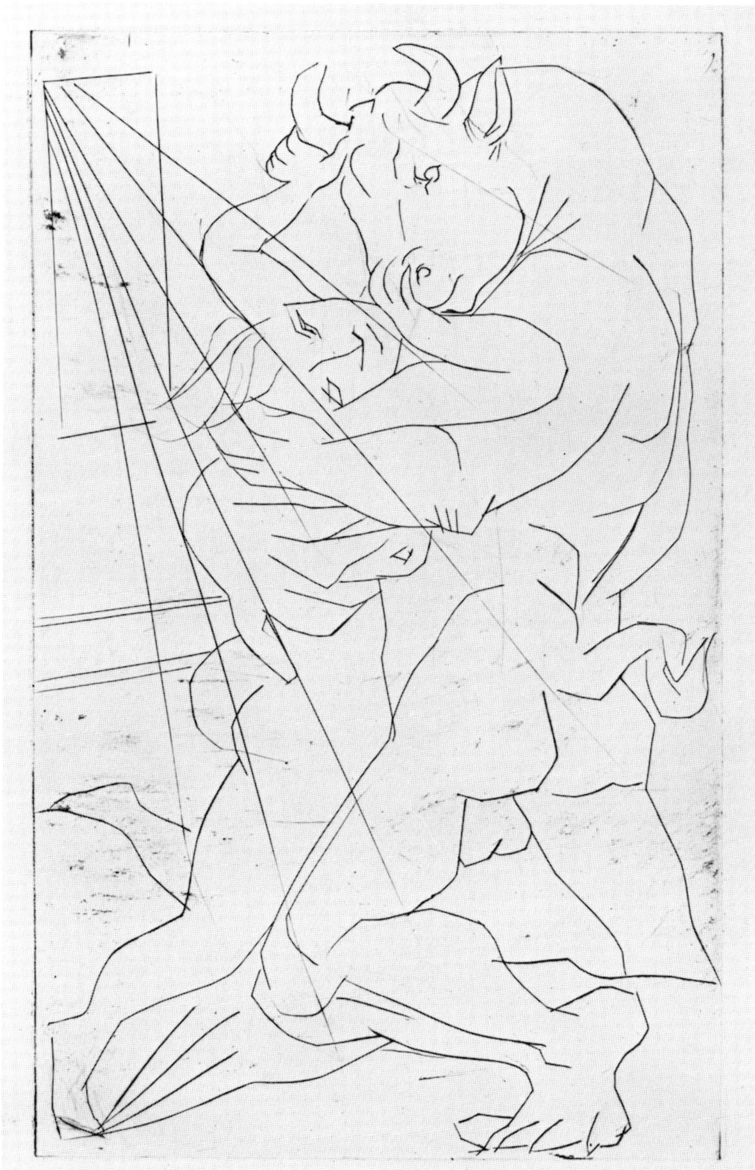

46.

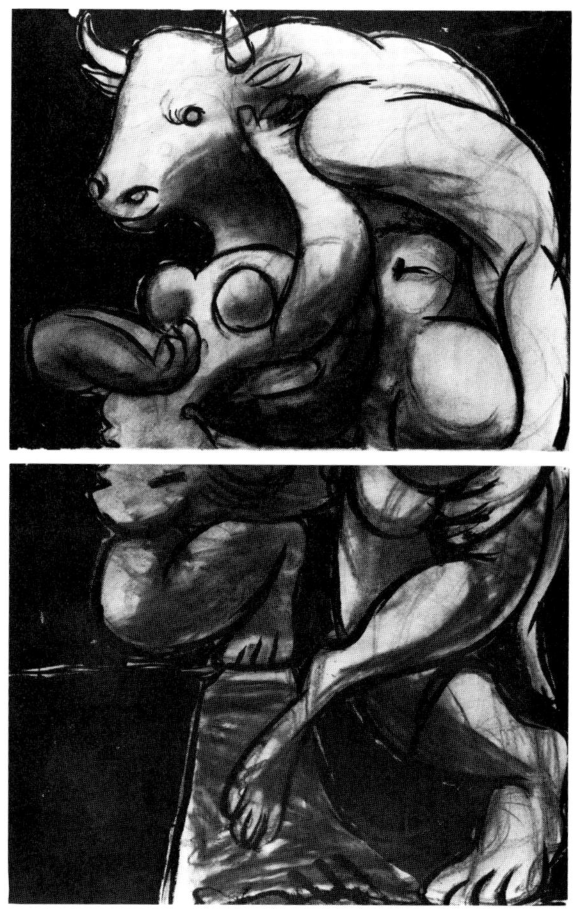

Fig. 2. Picasso, *Minotaur and Nude*, 1933, *encre de Chine* on paper, 96.5 × 61 cm., Marina Picasso Collection, Picasso Estate Inv. No. 3859.

In cat. no. 46 from August 1934, all doubt seems to have vanished once again. The Minotaur, bracing a foot against the bed, wrenches Marie-Thérèse out of it, and violently and lovingly embraces her. A comparison between the position of our two figures and those of the Barye bronze, cited above, is not without interest. In our drypoint, it is Marie-Thérèse who tries to repel the amorous violence of the Minotaur. In the Barye bronze, it is the Minotaur who, in a similar position, tries to repulse the death which Theseus is about to inflict on him. In the catalogue of the exhibition *The Romantics to Rodin* held at the Los Angeles County Museum, (1980, cat. no. 22), Glenn Benge points out "the oddly sexual overtone" of the embrace of Theseus and the Minotaur. The fighting embrace of Marie-Thérèse and the Minotaur, though sexual in content, has nevertheless a message of possible death. Eros and Thanatos again intermix.

Included here is a photograph of an extremely large undated drawing (fig. 2), where the same motif is seen, but in this case the Minotaur has already conquered and is in the process of carrying off his beloved victim, who has fainted. Thus it represents an abduction, not a rape.

46.
Minotaure embrassant une femme
Minotaur Embracing a Woman

1934 (August 4, Boisgeloup)

Drypoint on copper

396 × 244 mm.

A proof on Arches wove paper pulled by the artist.

G.431.A.

The copperplate (on exhibition) was cancelled in 1979.

This drypoint should be dated August 4, since one out of the three proofs pulled by Picasso, now in the Musée Picasso, Paris, is annotated top left "Boisgeloup, 4 aout XXXIV." In 1942, Lacourière pulled from the unsteelfaced plate 57 proofs on the paper left over from the *Suite Vollard* with the "Picasso" or "Vollard" watermark. No edition has yet been published.

From June 12 to June 22, 1934, Picasso, as was perhaps foreshadowed by our no. 45, gave up the Minotaur, and came back to "reality" with the theme of the bull from the arena and that of the woman torero. All this happened before the journey to Spain with Olga and Paulo at the end of August, which was perhaps provoked by his nostalgia for the bullrings. We know that he was an *aficionado*, following the *corridas* from San Sebastian to Burgos and on to Madrid. Bull or Minotaur? There is no real difference and, if we examine closely the big etching of June 12 (G.425; B.1329), we realize that the bull and the Marie-Thérèse torera are in fact kissing each other. This is a kiss of death no doubt, but also a lover's kiss. Everybody understands the mythological symbolism of the *corrida* in Spain: toro and torero perform an amorous ritualized struggle which results in the death of one or the other, or both of them. In this conflict, it is the man, feeble as he is, who represents the masculine principle, whereas, despite appearances, the bull represents the feminine one. This duality of love/destruction is still present in Picasso's *corridas,* even if the roles seem reversed, and it is Marie-Thérèse who is always the wounded torera. As is well-known, role reversal is archetypical of dream symbolism.

Well before the Spanish trip, Olga's jealousy took the same road as Picasso's passion for Marie-Thérèse, if we judge from his work, i.e. from bad to worse, and the situation became increasingly intolerable. In one of his most famous drawings, made on the 7th of July (Z.VIII.216), the artist has drawn his inspiration from David's *Death of Marat* repeating the subject in a small print from July (G.430; B.282). It is Marie-Thérèse who lies in the bath with her head thrown back as in the David. But Picasso adds a Charlotte Corday, in the guise of a delirious sorceress, the epitome of murderous revenge, who hurls herself at the woman in the bath while brandishing a butcher's knife. Scholars have always seen here a depiction of Olga's jealous fury and the artist's fears for his mistress.

After the journey to Spain came a new *corrida* (cat. no. 47, dated September 8), followed the next day by a drawing of the same subject which is equally disturbing (Z.VIII.233). The composition is literally terrifying and seems to show, this time in the execution rather than in the subject matter, such a paroxysmal crisis that all contents are totally intermixed and confused: the bull, the torera, the picador, the public as aggressor, victim, voyeur. In the general confusion, it is difficult to make out what parts belong to the bull, what to the torera, and what to the picador. The minute scale of the *barrera* with the spectators, of the arena itself, and even of the torera's assistant running about in the foreground is significant. It is indeed a battle of Titans. Only the head of Marie-Thérèse stands apart as calm, beautiful and delineated with a continuous stroke. Impetuous force and confusion are at their acme: no more Eros, simply Thanatos.

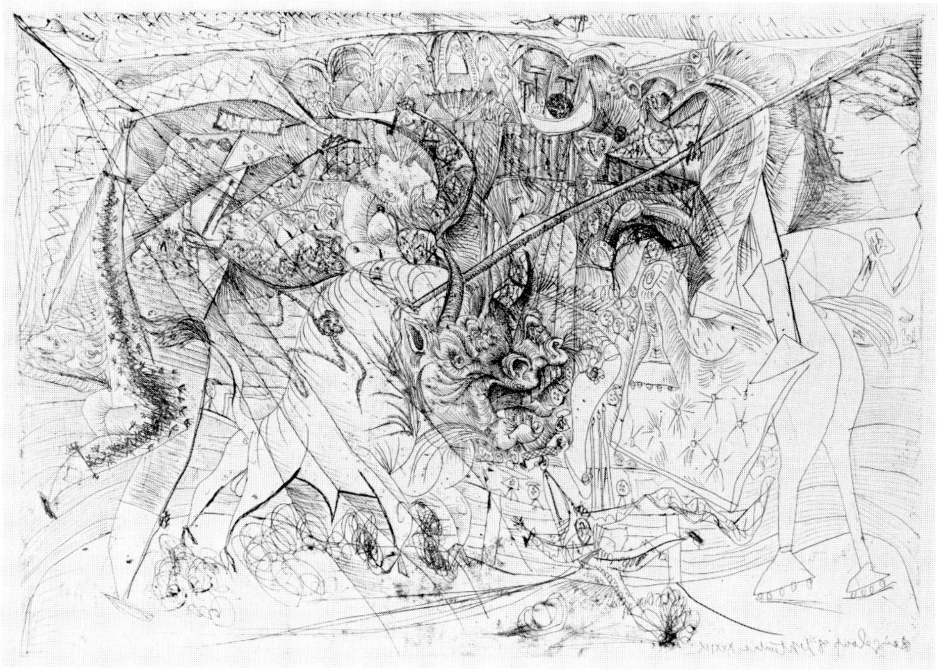

47.

47.

Femme torero
Woman Bull Fighter

1934 (September 8, Boisgeloup)

Etching on copper

495 × 697 mm.

One of the four proofs on wove, Arches or Rives, paper catalogued by Geiser (here on a wove paper without watermark).

G.433 ("*Corrida*"); B.1330.

From this plate, as in the case of G.425 (B.1329), 50 to 55 impressions were pulled on laid Montval paper before or after Vollard's death. As we have seen, two proofs on parchment of G.425 were signed by Picasso before Vollard's death; as for the remaining impressions, dates are not known. To this point, we have no knowledge of a *bon à tirer* state. Were these two plates and their printing the result of a contract with Vollard? It seems unlikely as Vollard always had his plates steelfaced and these have not been. The parcels of impressions were probably carried off by Fabiani who is said to have negotiated the purchase of the Vollard Estate, and through whom all the other transactions were made. A few proofs, probably printers' proofs, had been signed in the '40s (pre-1947): Art Institute, Chicago, and the Museum of Modern Art, New York. Much later, the artist signed the proofs belonging to Georges Bloch on the latter's request. As far as the writer of this catalogue knows there are no other signed proofs in existence. The remaining unsigned impressions only appeared on the market after Picasso's death and belong to a dealer in Paris. The copperplate exists.

We can draw a parallel between the theme of the dying Minotaur in the arena and the *corridas* with the "circus" games of the Cretan cycle of the Theseid, as described in the IVth century B.C. by Pausanias who already gives a more "civilized" version of the actual ritual. The young Athenians, sent as tribute to the Minotaur, had to fight bare-handed with an enraged bull. The archaeological evidence confirms that they were supposed to run at the bull, grasp its horns and execute a somersault, arriving upright on the animal's back.

Nevertheless, it was only from September 22 onward that Picasso made a more direct reference to Greek myths, those of Theseus and Oedipus. We are taking certain liberties with chronology in exhibiting here first the etching of November 29, 1934, which seems to confirm the storytelling element in Picasso's approach.

Two sailors, wearing Phrygian caps, are drinking at a table. One of them, heavily worked in line, is smoking his pipe while listening to a story told by the other, who is merely sketched in outline. What sort of tales do sailors recount in their bars? Fantastic ones, such as Sinbad the Sailor, Ulysses, Lord Jim, or that of Theseus. The fact that the storyteller is reduced here to his simplest form shows that it is the story he is telling and the interest of the pipe-smoker which are the most important elements. His tale, perhaps easily understandable, may also combine well-known stories and lead into new meanings, while maintaining the outline of the old.

48.
Histoire de marins
A Sailor's Story

1934 (November 29, Paris)

Etching on copper

237 × 299 mm.

Proof on Montval laid paper with the "Picasso" watermark. Plate is dated on the back.

G.442.II.c (*"Deux buveurs catalans"*); B.228; S.V.12.

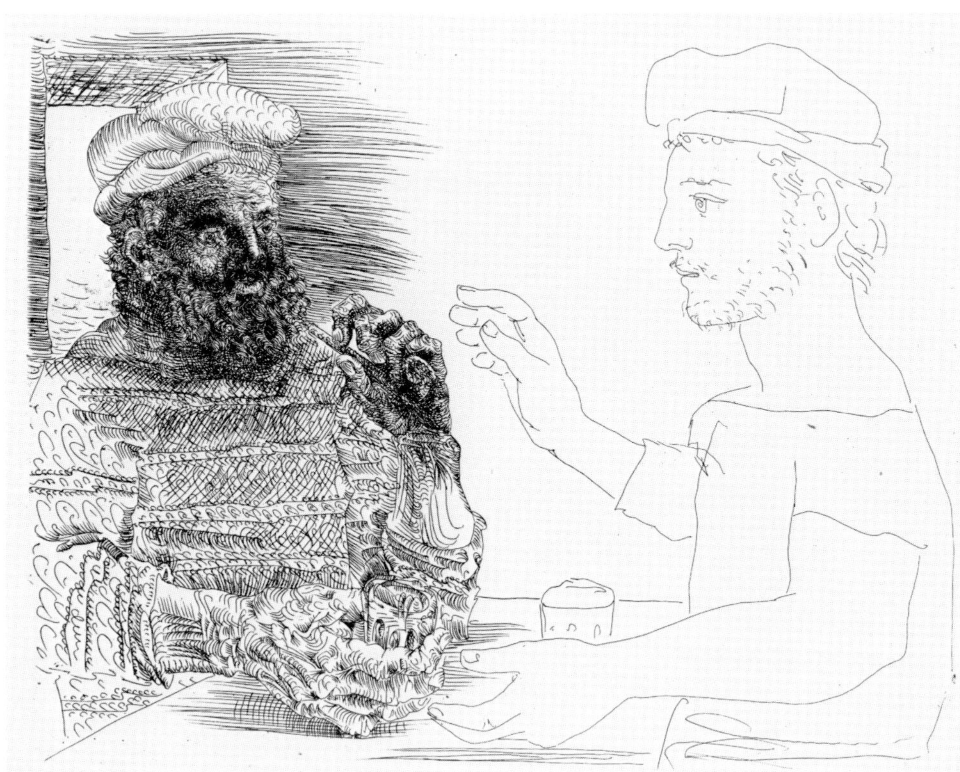

48.

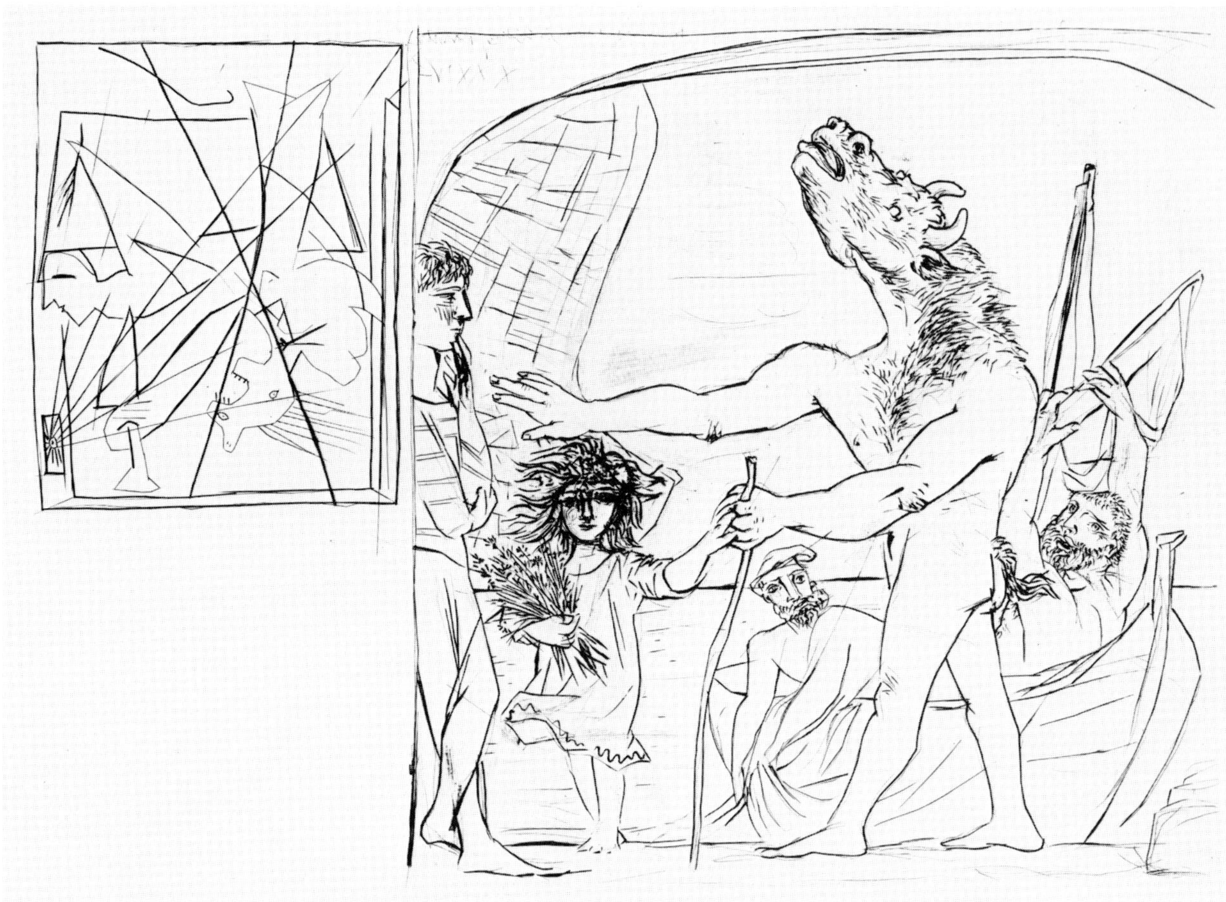

49.

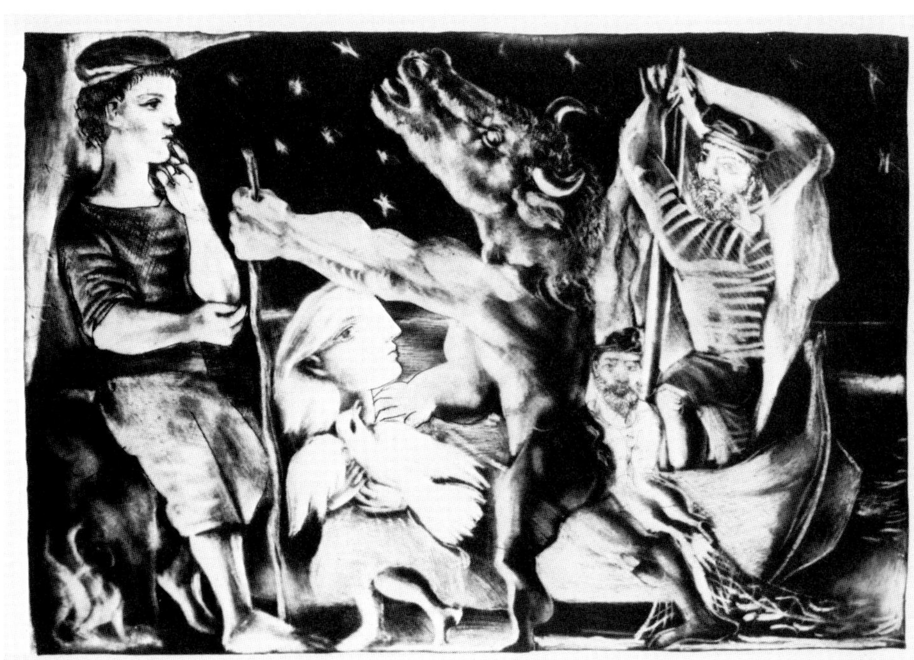

50.

49.
Minotaure aveugle guidé par une fillette, I
The Blind Minotaur Guided by a Little Girl, I

1934 (September 22, Boisgeloup)

Burin and etching on copper

252 × 348 mm.

Proof on Montval laid paper with the "Vollard" watermark.

G.434.XIII.c; B.222; S.V.94.

The blind Minotaur, who has been compared with reason to Picasso's series of blind people of 1903, is being guided just as Theseus was guided by Ariadne's thread and as Oedipus was guided by Antigone towards Colonus, where in fact he would meet Theseus and his death. The little girl has Marie-Thérèse's face and carries the bunch of flowers which is her symbol. A young sailor is leaning against a wall in a posture which repeats exactly the ritualized stance which Oedipus always assumes before the Sphinx, thus obliging us to associate the two myths. He is the spectator, the Minotaur's double, the one who has replaced the sculptor, Theseus. In the background, fishermen are hauling down their sail and bringing in their nets full of fish. The color of the boat's sail, black or white, is of vital importance in the Theseus myth, as seen below. The fish are an evident symbol of masculinity. On the left, we can see the *Death of Marat*, upside down and cancelled (see the description preceding cat. no. 47).

It is without doubt the confusion already apparent in no. 47 which led to the theme of the blind Minotaur. The inference to be drawn from the autobiographical aspect is clear. His love for Marie-Thérèse, watched over by Oedipus/Theseus, is leading him on blindly. Is it not towards Olga's jealous violence, repressed but latent, that the Minotaur is walking? But also the anguish inherent in the femininity of the Minotaur is an important factor here, that anguish present both in the Cretan cycle of the Theseid as well as in Picasso's iconography. Femininity has two contradictory aspects: on the one hand, the weak child, gentle and full of affection, and on the other, the witch armed with a murderous knife. Primary femininity (a product of the primary relationship with the mother and the defense mechanisms provoked by it) is impotence (the impotence of an infant) and also the inherent destructive rage which always attacks the best loved and most vital object of its affections. This destructive rage, present during the preceding months in the iconography of the Minotaur, is intolerable to look at in the "mirror" which is the other, the mother and the wife (here Olga), just as Perseus needed the gift of Athena, the polished shield, to use as a double mirror in order to kill Medusa. The Minotaur prefers to be blind and his shield is the child. But when a man allows himself to become weak and dependent, to be led, it means that once again destructive fury is not very far away. Theseus will abandon Ariadne (herself rather witch-like) pregnant on the beach at Naxos, because it is better to run off than to kill. What will the Minotaur/Picasso do?

50. (see color plate)
Minotaur aveugle guidé par une fillette dans la nuit
Blind Minotaur Led by a Young Girl in the Night

1934 (November)

Aquatint, additional work with the scraper as in a mezzotint, and burin on copper

247 × 347 mm.

Proof on Arches wove paper, pulled by Lacourière, but inked in colors by Picasso with dabber.

G.437.III.a.

This is in fact the 4th state, as there is an intermediary state between Geiser's 2nd and 3rd states.

As in the case of nos. 13 and 14, in the 1st state, the proof has a rectangular black, uniform surface. Little by little the artist "freed" the composition with the scraper.

There is one other proof, inked with the dabber and printed in colors. That proof, with more strident colors, is in the Musée Picasso, Paris.

After steelfacing of the plate, the *Suite Vollard* proof was printed: G.437.IV (in fact, 5th state); B.225; S.V. 97.

This is the same subject as no. 49 and the other two blind Minotaurs, G.435 and 436. *The Death of Marat* is no longer present, but one should not forget it. The little girl, in an even more pronounced fashion than in the preceding number, has Marie-Thérèse's features. The fish are much more visible. The sail is much more clearly a dark sail. The stars in the sky remind us of Ariadne, turned into a constellation as Marie-Thérèse was transformed into a Muse. The little girl is carrying a white dove in place of flowers: the dove which announces the end of God's wrath and the end of the Flood, the emblem of purity and one of those white pigeons which Marie-Thérèse loved so much. (Further, we cannot forget the meaning it will acquire as a symbol of peace.)

After abandoning Ariadne at Naxos, Theseus on his way home stopped at Delos and celebrated so heartily that he ''forgot'' a detail. He neglected to change the black sail on his boat for a white one. As a result, his father, Aegeus, who had been obliged to consult the oracle in his search for a cure for his sterility and who finally had come to love his only offspring, thought that Theseus had perished in the Cretan expedition and, in despair, hurled himself from a cliff into the sea. Theseus then became king. A print from November 11, *Au cabaret* (G.439; B.286), depicts a young sailor, onlooker but also participant, ''celebrating'' if not at Delos, at least in a sailors' nightclub. Thus is completed a return to the theme of the father. If the father is the Law, and if the Law in Spain prohibits divorce, must one submit like a child and so be prey to the rage of destruction? Or is it not more economical, like Theseus, to go from woman to woman, abandoning each in turn, ceaselessly to found cities (or households, which is the same thing), only to leave them once they have been constructed?

On November 18, Picasso again took up the theme of loneliness. The young man, who has been watching the blind Minotaur and drinking in the cabaret, takes on more and more the aspect he will keep not only in the first drawings for the *Homme au mouton*, but also in the related lithograph (M.7) and linocut (B.1025 and 1026). Also he reminds us of the young boy continually present in the Pink period. In cat. no. 51, he is sitting pensively while Marie-Thérèse, whose position already evokes the one she will have in the *Faune dévoilant une femme*, is plunged into a deep, deep sleep. The subject is not a new one. But the scene is illuminated this time by the candle of the *Minotauromachie*, and the atmosphere of calm melancholy which emanates from this superb plate is nonetheless a little bizarre. The boy looks more worried than thoughtful. What thoughts are passing through the head of the young man with the Minotaur's premonitory vision? What forebodings? Does he desire even irrationally a child from this woman who is everything to him for the moment? As for the Minotaur, he is not capable of assuming the division which a child's presence inevitably creates. He is too possessive, too madly and incurably intolerant.

51.
Garçon et dormeuse à la chandelle
Boy and Sleeping Woman with a Candle

1934 (November 18, Paris)

Etching, sugar-lift aquatint, scraper and burin on copper

237 × 300 mm.

Proof on Montval laid paper with the ''Vollard'' watermark. Plate is annotated on the back.

G.440.IV.c; B.226; S.V.26.

The next day, November 19, Picasso made an aquatint that is mysterious and fascinating in many ways. First, there is the question of technique. For the first time Picasso used a type of aquatint which we shall see time and time again from 1963 onwards. The ''drawing'' medium is the varnish. This means that the composition is painted with the varnish onto a clean copperplate or onto a plate grained with resin, but not yet bitten with acid. The painted areas - once the copperplate is either grained or bitten, or simply bitten - remain untouched and appear white on the proof. As here, the artist can also etch into the areas covered by the varnish. The French term for this technique is *aquatinte avec réserves au vernis*. Literally, the word *réserve* can be translated as ''area left apart.'' In our proof, the biting with acid has been made by hand and not in the acid bath.

Iconographically, the composition is complex. On a column sits a sphinx or pythia. A man (Oedipus or the young Aegeus, perhaps) is pouring a libation, asking questions and making replies. But in a way, the riddle of the Sphinx was a sort of reply from the Pythia. From the outset, it was up to Oedipus to solve the riddle, instead of interpreting as did Aegeus an answer. The two characters who are central to the composition, and vital also for the question and the answer, both wear masks. The man wears the mask of the Minotaur, whereas the woman wears the mask of the sculptor.

The problem of femininity is posed once again. We have seen that ''primary'' femininity (passivity, helplessness and the resulting destructive fury) was implicated in the personage of the Minotaur, the sculptor being the creative force without doubt, but also capable of rationalization and of sublimation. Here everything

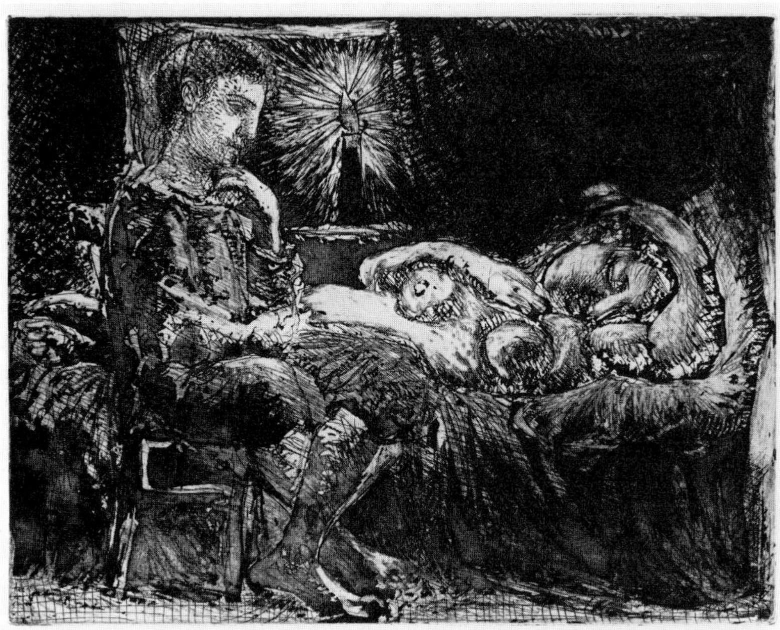

51.

52.

Personnages masqués et femme-oiseau
Masked Characters with a Bird-Woman

1934 (November 19, Paris)

Aquatint with *réserves au vernis*, bitten by hand, and etching on copper

249 × 348 mm.

Proof on Montval laid paper with the "Picasso" watermark. Plate is annotated on the back.

G.441.II.c; B.227; S.V.24.

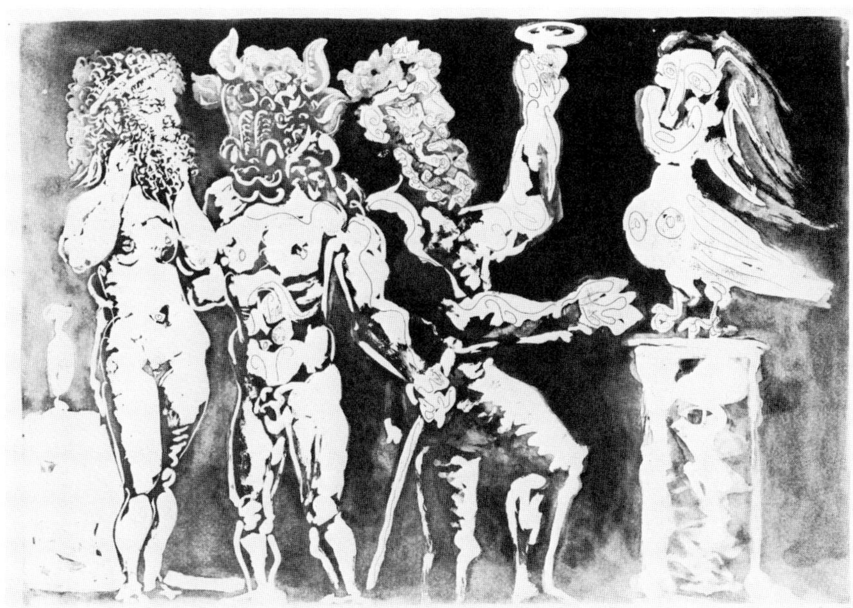

52.

seems to have been turned upside-down. Are we going back again to the theme of the sculptor and his model? Is the artist asking himself the question - linked to the motif of avidity and of envy - of whether it is the model, the Muse, who creates rather than the hand of the sculptor? In this case, it is logical that the sculptor should have the features of the Minotaur, since this idea is unbearable for him.

We have the feeling that a deep and complex question is being posed to the Pythia, such as, is not a child the perfect creation in itself which men envy women for, even if they partially solve the problem by creating works of art? If the masks are there to deceive the Pythia, then there is another possible question: how can one reconcile the destructive femininity of the Minotaur with the creative femininity of the artist? If one abandons the former, what will remain of the latter?

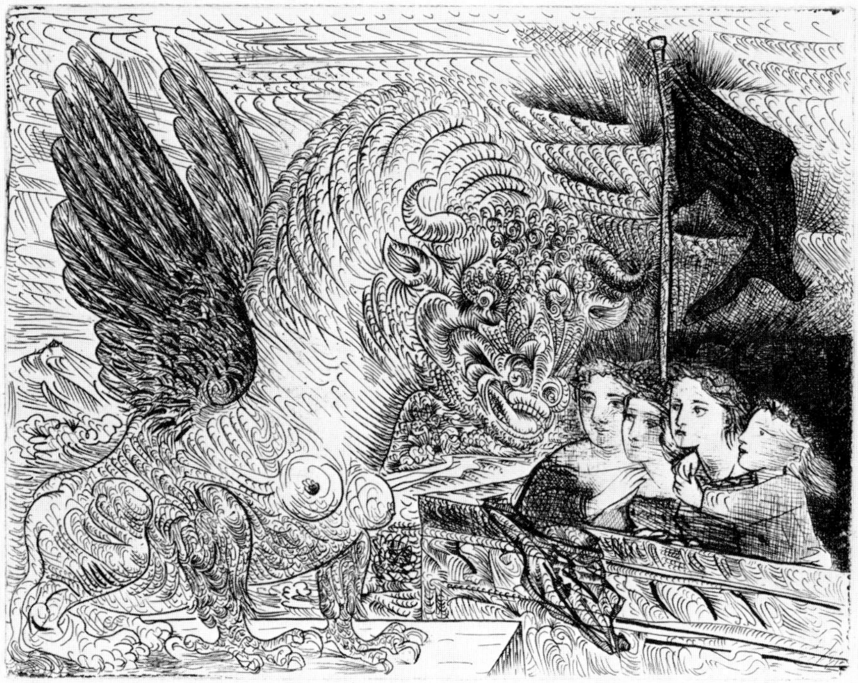

53.

During the month of December (the plate is simply annotated ''Paris Decembre XXXIV''), Picasso etched a superb composition which combines the stories of Oedipus and Theseus. On the black-sailed boat a group of small children are standing. All wear wreaths of flowers, as so often Marie-Thérèse does in Picasso's work, and as, it is said, the young Athenian boys and girls had to wear as they were offered to the Minotaur. In an attitude of terror, they implore a double monster, half-Minotaur, half-sphinx, whose femininity is emphasized by her full, rounded breasts. Here, the artist himself mixes the two stories and clearly shows that we are not mistaken in giving the Minotaur a strongly feminine and, if one can say so, pre-Oedipal connotation. Impotence and omnipotence, weakness and destructive rage - all go together and are present in this marvelous etching. The Minotaur-sphinx seems to be horrified by the idea that, under an inescapable compulsion, it will be obliged to devour the children. And what if the plate was engraved after Christmas, after Marie-Thérèse had told Picasso she was pregnant? In that case, we could add an anecdotal allusion: what is going to happen to the child? Will it be consumed by this Minotaur, who is so decidedly feminine and all the more frightening?

53.
Taureau ailé contemplé par quatre enfants
Winged Bull with Four Children Looking On

1934 (December)

Etching on copper

238 × 298 mm.

Proof on Montval laid paper with the ''Vollard'' watermark.

G.444.II.c; B.229; S.V.13.

Picasso abandoned copperplates between this etching and the *Minotauromachie*, as the *Petite baigneuse* (B.287) must in fact be dated 1939, *pace* Bloch.

The *Minotauromachie* dates from March 23, 1935. Picasso began it on a Saturday in Lacourière's workshop. Although it was heavily worked in seven states, it should be pointed out from the start that all the work did not modify in any significant way the composition. The only changes are that the tower, from whose window the two Marie-Thérèses lean as spectators with their doves, is seen in perspective from the 4th state onwards, and the little girl wearing a round hat in the 3rd state had previously been bareheaded. The herculean work of the artist consisted only in dramatizing, perfecting and making more precise certain details.

It is not our intention here to constitute a technical dossier of all the states, of the date of the steelfacing, or a topographical index of all the known proofs. It is quite enough to note that there are extremely few proofs before the steelfacing of the 7th and final state in existence: two proofs known on old paper, and one or perhaps two on laid Montval paper. All the others, even those marked "trial proof for . . . ," were printed after steelfacing. Of the latter, the locations of 55 of the impressions are now known. This figure includes those with a dedication by Picasso, the *bon à tirer*, the impressions numbered out of 50, those which are annotated "one of the thirty proofs of the edition," those impressions which their owners later asked Picasso to sign, and, finally, those unsigned ones which were in the Picasso Estate. All these proofs were pulled by Lacourière at the same time on Montval laid paper, although no watermark is visible on some of the trial proofs. No edition was ever published. Picasso used to give them as presents, one by one, hence the somewhat disturbing numeration. We are convinced that the four numbered impressions we have not yet been able to locate among those between 1/50 and 15/50, must have existed. Either they were lost or destroyed during the war, or they will reappear in time. We may assume that there were about 60 impressions printed after steelfacing. We shall give full details, list of the proofs, etc., in the forthcoming volume of the catalogue raisonné, begun by Dr. Geiser, on which we are working. (The above count does not include the two proofs printed in color with the dabber.)

Let us now examine more closely our proof of the *Minotauromachie*. Nothing remains of the confusion we saw in no. 47. Clearly there is violence, but so restrained that it is easy to overlook. The characters seem to have been petrified in the middle of their gestures as through the fairy from *Sleeping Beauty* or the lava of Pompeii.

Let us begin with a few brief words about the chronology. Marie-Thérèse had been pregnant since the end of November. Picasso, who had known about it since December the 24th, had already, on December 30, humorously shown in a superb drawing (fig. 3) that he now knew where the blind Minotaur's little girl was leading him. In this drawing, the blind Minotaur has been replaced by a man, wearing a *mask* of a blind Minotaur, who is led by the same little girl with a dove as in no. 50. However, in the mask there are two little holes to see through. Walking alongside them are two men carrying his few pathetic belongings, the chair and the lamp, which French bailiffs always leave after a seizure, a bullfighter's sword, a sculpture wrapped up in a cloth, another sculpture depicting the sculptor and Marie-Thérèse's vase of flowers. She and her future child were leading him toward a separation from Olga and toward the pathetic moving-out of a man rejected and deprived of all his earthly possessions.

Let us go back to the *Minotauromachie*. On the left, a serious and "human" man, bearded like the sculptor and dressed like the crucified Christ, is calmly climbing a ladder with a lingering backward look. (There is an obvious visual reference here to the iconography of the Crucifixion, where in the scenes of the Descent from the Cross, Joseph of Arimathea is shown on a ladder as he unnails the body of Christ.) Toward the upper corner, on the ramparts of the tower, thus out of reach, stands the doubled Marie-Thérèse, calm and serene with her two doves. In the center, the main action is comprised of a mare, with her entrails hanging out of a gaping hole, carrying across her back a Marie-Thérèse torera, whose bared stomach and breasts are already swollen. In a dead faint she seems to be drawing her sword against herself, but this is not immediately clear as the sword also touches the Minotaur's left hand. On the left, the little girl with the bunch of flowers is holding aloft a feeble candle whose pure light nevertheless manages to blind the Minotaur. The little girl is wearing the hat that Marie-Thérèse had on when photographed as an adolescent girl at the age of 14 on October 20, 1922 (fig. 4). This photograph was in the artist's possession and now belongs to Maya Picasso. Finally, on the right, the Minotaur. His fear of the light betrays his anguish and, we are tempted to say, his aggressive fantasies. He carries a bundle in a big, knotted red handkerchief (known from the colored proofs), red as a bullfighter's cape, red as blood. He has come to find something, to steal something, before escaping like the man on the left. The distant boat will carry him away. He is ready for the voyage with his belongings on his back. They are not heavy, however, since the arm which carries them is very small. The bundle, in fact, seems almost empty.

Thus Marie-Thérèse is depicted five times: doubled, a spectator, unconscious of the passions unleashed by her condition; a little girl hardly younger than when Picasso met her (at least in the eyes of a man who was

53 and easily old enough to be her father), seen as childish and pure, trusting and naive, capable because of this very naivety of protecting her other persona; the wounded Marie-Thérèse, symbolized by the mare; and the torera about to transfix herself with her own sword. (The fact that it is difficult to distinguish whose hand is holding the sword is clearly not without significance). What the mare is losing out of the hole in her belly, what is already in the Minotaur's bundle or what he desires to put there, is quite simply the baby of which he is madly jealous, and which he wants to destroy, and/or to wrench away so that he can have it for himself alone. (Here, we refer to the Kleinian fantasy, often misunderstood, but nonetheless true, which joins up with the theme of destructive rage and envy inherent in primal femininity.) His double, the man, understanding like Christ, prefers to leave. He does not run away, however, but cedes his protective role to the innocent child, which is enough to prevent the tragedy. On the other hand, he, in his persona of the sculptor, cannot but be envious: what price a lump of dead stone when compared with a living child? Therefore, we are given the destructive jealousy of the child/Minotaur whose place has been taken, the jealousy of the man/Minotaur who wants to carry off what he can never possess, and the jealousy of the sculptor who is unable to compete.

If we look carefully at the wound in the mare we realize full well that it is a baby pouring out. It is not a wound gored by a bull, but rather, a birth or miscarriage. There can be no doubt that there is a direct reference to the female genital organs.

It is a crisis, but it is the final crisis. The Minotaur's mad urge to destroy has been exorcized by the immense toil of the print. Evidently, the mad passion for Marie-Thérèse has been exorcized as well. She stays the Muse, but she is about to be a mother, and, from the very instant of birth, Picasso made no distinction between the mother and daughter, Maya, calling them both "my girls." It will not be long before he goes off, just like Theseus, just like the sculptor, just like the Minotaur who will rapidly vanish from the scene and gradually turn into a humanized faun. Even in the majestic series of gouaches of May 1936 his metamorphosis has already begun and the face of the Minotaur is anthropomorphic. Strangely enough, on one more occasion we find him again, this time loving Dora Maar (Z.VIII.296; September 1, 1936). Is this a final exorcism of the kind of passionate relationship that Picasso no longer had any use for? In the series entitled *The End of a Monster*, from 1938, the protagonist is a faun and ends up as a souvenir, a sculpture placed on a table next to Marie-Thérèse's bouquet of three flowers, or next to the palette, the brushes, and the papers which evoke this passionate, painful, happy and past era. (See e.g. Z.VIII.360 and Z.IX.239.)

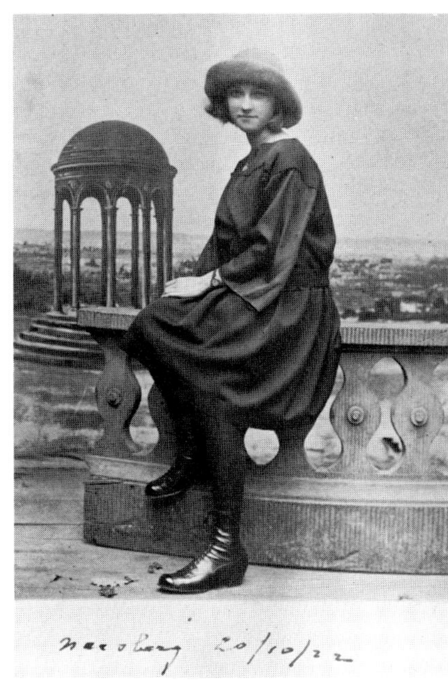

Fig. 4. *Marie-Thérèse at Age 14*, Oct. 20, 1922, photograph, Maya Picasso Collection (courtesy of Maya Picasso).

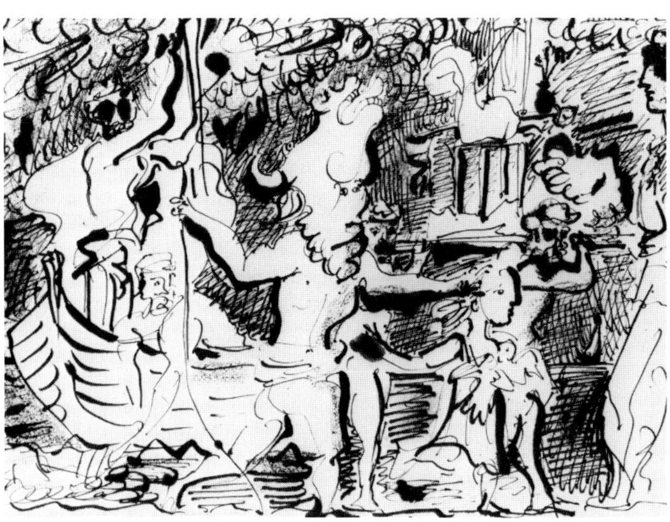

Fig. 3. Picasso, *Blind Minotaur led by a Little Girl*, Dec. 30, 1934, *encre de Chine* and crayon on paper, 25 × 32 cm., Maya Picasso Collection, Picasso Estate Inv. No. 3864 (courtesy of Maya Picasso).

54.

La Minotauromachie

The Minotauromachia

1935 (September 23, Paris)

Etching, scraper and burin on copper

498 × 693 mm.

Proof of the 7th state, after steelfacing, on laid Montval paper.

B.288.

The cancelled copperplate is in the Musée Picasso, Paris.

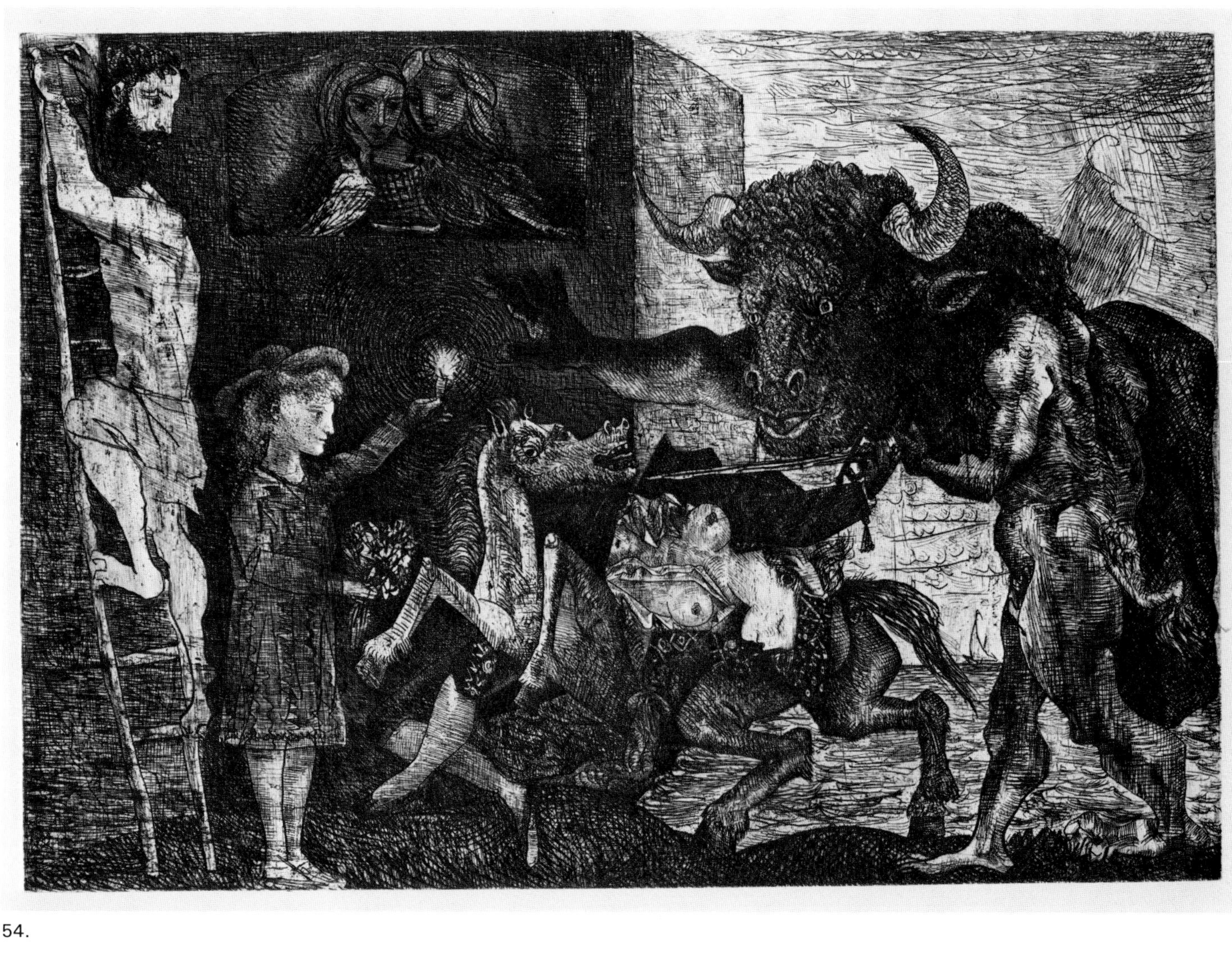

54.

Picasso would continue to love, paint and draw Marie-Thérèse for many years to come, and some of these portraits are among the finest of his career. He evoked their ''family'' clandestinely reunited at Juan-les-Pins in the marvelous drawings of April 1936, and he depicted the sad eyes of Marie-Thérèse as she showed to him, in a mirror, his own image of a dying faun (which no doubt she regreted as he regreted the Minotaur he was) in the *Death of a Monster* series. But his passion for her was that of the Minotaur and a Minotaur cannot share anything with a child; he is too afraid to destroy. Without passion, there is no more Muse. Marie-Thérèse disappeared from the engraved work in 1936 with the *Jeune fille regardent fuir une hirondelle dans un miroir* (B.290) and above all, so magnificently, with the *Faune dévoilant une femme* of the 12th of June (cat. no. 55), a work that looks back nostalgically on their stay in Juan-les-Pins and on a passion that had changed. This aquatint, the most successful print in the *Suite Vollard* and one of the most beautiful in the artist's engraved work, has a special quality: the more one studies it - the six states pose many technical and other problems - the more lyrical and mysterious it becomes, claiming clear title to the label of ''masterpiece.''

Although unhappily we cannot exhibit the six states of the print here, they tell a kind of fairy tale. The sleeping (dreaming?) woman hardly changes at all. Step by step, however, the light streaming in from the balcony and washing over the room becomes more and more lunar until it takes on that pale mysterious tonality of the full moon. (Picasso continually reworked the aquatint in every conceivable way in order to perfect the lighting via a process which certainly must have bored such an impatient man as he). There is another interesting detail: in the 1st state, on the balcony, stands a flower-pot with a strawberry plant in it. Picasso, who had not the vaguest idea about flowers or plants or the countryside in general changed this in the 3rd state into a pot filled with basil. According to Mediterranean folklore, basil has the power to change, particularly at the time of a full moon, any ordinary animal into a wonderful creature, a sort of Prince Charming. Throughout the six states, the young faun, beardless and slightly ugly, will gradually become more and more handsome, ending up, in the 6th state, as a god-like personification of beauty.

Le faune dévoilant une femme is directly based on Rembrandt's engraving of 1659, *Jupiter and Antiope* (Bartsch, 203; fig. 5), which in turn is based on a prior engraving by Rembrandt dating from 1631 (Bartsch, 204). As Christopher White points out in his *Rembrandt as an Etcher* (London, 1969, p. 185), the Dutch artist himself may well have known the Carracci etching of the same subject. The position of Antiope in all of these prints is almost exactly the same as that of Marie-Thérèse in our print.

As usual, however, Picasso makes the subject his own and changes the technique, the setting and the meaning. On the one hand, the balcony in Juan-les-Pins is perfectly real and exists but, whereas Rembrandt depicts Jupiter in his disguise of a faun as a rather disgusting, lecherous old creature, Picasso gives us a faun who is even more handsome and god-like than Jupiter himself. Once again, we are obliged to deal with another conflation. Given that this aquatint is a farewell to the passionate relationship between Picasso and Marie-Thérèse, we are inevitably reminded of Psyche who, when compelled to confront the real nature of her lover, Eros, lost him forever. But a faun, even one as handsome as a god, is not a Minotaur. As we have seen in the series of gouaches which antedate our aquatint by a month, the Minotaur dies and takes his leave. A large gouache, a project for the drop-curtain of Romain Rolland's *Le 14 juillet* (Z.VIII.287), shows us the Minotaur as a hollow doll, dressed in the costume of Harlequin and slung over the arm, like an overcoat, of a figure with the head of a griffon. That destructive passion that Picasso felt for Marie-Thérèse is now changed into love and tenderness. A new love affair is not far away. Like Theseus, Picasso made his choice: he found a solution for the anguish and the crisis, but in human terms, this is both a victory and a defeat. Doubtless his art, a new inspiration, a new stimulus, called him away. Figuratively speaking, he ''abandoned'' the woman with her child on the beach at Naxos. His sentiments changed towards Marie-Thérèse, but he needed the stimulus of feelings which approximate passion. It would not be the same type of passion this time, but another form of it, less violent, more human, less productive. For if, with the birth of this child, Marie-Thérèse made him more mature and so gave him the chance to exorcize that angst wed in all of us to our fear of primal femininity, she at the same time lost the Minotaur, her passionate lover.[1]

We should not forget that, mythologically speaking, the theme of Antiope has certain common features with our story. After Jupiter's visitation as a faun, Antiope bore twins, who were then exposed on the mountain side, like Oedipus. The wretched Antiope had to flee from her father who died from shame and anger. There is no space here to relate her long life of misery. Suffice it to say that her aunt, Dirce, who was jealous of her beauty and had been her principal tormentor, was punished by the grown-up twins in a way that reminds us of both the toreras and the *Minotauromachie*: Dirce was strapped to the back of a bull which dashed her to death against the rocky cliffs.

55.

Faune dévoilant une femme. Jupiter et Antiope

Faun Uncovering a Sleeping Woman. Jupiter and Antiope

1936 (June 12)

Aquatint: sugar-lift with *réserves au vernis*, scraper and burin on copper

316 × 417 mm.

Proof of the 6th state, after steelfacing, on laid Montval paper. No watermark is visible.

B.230; S.V.27.

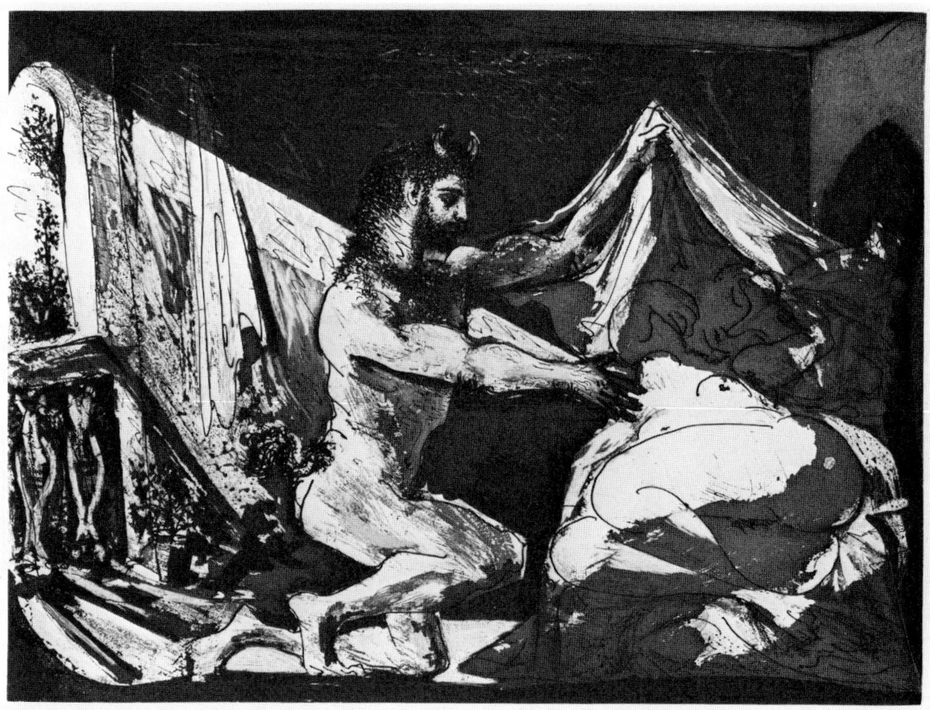

55.

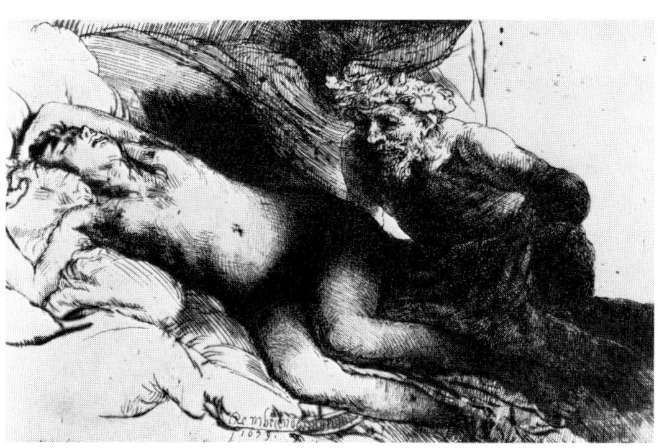

Fig. 5. Rembrandt, *Jupiter and Antiope*, 1659, etching (Bartsch, 203).

Note

[1]Certain parallels can be drawn between the legends of Theseus and Oedipus and the life and character of Picasso:

Like Oedipus and Theseus, he was a ''stranger,'' who felt, in France and possibly everywhere, the role of the alien.

Like Theseus and the Minotaur, because of his art, he too had a ''divine'' origin. (Cf. In the Cretan cycle, the role of Daedalos, the archetype of the artist.) Lack of space has prevented us from enlarging on this theme, but Oedipus also had a ''divine'' aspect. Owing to his exemplary fate and the courage he showed in facing it, Oedipus took on the quality of a Prometheus. At the same time, Picasso, like Oedipus, Theseus and the Minotaur, was an ''outsider'' (cf. the themes of the blind man, the Harlequin, etc.)

Like the Minotaur and like Oedipus, Picasso had the gift of prophetic sight in his role as a ''visionary'' artist.

Both Theseus and Oedipus had been abandoned by their fathers. As we have seen, at the end of his life, Picasso's father no longer tried to understand his son's painting, resulting in a type of abandonment. The father of Theseus finally ''recognized'' his son; the father of Oedipus died by his son's hand without having ''recognized'' him. Contemporary eyewitnesses have told how the old Don Jose was driven into a state of sadness and total indifference by his son's painting and died in acute depression. This was for the artist an extremely painful fact and a sort of accidental ''murder'' by melancholia.

Marie-Thérèse was of the age to be his daughter, and people often remarked that their profiles were strangely alike. A parallel can be drawn with Oedipus-Antigone and also the theme of Theseus's duplication with the Minotaur-Ariadne, its half-sister. Consider also the theme of Helen's abduction by Theseus.

Picasso had a ''privileged'' relationship with Marie-Thérèse, who sacrificed for him but was eternally abandoned (he was married) and whom he finally ''left behind,'' like Ariadne on the beach at Naxos, in order to pursue a new love affair. He must have had this in mind at the time of the *Faune dévoilant une femme* but did not enact it until the summer of 1936.

We have seen that at the end of 1934/summer of 1935, Picasso sometimes considered Olga as a destructive sorceress (theme of Pasiphaë). He certainly had no intention, if it came to a divorce, to cede to her half of his works (the greed of the Minotaur). He also must have been concerned about little Paulo (cf. the tragic fate of the male children abandoned by their fathers in the myths referred to above).

IX.

Dora Maar

Picasso met Dora Maar as early as January 1936 when he struck up a friendship with Paul Eluard. Although Dora Maar visited Picasso's studio several times during the first half of the year, the liaison between her and the artist (as we have seen, the drawings of May 1936 foretell the change) only began during the summer.

Dora Maar was part of the group of sophisticates that included René Char, Paul and Nush Eluard, Man Ray and Roland Penrose. If Marie-Thérèse was a private person, Dora Maar, who spoke fluent Spanish, was a very ''with it'' young lady. Her arrival in the life of Picasso cannot be disassociated from a certain atmosphere of ''the group,'' the reintegration of the artist into a close circle of friends who saw each other regularly and even traveled together.

On November 12, 1935, Picasso's old friend Sabartés had come back to Paris on Picasso's request and had settled into the apartment in the Rue la Boétie. Olga and Paulo had moved out in June, because of the scandal provoked by Marie-Thérèse's pregnancy and since then, Picasso had been living there alone.

By the same token, Picasso's relationship with Dora Maar did not prevent the artist from continuing to see and to love - and to paint - Marie-Thérèse. In the autumn of 1936, Picasso ceased working at Boisgeloup and installed a studio in the house lent to him by Vollard, where Marie-Thérèse and her baby came to live. Picasso divided his time between Paris and this house in Tremblay-sur-Mauldre, where he spent all of his weekends.

Some time later, in January 1937 and with the help of Dora Maar, the artist found a studio in the Rue des Grands Augustins where he painted *Guernica*. At the age of 54, therefore, Picasso once again took up a bohemian way of life: several ''homes,'' several ''wives,'' a ''gang.''

These few biographical landmarks are traced because, as was always the case with Picasso, when his life changed, his work did also. Despite several sudden leaps, where he turned into the faun, the Minotaur was dead, and so was mythology as a driving force in his art. Picasso had returned to a more current ''mythology.'' In his work, he participated more in the events of the moment. It must be said that events were moving quickly, as much in France as around the world, but especially in Spain. There, the Civil War was raging. In the beginning of 1937, Picasso's mother wrote to him that Barcelona was choked by the smoke of burning convents, and the Spanish Republican government asked him to paint a mural for the Spanish Pavilion of the World's Fair scheduled to open in Paris in June. On the 26th of April, the Germans bombed Guernica.

In the imagery dealing with Picasso's private world, we find numerous portraits of Dora Maar, in the painted work as well as in prints. It must be noted, however, that unlike Marie-Thérèse, Dora did not ''haunt'' his compositions. When the artist needed a feminine ''image'' in the graphic work, he returned, in fact, to Marie-Thérèse. Consider, for example, the *Faun Playing a Flute and Dancer* (B.306, 1938), *The Flea* in the Buffon illustrations (B.359, 1936), as well as the etching for Paul Eluard's *La Barre d'appui*, featuring a sleeping Marie-Thérèse. Dora Maar was represented as herself, and then only in portraits. People say that the *Weeping Woman* (B.1333) ''is'' Dora Maar, and it is well-known that she was a rather tearful person. After all, Picasso, still a married man, had created another family with Marie-Thérèse and the baby María de la Concepción, not yet called Maya, and he was still writing and receiving daily love letters to and from Marie-Thérèse. Dora Maar must have felt frequently sad and depressed, for she was in love with Picasso. Penrose points out, however, that Picasso's mother had written him that the smoke of the burning houses and convents made her eyes red with weeping and her face black with soot. And while the hair style of the *Weeping Woman* does, of course, remind us of Dora Maar's, the straightness of the hair is like Marie-Thérèse's, and Marie-Thérèse also was certainly crying. The identity of the *Weeping Woman* therefore is moot.

The only graphic work published between 1936 and 1942 aside from book illustrations - Eluard's *La Barre d'appui* and *Les Yeux fertiles* (1936), Iliazd's *Afat* (1938), André Breton's *Anthologie de l'humour noir* (1940, see cat. no. 70), or Luc Decaunes' *L'Indicatif present* (1938) - was *Sueño y Mentira de Franco* (cat. nos. 58-60). Actually, however, beginning in 1936 and up until his departure in July 1939 for Antibes and then Royan, Picasso was working nonstop in the Lacourière workshop in an atmosphere conducive to the creation of masterpieces. It was only in the beginning of 1939 that the Fort press was removed from the Boisgeloup to the Grands Augustins studio. There, the young Frélaut was in charge of assembling all the necessary odds and ends, but the press was never used.

Early in 1936, a rather perturbed Picasso began to spend every day in the womanless atmosphere of Lacourière's workshop. He plunged himself into the obviously calming process of ''aquatinting'' animals. Vollard had commissioned what he intended to be an album, based on Georges Louis Leclerc de Buffon's *Histoire naturelle*. (Buffon lived from 1707 to 1788. His *Histoire naturelle*, though scientifically out of date, remains nevertheless a well-known monument of eighteenth century French literature for its lively style, both classical and innovative.)

The sugar-lift aquatints of the Buffon series are the *chefs-d'oeuvre* of this special technique. Sometimes Picasso would rework one plate, producing four or five states (*The Donkey*); sometimes the work was perfect the first time (*The Pigeon*). Most of the aquatints went through two states. Picasso mischievously left out the cat. He knew how devoted Vollard was to his own cat and thus obliged him to make a special request for the cat's portrait. The dated aquatints were made on the 7th (*The Cock, The Pigeon*) and on the 9th (*The Donkey, The Monkey, The White Eagle*) of February, 1936. The others were made in the following weeks. As an example of the aquatints in the Buffon series, we have chosen to exhibit the amusing ostrich. In its two states, it shows exactly the way in which most of the plates were masterfully created (cat. no. 57).

At the time of Vollard's death in July 1939, no complete edition yet existed. It is still not known how Vollard planned to produce the 32 aquatints, as an integral part of the Buffon text or as an album apart from the text. Of the 32 aquatints, ten had been pulled on Montval laid paper, with plate marks and margins. This was surely done before the death of Vollard, although it is difficult to be certain. All ten of these plates were bevelled, while those which were only pulled for the book did not have to be bevelled, as the paper was smaller than the copperplates. However, all of the plates were steelfaced, even before the ten plates mentioned above were printed. There were 47 proofs pulled from each of these ten plates. The large-sheet proofs of the ten plates before bevelling, and those of the 22 other aquatints must be looked upon as trial proofs. It should be added that the first proofs of each state are on Arches wove paper, often even without margins.

After Vollard's death, Fabiani bought most, or perhaps even all of Vollard's estate. As Fabiani was clever at arranging things and a collaborator during the war, and since the paper with the "Ambroise Vollard" watermark was available, he managed to have the Buffon series printed by Lacourière during the darkest days of the war years in 1942. Madame Lacourière went searching among the bookstalls on the banks of the Seine to find an abridged copy of Buffon that could be used for texts to accompany the illustrations. Fabiani did not bother to look, and there are those who say that he did not even know who Buffon was. No text was found for *The Flea*, which therefore appears only in the *Suites*.

The details of another book project also remain obscure, a Don Quixote. It is impossible to know whether Fabiani found some sort of agreement in Vollard's papers for the illustration of Cervantes' masterpiece. All that is known is that, first of all, two aquatints do exist with Don Quixote and Sancho Panza as their subject (see nos. 65-69). Given the technique, they were probably made around 1937. Secondly, Picasso never wanted to take up his tools again to make a print of Don Quixote. He told Lacourière and his wife that Fabiani, whom he did not like, and even despised during the war and the years that followed, was always bothering him to work on this subject since he had some kind of rights to possible illustrations.

And finally, there was a "dream" project. In *Picasso: Portraits and Souvenirs* (Paris, 1946), Sabartés recounts that when he arrived at the Rue la Boétie in 1935, Picasso asked him to type his manuscripts complete with spelling errors and lack of punctuation (now in the Musée Picasso, Paris). In 1939, while working on the aquatints with four and five colors of Dora Maar's portraits, Picasso suddenly came up with a great idea: he would have the manuscripts transferred to copperplates by means of heliogravure, even etching some of the lines or engraving them with a burin. He would adorn the margins with etched and engraved *remarques*. He even dreamt of having these *remarques* etched and printed in several colors. The Dora Maar portraits and other aquatints in color would serve as the *hors-texte* plates. Vollard got very excited about the project. He and Picasso discussed the details, such as paper, publication and size of the book, and Picasso began to work. Then Picasso decided that it was too complicated.

He told Sabartés that he was satisfied with the concept, but that carrying it out was boring. It was at this time that Frélaut transported and set up the Boisgeloup press, Rue des Grands Augustins.

What remains of this aborted project?
1. One intaglio print (and the copperplate) of a page of manuscript (dated 1935) reproduced by means of heliogravure. Picasso etched bathers around the text, then scraped out some of the etched lines and added, with a burin, a goat-skull. It is dated 9 May 1939. The manuscript text begins ''El clarin...''
2. The burin engraving he later gave to Gili to serve as frontispiece for *El Entierro del Conde de Orgaz*, the *Trozo de Almibar*, dated 9 June 1939 (B.1465).
3. The seven aquatints (which were printed in colors) of the head of Dora Maar (B.1335 to 1340, and B.2024) which were to be *hors-texte* plates in the book.
4. Perhaps also a small copperplate with text beginning: ''Aux quatre coins de la pièce.'' The manuscripts, copied by Picasso around 1939 in reversed etched capital letters (1st state), then in reversed burin-engraved capital letters (the three last lines; 2nd state), are both dated 1938. The full text was set in type by Iliazd for *Rogelio Lacourière pêcheur de cuivres. Hommage à Lacourière*, 1968, as Picasso had given to him a proof of the text, telling him the plate was lost.
5. Finally, there is a group of small prints, all engraved on long, narrow copperplates. They were either intended as *remarques*, to be placed near the text or as *hors-texte* plates. Two of them can be seen in cat. no. 74. Among the five others, all small bathers (for we come back again to bathers), only one was catalogued by Bloch (B.1832) who saw it in the Picasso Museum in Barcelona. It was to have been printed in color using a dabber, and the two plates exist. Another was made on four copperplates and printed (only once) in four colors. It seems to fit Sabartés' description of the intended color *remarques*.

The tone of Picasso's work shifted radically with his *Sueño y mentira de Franco* (*Dreams and Lies of Franco*). The two big copperplates of this series were each divided into nine compartments. Each compartment contained an etching reworked in aquatint that Picasso intended to sell as a kind of postcard. The profits were to be given to Spaniards in need, those ruined by Franco's actions. Both plates were begun on January 8 and 9, 1937, before the bombing of Guernica. One of them was already finished by the time of the bombing in April, the other had been left unfinished and, on the 7th of June, Picasso filled the four empty compartments with subjects related to Guernica.

The best interpretation of these etchings is that by Sir Anthony Blunt in *Picasso's Guernica*, New York, 1968. The author explains that the subjects, which were intended to be cut out, should be read from right to left: Franco is a kind of loathsome polyp or root-shaped figure and his nasty adventures read like a child's comic book or like the old Spanish *Alleluias*.

In the first plate (B.297; cat. no. 58), reading right to left: Franco rides out to war wearing a crown and carrying a sword as well as a banner adorned with the Virgin Mary (Monarchy, Army and Church). Then, as Blunt points out, Picasso parodies Goya's *Desastres de la Guerra*, ''Que se rompe la cuerda'' (Desastres, 77; G.W.1128): the polyp-like form, walking on a tightrope, is still carrying the banner of the Madonna but it is at the end of his enormous penis. He goes on to do battle with a classical sculpted bust, perhaps an allusion to the works of art destroyed or to the destruction of the Spanish Republic or Truth.

On the second line, the *Caudillo*, dressed up like one of Goya's *Majas*, parades about with a fan decorated with the image of the Virgin. Franco is then attacked by a Spanish toro. He loses both crown and sword and is sent kneeling, a bishop's miter on his head, before money (a Spanish *douro*). The money is protected by barbed wire.

In the third line, the first subject is somewhat difficult to understand: Franco is in trouble, but he extricates himself and is soon riding a winged horse, perhaps a reference to Pegasus. The winged horse then turns into a pig, but Franco is still carrying the banner with the image of the Virgin.

In the second plate (see cat. nos. 59-60), Franco has killed the winged horse. The next two sections show real disasters. The first can be related to Goya's *Murio la verdad* (Desastres, 79; G.W.1132). The next depicts a *gitano* lying dead with his head tenderly cradled against his dead horse's neck. Then we see Franco facing the powerful Spanish toro. Franco, now represented by a root-shaped horse is gored by the toro. His torn belly spews out the banner, the sword and the flag. The rest of the plate, as mentioned above, was etched in June and is related to *Guernica*.

From this scathing image of international politics, villany and war, closely linked to some of Picasso's most powerful work in painting and drawing, we move to two masterpieces of a more personal sort, the first on the theme of *The Weeping Woman* (cat. nos. 61-64). Picasso began two different, large engravings on the first of July. Both used drypoint and were images of a woman crying with a handkerchief held to her face. He chose to develop on the first one (the other is annotated "1er juillet (II)"). We are showing four of the seven states that he produced, finally working the copperplate to death. The 3rd and 6th states were pulled and signed and numbered 1/15 to 15/15 by Picasso. After the 6th state, the artist made the image even darker and more tragic. Was all the work done on the copperplate, like the work done on the *Minotauromachie*, a kind of exorcism? Although he had painted *Guernica*, Picasso was living peaceably in Paris, while Spain was bathed in blood and torture was rampant. People from all over the world were beginning to enlist to help the Republicans fight against tyranny and oppression, yet, Picasso expressed himself only through his work. At any rate, on July 4th, Picasso made two other smaller plates of weeping women which were never printed even as trial proofs until 1949. The second large copperplate executed on July 1 was untouched after the 1st state until 1946 (see cat. no. 76).

In chronological order, his next masterpiece is *La Femme au tambourin* (cat. no. 71). The plate must have been worked on at about the same time as the small work discussed below. This remarkably successful interplay of equilibrium, movement and a wild kind of desperate joy was achieved through the use of aquatint and scraper alone. The 1st state is a mere sketch drawn with wide scraper lines in the varnish, then grained and bitten. Next, Picasso worked on the aquatint in the background and in the contrast of light and shadow on the body and the limbs, lightening up the areas he had just darkened and darkening the light areas over and over again, seeking a kind of dancing "dismemberment." But Picasso sensed a problem. In the first three states the bacchante is standing on her right foot (left on the proof) and her other leg is bent with the sole of the foot stuck on the calf of the straight leg. Then comes the 4th state and a stroke of genius! Suddenly the woman finds her balance. She is a visionary, embodying the spirit of a maenad in a sensual fluttering movement. Picasso has thrust away the left leg (right on the proof). He has freed its form, scraping it out of the layers of aquatint, slightly correcting the shape of the thigh and the buttock as he drew upon his strong, educated sense of anatomy. He once again covered the background with a layer of aquatint in order to delineate the new-found shape of his creation. Details were worked with the scraper in the 5th state and the result is prodigious. Notice how he deliberately avoided completely scraping away the aquatint and the wide strokes of the 1st state on the new leg, therefore giving it a movement of its own.

In technical terms, too, the print is a masterpiece. First by the economy of its means and then by its resolution of all the technical difficulties inherent in evenly graining and biting such a large plate since it does not fit in either the dusting box or in the acid bath.

It should be noted that Picasso may have remembered the dancing bacchante on the left of Poussin's *Bacchanal Before a Herm* (about 1637) in the National Gallery, London, when he suddenly decided to have his dancer toss her foot behind her.

Finally, another *chef-d'oeuvre*, though not yet recognized as such, is the small portrait of Dora Maar (cat. no. 70) which would be used later, in 1940, as the frontispiece for the *édition de luxe* of the *Anthologie de l'humour noir* by André Breton. Once again, Picasso, who began with a line-etching of his subject, retouched his aquatint, layer by layer, taking it through eight states. In the 9th and 10th states, Lacourière traced a line in drypoint to show where the copperplate should be cut and then removed the written part of the plate.

Picasso took a great amount of trouble with that small plate. He used tarlatan to lay down his sugar-lift aquatint on the bodice of the dress, worked and worked again on the aquatint of the background, scraped, and reworked the portrait with the burin, then went back again to the aquatint of the background, deciding to make the right side of it darker than the left side. He then had the idea of lightly coloring the triangular neck with aquatint and finally used his burin again to perfect his work. Despite its small size, the print is a highly successful and ''monumental'' portrait.

The reversed lines under the print read: ''déplacer à gauche de la pièce l'amidon de la couleur de la porte entre ouverte et jeter la cendre de la lumière du plafon (*sic*), dans la gueule du dessin qui voudrai (*sic*) déchirer l'illusion du sabot d'ombre soutenant le pié (*sic*) de nez vert amande.'' This can be translated as: ''shift the starch of the color of the half-opened door to the left side of the room and toss the ash of the ceiling into the mouth of the drawing which would like to tear the illusion of the shoe of shadow supporting the defiant kick of the almond green.'' Here, there is a kind of pun, difficult to translate: ''pied de nez'' in literal translation is ''foot of nose,'' which means ''thumbing his nose.'' ''Pied,'' i.e. foot, is related to ''sabot,'' i.e. wooden shoe. This typically Picassoesque literature was, as mentioned above, cut away when the plate was pulled for André Breton's book.

The Germans entered Paris on June 14th, 1940. On the 23rd, they were in Royan where Picasso, like many others, had retreated. On August 25th, Picasso decided to return to Paris and to stay in France. In the autumn, he left his apartment on the Rue la Boétie and settled into the studio on the Rue des Grands Augustins, where he would remain during the entire period of the Occupation. In the spring of 1941, Marie-Thérèse and Maya left Royan and Picasso found them an apartment right across the Seine within a short walking distance.

Everything was scarce, food, coal and wood, but also paper and copperplates, ink and tarlatan, so Picasso's graphic work naturally suffered. The Lacourière workshop was partially closed down at the beginning of 1940 and completely closed for quite a long time after the Germans invaded France. However, once Lacourière and Picasso had met again, the latter as we saw (cat. no. 22) decided to help his friend and to print some of the old plates. It is entirely possible that the beautiful color aquatints, the Dora Maar portraits, were also pulled at this time, although it is difficult to be certain. Madeleine Lacourière remembers that Picasso had not wanted them pulled immediately in 1939 but, on the other hand, she had thought that Fabiani might have secured the proofs. Luckily they were safely put away in Picasso's portfolios. As Fabiani took away from Lacourière's workshop all the remnants of the Vollard estate, it must mean that the proofs were only pulled in 1942. At the same time, *La Femme au tambourin* was also pulled. The smallness of the edition of the latter reflects the scarcity of paper. The Galerie Louise Leiris managed to publish it, as well as B.301, in 1943.

During the war years, Picasso engraved very few plates. Besides the large zincplate of 1942, where we can see the first ideas for the well-known sculpture, *The Man with a Sheep*, he did some small prints for his friends' books. The problem of censorship must not, however, be forgotten. All books had to be reviewed by the Franco-German administration before being printed and published. And, of course, Picasso's friends were generally classed as subversive and degenerate writers.

In 1940, the artist managed to engrave a copperplate for Dr. Mabille's book, *Le Miroir du merveilleux* (cat. no. 75). Then, in April 1942, using the hard zincplates which are used for commercial book illustration, Picasso made three portraits of Eluard. One (B.296) was used at the end of 1944 as the frontispiece for Eluard's *Au Rendez-vous allemand*. Also in April 1942, he experimented with small copperplates producing three portraits of women, still unknown to the public today. At the same time, he made a burin engraving (B.360) which was used as the frontispiece for Hugnet's *Non vouloir*, published half clandestinely as early as 1942. He also utilized again the technique which he had explored in 1936-1937, on the halftone plate reproducing a photograph for *Cahiers d'Art* (see cat. no. 55). Thus, in 1942, he engraved on commercial lineblock zincplates the illustrations, to be printed in letterpress, for Hugnet's *Non vouloir*. Then, in 1943, using commercial halftone copperplates, on which some drawings of his had been reproduced, he etched the six illustrations for Hugnet's *La Chèvre-feuille* (B.361), which were to be printed either in intaglio or letterpress. Picasso etched a small copperplate for his friend Desnos on December 23, 1943 (B. 362). But Desnos never saw his book, *Contrée*, printed. On February 22, 1944, just a few days before Max Jacob was arrested, Desnos was captured by the Gestapo. He died on June 8, 1945, in the Czechoslovakian concentration camp of Terezine.

56.
Portrait de Dora Maar
Portrait of Dora Maar

1936 (October 21)

Burin and drypoint on copper

348 × 248 mm.

Proof on Montval laid paper, with ''Vollard'' watermark.

B.291.

This is one of the fifty-seven impressions pulled by Lacourière in 1942, using leftover *Suite Vollard* paper. The copperplate was then steelfaced and, in 1961, pulled again: it is part of the 1981 Galerie Leiris edition of *La Caisse à remords*. The impressions pulled in 1942 have been distributed among the heirs of the Picasso Estate.

Notice the similarity between this portrait and the photograph which Picasso took and reworked, which was reproduced in *Cahiers d'Art*, volume 12, number VI-VII, 1937 (fig. 6).

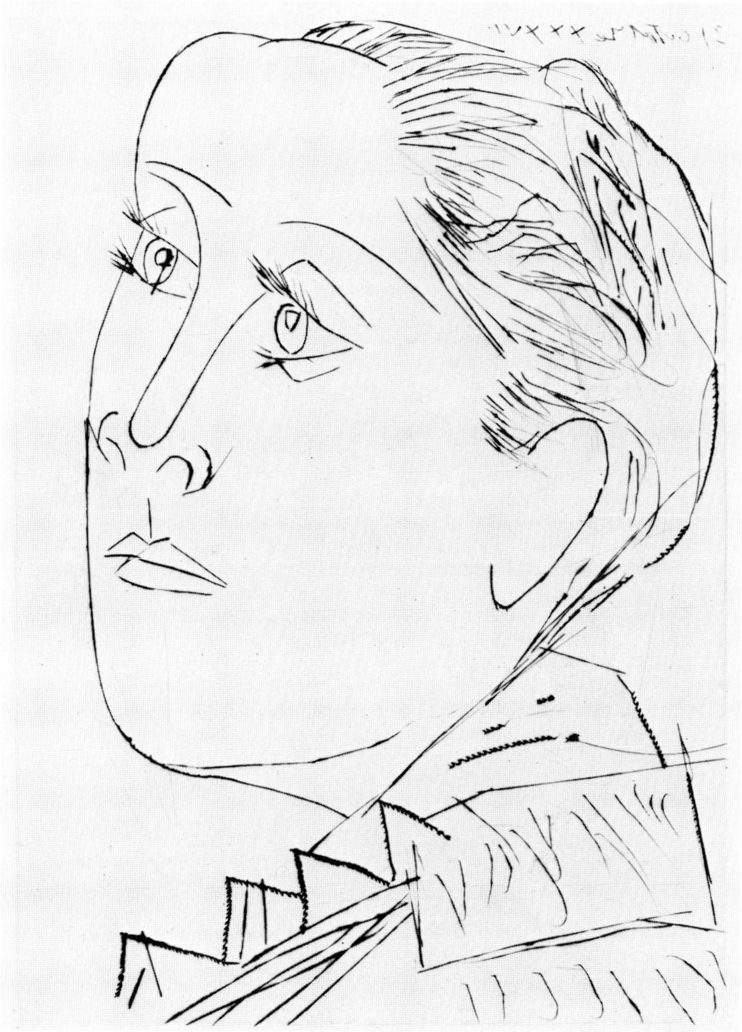

56.

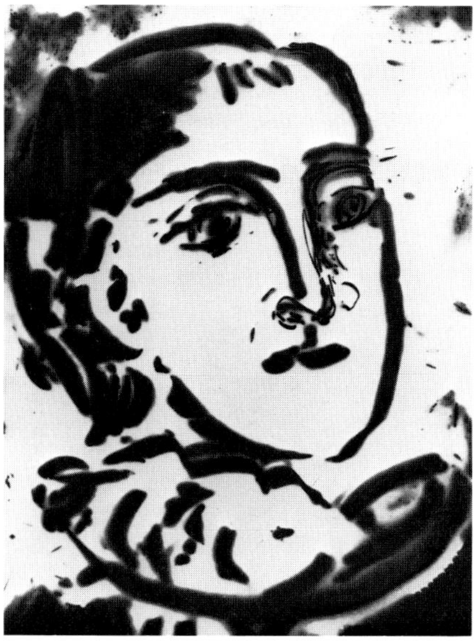

Fig. 6. *Photograph of Dora Maar, reworked by Picasso*, 1936-37 (courtesy of *Cahiers d'Art*, copyright Cahiers d'Art, Paris).

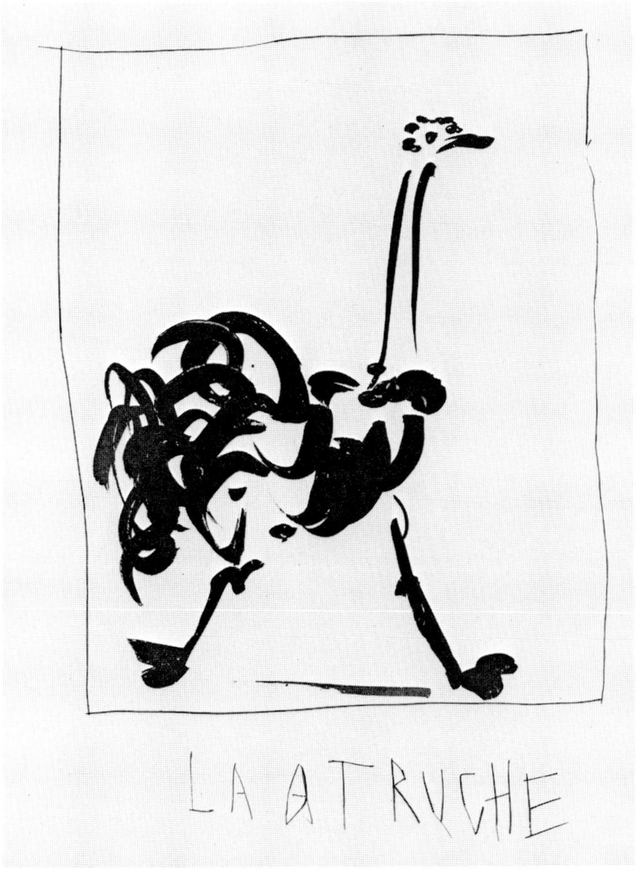

57a.

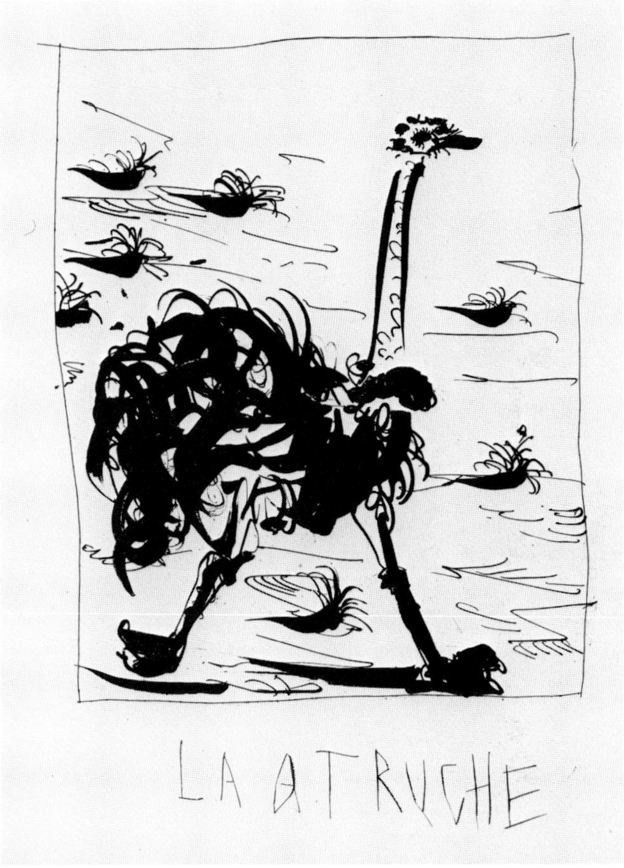

57b.

57a&b.
La A/OTRUCHE (L'Autruche)
The Ostrich

1936

Sugar-lift aquatint on copper

415 × 315 mm.

a. One proof, 1st state, on Arches wove paper.

b. One proof, 2nd state, on Arches wove paper.

B.343.

Both are the first of the few trial proofs that Lacourière usually pulled of the 1st and 2nd states of the Buffon series. In each case, the paper is slightly smaller than the copperplate. After the trial proofs on Arches paper, Lacourière generally printed four or five better impressions on Montval laid paper. *The Ostrich* is among the group of ten plates which were bevelled and then pulled on Montval laid paper, producing as many as 47 proofs with margins and plate marks.

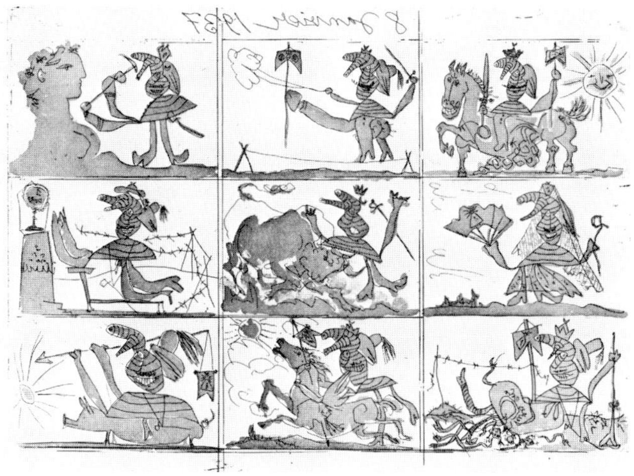

58.

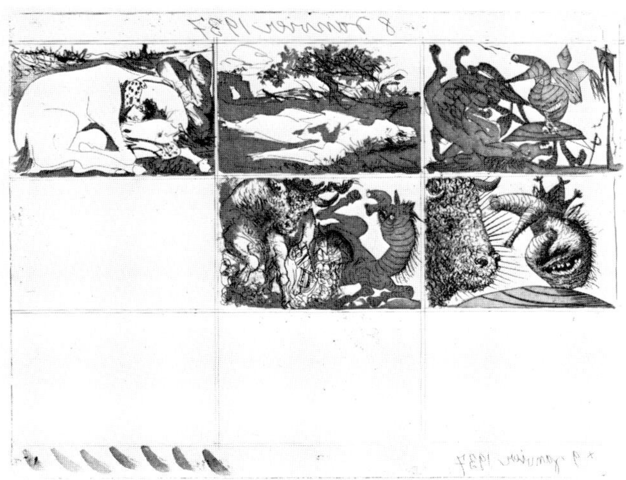

59.

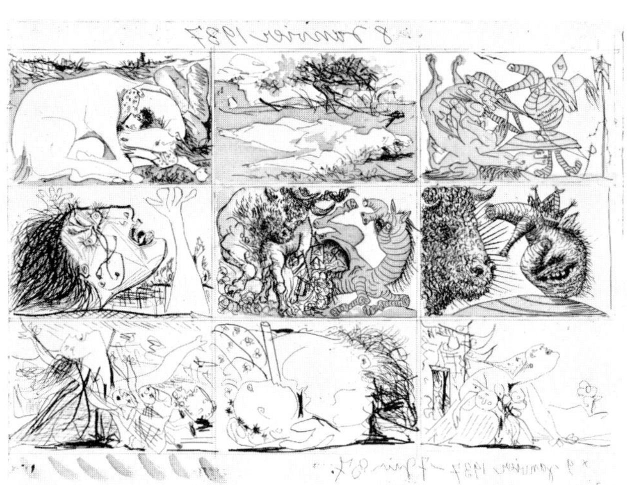

60.

58.
Sueño y Mentira de Franco, I
Dreams and Lies of Franco, I

1937 (January 8)

Etching and sugar-lift aquatint on copper

317 × 422 mm.

2nd state.

One of the seven trial proofs on Montval laid paper, pulled before the plate was steelfaced.

The copperplate (on exhibition) was cancelled in 1983.

B.297.

In the 1st state, which lack of space unfortunately prevents us from showing here, the subject is already detailed, but the aquatint has not yet been added.

59.
Sueño y Mentira de Franco, II

1937 (January 8 and 9)

Etching, sugar-lift aquatint and scraper on copper

318 × 422 mm.

4th state.

One of six proofs on Montval laid paper.

60.
Sueño y Mentira de Franco, II

1937 (January 8 and 9; June 7)

Etching, sugar-lift aquatint and scraper on copper

5th state.

One of the six trial proofs on Montval laid paper, pulled before the plate was steelfaced.

The copperplate (on exhibition) was cancelled in 1983.

B.298.

As with the first plate, Picasso only etched in the 1st state. However, on the second plate he drew only five of the compartments, which he then reworked with aquatint in the 2nd state, etched again in the 3rd state and worked with the scraper in the 4th state, our no. 59. It was only on the 7th of June that he etched the last four compartments.

As in the case of no. 58, lack of space prevents our showing the first three states. All the trial proofs of both plates were pulled by Lacourière.

Edition: after steelfacing; printed by Lacourière.

Albums with white covers: Both prints, plus a Picasso manuscript reproduced in heliogravure. Signed and numbered 1/150 to 150/150 and 1/XXX to 30/XXX; on *Chine collé* on old Japan paper.

Albums with blue covers: As above. Numbered 1/850 to 850/850 and stamped with a seal reproducing Picasso's signature; on Montval laid paper.

61.
La Femme qui pleure
The Weeping Woman

1937 (July 1)

Drypoint, sugar-lift aquatint, etching and scraper on copper

692 × 495 mm.

1st state: drypoint.

One of two proofs on Montval laid paper. Plate is annotated on back "I."

62.
La Femme qui pleure

See no. 61.

3rd state: etching and scraper-etched lines, grained with aquatint.

One of 15 signed and numbered impressions on Montval laid paper.

Numbered 11/15.

B.1333.

In the 2nd state, sugar-lift aquatint was added and only one proof was pulled. For the 3rd state there is one trial proof as well as the 15 numbered proofs. The wide etched lines made with a scraper were grained with aquatint before being bitten in order to make them darker. The irregularities in some of the lines were produced by using pitch varnish.

63.
La Femme qui pleure

See no. 61.

6th state: scraper, drypoint and *velo* (drypoint with several needles) added.

One of the 15 signed and numbered impressions on Montval laid paper.

Numbered 11/15.

B.1333.

In the 4th state, there is new work with the etching needle. The 5th state has part of the aquatint scraped away. There is one trial proof of the 6th state, as well as the 15 numbered proofs.

64.
La Femme qui pleure

See no. 61.

7th state: more drypoint and *velo* added.

One of two proofs on Montval laid paper.

The subject becomes even darker and more dramatic in this state, as Picasso literally destroyed his copperplate.

The first proofs of the 1st and the 7th states, the unique trial proofs of the remaining five states and the cancelled copperplates are in the Musée Picasso in Paris. The two proofs which were on loan to the Museum of Modern Art in New York (6/15 of the 3rd state and 4/15 of the 6th state) are now in the Prado Cason in Madrid.

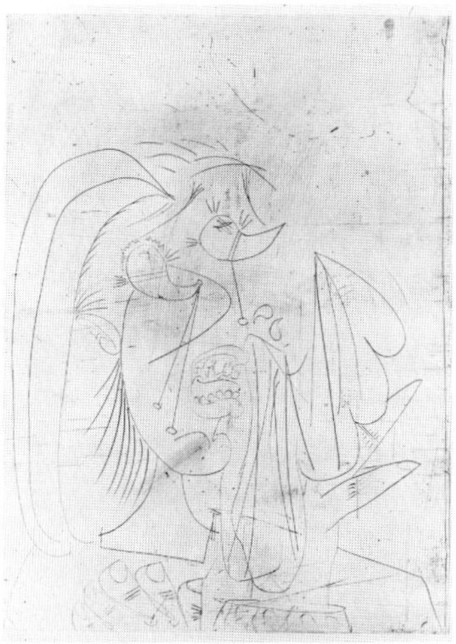

61.

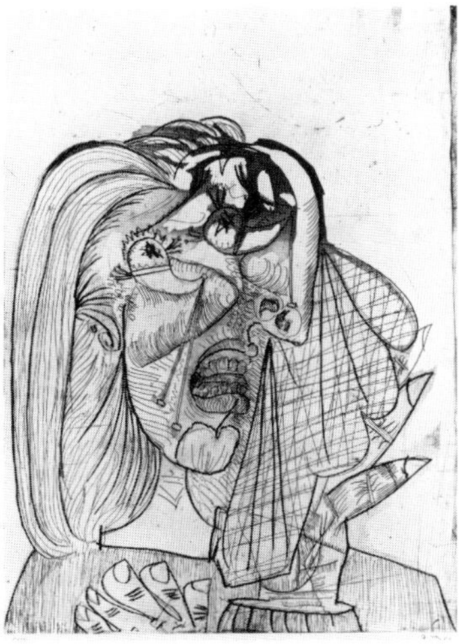

62.

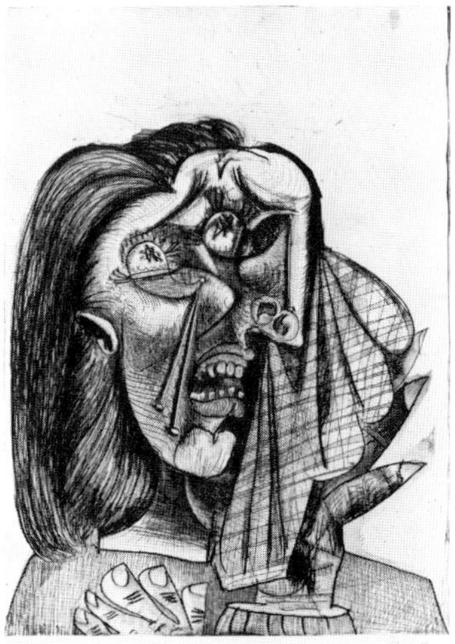

63.

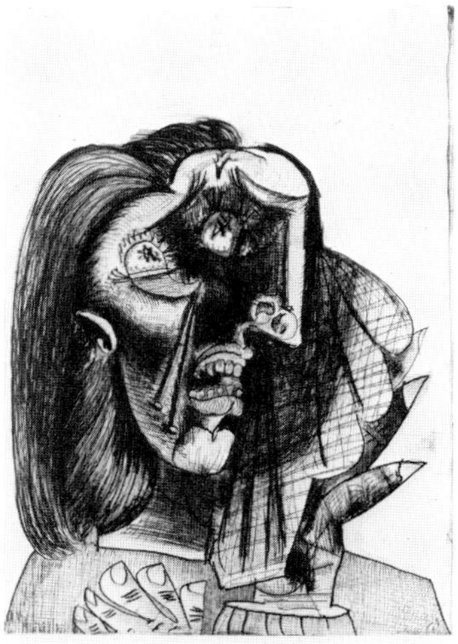

64.

65a&b. (see color plate)
Don Quijote y Sancho Panza
Don Quixote and Sancho Panza

c. 1937

Sugar-lift aquatint, scraper and burin on copper

348 × 246 mm.

1st state: sugar-lift aquatint.

a. One proof on Montval laid paper.

b. One proof on Montval laid paper, printed with three plates: one plate for the reddish brown, printed first, then one plate for the green printed over the first and finally the plate for the black.

This is apparently the first time that the artist worked on several intaglio plates in order to make color prints. He had two proofs pulled by Lacourière in color and then put aside the two copperplates that had been used for the colors. He did not rework these but did continue to work on the plate that had been used for the black. The two abandoned copperplates are still in existence.

66.
Don Quijote y Sancho Panza

See no. 65.

2nd state: scraper and burin.

Proof on Montval laid paper; there are four in all as well as one proof on Montval wove paper.

67.
Don Quijote y Sancho Panza

See no. 65.

3rd state: scraper and burin.

Unique proof, on Montval wove paper.

68.
Don Quijote y Sancho Panza

See no. 65.

4th state: scraper and burin.

Unique proof, on Montval wove paper.

69.
Don Quijote y Sancho Panza

See no. 65.

5th (and last) state: scraper and burin.

Proof on Montval wove paper, with dry stamp ''Picasso'' bottom right.

Another proof, on Montval laid paper, with large margins, is known. In 1960, Picasso had Frélaut pull a trial proof on Rives wove paper with holes punched in order to fit in the ring-binder.

All the proofs pulled, before Frélaut's, were printed by Lacourière. The copperplate still exists.

Notice the way Picasso scrapes and scrapes the aquatint until it almost disappears.

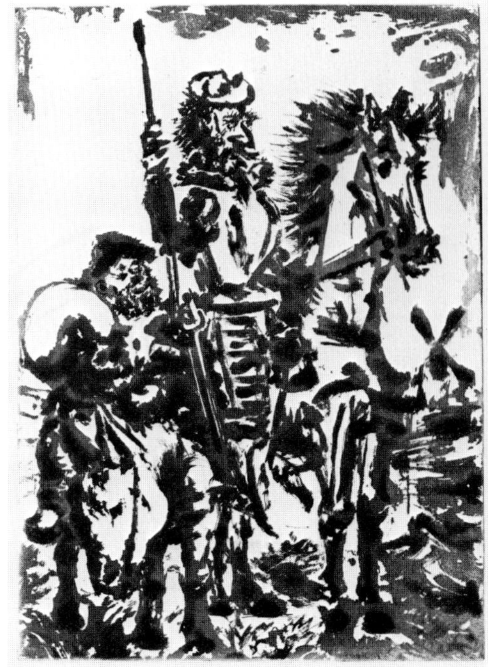

65a.

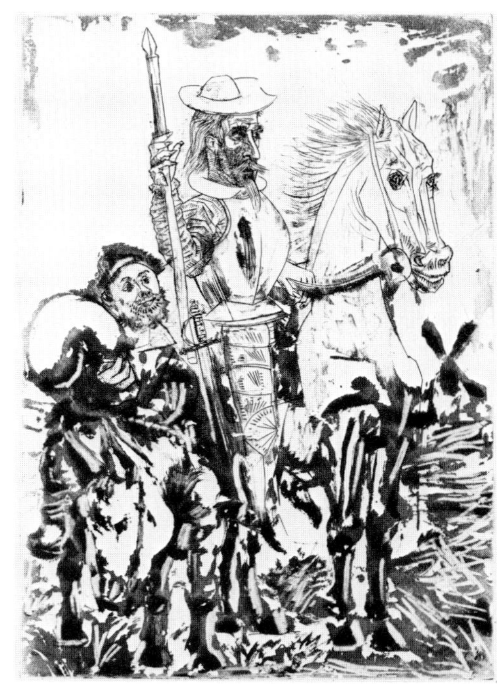

67.

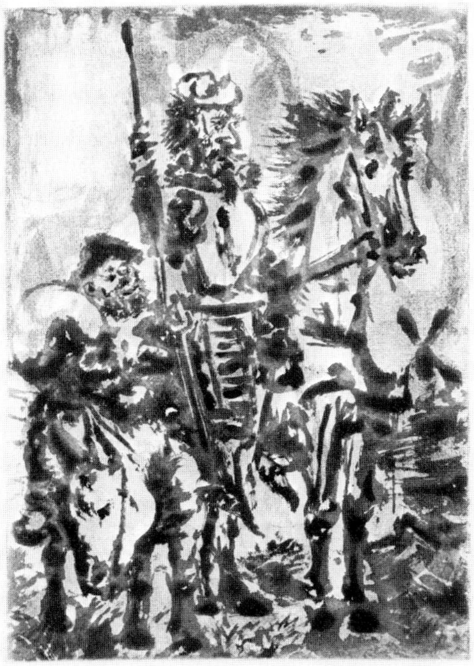
65b.

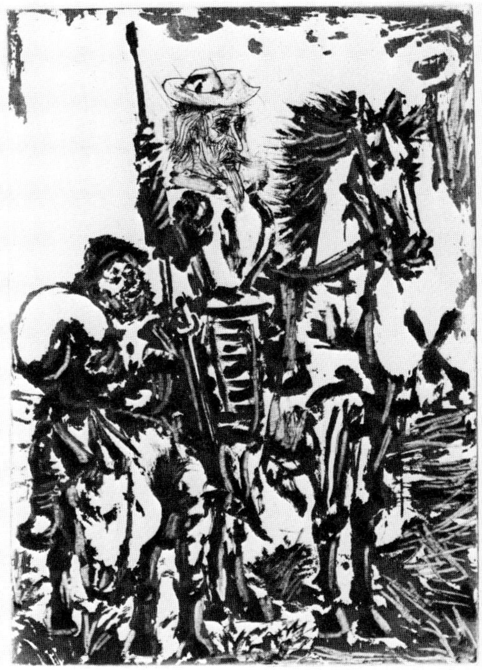
66.

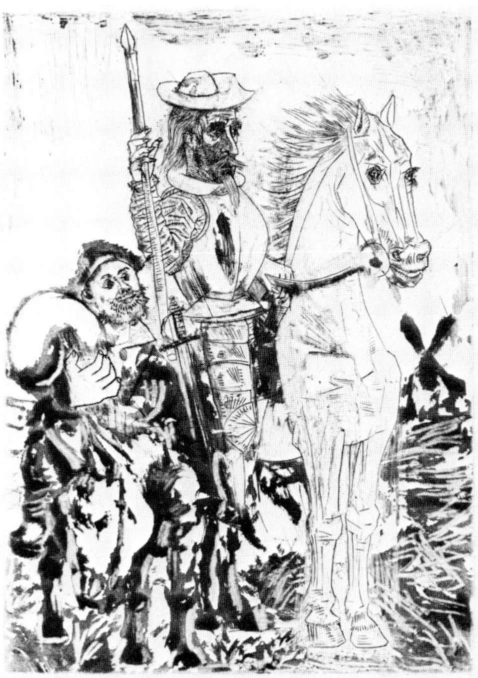
68.

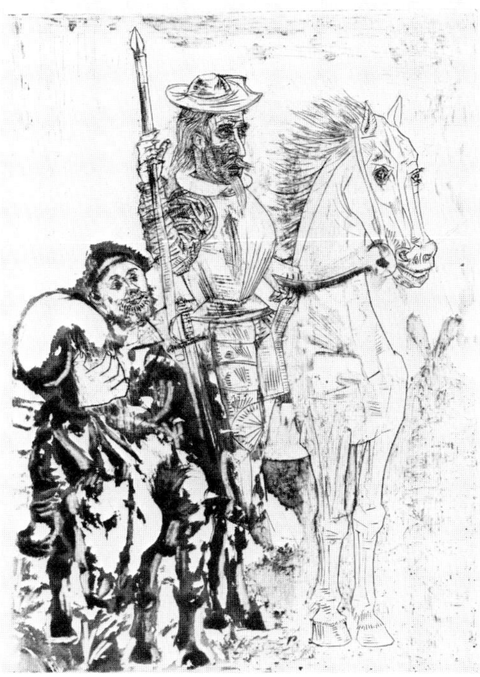
69.

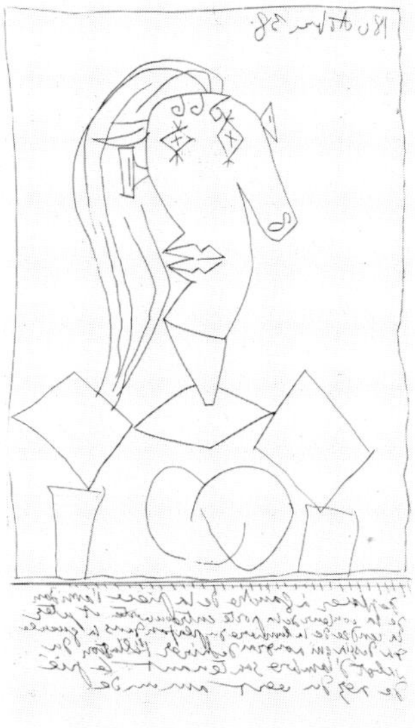

70a.

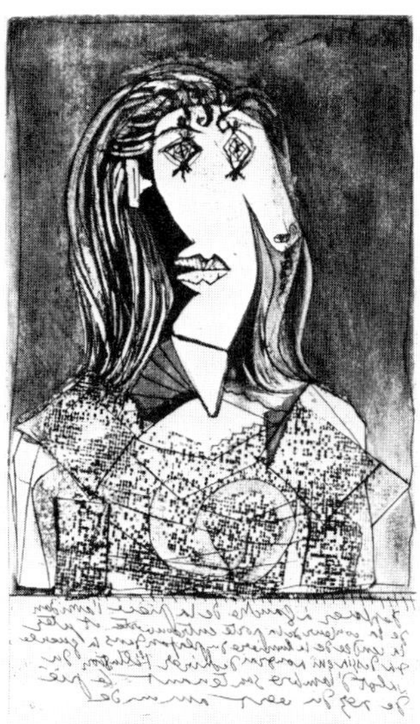

70b.

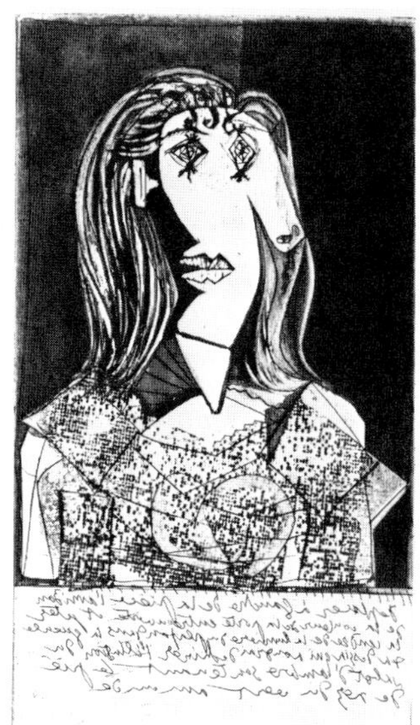

70c.

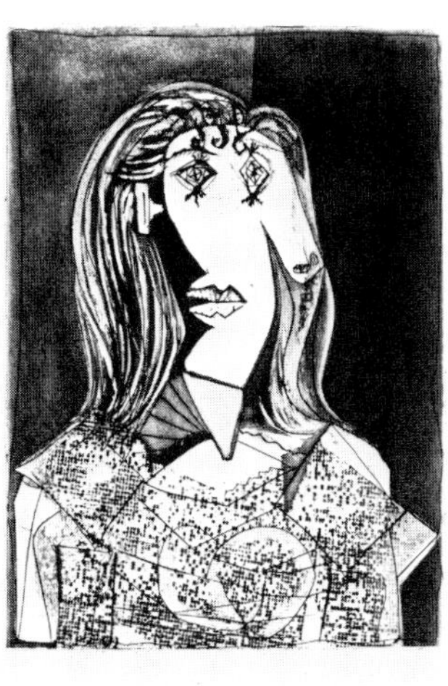

70d.

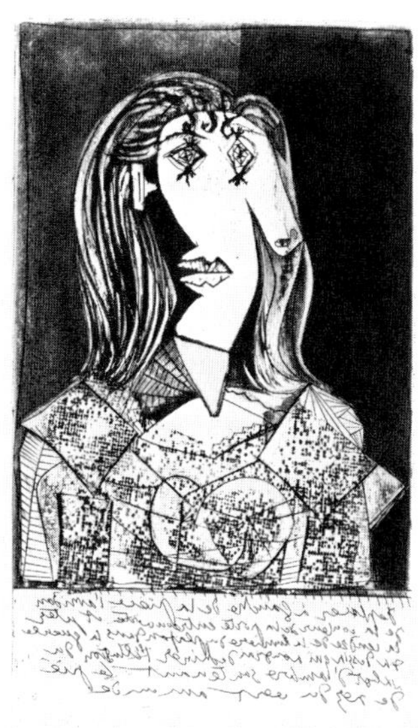

70e.

70a-e.
Buste de femme à la chaise
Seated Woman: Dora Maar

1938 (October 18)

Etching, aquatint, scraper and burin on copper

248 × 138 mm.

B.308.

a. 1st state: etching.

Proof on *Chine collé* on Montval laid paper.

15 proofs of the 1st state are known to exist on different kinds of paper.

b. 4th state: scraper and burin.

One of two known proofs, on Montval laid paper.

In the 2nd state, the background was unevenly covered with sugar-lift aquatint. In the 3rd, there is a new layer of sugar-lift aquatint. The bodice of the dress was obtained by laying the sugar with a piece of starched tarlatan.

c. 6th state: aquatint.

One of the two known proofs, on Montval laid paper, watermarked "Picasso."

In the 5th state the entire background was covered with an even layer of aquatint. In the 6th state there is a new layer of aquatint added on the right side.

d. 7th state: aquatint (probably sugar-lift).

One of the four known proofs, on Montval laid paper, watermarked "Picasso."

The written lines have not been inked. The triangular neck is now covered with very light aquatint.

e. 8th state: scraper and burin.

One of four known proofs, on Montval laid paper.

10th state: the copperplate (on exhibition), cut down for Breton's book, was cancelled in 1979.

The only difference between the 8th and 9th states is a drypoint line drawn by Lacourière between the seated woman and the written lines. One of these proofs was marked *bon à tirer* in 1940. Some 20 proofs, pulled in 1940, exist and there are two more printed by Lacourière on cut-out bits of ''collaged'' paper (Musée Picasso, Paris). All the proofs were pulled by Lacourière without steelfacing the plate.

Edition: Frontispiece, Breton's *Anthologie de l'humour noir*, Paris, 1940, Editions du Sagittaire.

10th state; copperplate cut down to 195 mm. high.

Five copies on Japan paper (nos. 1 to 3 and I and II)

Twelve copies on Van Gelde laid paper (nos. 4 to 13 and III and IV).

71.
La Femme au tambourin
Woman with a Tambourine

1938

Aquatint and scraper on copper

665 × 512 mm.

One of 30 impressions of the 1943 Galerie Louise Leiris edition, signed and numbered 30/30, on Arches wove paper.

B.310.

The proofs pulled in 1938, proofs of the states as well as two trial proofs of the last and the 5th state, were pulled on Montval laid paper. The few trial proofs pulled in 1942 are on Arches wove paper. No artist's proofs are known. The copperplate was never steelfaced. It was cancelled in 1979 and is in the Musée Picasso in Paris. All the proofs were pulled by Lacourière.

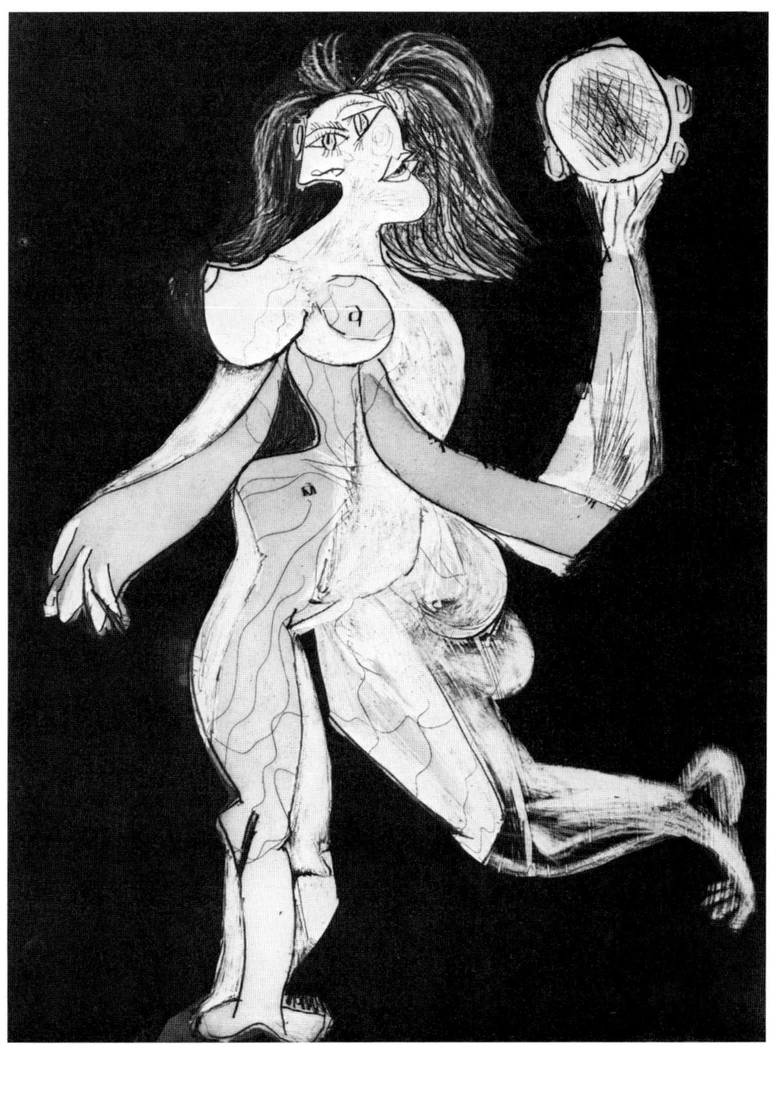

71.

72. (see color plate)

Tête de femme no. 6 - Portrait de Dora Maar
Portrait of Dora Maar, no. 6

1939 (between January and June, Paris)

Aquatint and scraper, four colors, on four copperplates

298 × 237 mm.

B.1338.

One of 106 proofs pulled by Lacourière in 1939 or 1942, on leftover Montval laid paper, watermarked either "Picasso" or "Vollard."

The four copperplates are on exhibition: the order of the printing of the colors was pink, green, blue, and then black. The copperplates were steelfaced and, in 1979, cancelled.

Our aquatint is one of the simplest of the group. There is only one state for each plate. Some of the other portraits were reworked and reworked, plate by plate. Actually seeing the copperplates helps one to understand much more clearly how these color aquatints were made.

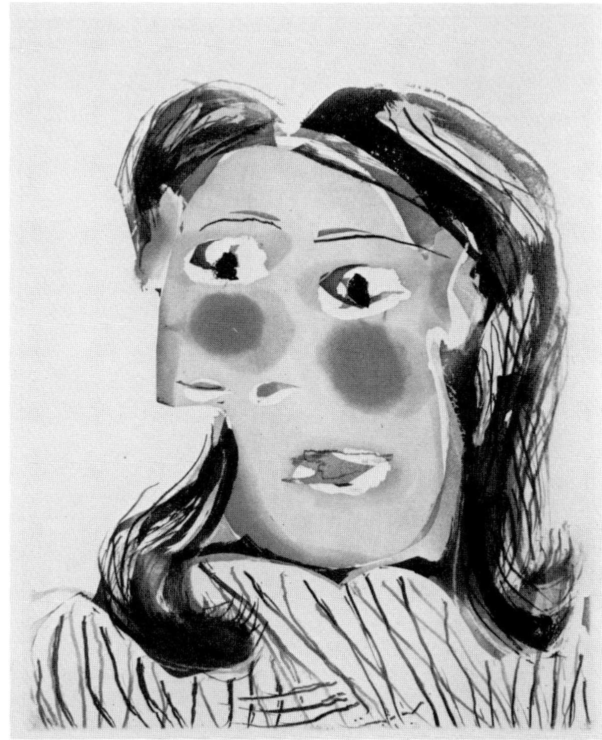

72.

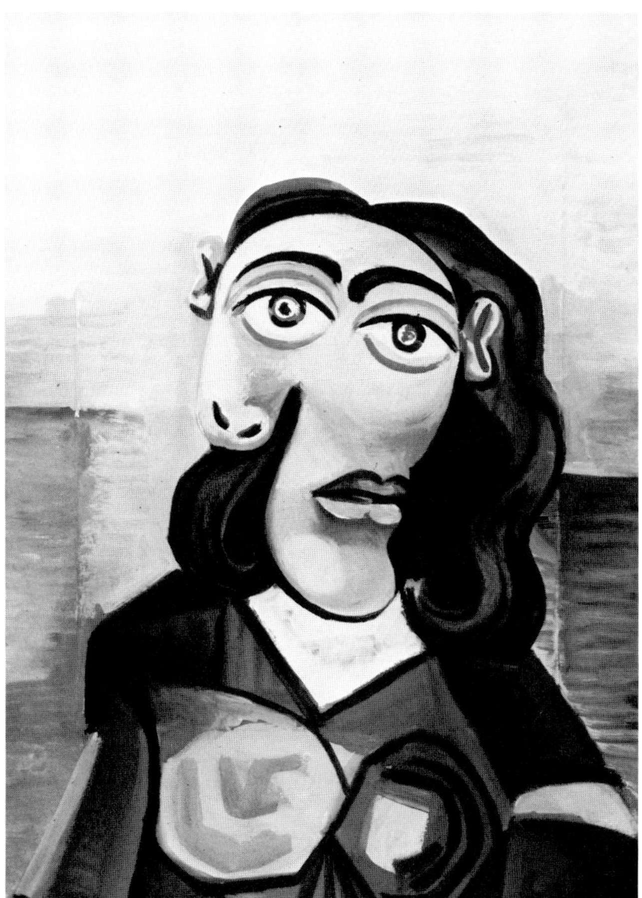

73.

73.

Portrait de Dora Maar aux yeux bleus
Portrait of Dora Maar with Blue Eyes

1939 (March 21)

Monotype on copper

429 × 332 mm.; paper measures 642 × 452 mm.

Picasso Estate inventory number: 4.027.

Second proof of a monotype (Z.IX.271), pulled with gouache, then retouched with oil paint over the whole surface of the paper, which is Arches wove. The original monotype is still visible in some areas, especially on the white collar.

Z.IX.277.

During the process of working on aquatints in several colors (cat.no. 72, for example), Picasso suddenly turned to monotypes and produced three. He made second proofs of two of these monotypes and retouched these proofs with oil paint. Only one proof was printed of the third monotype.

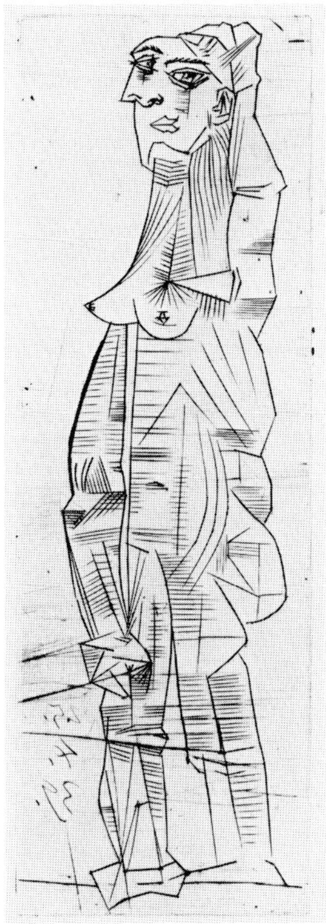

74a.

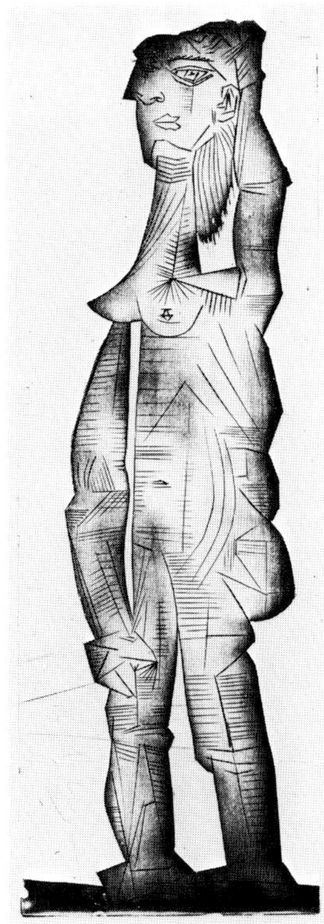

74c.

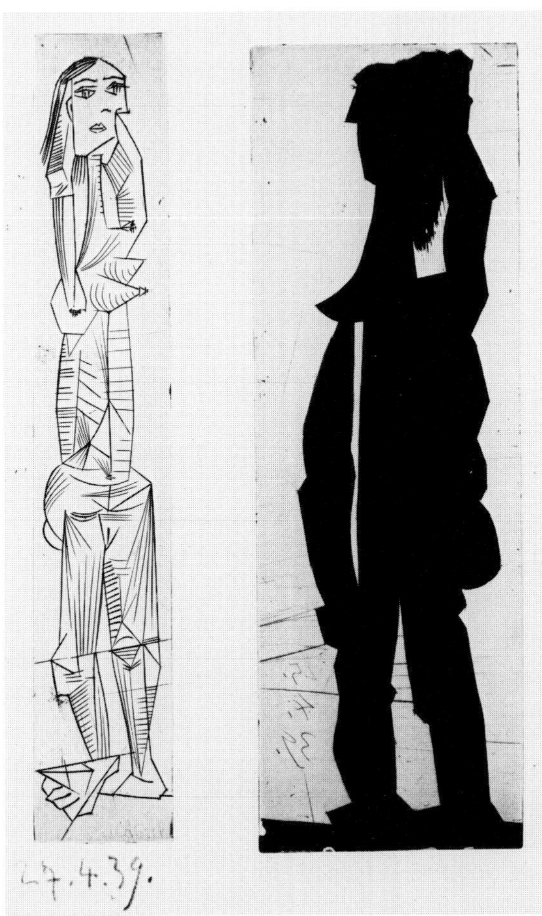

74b.

74a,b,c.
Baigneuses
Bathers

Bather I

1939 (April 25-27)

Burin and aquatint on copper

295 × 96 mm.

1st, 3rd and 4th states (see below).

Bather II

1939 (April 27)

Burin on copper

296 × 51 mm.

One state, printed on the same sheet as *Bather I*, 3rd state (see below).

a. *Bather I*: 1st state: burin.

Unique proof on Montval laid paper, watermarked "Vollard."

b. *Bathers I & II*: 3rd state: body and ground are covered with dark aquatint.

Proof on Montval laid paper.

Printed on same sheet as *Bather II*, dated below by the artist "27.4.39."

Bather I, 2nd state, has very light aquatint in the sky while the body and the ground remain untouched (unique proof in the Musée Picasso, Paris). There exists another proof of *Bather I*, 3rd state without *Bather II* (Musée Picasso, Paris).

c. *Bather I*: 4th state: aquatint lightened with willow wood charcoal.

Proof on Montval laid paper.

Another proof of *Bather I*, 4th state printed on the same sheet as *Bather II* can be found in the Musée Picasso, Paris. *Bather II* was pulled in 1960 by Frélaut, on Rives wove paper, with holes punched to fit in the ring-binder.

All proofs were pulled by Lacourière.

The two copperplates still exist.

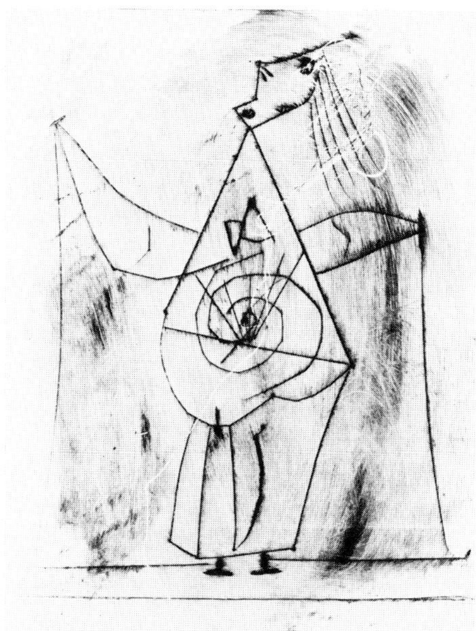

75a.

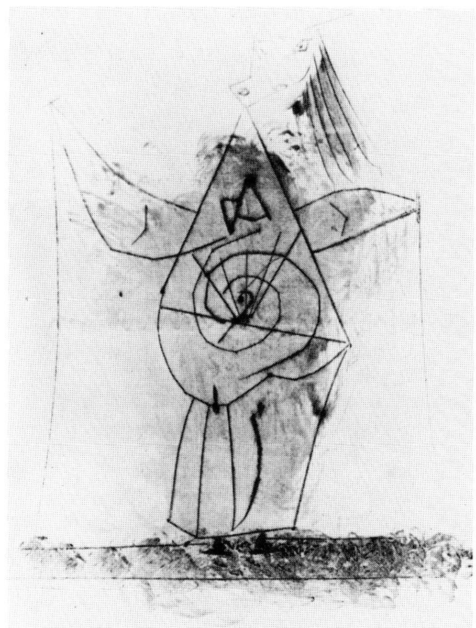

75b.

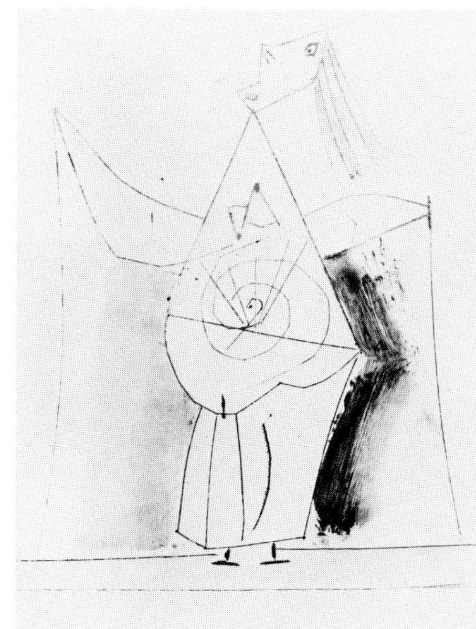

75c.

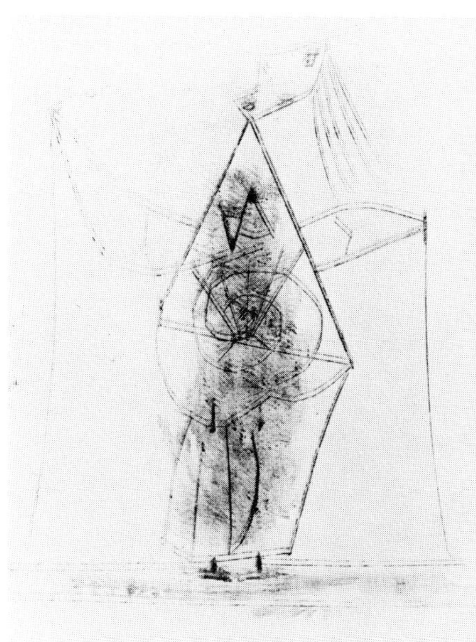

75d.

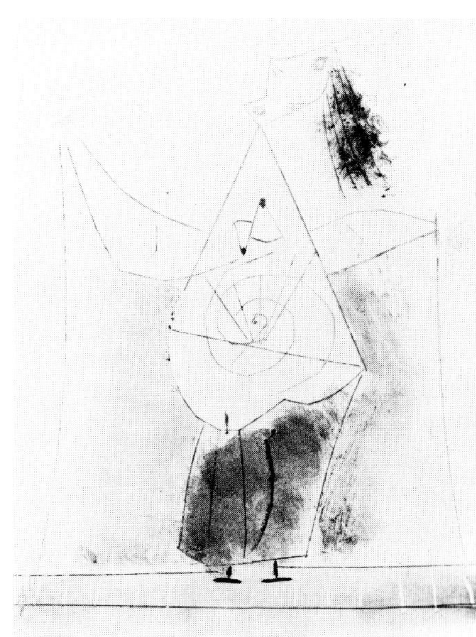

75e.

75a-e.
Baigneuse à la serviette de bain
Bather with a Towel

1940 (April 5)

Burin and drypoint on copper

251 × 140 mm.

a-e. Five proofs on mock Japan paper, watermarked "Lafuma Navarre Madagasc (ar)." All were printed by the artist, who added monotype-like details by painting on the plate before each printing. Plate is dated on the back.

The paper is smaller than the copperplate.

The copperplate (on exhibition), never steelfaced, was cancelled in 1979.

B.327

The existing proofs of this small engraving are all printed on the same paper cut down to approximately 190 × 142 mm. The engraving was intended to be the frontispiece for Mabille's *Le Miroir du merveilleux*, Paris, 1940, published by Le Sagittaire. The first 12 copies were numbered 3 to 14.

Between September 1939 and the end of August, 1940, Picasso made several brief trips back to Paris from Royan. In the middle of February, 1940, when the printing of Mabille's book was terminated, Picasso was in Paris. Perhaps he had already promised an engraving for it, or perhaps he decided then and there to help out the author. At any rate, it was only on April 5 during his next stay in Paris (around March 14 to May 16), that he engraved what must have been the only copperplate he had at hand, since it was bigger than the paper size of the book. It is not known when he pulled the few proofs in existence, nor whether he pulled them with his own press or, and it seems more likely, if he made them in the half-closed Lacourière workshop. Given the use of colored inks in three of the proofs, it may be assumed that he pulled them or inked them and had them pulled by Lacourière.

However, the book was never actually sold. Although it had passed the censors, it nevertheless seemed too dangerous in those war years. The first fourteen copies of *Le Miroir du merveilleux* were supposed to include a proof of our engraving for the frontispiece, and Mabille and Picasso were to receive the first two copies.

After the war, copies of the ordinary edition began to show up at rare bookdealers' shops. But up to the present time, only one copy of the special edition has been found. It belonged to Eluard, was signed by Picasso and is number five. The engraving, as planned, was unsigned. Eluard undoubtedly received this copy from his friend Mabille, upon the former's return from the "phony war" in June 1940. Picasso's signature dates from around 1940 - 1942. He could have signed the book when he returned from Royan in the autumn of 1940.

Some detective work on the part of the present writer has helped clarify the facts behind this scenerio. Antoine Coron, curator at the Bibliothèque Nationale, Réserve des Imprimés, found a letter from Madame Mabille in the archives of the Edition du Sagittaire. The letter, dated November 11, 1956, four years after Mabille's death (October 30, 1952), suggests that the special edition of the book should be completed and sold. She states that she still had the proofs of the Picasso engraving and adds that no copy was ever given to Picasso (which is true).

One wonders if the copies of the book for the special edition were lost, for they were not to be found at Le Sagittaire. Nine prints, one an impression in color, were sold in the 1960s by Galerie Leiris. The signature on them is from 1960. Just by chance, this writer found another signed proof in a collection of rare books. The owner said that he had succeeded in getting the print from the estate of Dr. Mabille in the 1960s, in order to grangerize his own non-illustrated copy.

All these clues seemed to add up to an idea that then had to be verified. The Mabilles had been closely tied to the circle of Michel Leiris. Perhaps Mme. Mabille, seeing that she could not realize her project of putting together books and prints, thought of selling the proofs separately. The Galerie Leiris, then, had them signed by the artist in order to be able to sell them at a better price, and returned at least one, and maybe several signed proofs to Mme. Mabille. The idea proved accurate: the Leiris proofs had come from Mme. Mabille.

It is most probable that the only existing copy of the special edition of Mabille's *Le Miroir du merveilleux* is the one that was given to Eluard. Both Picasso and Mabille each had a proof printed in color, so it can be assumed that their copies (nos. 1 and 2) would have had a frontispiece printed in color.

Actually, Picasso owned two proofs printed in color. The second, much weaker than the first, is now in the Musée Picasso in Paris. All of the proofs were printed on the same size paper. As far as is known, 17 proofs were pulled in black ink (nine of them signed in 1960) and three were pulled with dabber color inking (one of them signed in 1960). It is possible that two or three other proofs are still to be found.

X.

Françoise

Picasso met Françoise Gilot in May 1943. The first recognizable drawing of her would seem to be the rather conventional one drawn from life and dated January 1, 1944 (Z.XIII.208), in which the resemblance to Paloma Picasso is striking. It was only in 1945 that Françoise began to appear regularly in the artist's canvases, drawings, engravings and lithographs.

Dora Maar was sick and depressed in the spring of 1945. In a thick notebook filled with manuscripts from 1941 and drawings from later years, Picasso noted important dates such as: ''1947, le 15 mai à 1h.½ après midi Claude'' (Claude's time of birth), ''Boulogne sur Seine 19 avril 1949 à 19h.40 Paloma'' (Paloma's time of birth), or ''2.3.61. Vallauris 7h.½'' (the date of his marriage with Jacqueline). He even noted, ''Mercredi 16 mai 1945 folle?'' and above, with a different colored pencil, ''D.M.'' Picasso and Dora Maar stayed in Antibes in July 1945. It was not until the autumn that he rejoined Françoise Gilot.

Between September 24 and October 5, Picasso was once again in Antibes, at least for several days. There he etched a series of small plates, some of which are still more or less unknown. One of them was *Faune flûtiste et danseuse à l'almaraca et au tambourin* (cat. no. 78). Was he in Antibes with Françoise? She appears in this series of fauns and dancers that Fort, now in retirement in Golfe-Juan, pulled in several trial proofs.

As we have seen before, new *joie de vivre* for the artist led to new inspiration. Françoise was young, pretty, gay, headstrong and was herself a painter. The theme of the ''flower-woman'' found in other media was not reflected in the graphic work but it is amusing to note that the theme of *La Joie de vivre*, most closely linked to Antibes in the artist's mind, was already apparent a year before the mural for the Musée d'Antibes in the flute-playing faun and the dancer mentioned above. *Les*

Pipeaux (B.1347 to 1349) should be dated August 26-28 or during the first days of September 1946, when Picasso and Françoise were the guests of Louis Fort in Golfe-Jaun. As we know, beginning on November 2, 1945, Picasso resumed making lithographs, which he had not done since 1930. However, he also continued to work on intaglio copperplates.

A number of prints that he gave to friends wound up as illustrations: portraits of Françoise for Aragon's translation of Petrarch (B.370) and for Paul Eluard's *A Pablo Picasso* (B.373), the head of a woman wearing an anvil-shaped hat for René Char's *Le Marteau sans maitre* (cat. no. 77), just as prints made in 1944 were given, many years later, to Goder for *L'Age de soleil* (B. 369) as well as to the publisher Flammarion for *Six contes fantasques* by Maurice Toesca (B.363 to 368). Later, however, in 1947-48, Picasso began to concentrate his energy on a few books, which probably were more important to him since they were in Spanish.

Iliazd asked Picasso to illustrate his book *Pismo*, written in Russian. Picasso agreed to engrave the copperplates that Iliazd gave him, the size of which was carefully planned to suit the complicated layout of the book. This required considerable effort for someone like Picasso who did not easily bend his will to the dictates of others. On the other hand, he must have worked joyfully to provide the illustrations for the Spanish version of his friend Reventos' book *Dos Contes*, as well as for the French translation *Deux contes*. From February 9 to February 13, 1947, Picasso copied the whole text into the notebook mentioned above.

He made drawings related to the text, which were then transformed into engravings. At around the same date, he worked even harder on *Gongora*, copying the sonnets that he chose into the same notebook used for *Dos Contes*. He then copied them again on a special translucent plastic called Kodatrace, which was used to transfer the text onto the copperplates by means of heliogravure. He decorated the margins with *remarques*, which are always related to the given sonnet. However, he did not add any ornamentation to the sonnet dedicated to El Greco. He told Frélaut that he did not feel great enough himself to measure up to Gongora talking about El Greco and that El Greco did not need any embellishment. With Gongora, he realized the project he had envisaged in 1939 for his own manuscripts.

Soon after he worked on two other large book projects, *Carmen* and *Corps perdu*. He engraved a great many plates, but his heart was not in the work and he himself had to admit to Madeleine Lacourière that he had done slipshod work for *Carmen*. Then in 1952, he gave an exquisite small etching of a goat to his friend André Verlet, for his book, *La Chèvre* (cat. no. 122).

Aside from the book illustrations, Picasso did not devote much time to intaglio printmaking until 1949. Around 1946, however, he again took up the copperplate for *La Femme qui pleure II*, executed on July 1, 1937. He turned it upside down, and using the scraper and then graining the etched lines with aquatint to make them even blacker, he firmly etched a large portrait of Françoise. Exorcism again? Turning the copperplate around, he used the verso to produce a drypoint portrait of Françoise, directly related to the many groups of Matisse-like Françoises he was drawing at that time. Then in 1947 he added an aquatint portrait of her (B.457).

It was not until 1949 that he created the masterful *Vénus et l'Amour, d'après Cranach* (cat. no. 112). It has traditionally been said that Picasso was inspired by a postcard sent to him by Kahnweiler picturing a reproduction of *Venus and Cupid* by Cranach the Elder (1472-1553) in the Staatliche Museen, Berlin. On a page dated March 22, 1949, in the notebook already mentioned above, there are sketches of Cranach-style women with several annotations, ''Lucas Cranach d.A'', ''Baddsche (*sic*) Kunsthalle Karlsruhe,'' ''Der Traum das Paris.''

Picasso worked on the sugar-lift aquatint of the 1st state, only using scraper, drypoint and burin, until by the 6th state, his print was close enough to the model. His nephew, Vilato, recalls that he worked on it for a very long time. Frélaut pulled all the trial proofs for the six states. The plate was then put aside. Just a few months before the death of the artist, the *bon à tirer* proof was given to the Crommelynck brothers. Galerie Leiris published the print in 1979 after Picasso's death, signed with a stamp of the artist's signature.

In 1951, Picasso etched *Corrida en Arles* (cat. nos. 113-120), a large plate, printed first in two then three colors. Two of the plates exist in two states. Both 1st states were executed in 1951, and the 2nd states, as well as the only state of the third plate, were done in 1952. Frélaut pulled numerous trial proofs with different inkings and different colors. Madeleine Lacourière brought the portfolio with all these trial proofs to Picasso in the south of France, and although she says that she insisted vehemently, Picasso never agreed to have the plate published.

In May 1952, perhaps out of boredom with the lithographic process which he had already squeezed dry, Picasso returned to copperplates, working on a large scale and using sugar-lift aquatint. On May 14, he produced an aquatint of a goat skull (B.691), then on May 17, the big portrait of Françoise, *La Femme à la fenêtre* (cat. no. 121). On June 17, Picasso began to struggle with a large copperplate depicting a picador and bull, working it through twenty states and ultimately destroying it. He scraped the aquatint, reworked the toro with new layers of aquatint, used scraper, burin, and scraper again. The resulting print is virtually unknown today, although some of the state proofs have appeared on the print market during the past few years. Then on June 18 and June 20, he made new, quieter picador scenes (B.692 and 693). In July, he began a large portrait of Françoise, which he developed through ten states and finished at the end of November. It remains unknown to the public. Once again, as with G.287, it would seem that after working and reworking the same plate, producing many states, Picasso lost interest and did not bother to print it. Both the plate and subject were dead for him.

Early the next year, he came upon a plate Lacourière was using in order to etch a reproduction of one of his paintings in sugar-lift aquatint. He told Lacourière that it was awful and he took it over completely, producing *Le Crâne de chevre sur la table* (B.696) which is dated January 17, 18 and 20, 1953. Meanwhile, Lacourière had to start all over again on another plate to produce his reproductive print.

On May 9, Picasso made a burin engraving on zinc of Françoise with a very Egyptian hairdo. Since the plate did not print properly when it was proofed, the artist had it pulled as a lithograph (see cat. no. 123). The artist returned to the idea and two days later, on June 11, 1953, created the superb *Torse de femme* (B.746), always called *L'Egyptienne* in the Lacourière workshop. In the autumn, Françoise took her children and left.

Here it is necessary to backtrack a bit to consider the connection between Picasso, Françoise, lithography and the Mourlot workshop. Although he had already tried out the technique, Picasso had completely turned away from lithography and had not used it since 1930. Mourlot explained that Picasso only began his daily visits to the workshop after November 2, 1945, because there was enough wood and it was warm, while everywhere else in Paris was freezing cold. Inspiration and the desire to experiment must also be credited, however, to the new love of his life.

In the Mourlot catalogue raisonné, *Picasso Lithographs*, the interested reader can find detailed descriptions of nearly all the lithographs, with reproductions of the states and notes on technique. Unfortunately, some of the trial proofs have been overlooked and some of the intermediary states are missing, as for example with the *Two Nude Women* (M.16), the *Bull* (M.17), as well as the two intermediary states of the superb *David and Bathsheba* (M.109), or the 3rd state of the *Table with Fish, Black Background* (M.140). As a whole, the Mourlot catalogue is accurate and does not require revision. For this reason, the volumes soon to be published by the author of this exhibition catalogue, which complete the work undertaken by Dr. Geiser to catalogue Picasso's entire graphic work, will not include lithographs, with the exception of one dated 1962 which was inadvertently omitted in Mourlot.

From the very beginning of Picasso's activity in his workshop, Mourlot developed the habit of placing the proofs of all the states of his lithographs in boxes. Therefore the artist had a few complete sets of the proofs. He had 18 proofs of each of the lithographs M.1 to M.35 and five proofs each from M.35 to M.316. Mourlot kept one print of each proof for himself and thus was able to put together the catalogue raisonné. The proofs of M.35 to M.316 are numbered 1/6 to 6/6 on the verso and are signed by Mourlot. Sometimes the stone could not be printed 18 times, or even five times and so some states are missing from the boxes. Sometimes Mourlot simply did not have the time to pull five proofs before Picasso set to reworking the stone or the zincplate.

As far as Picasso's work itself is concerned, lithography was relatively new to him and his approach was, as usual, charged with curiosity and passion. He changed traditional ways of doing things and manipulated the technique to obtain the results desired. It must be assumed that Mourlot is correct when he says that Picasso was tempted by the endless variations between pure white and pure black that lithography afforded. Ultimately, though, lithography was but a passing fancy for Picasso; intaglio printmaking was truly his lifelong passion.

After a period of experimenting with all the possibilities of the lithographic technique, Picasso mastered the process and his enthusiasm was at its peak. In 1947 he produced the *David and Bathsheba*. In 1948, he worked at home, sending everyone from Mourlot running back and forth between his studio and the workshop, carrying fresh zincplates and pulling the states. The results were outstanding. First there was the group of large women's heads, and then, in 1949, the masterful *La Femme au fauteuil* (M.133 to 138) featuring Françoise wearing the coat Picasso had brought back for her from Warsaw. There were also the great still lifes, as for example the huge lobster, and then later the portrait of Paloma with her doll in 1952 (cat. no. 123). By 1952, however, the intensity of his interest in this medium was beginning to cool, although he never abandoned it again altogether and we can see later fruitful efforts in, for example, the group of beautiful portraits of Jacqueline (M.306 to 311) from 1957 and the last group of pure lithographs such as cat. no. 178.

It is common knowledge that the lithography technique is based on the antagonism between grease and water. When areas of the stone are covered with greasy lithographic crayon or greasy lithographic ink, those areas will hold the ink rolled over the surface of the stone. As the printing ink itself is greasy, it is repelled by the wet parts of the stone without ink or crayon, which produce empty areas on the proof. By scratching or even digging into the stone surface, Picasso produced white surfaces on the proofs. Textured zincplates produce similar results and offer large possibilities for wash drawing in litho-ink. When Picasso began working at home, he used zincplates since lithographic stones were too heavy to be easily carried from one place to another.

An overview of the graphic work of this period reveals that it contained practically no narrative element. There are portraits, subjects from daily life, still lifes and bullfights. In 1951, the artist did make allusions to chivalric epics, probably because of his work for Montluc's *La Maigre*, which he executed for Iliazd on April 13. Then he did some medieval subjects such as the departure of the knight, where we see a lady, resembling Françoise, watching from the top of the castle wall while her faithful knight goes out to war (M.199 to 201). Myths and mythology, however, do not reappear until later.

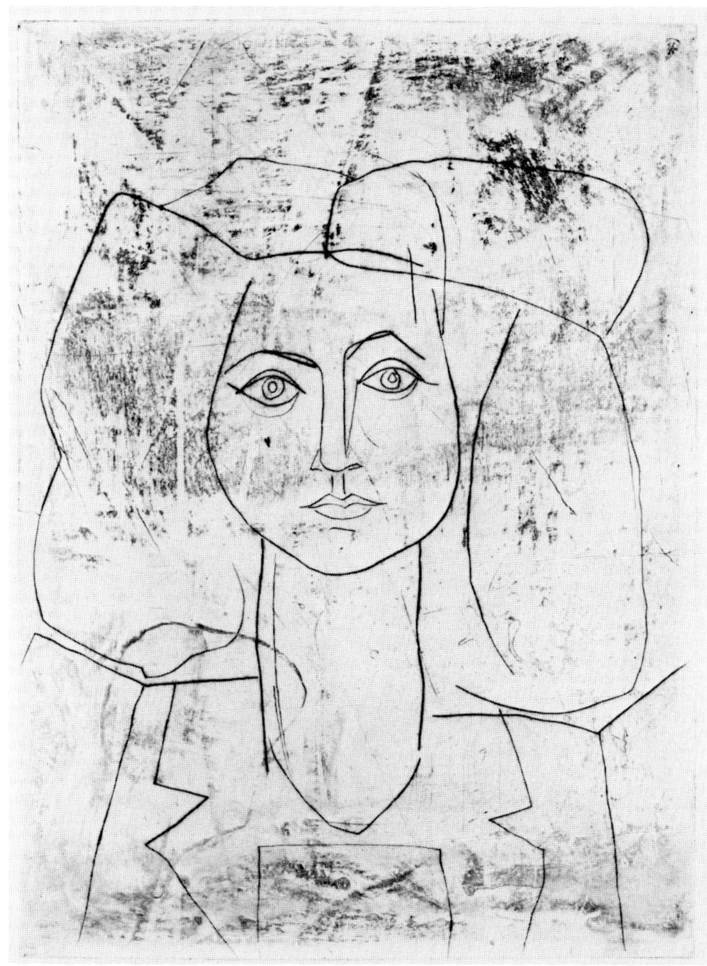

76.

76.
Portrait de Françoise
Portrait of Françoise

c. 1946

Drypoint on copper

696 × 496 mm.

Proof on Montval laid paper, pulled by Lacourière.

The drypoint was executed on the verso of the copperplate used in July 1937 for *Weeping Woman II*. In 1946, the plate was turned upside down, and the recto was re-etched with a portrait of Françoise. Visible in the upper right corner of the proof is the stamp of the copperplate maker. Our drypoint can be related to a group of eight drawings dated April 23, in which Françoise wears the same blouse and jacket with a tailored collar (Picasso Estate, not in Zervos).

As far as can be known only eight proofs of our drypoint are in existence; one is in the Musée Picasso, Paris, which also owns the copperplate.

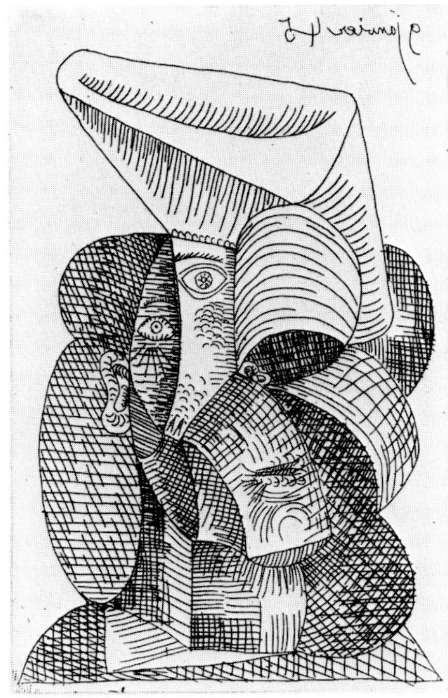

77d.

77a-d.
Tête de femme au chapeau
Head of a Woman Wearing a Hat
[only one proof is illustrated]

1945 (January 9)

Etching on copper

165 × 107 mm.

a. One trial proof printed with blue ink, on Montval laid paper.

[not illustrated]

b. One trial proof printed with green ink, on Montval laid paper.

[not illustrated]

c. One trial proof printed with red ink, on laid paper watermarked ''LES CENT UNE.''

[not illustrated]

d. One trial proof printed in black on Montval laid paper.

The copperplate (on exhibition), never steelfaced, and cancelled in 1983.

B.374.

All these proofs have large margins.

Perhaps the anvil-shaped hat is related to the title of René Char's book *Le Marteau sans maitre*, for which Picasso etched the plate (*marteau* = hammer, hence the anvil-shaped hat). But this is not at all certain. In 1955, Pierre Boulez put his friend's poem to music.

Edition of the book: published by Jose Corti, Paris, 1945. The colophon states that the first 25 copies, numbered from 1 to 25, on Arches laid paper include a ''drypoint'' by Picasso, pulled by Lacourière, but: 1. The ''drypoint'' is an etching; 2. The paper is Arches wove paper; 3. The first three copies are different: three more impressions of the etching were added to them; the proofs were pulled in three different colors (see our proofs) on Imperial Japan paper.

One of these copies was René Char's copy (no. 3, now in the Solvay collection, Biblioth`eque Royale Albert Ier, Brussels). One was Yvonne Zervos's copy (she either introduced Picasso to Char, or asked the former to be kind enough to give the frontispiece (no. 1, now in the Bibliothèque Litteraire Jacques Doucet, Paris: *fond* Char-Zervos). The last one was Picasso's copy (no. 2). This copy appears to have been lost, but the four proofs had been put aside by the artist and are now in the Musée Picasso, Paris.

The proofs in the exhibition are the only trial proofs known to exist, at least as a coherent group of four proofs, on the same kind of paper, each pulled with a different color ink.

A group of proofs, similar to the four in the first three copies of the book, is known to exist.

Matarasso, 40; Bloch, Livre, 42.

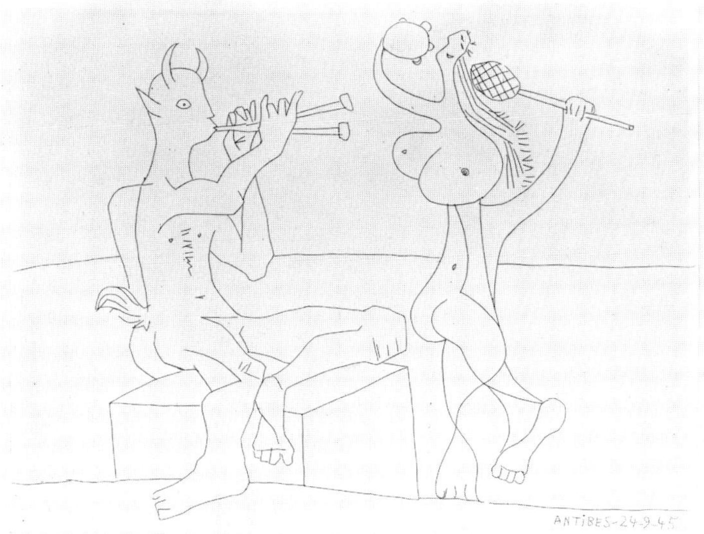

78a.

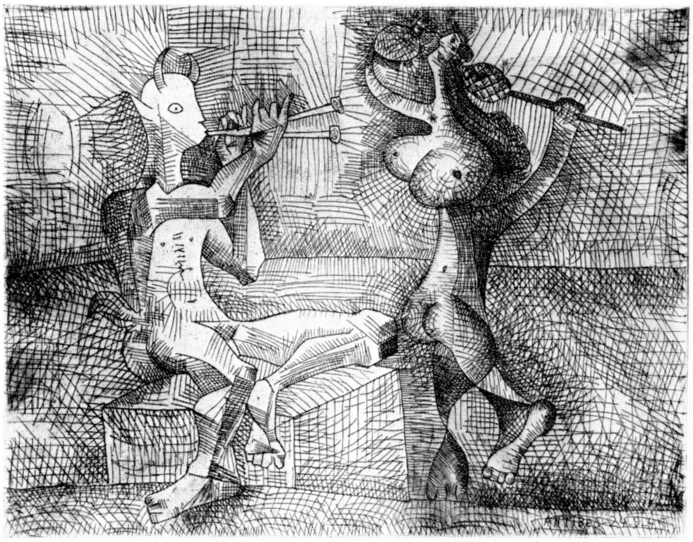

78b.

78a&b.

Faune flûtiste et danseuse à l'almaraca et au tambourin

Faun Playing the Flute and Dancer with Maraca and Tambourine

1945 (September 24, Antibes)

Etching on copper

265 × 348 mm.

a. 1st state: proof on Arches wove paper (slightly colored).

b. 2nd state: proof on Arches wove paper, watermarked "Perrigot," pulled with tone.

B.1341.

All the existing proofs of this etching were pulled by Fort, in Golfe-Juan. Seven proofs of the 1st state, including one pulled in negative, are known.

Nine proofs of the 2nd state are known: in 1953 one was stolen from a Paris print dealer and has never been located. One proof of the 2nd state was pulled in two colors, with two plates: first plate inked and printed in yellow (a simple aquatint background with scraped areas on the face, breasts and buttocks of the dancer); second plate: our plate, inked and printed in black. It is possible that this proof was pulled in the Lacourière workshop.

The background copperplate is lost. The copperplate of the etching exists. Note the artist's return to traditional etching techniques. The subject can be linked to the later *Joie de vivre* mural (1946, Antibes Museum).

79.
Les Deux femmes nues
Two Nude Women

1945 (November 21)

Lithograph on stone

Size of the image: 265 × 342 mm.

Mourlot's 3rd state: proof on Arches wove paper.

M.16.3rd state.

Actually, this is not the 3rd state but the 4th.

80a&b.
Les Deux femmes nues

1946 (January 5)

See no. 79.

Size of the image: 314 × 415 mm.

a. A proof on Arches wove paper of an intermediary state between Mourlot's 7th and 8th states. In fact not the 8th but the 10th state.

b. A proof pulled in brownish red, on thin laid paper, of what Mourlot calls the 8th state. It is, in fact, the 11th state.

M.16.8th state.

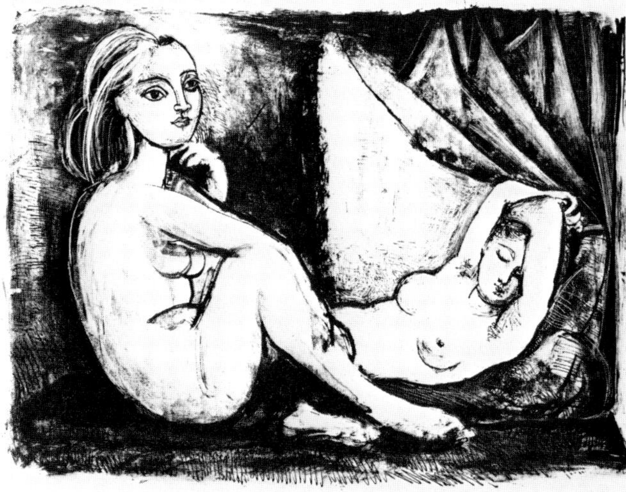

79.

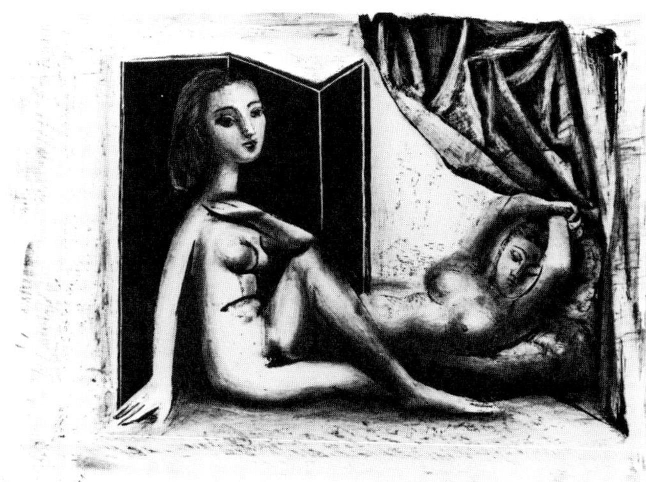

80a.

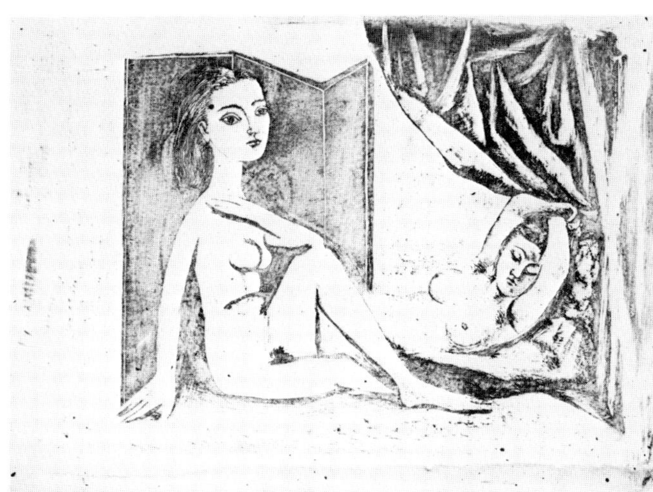

80b.

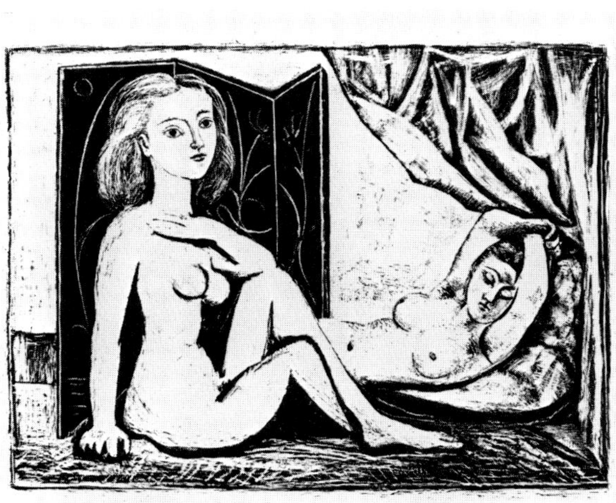

81.

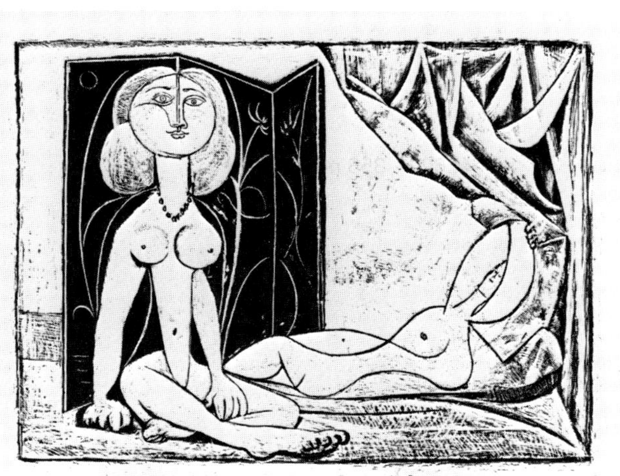

82.

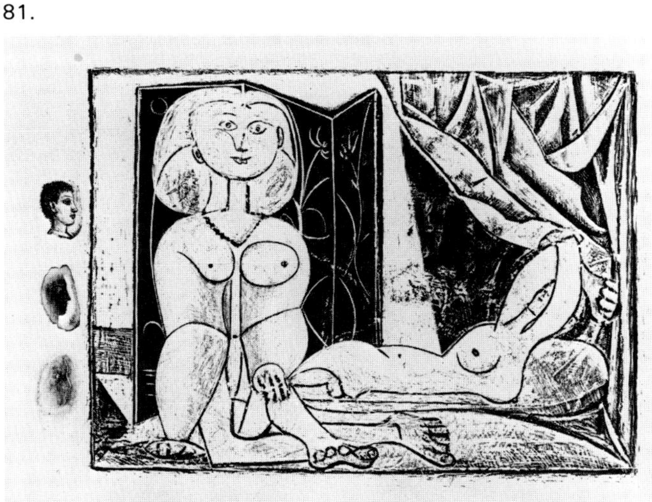

83.

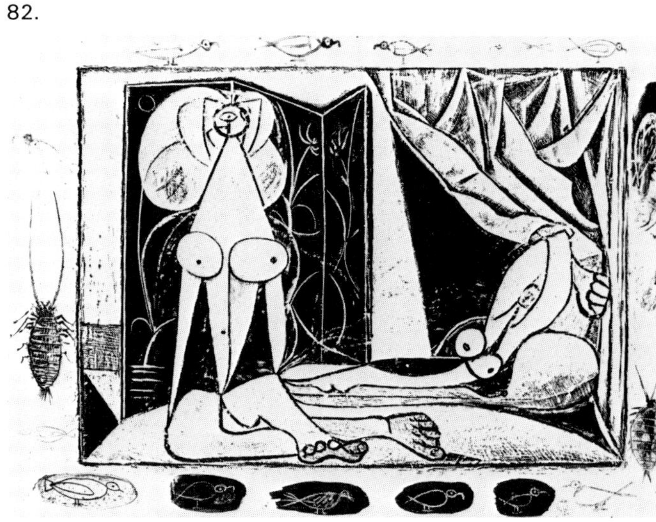

84.

81.
Les Deux femmes nues

1946 (January 10)

See no. 79.

Size of the image: 262 × 360 mm.

Mourlot's 9th state: proof on Arches wove paper.

M.16.9th state.

In fact, not the 9th but the 12th state.

82.
Les Deux femmes nues

1946 (January 21)

See no. 79.

Size of the image: 262 × 358 mm.

Mourlot's 12th state (photograph of 12th state).

M.16.11th state.

Mourlot got mixed up in his photographs: the photograph of the 11th state is the reproduction of his 12th state, and the photograph bearing the mention ''12th state'' is the reproduction of his 11th state. Hence, our proof should correspond to the text of Mourlot's 11th state, but is, in fact, a proof of the 14th state.

83.
Les Deux femmes nues

1946 (February 6)

See no. 79.

Size of the image: 263 × 392 mm.

Mourlot's 16th state: proof on Arches wove paper.

M.16.16th state.

In fact, not the 16th but the 19th state.

The size given by Mourlot does not include the *remarques* on the left margin, *remarques* which will eventually disappear in the Mourlot 17th state.

84.
Les Deux femmes nues

1946 (February 12)

See no. 79.

Size of the image: 315 × 423 mm.

Mourlot's 18th state: a trial proof on Arches wove paper.

M.16.18th state; B.390.

In fact, not the 18th but the 21st state.

The size given by Mourlot does not include the *remarques* in the margin. Apart from the trial proofs, of which 17 (various states) have been reworked with watercolor, crayon and gouache, 18 proofs of each of the Mourlot 18 states were given to the artist in the boxes mentioned above. The last state was published in an edition of 50, signed and numbered.

Concerning nos. 79-84: Because of the lack of space, we unfortunately had to choose only a few states from the complete group of Mourlot's eighteen states. We tried to choose the states which show the most drastic changes in the form or position of the two women. The work was begun on the stone on November 10, 1945. The artist employed ink wash, pen and ink and scraper.

To make it easier for the reader, we have used Mourlot's numeration of the states. Actually, there are intermediary states, the proofs that Mourlot says Picasso took home with him, which Mourlot did not remember and could not photograph. We show one as an example (no. 80, first proof). Usually the intermediary states do not show drastic changes, but merely imperfections in the ink wash or in the scraping of the stone. It is still possible that there could be more than 21 states.

As for the subject of ''women together'' see the introductory notes for cat. nos. 31 and 32. For the recurrent theme of ''someone sitting, fully awake, near someone soundly asleep,'' see cat. no. 22. The sitting woman obviously resembles Françoise. In Mourlot's 6th state, the likeness to Paloma is striking.

85.
Le Taureau
The Bull

1945 (December 5)

Lithograph on stone

Size of the image: 290 × 420 mm.

Mourlot's 1st state: proof on Arches wove paper.

M.17.1st state.

86.
Le Taureau

1945 (December 12)

See no. 85.

Mourlot's 2nd state: proof on Arches wove paper.

M.17.2nd state.

In fact, not the 2nd but the 3rd state.

87.
Le Taureau

1945 (December 18)

See no. 85.

Mourlot's 3rd state: proof on Arches wove paper.

M.17.3rd state.

In fact, not the 3rd but the 4th state.

88.
Le Taureau

1945 (December 22)

See no. 85.

Mourlot's 4th state: proof on Arches wove paper.

M.17.4th state.

In fact, not the 4th but the 5th state.

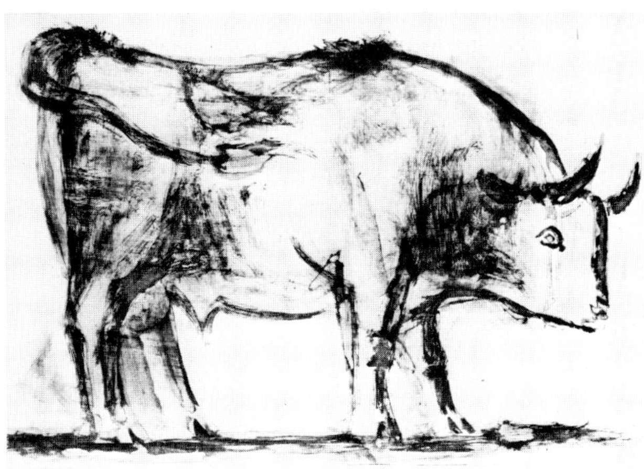

85.

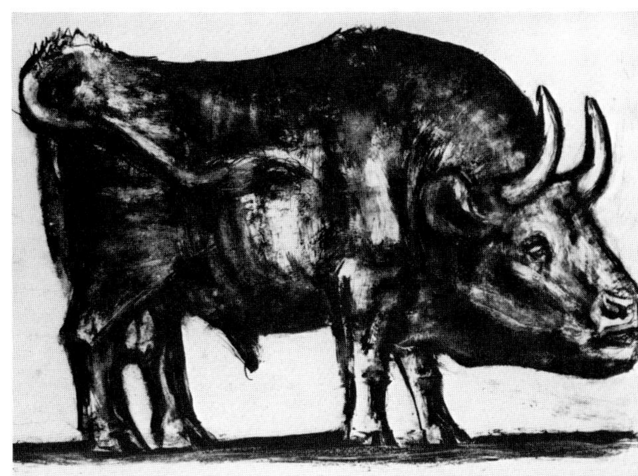

86.

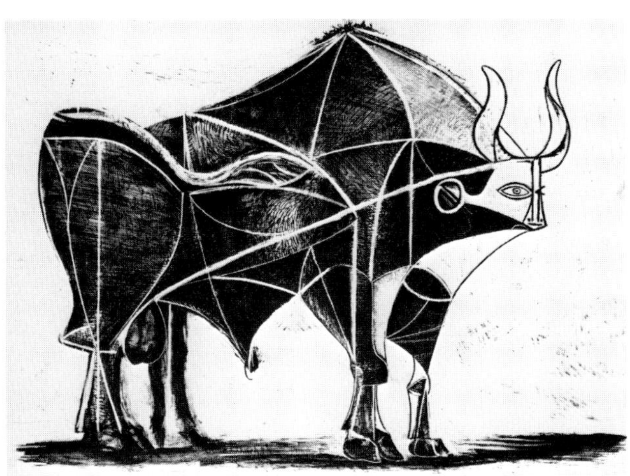

89.

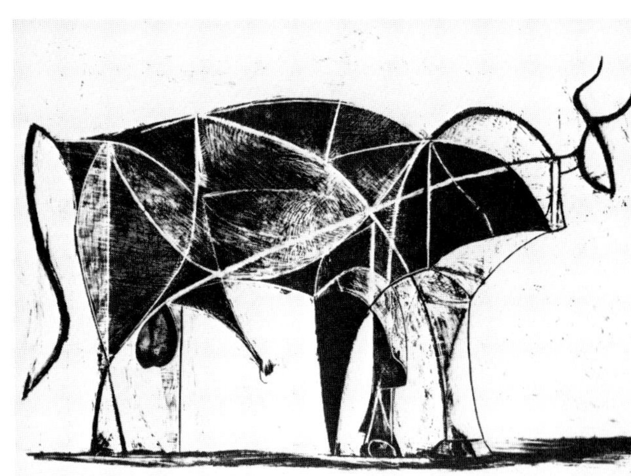

90.

89.
Le Taureau

1945 (December 24)

See no. 85.

Mourlot's 5th state: proof on Arches wove paper.

M.17.5th state.

In fact, not the 5th but the 6th state.

90.
Le Taureau

1945 (December 26)

See no. 85.

Mourlot's 6th state: proof on Arches wove paper.

M.17.6th state.

In fact, not the 6th but the 7th.

91.
Le Taureau

1945 (December 28)

See no. 85.

Mourlot's 7th state: proof on Arches wove paper.

M.17.7th state.

In fact, not the 7th but the 10th state.

92.
Le Taureau

1946 (January 2)

See no. 85.

Mourlot's 8th state: proof on Arches wove paper.

M.17.8th state.

In fact, not the 8th but the 11th state.

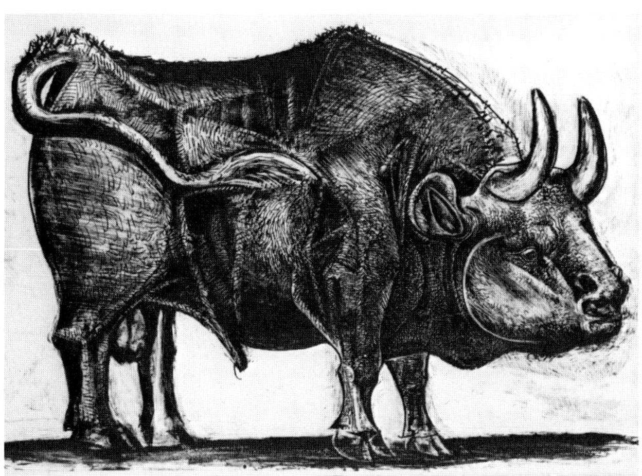

87.

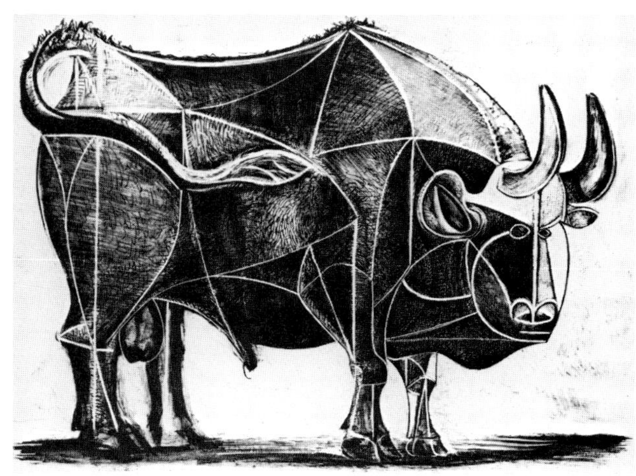

88.

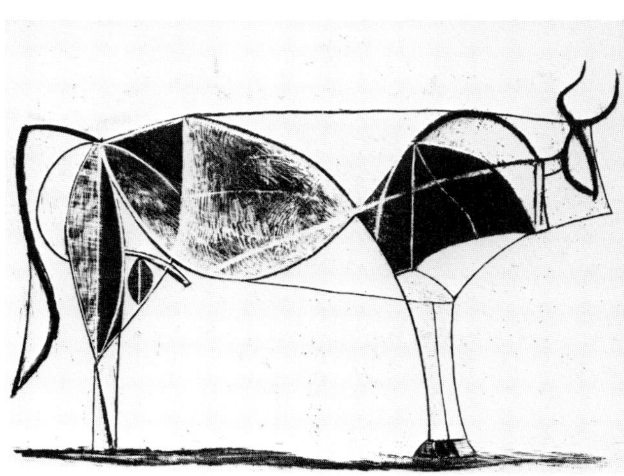

91.

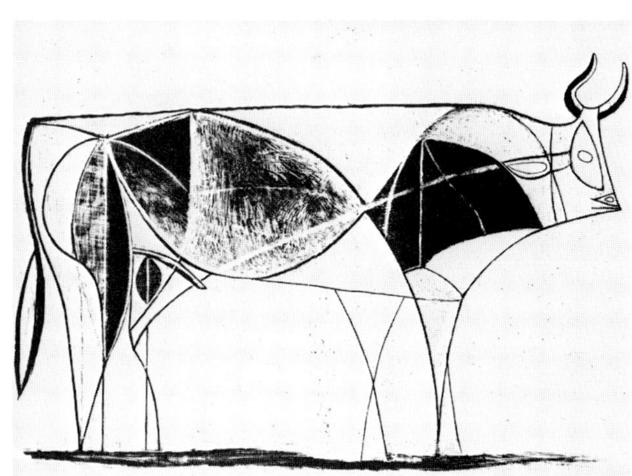

92.

93.
Le Taureau

1946 (January 5)

See no. 85.

Mourlot's 9th state: proof on Arches wove paper.

M.17.9th state.

In fact, not the 9th but the 12th state.

94.
Le Taureau

1946 (January 10)

See no. 85.

Mourlot's 10th state: proof on Arches wove paper.

M.17.10th state.

In fact, not the 10th but the 13th state.

95.
Le Taureau

1946 (January 17)

See no. 85.

The size of the image is now: 290 × 375 mm. approximately

Mourlot's 11th state: trial proof on Arches wove paper.

M.17.11th state.

In fact, not the 11th but the 14th state.

Between the 1st state and the last state, the dimensions of the bull change. Apart from a few trial proofs, 18 proofs of each of the Mourlot 11 states were given to the artist (see no. 84). The last state was published in an edition of 50 signed and numbered impressions.

On nos. 85 - 95: The artist worked on the stone with ink wash, pen and ink and with the scraper. The same remarks concerning the states apply as for nos. 79 to 84. As for the development of the *toro di corrida* -at first a mere *novillo*, then a full grown *Miura toro*, gradually transformed into the embodiment of the very conception of *toro* - it seems better simply to look at the progression in the various states. So much has been said about it that it would be needlessly repetitive to discuss it once again. However, we must never forget Picasso's predilection for jokes and even humbug, and we must be able to react to the humor implict in even so aggressive a series as the bulls.

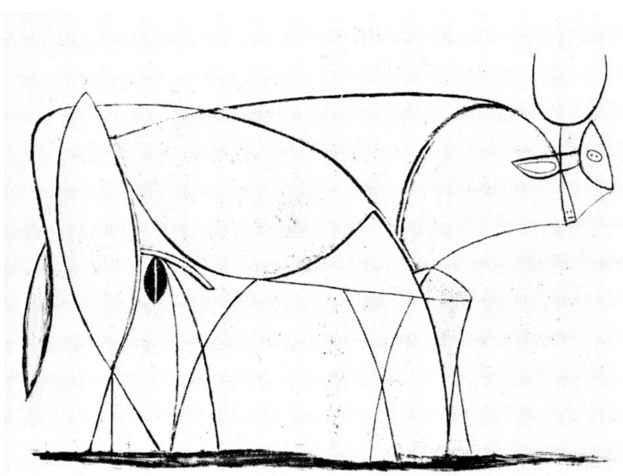

93.

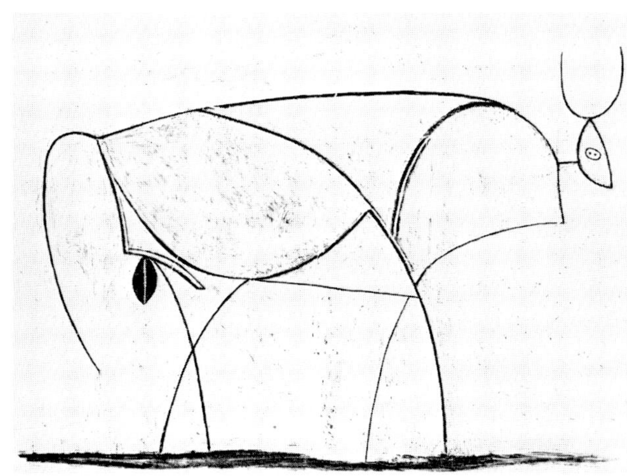

94.

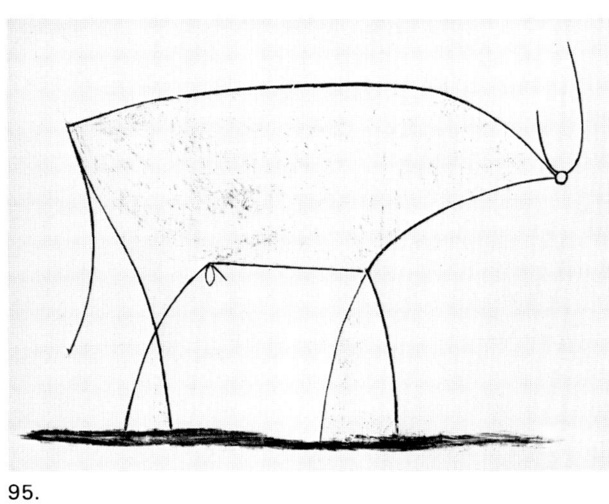

95.

96.
Tête de femme; portrait de Françoise
Portrait of a Woman: Françoise

1948 (November 10)

Lithograph on zinc: litho-ink wash

620 × 440 mm. approximately

Proof on Arches wove paper, annotated on the verso by Mourlot "5/6 F.M."

M.122.

The annotation on the verso means that this print was in the group of proofs that Mourlot put together in the number 5. Five of them were given to Picasso and Mourlot kept the sixth. The zinc of this superb portrait was somehow ruined. Apart from two or three trial proofs, the only existing ones are in Mourlot's six boxes. Note the quality of the scale of blacks and whites.

It is around this date, at the end of October, that Picasso decided not to work again - at least not continuously - in the Mourlot workshop, but to work quietly at home. Members of the Mourlot staff, like Celestin or Tutin, were constantly running from Mourlot's place to Picasso's studio and then back again. In the metamorphosis of the *Bull*, for example, there is a state on the 24th of December, then another one, right after on the 26th: Picasso always spent holidays like Christmas and New Year's day working. Apparently, he hated all festive celebrations. He must have been furious not to have been able to work on his bull on Christmas day. Working at home simplified the problem, as he could lock himself up with his work and forget about the rest of the world.

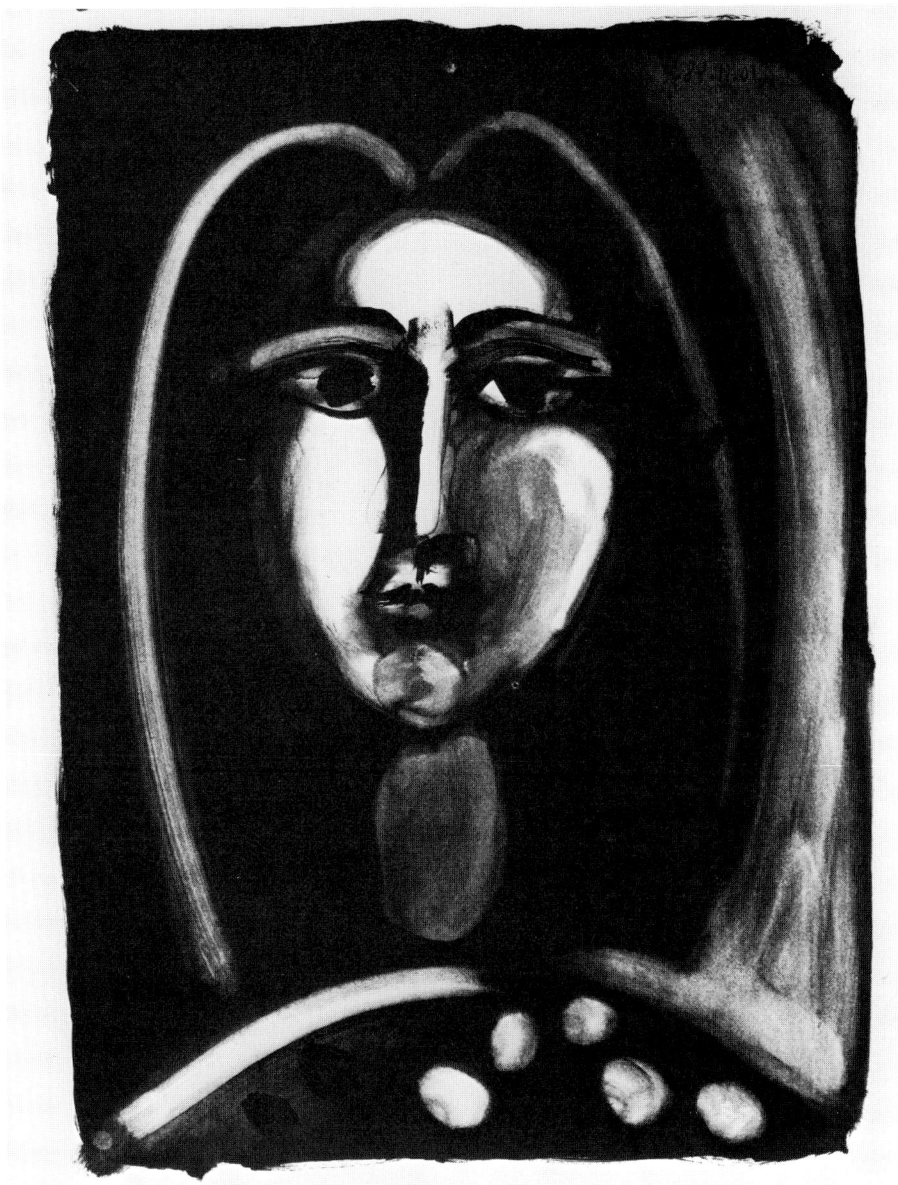

96.

97.
Figure noire
Black Face: Portrait of Françoise

1948 (November 20)

Lithograph on zinc

650 × 500 mm. approximately

Proof on Arches wove paper, annotated on the verso by Mourlot "2/6 F.M." (see no. 96).

M.126; B.577.

Flat tint of litho-ink. Ear, neck and dress left untouched. Scraping with scraper and sandpaper on the face, the outline of which is engraved with the sharp end of the scraper. Neck and dress are reworked with a lithographic crayon.

In the group of large women's heads (M.126-131), it is interesting to note how Picasso translated the aquatint technique he loved into the lithographic process. With the lithography technique, the *réserves* (see cat.no.52) are easier to make; it is possible to get halftones either with the scraper or with sandpaper, and further to obtain another half tone with lithographic crayon. Thus a descending scale of blacks, greys and whites can be produced, which are more subtle than those obtained with aquatint. In addition to the six proofs in the Mourlot boxes, the lithograph was published: edition of 50, signed and numbered, plus a few artist's proofs.

98.
Figure stylisée
Head of a Woman

1948 (November 21)

Lithograph on zinc

650 × 500 mm. approximately

1st state: proof on Arches wove paper, annotated on the verso by Mourlot "2/6 F.M." (see no. 96).

M.131.1st state.

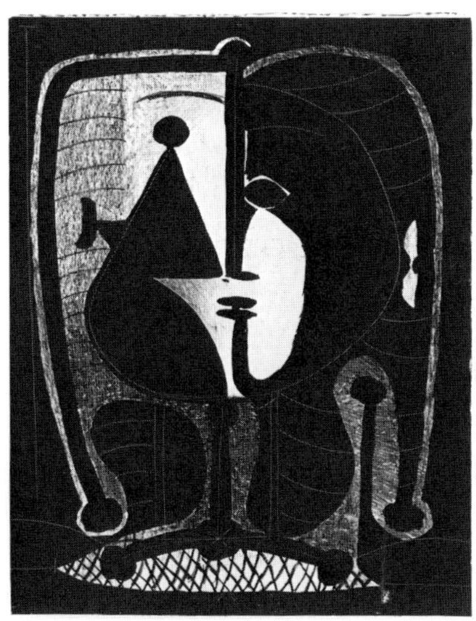

98.

99.
Figure stylisée

1948 (December 13)

See no. 98.

2nd state: proof on Arches wove paper, annotated on the verso by Mourlot "2/6 F.M." (see no. 96).

M.131.2nd state.

100.
Figure stylisée

1948 (December 21)

See no. 98.

3rd state: proof on Arches wove paper, annotated on the verso by Mourlot "2/6 F.M." (see no. 96).

M.131.3rd state.

Same technique as no. 97: flat tint of litho-ink, with *réserves*, engraved (white lines) with the sharp end of the scraper, shading with lithographic crayon. In the 2nd state, the right side of the head was erased with benzine and redrawn, and new work was done with the sharp end of the scraper and with the lithographic crayon. 3rd state: the background is cleaned and scraped and the whole composition is simplified (scraper and benzine).

Apart from one or two trial proofs of each state, there are six proofs of each in the Mourlot boxes. The 3rd state was printed: edition of 50, signed and numbered, plus a few artist's proofs.

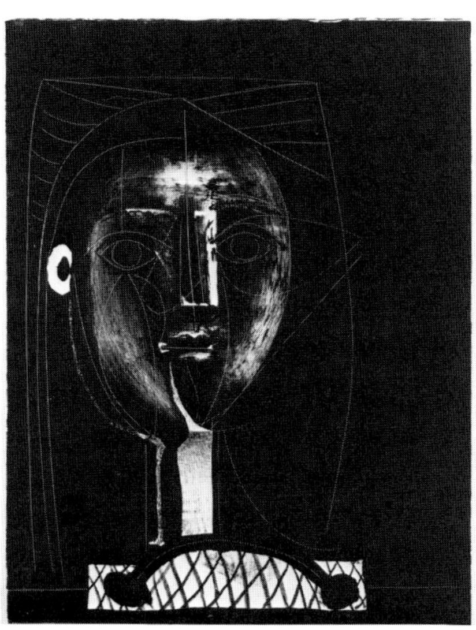

97.

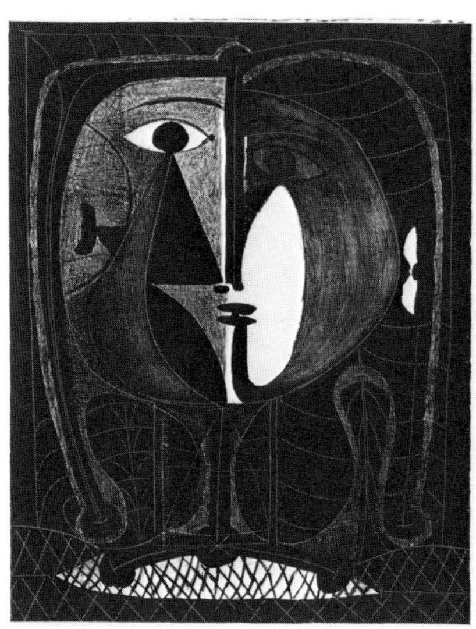

99.

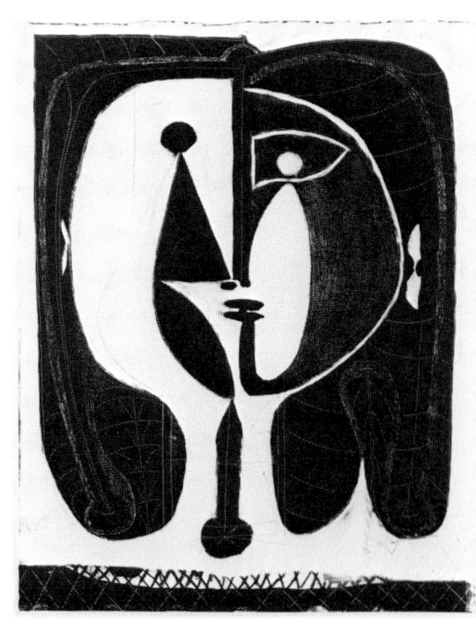

100.

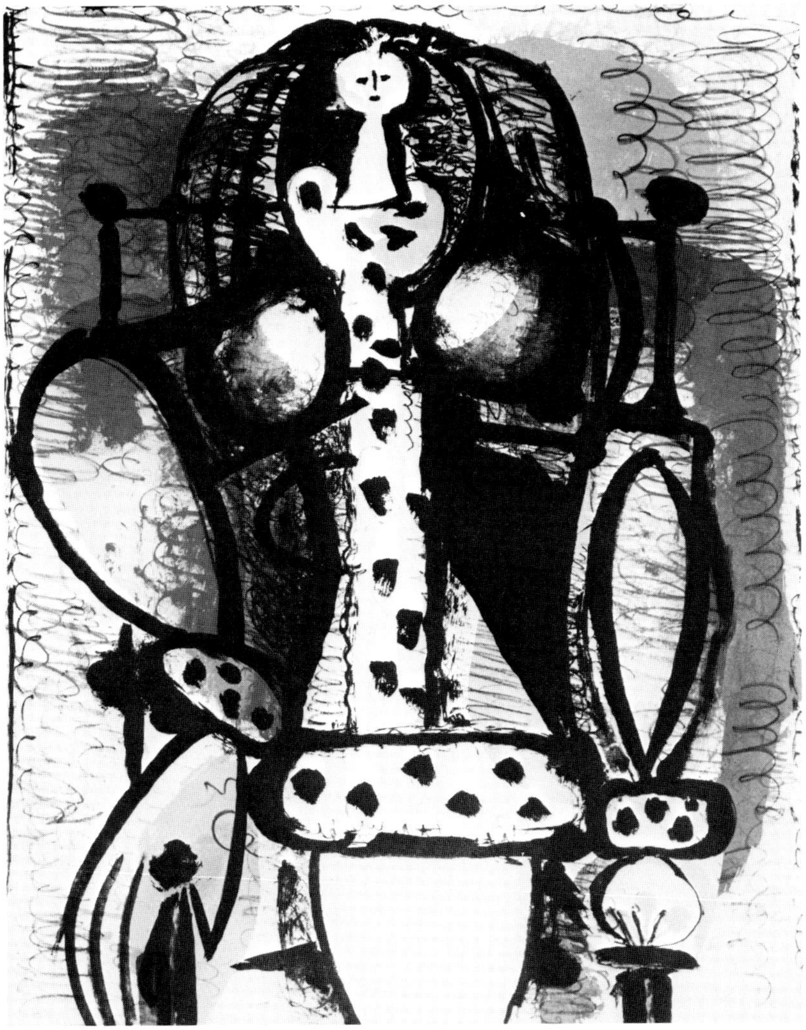

101.

101. (see color plate)
La Femme au fauteuil
Woman in an armchair

1948 (November)

Lithograph, in five colors, on five zincplates

660 × 500 mm.

2nd state of the five colors: trial proof on Arches wove paper.

M.133 (a).

Of this state not more than eight proofs exist: two trial proofs, one of which with the zincplate of the black printed in blue, and our proof. Then, six proofs in the Mourlot boxes.

Picasso intended to make a large portrait in five colors of Françoise wearing the Polish coat he had bought for her during his trip to Poland. This proof shows where he abandoned his idea, definitely preferring the scale of half tones given by black and white. He then began to work each of the five zincplates, creating the group of lithographs which are the acme of his work in that technique. From the red plate, for example, he first produced six states that were not published. Not satisfied with the 5th state, he then had it transferred onto another zincplate, where he reworked three states. But he had also made a "corrected tracing" on tracing paper. The drawing was transferred onto a third zincplate, then completely erased and reworked with ink wash. He intended to print it on the 3rd state of the first transfer-zincplate, which would be printed in grey. He abandoned the idea again, and only the ink wash figure was printed and published, in black and white (M.134). He worked day and night on this group, reworking some of the proofs with ink wash and even collaging onto them.

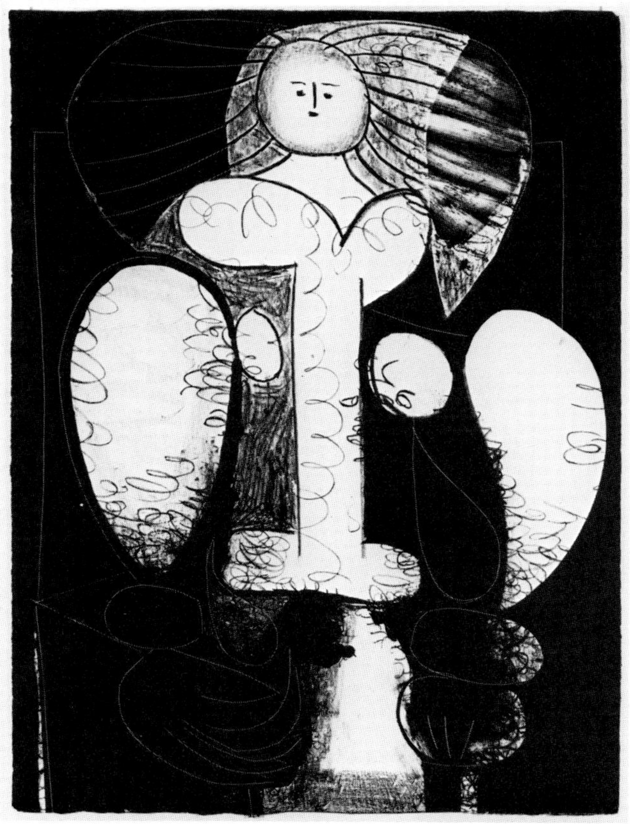

102.

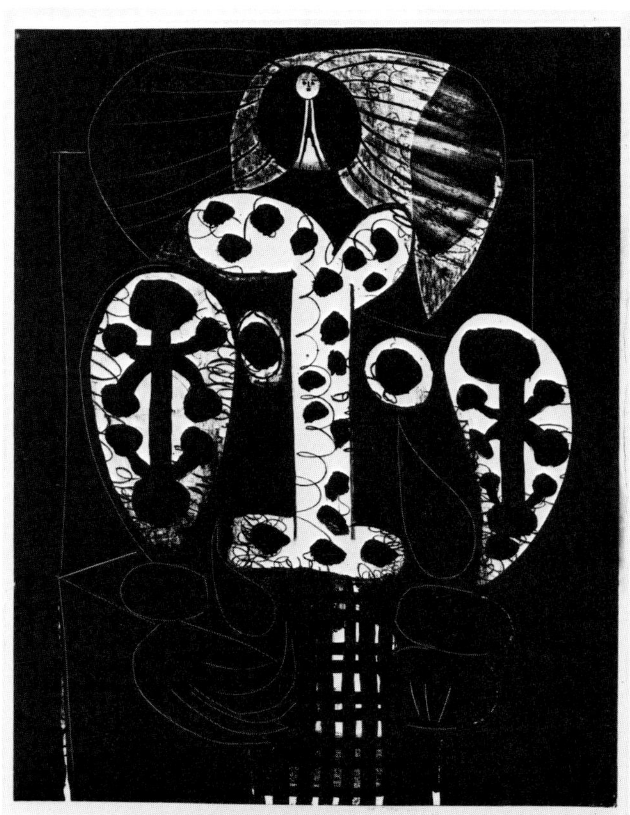

103.

102.
Femme au fauteuil No. 2 (d'après le vert)
Woman in an Armchair No. 2, Green Plate

1948 (December 10)

Lithograph on zinc

654 × 500 mm. approximately (the paper is smaller than the plate)

1st state: trial proof on Arches wove paper.

M. 135. 1st state.

103.
Femme au fauteuil No. 2 (d'après le vert)

1949 (April 5)

See no. 102.

696 × 544 mm.

2nd state: trial proof on Arches wove paper.

M. 135. 2nd state.

One or two trial proofs are known to exist of each of these two states, plus the six proofs in the Mourlot boxes.

It is difficult to find, in our 1st state, remnants of the green colored areas from no. 101. In fact, the Mourlot 1st state of M. 135, is the 3rd state of the Green plate, the 1st and 2nd states being registered as Mourlot no. 133 and 133 (a). The plate was completely reworked with a uniform layer of litho-ink, except for some areas which were left untouched and worked on with lithographic crayon. The sharp end of the scraper was used to engrave the plate.

In the Mourlot 2nd state, which is in fact the 4th state, new work with litho-ink on the sleeves of the Polish coat has been added to show the embroidery. The zincplate, abandoned at this point, is exhibited so as to understand the technique.

104.
Homard et poissons
Still Life with Lobster and Fish

1949 (January 7)

Lithograph on zinc: litho-ink wash

750 × 1050 mm.

Trial proof on Arches wove paper.

M.142; B. 582.

Given the size of the plate, Mourlot could not put the proofs in boxes as usual. Picasso had two trial proofs and surely a few signed artist's proofs, of which two were found in his portfolios.

The plate was printed and published: edition of 50, signed and numbered.

Note the infinite range of halftones between the black and white. The size of this work makes it even more of a technical exploit.

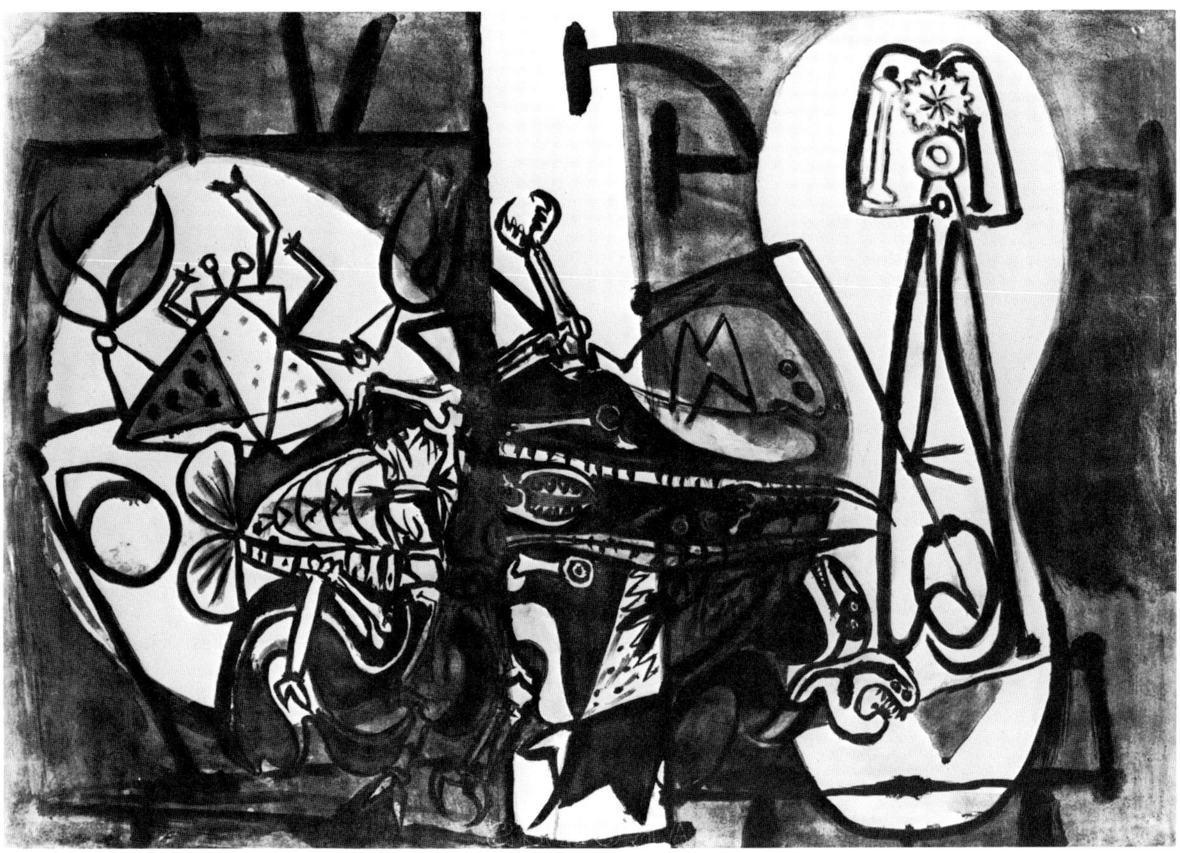

104.

105.
Buste de jeune femme
Young Woman: Portrait of Françoise

1949 (February 26)

Lithograph on zinc

620 × 480 mm. approximately

1st state: proof on Arches wove paper, annotated on the verso by Mourlot ''5/6 F.M.'' (see no. 96).

M.158.1st state.

106.
Buste de jeune femme

1949 (March 4)

See no. 105.

2nd state: proof on Arches wove paper, annotated on the verso by Mourlot ''2/6 F.M.'' (see no. 96).

M.158.2nd state.

Apart from one or two trial proofs, only the six proofs of each state in the Mourlot boxes exist. One proof of the first state was reworked in oil by the artist on February 26, 1949.

In the 1st state we find litho-ink wash, the sharp end of the scraper (outline of the cheek) and lithographic crayon held horizontally, whence the wide stripes on the dress. In the 2nd state, work was probably done with sandpaper to lighten the hair.

These plates provide a loving portrait with a true likeness of the model.

107.
Le Corsage à carreaux
The Checkered Blouse: Portrait of Françoise

1949 (March 26)

Lithograph in two colors, on two stones

646 × 497 mm.

Proof on Arches wove paper, annotated on the verso by Mourlot ''2/6 F.M.'' (see no. 96).

M. 175.

The stone of M.163 was first printed in a pinkish color. This lithograph dating from March 7 (although Picasso inscribed it ''7.4'') had been obtained by transferring a gouache and ink wash drawing onto a stone. Then M.175(a) was printed over it, in black. Like the first, this new lithograph was the result of a transfer onto a stone of an ink drawing, made on a sheet of lithographic paper on which the first lithograph (M.163) had been printed. Lithographs can be produced by transferring onto a stone a freshly drawn or ink-wash drawing, which normally is made with a greasy pencil or ink, preferably on special lithographic paper.

Picasso decided to publish only the composition on the second stone, without the first. Only one trial proof and the six proofs in the Mourlot boxes are known to exist of the two lithographs printed together.

108.
Femme aux cheveux verts
Woman with Green Hair: Portrait of Françoise

1949 (March 28)

Lithograph in three colors, on three zincplates

653 × 500 mm.

1st state of the three colors: purple, green and brown; the black is still lacking. Proof on Arches wove paper, annotated on the verso by Mourlot ''5/6 F.M.'' (see no. 96).

M.178, unrecorded state.

109. (see color plate)
Femme aux cheveux verts

1949 (March 28)

See no. 108.

Lithograph in four colors, on four zincplates

2nd state of purple, green and brown; 1st state of black. Purple and green reworked into flat tint. Brown has been erased over the shoulders and the cheeks were cleaned up.

M.178, unrecorded state. The proof in the exhibition does not correspond with the Mourlot photograph of the 1st state of the four colors.

110.
Femme aux cheveux verts

1949 (April 18)

See no. 108.

2nd state of the black: trial proof, printed in black, on Arches wove paper.

M.178 (a): in the Mourlot photograph, the reproduced proof is printed in four colors. The three other colors are in their second state, as they appear in no. 109.

The proof with only the second state of the black is not reproduced.

111. (see color plate)
Femme aux cheveux verts or Femme à la résille
Woman with a Hairnet

1956 (September)

Lithograph in four colors, on four zincplates

653 × 500 mm.

4th state of the black; 3rd state of the green; 2nd state of the brown and of the purple.

Artist's proof on Arches wove paper, signed.

M.178 (b); B.612.

In this last state the four-color lithograph was published: edition of 50, signed and numbered, plus a few artist's proofs.

The colors were printed in the following order: purple, green, brown and black. The first states of the four colors were obtained by the transfer of four drawings in ink wash on lithographic paper onto four zincplates. Then Picasso worked directly on the plates: litho-ink drawings, litho-ink wash, scraping and sandpaper erasing.

The Mourlot boxes comprise: one proof of no. 108, one proof of no. 109, one proof of M.178 (a), one proof of M. 178 (b) (3rd state of black, in black and white) and one proof M.178 (b) in four colors (no. 111). There are six proofs of each of these states. There must have been two proofs of the 1st state reproduced by Mourlot (M.178): one now in the Musée Picasso, Paris, and the one Mourlot kept and photographed. Two proofs of our no. 110 are known to exist.

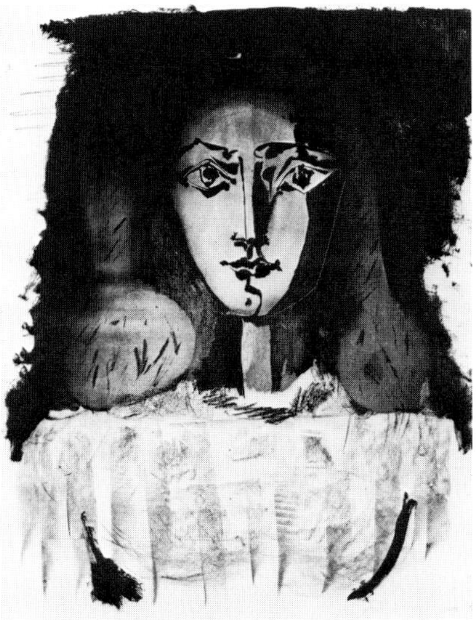
105.

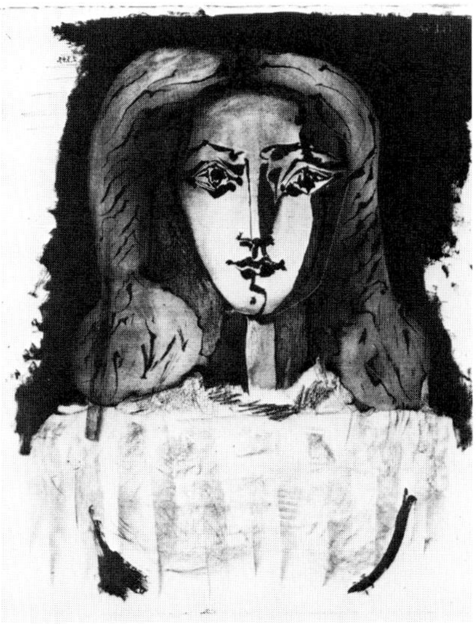
106.

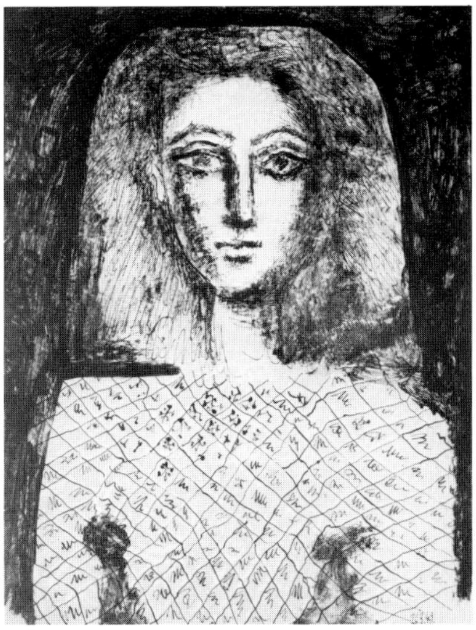
107.

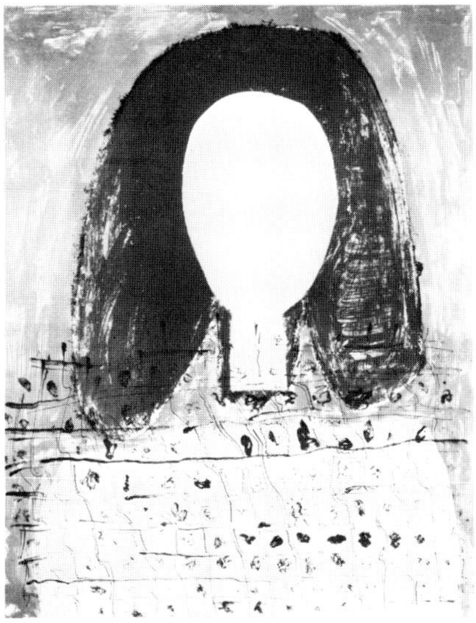
108.

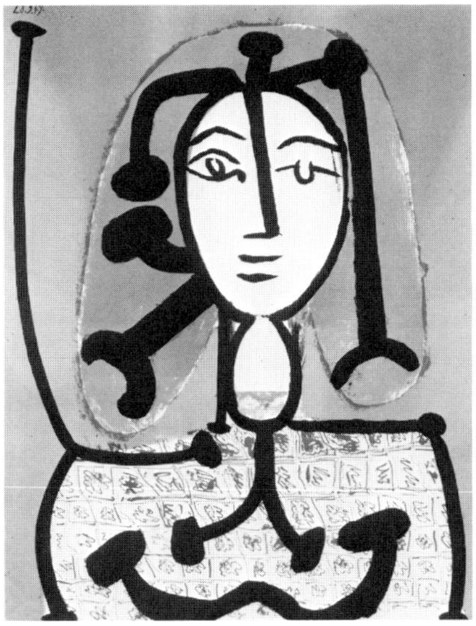
109.

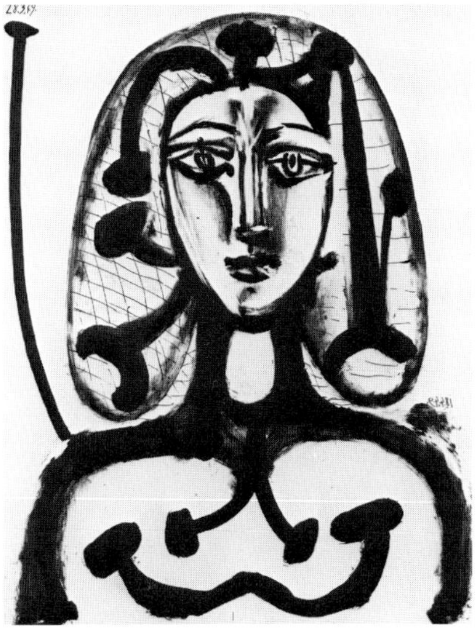
110.

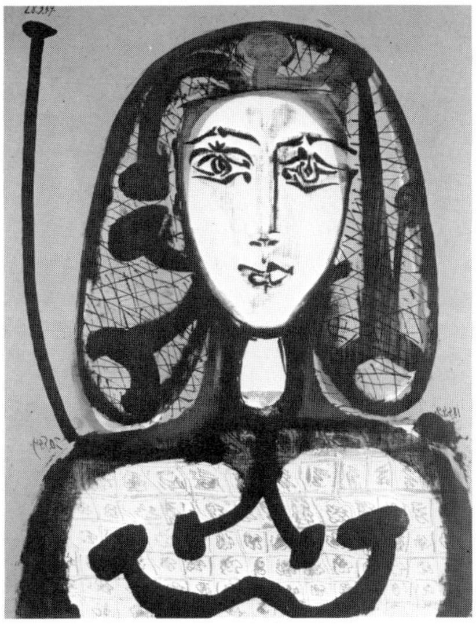
111.

112.
Vénus et l'Amour, d'après Cranach
Venus and Cupid, after Cranach

1949

Aquatint, scraper, burin and drypoint on copper

796 × 428 mm.

6th state: after steelfacing of the plate.

Artist's proof on Rives wove paper, printed by Crommelynck, numbered "E.A. VIII/XV" and marked with a stamp reproducing Picasso's signature.

B.1835.

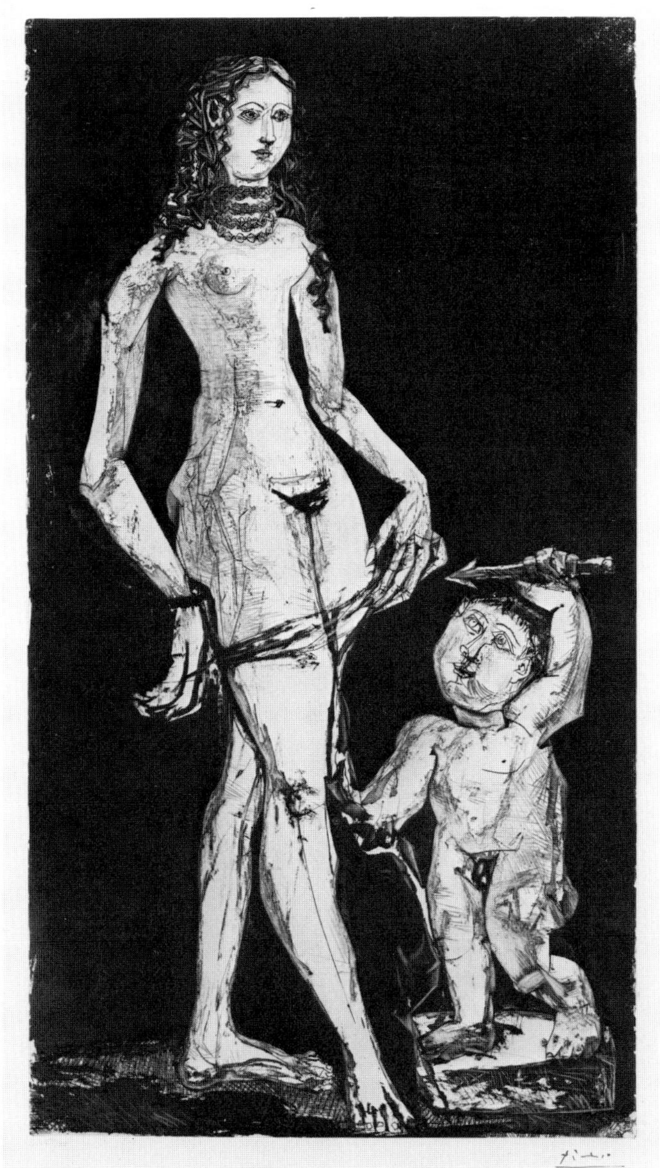

112.

The Galerie Louise Leiris edited this print at the same time they edited the group known as "the 156 prints," although there are only 155, a small copperplate having been somehow mislaid. The artist approved the *bon à tirer* proofs before he died. The edition was put on the print market in 1979. The usual artist's proofs are all numbered in roman numerals, with "E.A." meaning "artist's proof": *Epreuve d'Artiste*.

The copperplate is not inscribed on the back, as are most of the others; thus it is difficult to be more precise about the date. In 1949, Picasso made three lithographs of the same subject between May 25 and May 30. The quality of the print on exhibition is much finer than that of the lithograph. The 1st state is done only with aquatint. As the plate was so large, it would not fit in Lacourière's dusting-box and so was difficult to grain, and the background was not the uniform black surface that Picasso and Lacourière would have wished for. Picasso must have begun the plate around May 1949. It seems probable that he then thought of having it printed, since a small number of proofs were pulled. Then, maybe in the middle of the printing process, he decided to continue working on the plate. He took the trouble to blot out, with drypoint, all the white spots left in the aquatint of the background. Over and over again, Venus gets fatter, then thinner, fatter, then thinner. Her arm, on the left of the proof, swells, as if it had been stung by a squadron of wasps, then shrinks again. The artist could not capture the graceful posture he sought, the other arm was too close to the body, the hair was too long, etc. so Picasso worked and reworked the plate at Lacourière's. Frélaut printed and reprinted the trial proofs until the masterpiece was achieved. After the 1st state, Picasso never again used acid on the plate, only scraper, drypoint and burin.

The proofs before steelfacing, which were printed in Lacourière's workshop by Frélaut, have an unimpaired velvety quality, and the blackness of the background aquatint shows no trace of the drypoint patching. The whiteness of the two figures, especially Venus' slender body, truly glistens against this inky background.

113.
Corrida en Arles
Bullfight in Arles

1951 (May 17)

Aquatint (etching grained with aquatint) on copper

418 × 544 mm.

1st state of the black plate.

Proof on Montval laid paper.

B.1355.

The etching was made by the artist with a pocketknife on a special soft varnish called *vernis à la cire*; this kind of varnish melts when heated, making the graining process, done by Frélaut, extremely difficult to realize. A dozen proofs on different kinds of paper are known to exist.

114.
Corrida en Arles

1951 (May 28)

Aquatint with *réserves au vernis*

418 × 544 mm.

1st state of the yellow plate.

Unique proof on Montval laid paper, printed in black.

One can see the greyish outline of the transfer onto the new copperplate of a proof of the black. Frélaut admitted that he went a bit too far with the process.

115. (see color plate)
Corrida en Arles

See nos. 113 and 114.

Superimposition of the yellow plate, inked in brownish ochre, over the black plate.

1st state of both of the plates.

Unique proof on Montval laid paper, printed either in May 1951 or in June 1952.

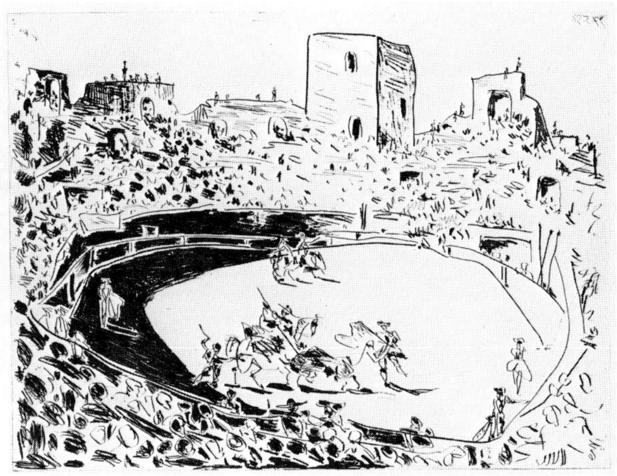

113.

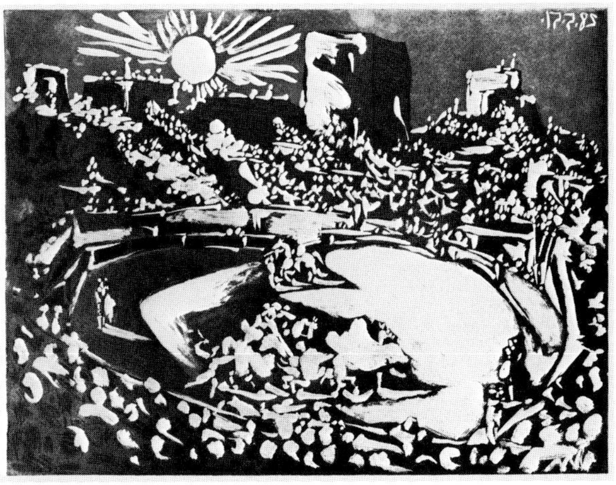

114.

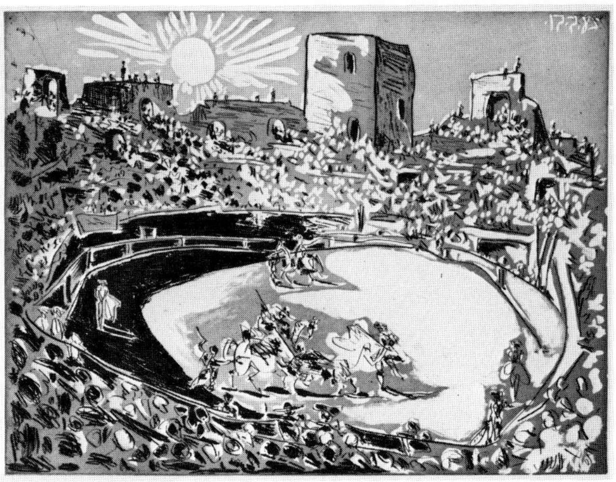

115.

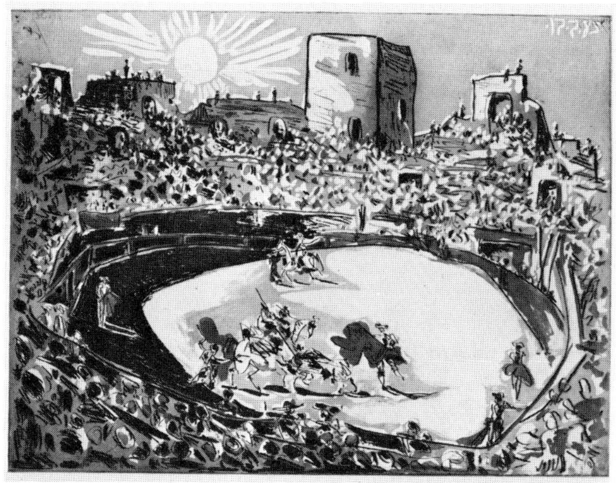

116.

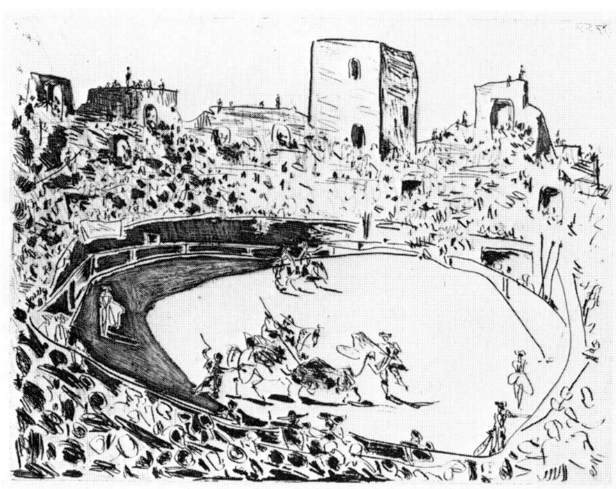

117.

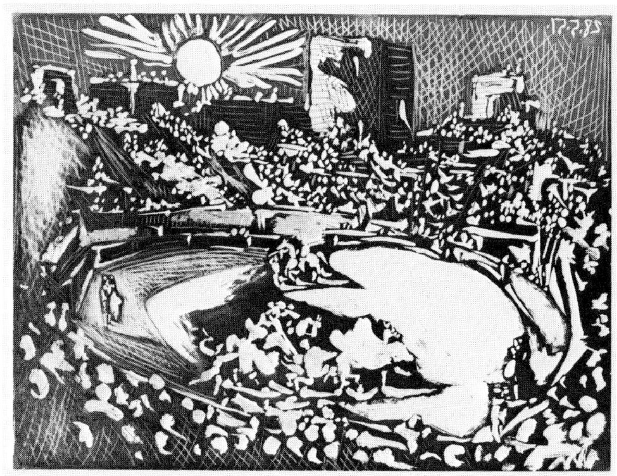

118.

116. (see color plate)
Corrida en Arles

1952 (June 28)

Aquatint, in three colors, on three copperplates

418 × 544 mm.

Superimposition of the yellow, the red and the black plates.

1st state of the yellow and of the black; unique state of the red.

Proof on wove paper without any watermark, probably Arches.

The red plate has been worked in sugar-lift aquatint. It is dated on the top left of the proof "28 juin 52." It is inked in red. The yellow plate has been inked with a dabber, or a brush, in two colors which are mixed together in some areas: blue, yellow and a mixture of both for a pale green in the sky.

Three proofs are known to exist, all with different inkings.

117.
Corrida en Arles

See no. 113.

2nd state of the black copperplate.

One of the two proofs on Arches wove paper.

The plate is worked on with the scraper.

118.
Corrida en Arles

See no. 114.

2nd state of the yellow copperplate.

Unique proof on Arches wove paper, printed in black.

Worked with the scraper, as well as with its sharp end (producing greyish drypoint-like strokes on some of the white areas of the proof: the tower, for instance).

119. (see color plate)
Corrida en Arles

Aquatint in three colors, on three copperplates

418 × 544 mm.

Superimposition of the yellow plate (2nd state), of the red plate (unique state) and of the black plate (2nd state).

Proof on Arches wove paper.

The red is inked in red; the black is inked in black. As for the yellow, it is inked with the dabber in blue and yellow. The sunny areas are in yellow.

120. (see color plate)
Corrida en Arles

See no. 119.

Same superimposition of the three colors: different inking.

Proof on wove paper without watermark, probably Arches.

The black plate is inked in dark purple. The red plate is inked with the dabber in red, blue (blue on the picador in the foreground and on the trousers of the man who holds the picador's horse in the background of the arena) and brown (*barrera* and details on the front row of the *barrera*). The yellow plate is inked in brown, in beige for the sunny areas, and in greenish blue in the sky.

Note that the inking with the dabber conveys the contrast between the *sol* and *sombra* in the *placa*. This difference is well known to *aficionados*: *sombra* seats are more expensive than the *sol y sombra* ones (sunny in the beginning of the corrida, then, as time passes, in the shade). The *sol* seats are the cheapest. *Corridas* always begin at five o'clock (*a las cinco de la tarde*). The red plate, only used to add color, was never printed without the others.

Concerning nos. 113-120: The above eight numbers all refer to a single aquatint made in three colors, using three different copperplates.

On May 17, 1951, Picasso executed the first state of the black plate (no. 113). On May 28th of the same year, using the technique of *réserves au vernis*, he made the aquatint which is the 1st state of the plate we shall call the yellow, although it was often inked with the dabber in other colors (no. 114, printed, as it is normally, in black). Either then, or just before resuming his work on these plates a year later, in June 1952, he had the two plates printed one over the other (no. 115). At that time, on June 28, 1952, he produced the third plate, the red, using sugar-lift aquatint which only colors the capes and clothing of the *torero* and his assistants, the outlines of the *barrera*, details in the *placa* and the heads of some of the spectators. He then had a few trial proofs printed of the superimposition of the three plates, some of them with dabber inking on the yellow plate (no. 116).

After that, he reworked the black plate (2nd state, no. 117) and the yellow plate (2nd state, no. 118, printed in black), only scraping the areas he wanted to be clear and adding, on the yellow plate, crisscross white scraper strokes in the sky, the tower and the crowd. After one or two trial proofs of the superimposition of the three plates (which were printed in the following order on the proofs: first, yellow, then red, and then black), Picasso put the plates aside in the Lacourière workshop. Later, the plates were steelfaced as this ensures the stability of the colored ink, preventing its oxidation due to chemical reactions with the copper. Frélaut, then, by himself, printed a dozen trial proofs, with dabber inking on the yellow plate (no. 119) and, eventually, even on the red plate (no. 120).

In spite of all the work undertaken in the Lacourière workshop, Picasso refused to sign any proof *bon à tirer* and Madeleine Lacourière had to be satisfied with only an affectionately annotated and dedicated proof which had been printed from the first state of the black plate. It is interesting to note the 1950s taste in the choice of the colors. The three copperplates still exist. The black and the yellow ones have had their steelfacings removed, surely in order to allow a possible reworking of them. The red plate is still steelfaced. All the proofs were pulled by Frélaut (Lacourière workshop).

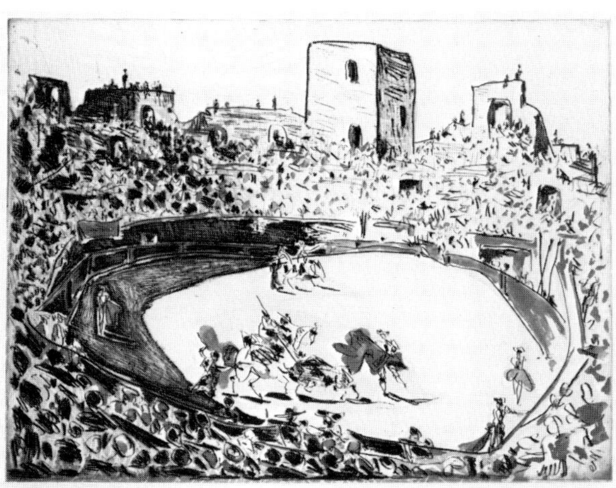

119.

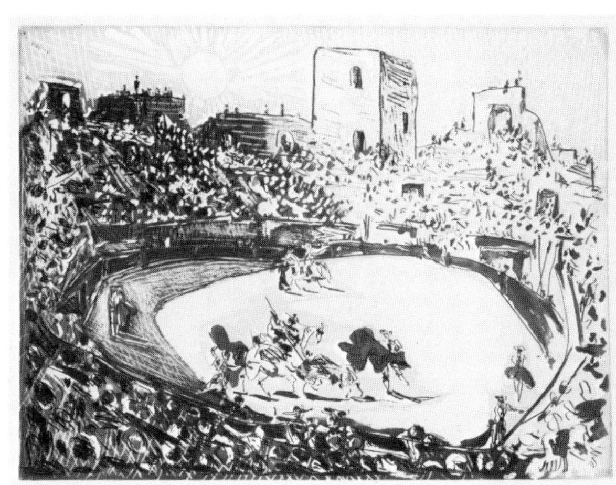

120.

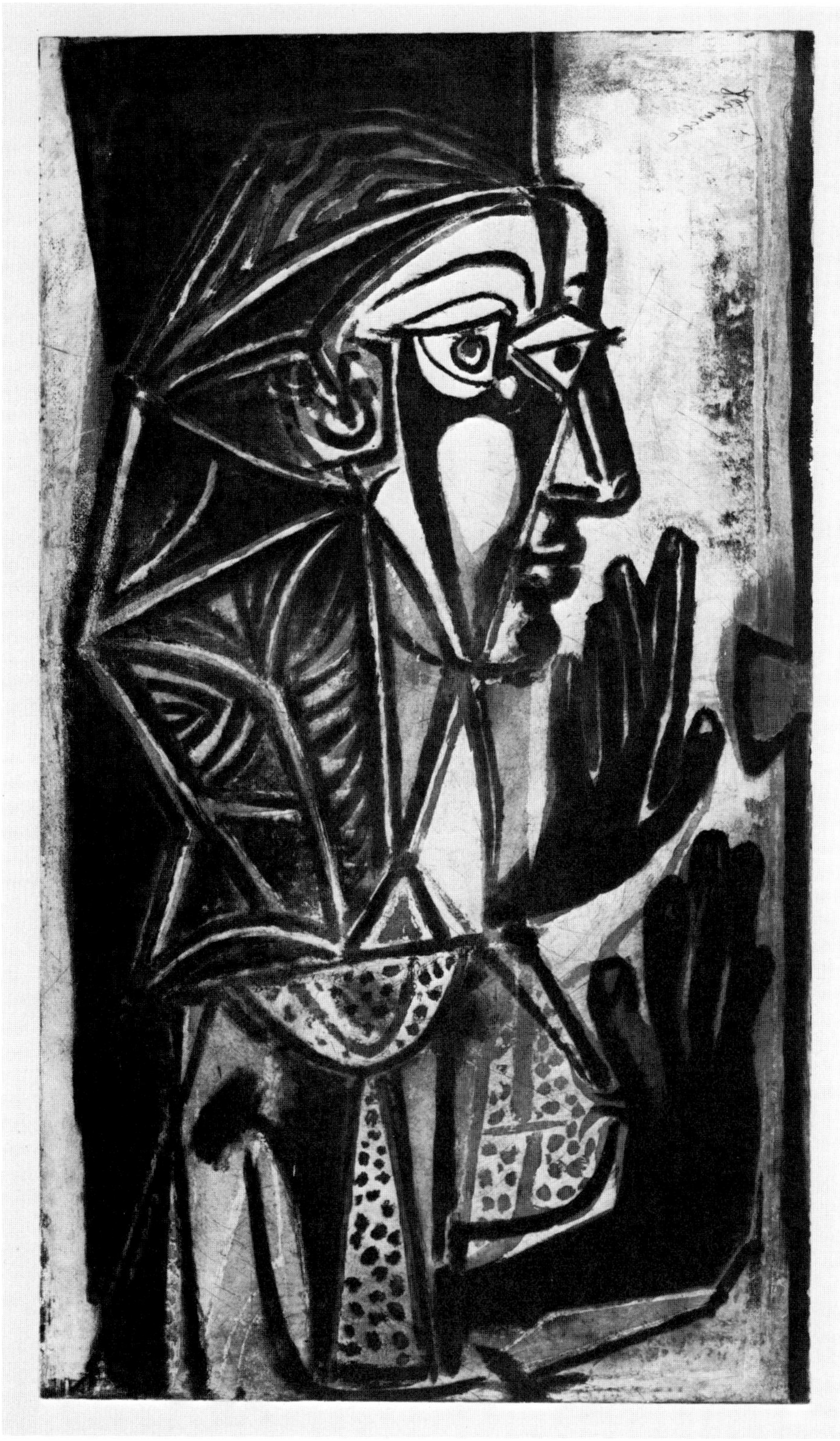

121.

121.

La Femme à la fenêtre

Woman Looking Out of a Window: Portrait of Françoise

1952 (May 17)

Sugar-lift aquatint on copper

836 × 475 mm.

2nd state: proof on Arches wove paper printed before steelfacing.

The copperplate (on exhibition) was cancelled in 1979.

B.695.

We know the exact date because the unique proof of the 1st state now in the Musée Picasso, Paris (MP 2990) is annotated on the top right ''17 mai 52.''

On the upper right corner of the proof can be read, in reverse (drypoint), ''Lacourière.'' The mark was made by the copperplate maker and it only means the copperplate was to be sent to Lacourière. Picasso made his aquatint on the verso of an engraved and steelfaced copperplate, which he found in the workshop. The writer of this catalogue does not know who etched the recto. After the printing of five or six trial proofs, the copperplate was steelfaced, printed on Arches wove paper and published by the Galerie Louise Leiris: edition of 50, signed and numbered, plus ten or 12 signed artist's proofs.

The first state was etched in large-grain aquatint, then the artist added a new layer of darker (thin-grain) aquatint in order to enhance certain details: hands, hair, windowknob, etc. The dark areas in the background changed slightly: in the 1st state you could almost read the date engraved on the upper right corner of the proof; then the shape of the shadow, or of the curtain, was modified and the date was covered with aquatint. The proofs printed before steelfacing, like the one in the exhibiton, show a softer, deeper texture in the aquatint. After steelfacing, the result is somewhat drier perhaps because the plate was easier to wipe clean. All the proofs and impressions were pulled by Lacourière.

122a&b.
La Chèvre
The She-Goat

1952 (June 16)

Sugar-lift aquatint and scraper on copper

94 × 124 mm.

a. 1st state: sugar-lift aquatint, and scraper in the varnish, before the graining and biting of the plate.

Unique proof, on Arches wove paper, annotated bottom left "Seule épreuve du 1er ETAT 16 juin 1952."

b. 2nd state: scraper, used conventionally to make some areas clearer, but equally handled like a drypoint.

One of the two proofs, on Arches wove paper, annotated bottom left "Une des deux premières épreuves du 2e ETAT 16 juin 1952."

A third proof, before steelfacing, exists on wove paper without watermark.

After steelfacing and bevelling, the plate was pulled and given to André Verdet, as a frontispiece for the limited edition of his book, *La Chèvre*, Paris, 1952: edition of 50 on wove paper signed and numbered 1/50 to 50/50: B.697; Bloch, Livre, 61; Matarasso, 62. All the proofs and impressions were pulled by Lacourière.

This small print is an example of the artist's effortless mastery. Moreover, it is, two years later, a portrait of his large sculpture dated 1950 (Spies, 409).

123.
Paloma et sa poupée, fond noir
Paloma with her Doll

1952 (December 14)

Lithograph on zinc: lithographic crayon

705 × 550 mm.

Artist's proof on Arches wove paper, signed.

The zincplate is on exhibition.

M.229; B. 727.

Apart from the six proofs in the Mourlot boxes, there are four trial proofs with small margins.

The plate was pulled and published by the Galerie Louise Leiris: edition of 50, signed and numbered, plus a dozen signed artist's proofs.

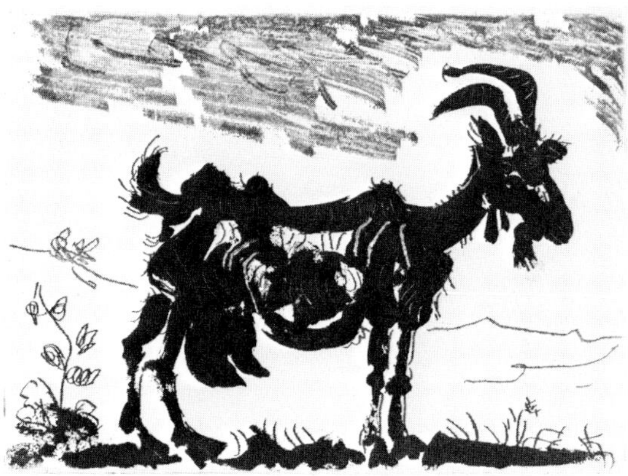

122a.

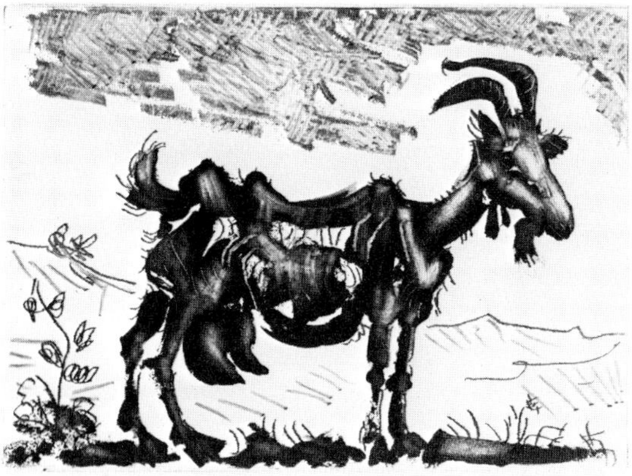

122b.

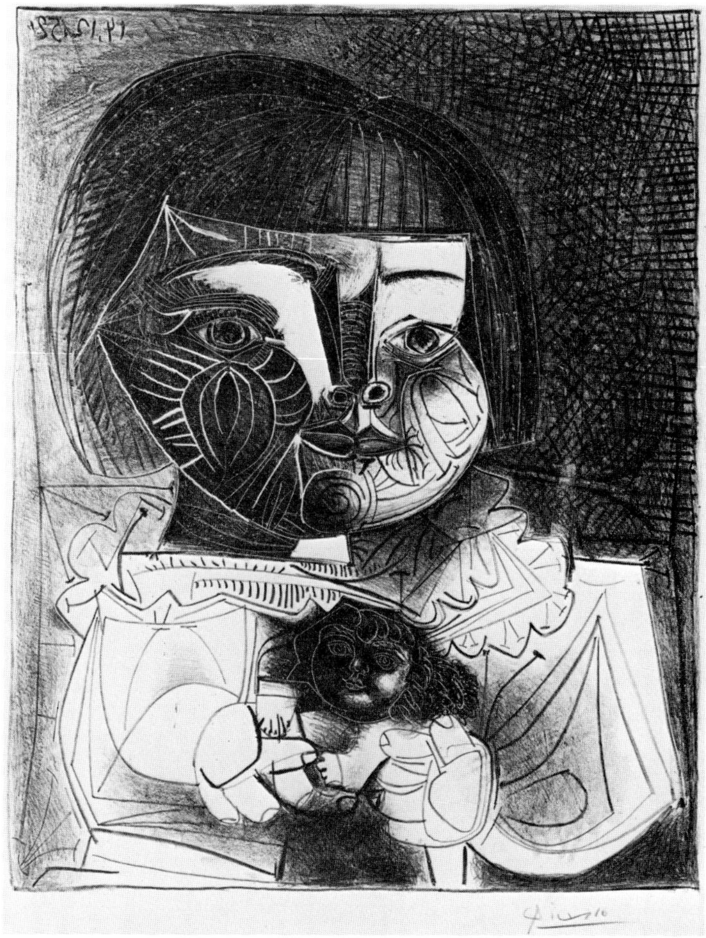

123.

124.
Tête sur fond noir
Woman's Head on a Black Background

1953 (May 9, Paris)

Lithograph on zinc

695 × 545 mm.

Trial proof on Arches wove paper.

M.241.

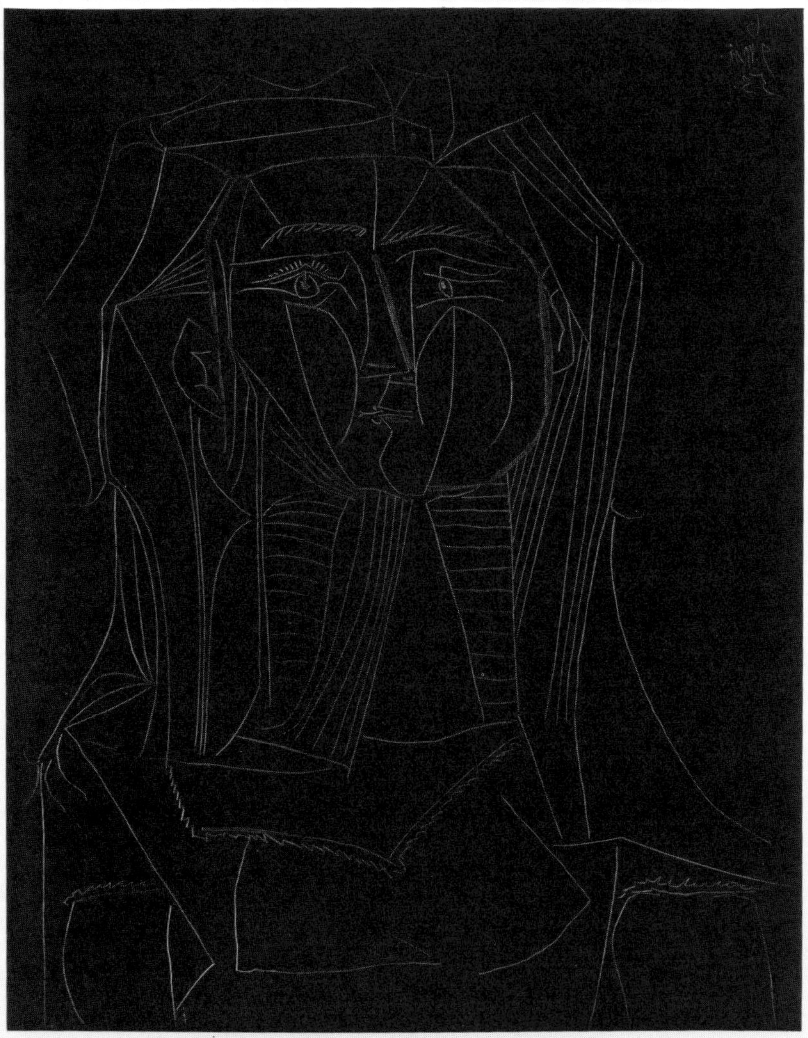

124.

Apart from the six proofs in the Mourlot boxes, there are four more trial proofs. The plate was printed and published by the Galerie Louise Leiris: edition of 50, signed and numbered, plus a dozen artist's proofs.

It should be noted that in this print Picasso first engraved a zincplate with a burin. He wanted to print it in intaglio. The surface of the plate was rough and textured and the results were not what he wanted. The background, instead of being whitish, came out grey and muddy. No proof printed in real intaglio is known to exist. Then he decided to pull the plate on the lithography press. Usually, and it seems to be the case here, an intaglio zincplate cannot be used as is, in the lithographic printing process. The image has to be transferred onto a lithographic zinc. A freshly printed proof is used in the transferring process.

Frélaut remembers that once a workman from Mourlot's workshop came to the Rue Foyatier, then rushed back to the other end of Paris with a fresh and still wet proof of an intaglio print in order to be able to transfer it onto a lithographic zinc. In our case, it was the zincplate which was carried to the Mourlot workshop.

A few proofs were printed in semi-intaglio, i.e. with the lithographic press. One of them, which seems to have been lost, but which had been photographed, was pulled in positive (black lines on light ground): it shows a very unclean background and is hardly legible. We can assume that it was pulled on the lithographic press because it shows the marks of the rough *carte de Lyon* used in the lithographic printing process, while in the intaglio printing a soft, felt-like cloth, called *les langes*, was used. A few more proofs must have been printed in negative (white lines on dark ground) in order to transfer one of them onto the lithographic zinc. The original intaglio zinc was either lost or destroyed.

Note the Egyptian hair style that Françoise has. Picasso reworked that idea in the *Torse de femme*, executed on the 11th of May three days later, and which, as we mentioned before, was called *L'Egyptienne* in Lacourière's workshop.

XI.
Jacqueline

Picasso met Jacqueline Roque at Perpignan during the summer of 1953. We can see her, young and beautiful, with her short hair and classical profile in a drawing from the 21st of January, 1954 (Z.XVI.203), where she appears between a musketeer and a monkey in a cameo profile. The fine oil portrait entitled *Jacqueline aux fleurs* (Z.XVI.325) dates from June 2, 1954. However, it was only in autumn of that year that Picasso and Jacqueline began to live together. Just as with Marie-Thérèse, the other great love in Picasso's life, so Jacqueline quickly became present in all the artist's work. Like Marie-Thérèse, Jacqueline, little by little, began to haunt the artist's hand whether he drew, painted, cut sheet metal, modeled clay or decorated pottery. And she became ever present in his prints.

Very rapidly one becomes familiar with her appearance, with the short hair she wore at the time, in the versions of the intaglio prints of the *Femmes d'Alger* after Delacroix (a blend from memory of the two versions, one in the Louvre, the other in the Musée Fabre at Montpellier). Between January 2nd and 31st, 1955, Picasso worked on this composition with nine different copperplates, using the whole gamut of possible techniques and once even reworking a plate in five states (B.1357-60, plus five additional). One of these was transferred onto a zincplate and Mourlot printed a few trial proofs (M.265). Then Picasso tried to ''extrude'' his subject out of a lithographic stone which he literally carved into through four states (M.226; 5th of February). Then, on the 21st of January, there follows a drypoint ''classical'' portrait of Jacqueline (unpublished), this followed on the 19th of March by a superb bust portrait in profile, where the artist attempted an extremely difficult technique: direct biting with the brush onto a copperplate which had been grained with resin (B.771).

Simultaneously, between the 9th and 11th of March, Picasso began a series of five large plates, four zincs and one copper, depicting scenes in a brothel, no doubt inspired by one of those Spanish picaresque novels which he liked so much. He had in his possession several versions of the *Diablo Cojuelo* (*The Limping Devil*) by Luis Velez de Guevara (1641) as well as a copy of the French adaptation by Le Sage (1707), entitled *Le Diable boiteux*. The latter, aided by an aura of scandal, became more famous than the original. In two of these prints (cat. nos. 125-129), an ancient female go-between, who already presages the reappearance of *La Célestine* and who carries on a tray the ritual cup and chocolate pot of the morning in Spain, puts herself between the two lovers. We shall have the occasion of saying more about *La Célestine* below. Here, it suffices to remind ourselves that the work of the same title by Fernando de Rojas is a monument in the history of Spanish literature (the definitive text is dated 1502) and that Picasso had already depicted the heroine of the novel under the guise of one of those proper ladies whom one used to pass in the streets of Barcelona, severe and dignified with her veiled eye, in his famous painting of 1903 (Z.1.183). In that work, Picasso shows us Célestine as a virtuous old lady who has suffered in her life and has kept all her dignity, but who ''works'' as a marriagebroker, a profession or ingrained custom still very widespread in Spain at his time and afterwards. Underneath this virtue and dignity, the artist sees the go-between in the pejorative sense of the word. The old woman who glides behind the lovers in our series of prints has nothing in common with the Célestine of 1903. It is clear that she is an old procuress or at best, the scheming *dueña*, old Marcella from the *Diable Cojuelo*, or possibly one of those harpies who play such an important role in the *Exemplary Novels* of Cervantes, for example. In the print of March 11 (nos. 127-129), one cannot fail to recognize in the young woman the clear and tidy profile of Jacqueline.

With the powerful emergence of Jacqueline as a source of inspiration in Picasso's art, we should focus briefly on the mechanisms, both understandable and somewhat disturbing, of repetitions and replicas in the themes dealing with his lovers. His works begin to repeat stories which had already been told with different actors. They are told in different ways perhaps, but with the same basic *mise-en-scenes*. We have seen, for example, how the theme of the artist and his model seemed to obsess Picasso from the outset of his passion for Marie-Thérèse and later in the *Suite Vollard*. If one can accept the idea that the theme of the *Déjeuner sur l'herbe*, after Manet, is linked to the idea of the artist and his model, we shall find the latter theme again recurring from 1963 to 1966 in an entire series of more than 100 prints. It would continue to be present later, sometimes with a much more direct allusion to the problem of creativity, as in B.1668 or B.1913, where the aritst paints directly on the model's body, caressing her as it were with his brush.

We have seen how the theme of abduction and rape was repeated over and over again in the prints of 1933-34. Once more we find numerous rapes or embraces (B.1110-1117, for example), as well as all the abduction scenes from the story of Calixtus and Melibea (*La Célestine*; *Suite 347*).

The *Chef-d'oeuvre inconnu* appears again (B.1824), as does Ingres with the series *Raphael et la Fornarina* (e.g. B.1776-1799), where Picasso brings together two of Ingres' subjects, *Raphael and the Fornarina* (1813) with *Paolo and Francesca*. Here, the motif of the ''voyeur'' already latent in 1934 (cat. nos. 38-41) also appears, but now much more openly treated and more frequent.

We have seen how Marie-Thérèse took many guises, how a complete mythology was created around her and her relationship with the artist, and how she entered into classical mythology with the story of the Minotaur. In the same way, Jacqueline becomes omnipresent in

Picasso's graphic work. There is hardly a single print in which she does not appear, her presence being felt even in the mythologies and narratives, whether it involves circus scenes (see e.g. cat. nos. 186-189), or harem scenes inspired by Ingres (see B.1769, 1770 or 1918), or the subjects of Raphael and the Fornarina or Paolo and Francesca. Jacqueline is ''implicated'' in the reminiscences of Rembrandt (e.g. cat. nos. 194-198), of Velasquez (e.g. B.1920), of Goya (cat. no. 193), of Delacroix and Manet (B.1884), and in an entire group of prints connected with Guy de Maupassant's *La Maison Tellier* (1881) and Degas' monotypes on the same subject (e.g. cat. nos. 202 and 203). We are also going to find her in a more obscure mythology when we come to the series *156 gravures*. As was Marie-Thérèse, so Jacqueline is transformed and becomes a ''creation'' of the artist, always different yet always the same. In order to flesh out the parallel we dare to draw here, it is interesting to compare our cat. no. 37 with B. 1613, where once again three heads of bearded men, under the watchful eye of the painter ''dream,'' this time in a more concrete fashion, of ''the woman'' who has Jacqueline's features.

Picasso's new love, which again brings up the problem of love/model, muse/mistress and mirror images, clearly reactivated many of his old preoccupations. These are expressed by analogous themes, even if the techniques have changed, even if the old mythologies have been replaced by new subjects and new attitudes. For if Marie-Thérèse was 17 years old when Picasso first met her, and if he often called her ''ma fille,'' Jacqueline was only 27 when they met and Picasso himself was more than 70 years old.

On February 11, 1955, Olga died at Cannes. After a summer largely consumed by Clouzot's film, *Le Mystère Picasso*, Picasso and Jacqueline took up residence in a marvelous baroque house situated on one of the hills overlooking Cannes, La Californie. For all intents and purposes, they abandoned Paris completely. In 1958, the artist bought the Château de Vauvenargues, which was his passion for a year or 18 months, but he did not move out of La Californie. On March 2, 1963, Picasso and Jacqueline got married at Vallauris. In June, after the construction of an enormous building which not only blocked their view of the sea but also dominated the superb garden, Picasso and Jacqueline left Cannes and moved into a traditional Provencal farm house, Notre-Dame de Vie, at Mougins.

In the execution of his prints, Picasso was no longer interested in pulling his own trial proofs. Fort's printing press was installed at La Californie, but no craftsmen were present to help. Mourlot and Frélaut therefore had to travel back and forth between Paris and the South of France.

Continuing his work in lithography, Picasso made a large number of works on transfer-paper, which were easy to transport, and then between December 1957 and December 1958, six wonderful portraits of Jacqueline executed directly on zincplates (M.306-311; see cat. nos. 134-136). We have to wait then until 1960 for the artist to return again to this medium with a series of large zincplates (wash and lithographic crayon) which will be his last true lithographs (M.389-397). They were never published and the zincplates have apparently disappeared (see cat. no. 178).

While lithography and later linocuts were simply fleeting passions in Picasso's life, intaglio printing was his constant love. He seized the opportunity granted by Frélaut's trips to the south of France to make, first in September 1955, a series of bacchanalias, published in the *Caisse à remords* (B.772-777), then in 1957 the series of sugar-lift aquatints for the *La Tauromaquia*, which were published by Gustau Gili in Barcelona in 1959 and which are works of brilliance and brio. Again profiting from Frélaut's presence, he executed a group of playful small aquatints, *The Story of Sabartés and the Woman Next Door*, where the theme of bull-fighting is coupled with ''amorous'' sports.

In 1960, while Frélaut was unpacking the copperplates which had arrived from Paris and was printing trial proofs, Picasso made a group of eight etchings, seven of which would have to wait for publication until after the artist's death (B.979-985). Between March 24 and April 11, Frélaut was again at La Californie and Picasso was involved in a series of 15 prints depicting fauns, centaurs and portraits of Jacqueline in her wedding hat and veil, none of which were published. In practically all of them, he employed aquatint, sometimes sugar-lift, other times by biting directly by hand the plate grained with resin. Then he began scraping away, bit by bit, nearly all the aquatint as he reworked the plate with the burin. Frélaut recounts how in the evening Picasso would show him a pile of copper shavings on the floor and would say, ''You see, I've worked well today.'' One of the plates depicting a centaur, a faun and a small man with a stick, was pushed through 14 successive states. The portrait of *Jacqueline en mariée*, presenting a fascinating history of metamorphosis, was ''ploughed over'' through a total of 18 states (cat. nos. 144-161). Because of the hospitalization of his wife Cécile, Frélaut was suddenly compelled to return to Paris, and the proofs of this print were left in the process of drying-out between the blotters. It was there that they were found after the artist's death. The Lacourière-Frélaut workshop would continue to print editions for Picasso, but the day-to-day collaboration with Frélaut was over.

In the meantime, Picasso went on making prints: small celluloids were done for P.A. Benoit, writer, typographer, intaglio-printer and publisher. It is relatively easy to engrave on celluloid, and Benoit, who had only a small lithographic press at his disposal and was not a professional printer, could pull these more easily.

Picasso also continued executing works in drypoint and burin for Iliazd. This important publisher, whose knowledge of literature was enormous, was constantly researching and tracking down historical documents which he translated after establishing the original texts. His publications were highly personal efforts and are outstanding in their class. In 1938, Picasso had illustrated *Afat* for him, and from then on their work together was never interrupted.

Iliazd (his full name was Ilia Zdanevitch) was not satisfied, like other people, with the ''gift'' of an illustration picked out at random by Picasso. His layouts were very elaborate and necessitated prints of a certain size, which could only fit into the decoration of the page in one way. He used to send his own plates to Picasso, wrapped up in red paper with yellow stripes, the national colors of Catalonia, to remind him that he had to work on these plates for Iliazd and no one else. At the beginning of 1955, Picasso made ten horses for the *Chevaux de minuit* and went on to complete the series with the cover (autumn 1955) and two *hors-textes* executed with the burin (beginning of 1956).

In the first months of 1958, Picasso threw himself into the illustrations for *Le Frère mendiant*, a text which Iliazd had found and which relates the journey to Africa of a Spanish Franciscan monk of the XIVth century. Iliazd had spent a long time in researching not only the actual route of the monk but also the correct nomenclature of the places he visited. For example, in the Biblioteca Nacional in Madrid, he secured photocopies of ancient manuscripts containing, in addition to a verbal description, illuminated texts showing the banners of each tribe or phratry. He gave these to Picasso to ensure that the banners engraved by the artist reproduced those of the illuminations faithfully. He had sent from Nigeria documentary photographs, among them one of two *Ife* terracotta heads, so that the artist could have as accurate a guideline as possible when he depicted the morphology of the various tribes who figured in the story. Picasso bowed to the demands of Iliazd as we can see in cat. no. 137 and the accompanying photograph.

Another medium which came into play at this time is the linocut. After Picasso had made his first linocut in 1939 (*Pour la Tchécoslovaquie. Hommage à un pays martyr*, B. 325), he did not use the technique again until 1952, when he produced the poster of *La Chèvre* for an exhibition at Vallauris (B.1257). The *Young Pigeon* which is normally dated 1939 (B.326) was made in fact in 1954 or 1955.

The printer Arnéra was close at hand in Vallauris with his workshop and printing presses, and Picasso, as was not unusual, attacked the technique of linocutting with habitual vigour and inventiveness until he exhausted both its possibilities and his enjoyment of it. Why, indeed, simply use it to make posters? There were certainly other possibilities to be explored. Picasso's beginnings in the technique were traditional, but he soon used it with a brio that only total control of his materials would permit.

Linocuts should be classified with relief prints and compared to woodcuts. As Riva Castleman so clearly put it in her catalogue *Prints from Blocks. Gauguin to Now* (New York, 1983), "The specific technique of block printing is based upon cutting into a flat-surfaced rigid material, covering the uncut surface with ink, and printing from that surface." Linoleum is a type of floorcovering made from canvas coated with a thick layer of oxidized linseed oil. The sort of linoleum used for linocuts is a bit harder and thicker than the normal floor-covering, but it is still relatively supple and has to be fixed firmly to a wooden panel for the printing process to be carried out. At the beginning, the plaques of linoleum that Picasso cut were nailed on a wooden panel, at least as far as the trial proofs are concerned (see the marks of the nails in cat. nos. 138-140); later, the panels came ready-made with the linoleum already fixed to them.

On December 28, 1955, Picasso began to make linocuts which were not destined to be posters. He had previously executed a small one circa 1953-1954 for the plaquette *U.A.P.54* (B.1839), but his first real linocut is our cat. no. 130, a portrait of Jacqueline. He took a proof of this print and on December 30-31, 1955, worked it up with *encre de Chine* into a very fine drawing (Z.XVI.525).

Later, in 1956, he attempted linocuts in two colors with two blocks, printed one over the other (cat. nos. 131-133). In 1958, he went further and tried to make linocuts in five colors, on five blocks, and from July 4 onwards, produced the *Buste de femme, d'après Cranach le jeune* (B.859). Then in December, he made another trial with a "seated Jacqueline" which finally he set aside out of impatience. The colors would react with one another, blue and yellow giving an unexpected green, blue and red turning into a strange kind of purple. Colors not yet dry would fuse together and the end result was a muddy coagulate. Moreover, he was bored with the necessity of employing registration marks, used to print one block over another accurately, as well as with the traditional process of transfer necessary to work on a new block in order to get another color. He had to find another solution.

It was at this moment that he invented a trick which he would elaborate and eventually exhaust. It must have been known previously that colors in the linocut printing process look much better when printed over a layer of very clear ink. An uncut block, inked in cream-white or beige, would first be printed on about 80 sheets of paper, thus preparing the sheets for further printing. Then the artist would cut away with a knife or a gouge the areas of the surface which were to remain clear; this is the first ''drawing'' and the 1st state. The block is then inked, generally in a darker color, and the 80 or so sheets are printed. Next, Picasso would resume work on the same block and cut away the parts of the surface which were to remain. After another inking, the proofs would be pulled again, although the original number would be reduced by now as a result of errors, trials, etc. This constitutes the third color and the 2nd state of the block.

For his first attempt with this technique, Picasso made a small group of linocuts (uniform beige background, chocolate brown and black) on the theme of the *corrida* (B.941-946, August 23-24, 1959). Then on the 26th of the same month, he undertook a large block, and it is in B.940 that he ''combined'' the technique of normal states (see cat. nos. 138-141). As the visitor can see from the exhibited linoblock, only the black areas remain untouched or, in our case, only lightly scraped. The remainder of the surface has been cut away.

Naturally this rather simple if very cunning solution could not satisfy Picasso. He had invented a new way to do linocuts, and he was determined to squeeze everything he could out of his discovery. Another new idea came to him, inspired by the woodcuts of Eduard Munch. Munch would cut his blocks into several segments to allow printing in different colors. As we have seen, at this point Picasso did not need this process, but what if, for example, he wanted a clear (white and blue) sky associated with a dark landscape (brown and green)? For the Bacchanalia dating from November 1959 (B.931, 934, 935), he worked with two linoblocks: one was cut away roughly under the skyline and corresponds to the top half of the composition; the other was cut away above the skyline and corresponds to the landscape. He worked on each of them using exactly the technique described above, and then printed the parts contingently. Sometimes there are two blocks for the sky, one giving only the white color over which the blue looks better, and at other times, there would be two versions of the landscape (one eventually being abandoned) as in B. 930. There were even occasions (B.934 and 935) when the artist added further small linocuts prior to printing the black in order to obtain a different brown on the flute-playing fauns or to superimpose the blue over the green on the lakes. Moreover, in B.934 an additional third linoblock gives a different caramel tone to the goat. Picasso could not leave these small blocks alone and would cut them into further small unpublished linocuts as a hobby.

In the *Déjeuner sur l'herbe* of 1962 (B.1027) he used six colors, leaving practically nothing of the cut-away block. In the case of B.1149 (1963), he decided to rework the linoblock of B.1076 and to produce a linocut in seven colors, that is, without the brown frame made on another linoblock which would be used also for B.1145-1148.

As for the *Nature morte à la pastèque* (cat. nos. 170-176) Picasso used two linoblocks and seven colors plus another linoblock (and color) for the grey frame, in ten states. He also had the idea of printing the linocut on a caramel background, but without giving up his intention of obtaining a white outline. Hence, he would use a second block only for the outline (see cat. nos. 164-169).

He experimented further by trying the superimposition of three or four different ''states,'' all printed in white, thus producing a tonal scale of grey, whitish grey, pure white, etc. (cf. B.1148 and 1147).

In 1963, having squeezed dry the technique of linocuts out of which he derived no further pleasure (the beautiful portrait of *Jacqueline with a Book*, B.1181, should be dated February 2, 1962), he buried as it were the whole process with a multi-layered joke which poses a riddle for the interested observer. This is seen in the linocut known as *The Old Clown*. Here he managed to add, one on top of the other, the remnants of three linocuts which had already been printed and published, after slight reworking. He not only printed underneath these a new linocut in brown, dated 18.1.63, but also added over them a further new linocut printed in black, dated 14-26.1.63. Over the bottom, brown linoblock, he added the remnants of B.1104 in pink, then the remnants of B.1106 in yellow and on top of this, the remnants of B.1107 in blue. Over all these colors, the new linocut printed in black provided for this heap of ''found objects'' a background and a few other features. Nevertheless, there is a problem: on the left, the pink eye cannot possibly come from the block of B.1104, and, on the right, there is the same problem with the blue eye. Perhaps two more blocks were completely cut away in order to add a small dot of pink (one eye) and a small dot of blue (the other eye). Inking with the dabber cannot be used in linocuts, and there is no other solution which could explain thse two anomalies. On the linoblocks B.1104 (pink) and B.1107 (blue) which still exist, there are no traces of the two little eyes, and, furthermore, there is no way little pieces of linoleum could have been stuck onto what remains of the cut away blocks. We must therefore assume that the artist used seven linoblocks, printed one on top of the other, as an ironic farewell to the medium. The unknown author of the title of this print was not too far from the mark.

The following year, Picasso made a few more linocuts as a sort of hobby, and when he did so, usually employed the traditional technique of simply cutting out his ''drawing'' from a single linoblock. And in 1963-64, having invented a new trick, he returned briefly to the medium, producing the so-called *épreuves rincées* (rinsed proofs). He had old or new linoblocks printed usually with a creamy white color. Then, on those areas where the paper was still untouched, he painted over them sketchily with a brush and *encre de Chine*. Then he and Jacqueline would rinse them under the shower. The printed areas (linocut ink provides a thick, uniform waterproof covering) were thus washed clean of the *encre de Chine*, and only the untouched absorbent paper retained the ink which took on a greyish color. In this way he obtained a type of negative proof of his linocuts. There were occasions when he added different colored inks, gold, watercolor, etc. Of course, the blocks which had been totally cut away, such as the *Déjeuner sur l'herbe* (B.1027), could not be treated in this way. In order ''to play this new game,'' he had a few proofs of some very early linocuts printed (see cat. nos. 132 and 136), or, on other occasions (cat. nos. 179 and 180), he would ''rinse'' proofs of linocuts which had never been intended to undergo this treatment and which had been printed in milk-chocolate (cat. no. 180) or in chocolate colors (cat. no. 179).

125.
Maison close: le matin
Brothel-Scene: Morning

1955 (March 9)

Sugar-lift aquatint, burin and scraper on zinc

495 x 645 mm.

1st state: sugar-lift aquatint and burin. Plate is annotated on back ''II.''

One of six proofs on Arches wove paper.

126.
Maison close: le matin

See no. 125.

2nd and last state: scraper.

One of six proofs on Arches wove paper.

The plate exists. The print was never published.

The burin engraving on the face of the old procuress was made in the 1st state. In the 2nd state, the artist only scraped it.

127.
Maison close: le client
Brothel-Scene: The Client

1955 (March 11)

Sugar-lift aquatint, with hand-biting, etching, scraper, burin and drypoint on zinc

448 x 645 mm.

1st state: sugar-lift aquatint with hand-biting, etching and burin. Plate is annotated on back ''I.''

One of six proofs on Arches wove paper.

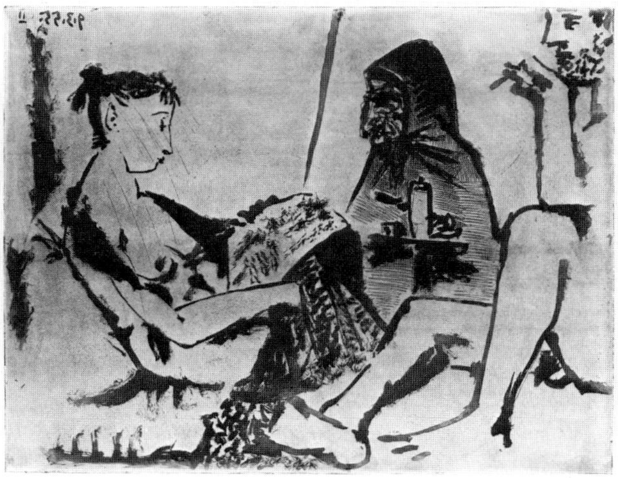

125.

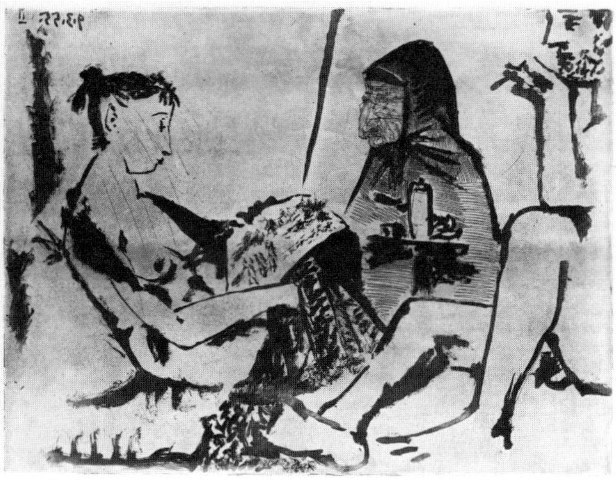

126.

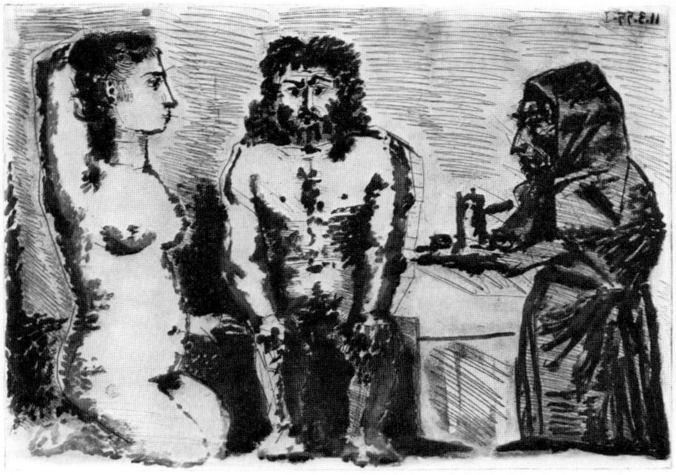

127.

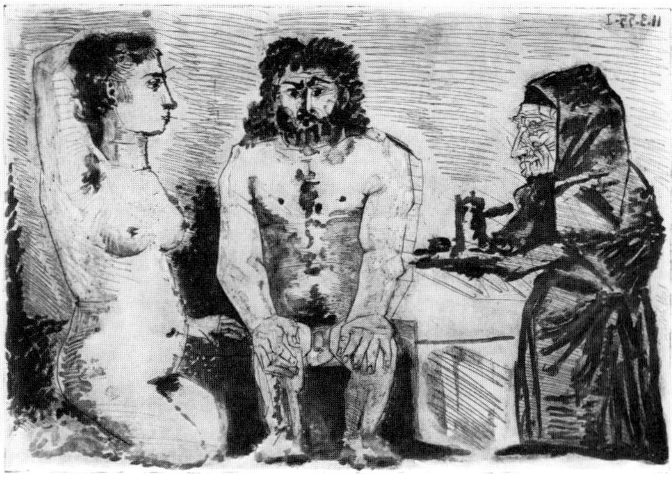

128.

128.
Maison close: le client

See no. 127.

2nd state: scraper.

One of six proofs on Arches wove paper.

129.
Maison close: le client

See no. 127.

3rd and last state: drypoint, burin and scraper.

One of five proofs on Arches wove paper.

The plate exists. The print was never published.

In the 2nd state, the face of the old woman is scraped clear, exactly as in no. 126. Same process on, for instance, the hand of the man, etc. In the 3rd state, new drypoint strokes in the background, and the old witch's clothes; scraper on the young woman who looks like Jacqueline; burin on the packing-box on which the man is seated. All proofs of nos. 125-129 were pulled by Lacourière.

In Spain, especially in the morning but all through the day, people used to drink very thick chocolate in small cups. The old "go-between" is obviously part of the household, a kind of *dueña*.

130.
Portrait de Jacqueline au foulard
Portrait of Jacqueline with a Scarf

1955 (December 28)

Linocut

549 x 511 mm.

Proof on ordinary thick wove paper.

Eight proofs exist, printed on different papers; one on Arches wove was reworked into a drawing. There are also three pencil-rubbings of the linoleum. The proofs were printed in black by Arnéra. The linoleum still exists.

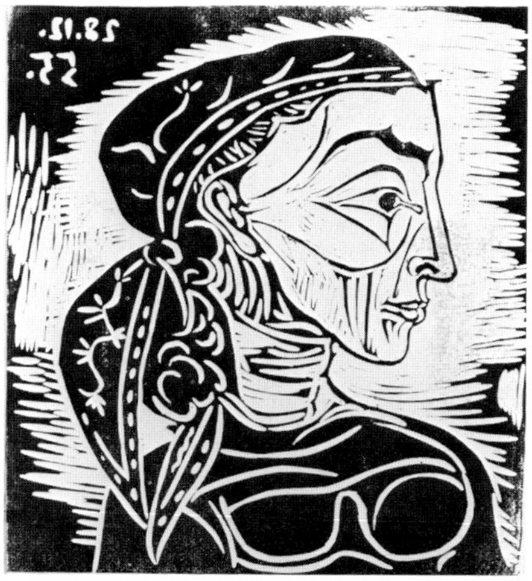

130.

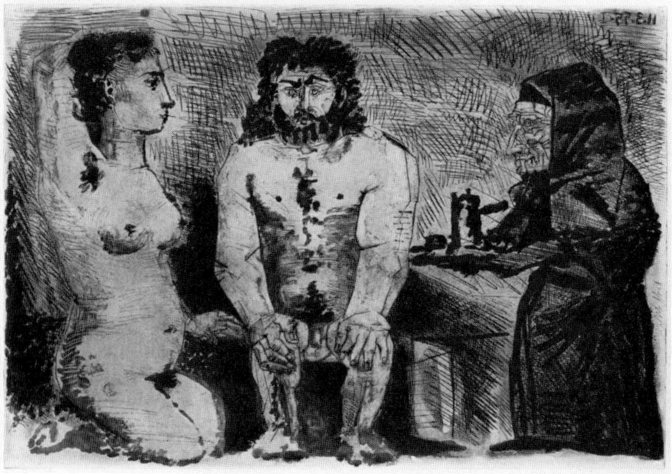

129.

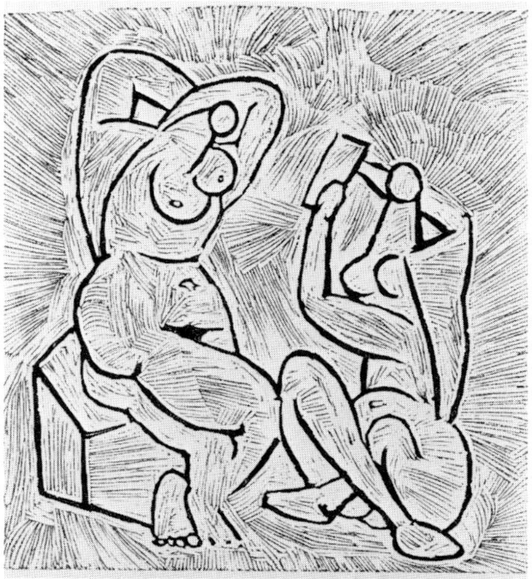

131.

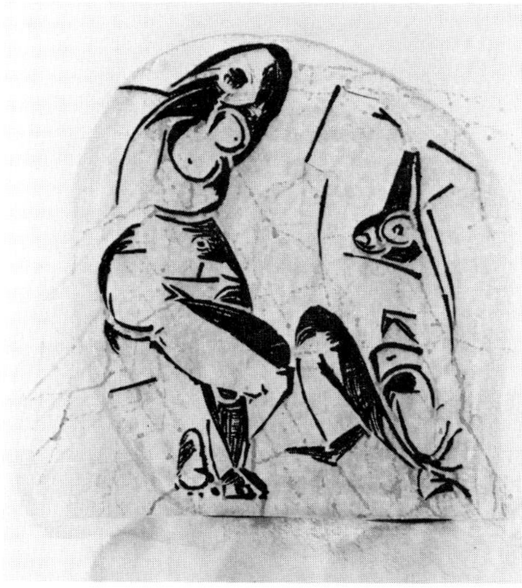

132.

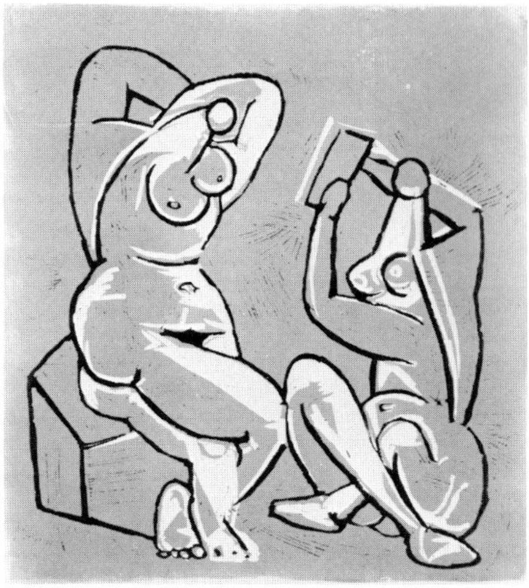

133.

131.
Femmes à leur toilette
Two Women with a Mirror

1956

Linocut in two colors, on two linoblocks

The Black: 551 x 517 mm.

The Brown: 542 x 499 mm.

Superimposition: first, the Brown, then the Black.

The Black: unique state.

Proof on Arches wove paper, pulled in intaglio on wet paper (probably letterpress with heavy pressure); hence, the plate mark and embossing of the paper. Three proofs, printed in brown in the usual linocut technique, exist.

This unique proof is interesting, as it shows all the details of the gouge-cutting of the surface; on the linoblock, the only remnants of the surface are the lines here printed in black. If the linoblock had been printed in the normal way, we would not have been able to see the details of the gouge strokes, which would not have been in contact with the paper. At least one ''rinsed'' and signed proof is in existence.

132.
Femmes à leur toilette

See no. 131.

The Brown: unique state.

Proof on Arches wove paper, printed in creamy white at the end of 1963 or beginning of 1964, and ''rinsed'' by the artist. On this proof Picasso not only employed *encre de Chine* but also red ink, which turned pink in the shower. Since another ''rinsed'' proof is dated 4.1.64, we may assume that our proof was probably ''rinsed'' at the same time (for the ''rinsing'' process, see introduction to this chapter, last paragraph).

Four proofs were printed in brown as normal linocuts; two other ''rinsed'' proofs also exist.

133. (see color plate)
Femmes à leur toilette

See no. 131.

Superimposition of Brown, printed in a pink-caramel color, and of the Black.

One of two proofs printed on ordinary paper.

The two linoblocks exist.

As is possible to see, the areas of the linoblock of the brown which were covered with ink in the ''rinsing'' process, remain white in the usual linocut printing. They were cut away from the surface of the block.

All the proofs were printed by Arnéra.

134.
Portrait de Jacqueline, de profil
Portrait of Jacqueline in Profile

1957 (December 16, Cannes)

Lithograph on zinc

640 x 490 mm. approximately

1st state: litho-ink wash and drypoint.

Proof on Arches wove paper, annotated on the verso by Mourlot "4/6 F.M."

M.306.1st state.

Apart from six proofs in the Mourlot boxes, there is an edition of 50 signed and numbered impressions, plus a few artist's proofs.

135.
Portrait de Jacqueline, de profil

1958 (January 11, Cannes)

See no. 134.

2nd state: litho-ink wash, drypoint and lithographic crayon.

Proof on Arches wove paper, annotated on the verso by Mourlot "4/6 F.M."

M.306.2nd state.

Apart from six proofs in the Mourlot boxes, four or five proofs exist.

136.
Portrait de Jacqueline, de profil

1958 (December 27, Cannes)

See no. 134.

3rd state: flat tint of litho-ink, scraper, sandpaper, drypoint.

Proof on Arches wove paper, annotated on the verso by Mourlot "4/6 F.M."

M.306.3rd state.

Apart from six proofs in the Mourlot boxes, nine or ten proofs exist, a few on bluish-grey laid paper.

Mourlot printed all the proofs and impressions.

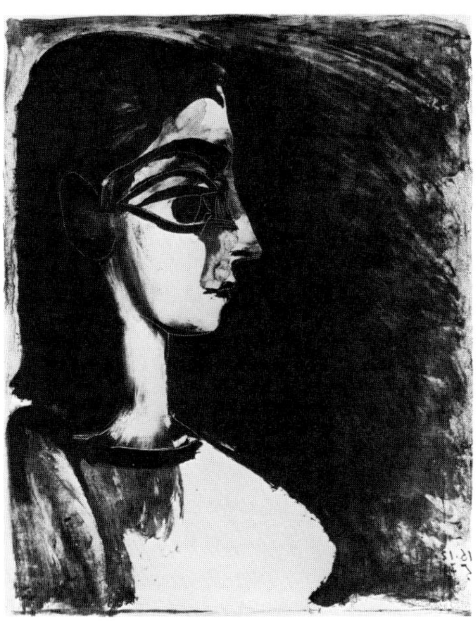
134.

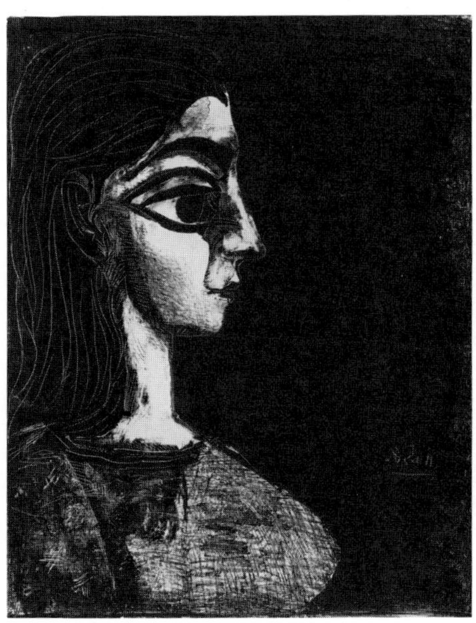
135.

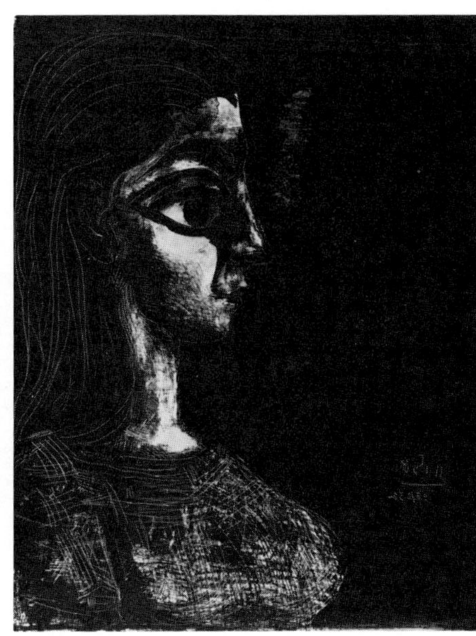
136.

137.
Los Hombres
The Men

1958 (before April 23)

Drypoint on copper

312 x 527 mm.

Proof on old Japan paper.

B.880.

This proof is part of a complete suite of 16 drypoints made by Picasso for Iliazd's edition of *Le Frère mendiant. Libro del conocimiento.* Lack of space unhappily prevents showing the full suite. The copperplates were never steelfaced and are cancelled.

After the edition of the book (54 numbered copies plus one annotated "ejemplar para Dépôt Légal," in the Bibliothèque Nationale, Paris, all of them on old Japan paper), Iliazd had a few suites pulled by Lacourière-Frélaut. As far as we know, there should exist: three suites on *Japon blanc à la forme*, one of which was signed by Picasso, the three of them annotated and signed by Iliazd; one suite on Imperial Japan paper annotated by Iliazd "Epreuves d'essai. Unique sur imperial;" five suites on China paper, which should all be signed and numbered by Iliazd; and finally, two suites belonging to Picasso on old Japan paper, with the drypoint for the cover on heavier Japan, not signed or inscribed by Iliazd apart from the print for the cover.

As mentioned before, Iliazd as well as Picasso took great pains to produce the right illustrations for this beautiful book. The banner-bearers engraved by Picasso carry exactly the same banners as those illustrated in an illuminated manuscript in the Biblioteca Nacional, Madrid (see introduction, above). As well, Iliazd had sent to Picasso a photograph of two African terracotta heads, so that he would have an idea of the morphology of the people the monk describes in his manuscript.

The writer of this catalogue found in Iliazd's archives the photograph which is reproduced here by courtesy of the owner, Hélène Iliazd (fig. 7): the similarity with Picasso's drypoint is striking. Nothing was inscribed on the photograph but the same writer traced the terracottas, from the *Ife* culture, to the Federal Department of Antiquities, Lagos, Nigeria, which meant that Iliazd went to great trouble, first to find the special ancient type he wanted, then to get the photographs made and sent. It was very unusual for Picasso to follow such sources so closely. We must not forget that it was a Spanish manuscript. The title we give to the drypoint is the title Iliazd gave to it in his notes.

138.
Les Banderilles
The Banderillas

1959 (August 26)

Linocut in three colors on one linoblock

540 x 658 mm. (states). Then: 530 x 640 mm.

1st state: superimposition of a uniform beige background and of the 1st state of the linoblock, printed in chocolate brown.

One of two proofs on ordinary coated paper, annotated in black pencil, top right "I E 2/2." The proof annotated "1/2" was reworked with black pencil, which delineates the black areas to be obtained in the final state.

Cf.B.940.

139.
Les Banderilles

See no. 138.

2nd state: superimposition of a uniform beige background and of the 2nd state of the linoblock printed in chocolate brown.

One of two proofs on ordinary coated paper, annotated in black pencil top left "IIe E 2/2." Same remark as in no. 138 about the proof annotated "1/2."

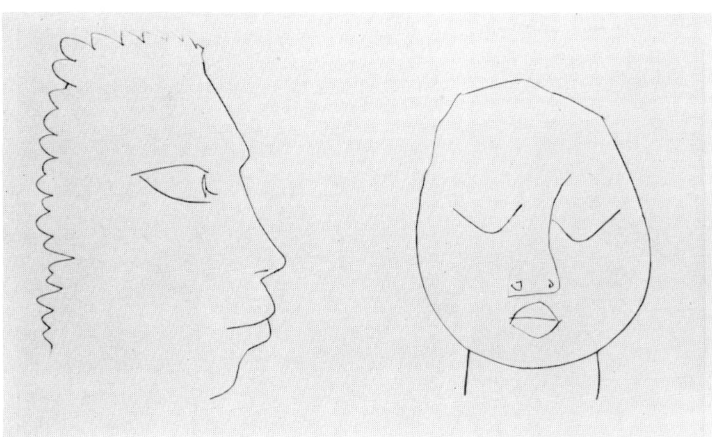

137.

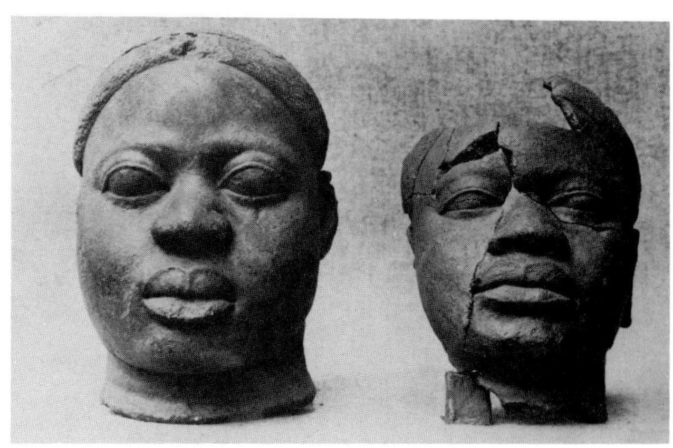

Fig. 7. *Two terracotta Ife heads*, 12th to 15th century, Federal Department of Antiquities, Lagos, Nigeria (courtesy of Hélène Iliazd).

140.
Les Banderilles

See no. 138.

3rd state: superimposition of a uniform beige background and of the 3rd state of the linoblock, printed in chocolate brown.

One of two proofs on ordinary coated paper, annotated in black pencil top left ''IIIe E 1/2.''

Two more proofs of the 3rd state exist: on Arches wove paper; one of them is stamped by Arnéra ''7 sept 59.''

141. (see color plate)
Les Banderilles

See no. 138.

530 x 640 mm.

4th state: superimposition of a uniform beige background, then of the 3rd state of the linoblock, printed in chocolate brown, then of the 4th state of the linoblock, printed in black.

Artist's proof on Arches wove paper, signed.

B.940.

The linoblock (on exhibition) is annotated on the back: ''26.8.59. no. 3.''

The 4th state was printed and published: an edition of 50 signed and numbered impressions, plus 15 or 18 signed artist's proofs. Two trial proofs also in exist.

As we saw before, this is the first large linoblock that Picasso worked on with his new technique. That some of the proofs of the 3rd state are stamped ''7.septembre 59'' means that Picasso went on working on the block for sometime. We must not forget that the proofs, for instance, here, of the 3rd state all had to be printed before he could cut away the linoblock to get another color. The date inscribed by him on the back is the day he began to work on the linoleum. Notice that here the second color is worked in three states. It was only after the 3rd state that the brown was completed, and that, after the printing of the approximately 80 sheets, Picasso could go on working on the block to get his black. The visitor can see that the only remaining surface on the linoblock corresponds exactly to the black on the proof.

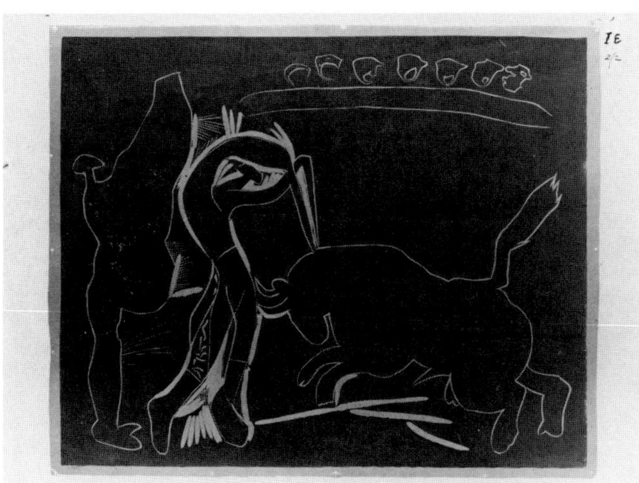

138.

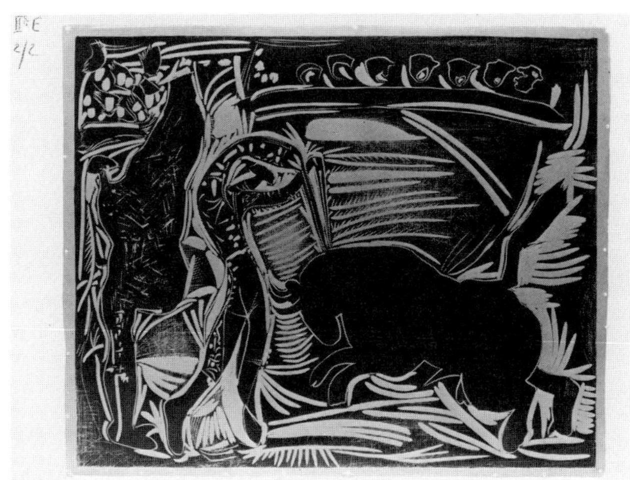

139.

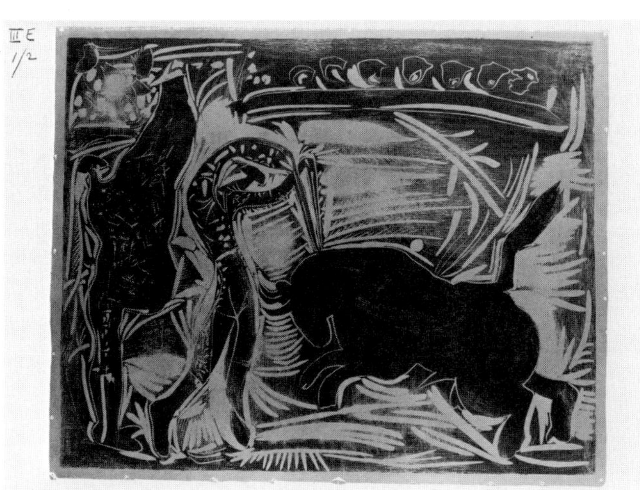

140.

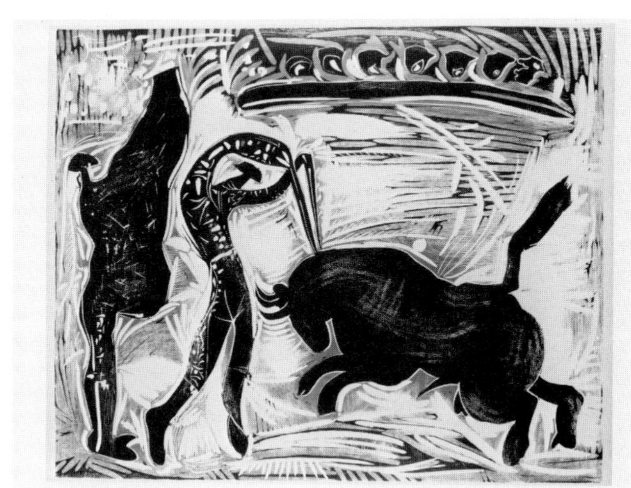

141.

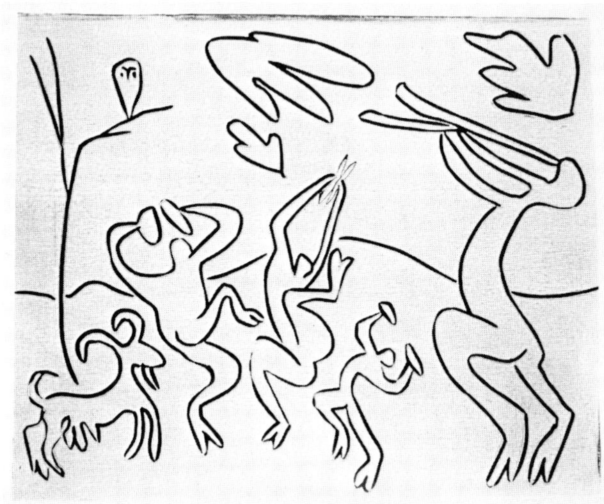

142.

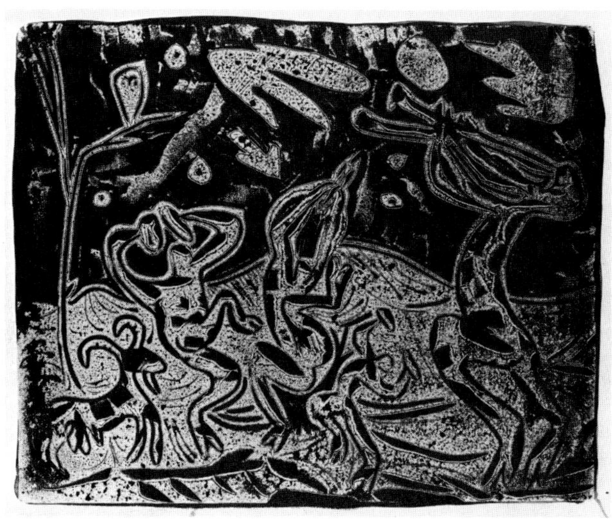

143.

142. (see color plate)
Les Danseurs au hibou
Bacchanalia with Goat and Owl

1959 (November 18)

Linocut in two colors on one linoblock

532 x 643 mm.

1st state: superimposition of a uniform black background and of the 1st state of the linoblock, printed in buttercup yellow which gives the effect of pale green.

Unique proof on Arches wove paper, annotated at right ''1er Etat (18.11.59).'' Plate annotated on the back ''II.''

Cf.B.936.

143.
Les Danseurs au hibou

See no. 142.

2nd state of the linoblock.

Proof on Arches paper, printed in cream white at the end of 1963 or in 1964 and ''rinsed'' by the artist at that time.

Cf.B.936.

The 2nd state of the linoblock was printed in two colors: first a uniform black background, then the linoblock, printed in chocolate brown: edition of 50, signed and numbered impressions and approximately 20 signed artist's proofs. The linoblock exists.

In this case, Picasso came back to a traditional technique, reworking the linoblock in the 2nd state only to get a more precise drawing.

Our use of the words ''rinsing,'' ''rinse,'' etc., comes from the explanations given orally by Picasso's wife, Jacqueline, who always helped the artist in the process and used to call the proofs *épreuves rincées*, as Picasso probably did also. As the known and published linocut is printed on a black background, the ''rinsed'' proof is more or less similar to the usual ones. Our proof was heavily painted with *encre de Chine* and only lightly ''rinsed.'' One can see small black dots on the printed surface: the waxy or greasy linocut inking produces a kind of waterproof surface which repels water as well as *encre de Chine*; in this case, the drops of ink so produced dried where they were.

Another ''rinsed'' proof exists, dated 1964 and signed. Three trial proofs of the 2nd state were printed, two in the known colors and one where the block was printed in pale blue on the black background (annotated ''II Etat du 19.11.59''). All the proofs (nos. 138-143) were printed by Arnéra.

144.
Portrait de Jacqueline en mariée
Portrait of Jacqueline as a Bride

1961 (March 24)

Sugar-lift aquatint, scraper, drypoint, burin and direct biting with acid on copper

399 x 299 mm.

1st state: sugar-lift aquatint and scraper.

Proof on wove paper without watermark.

Four more proofs exist.

In many of the states of this print, the scraper is used both to take away some of the aquatint and the strokes and to produce drypoint-like strokes (white on the aquatint, black on the white areas on the proof). Picasso would often employ the sharp end of the tool.

145.
Portrait de Jacqueline en mariée

See no. 144.

2nd state: drypoint or sharp end of the scraper.

Proof on wove paper without watermark.

Six more proofs exist.

146.
Portrait de Jacqueline en mariée

See no. 144.

3rd state: drypoint or sharp end of the scraper.

One of five proofs on handmade laid Auvergne paper.

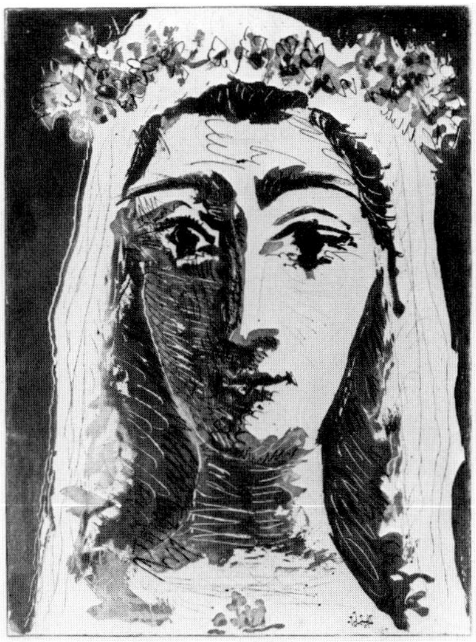

145.

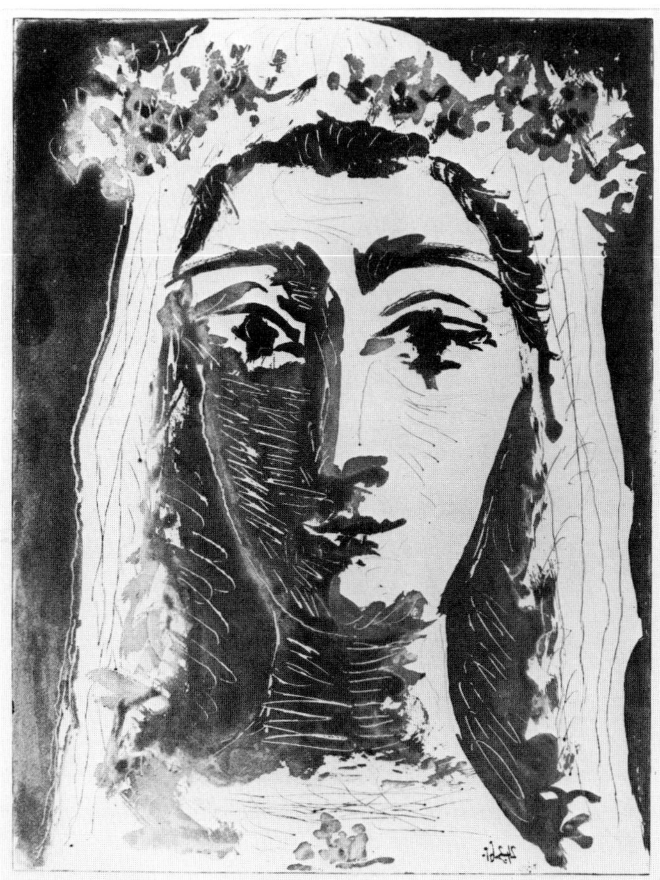

144.

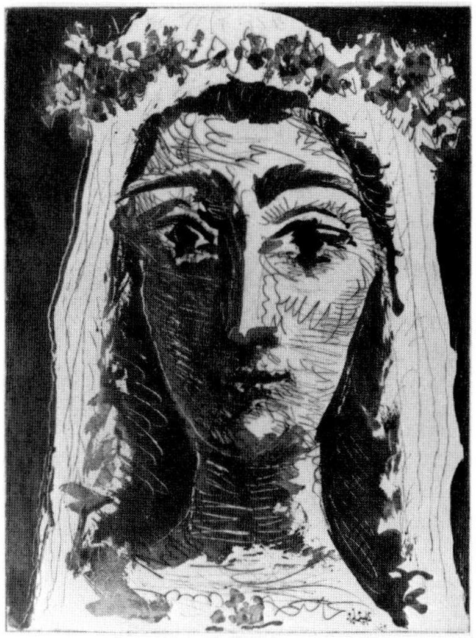

146.

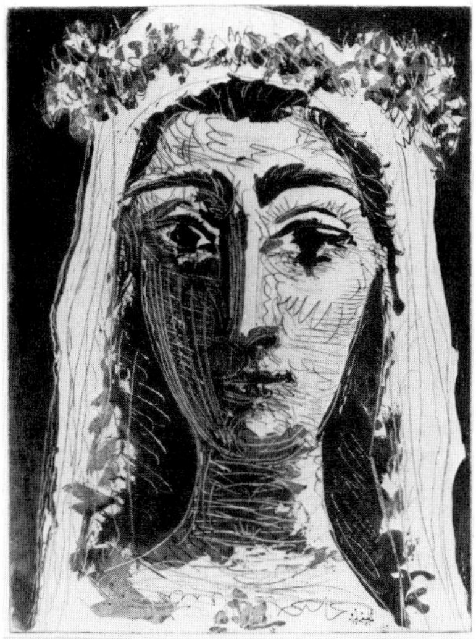
147.

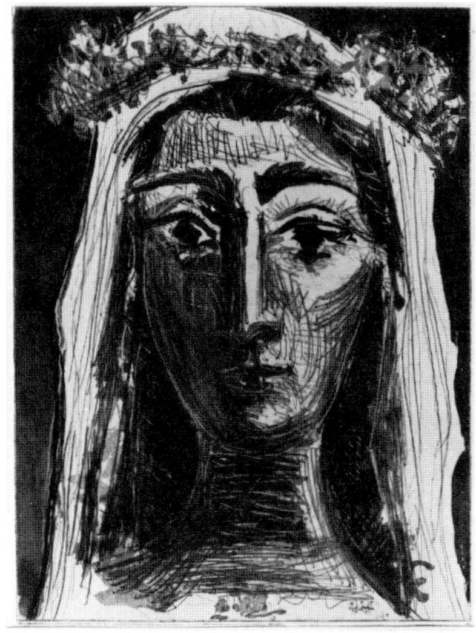
148.

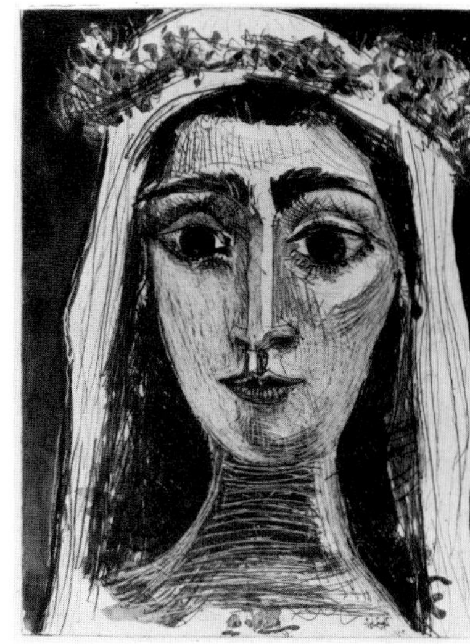
149.

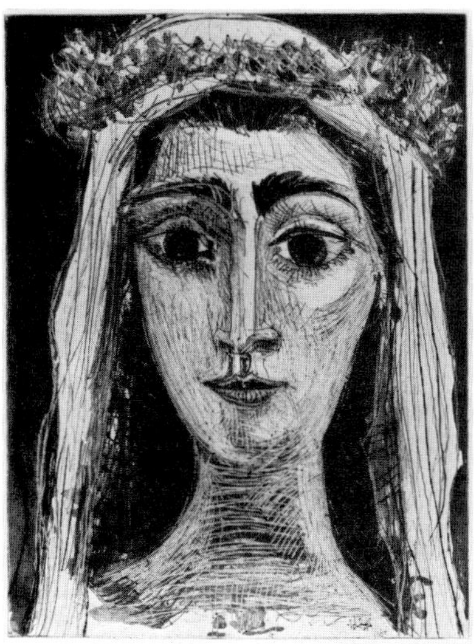
150.

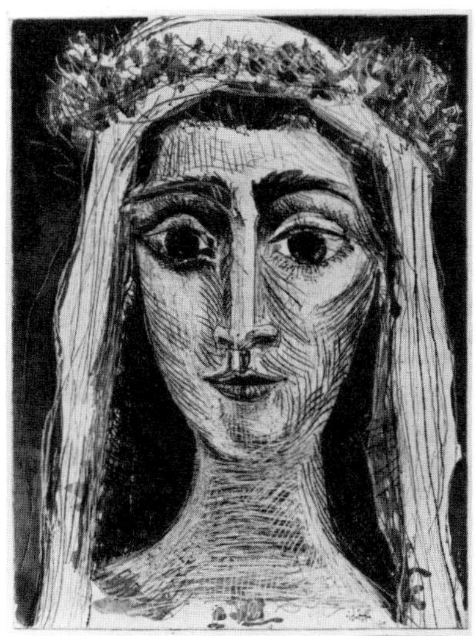
151.

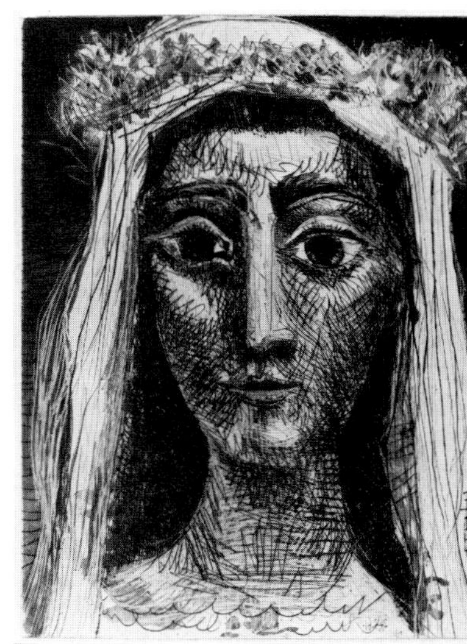
152.

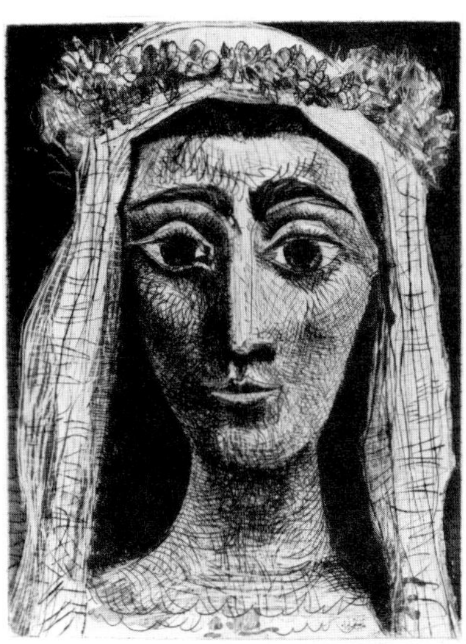
153.

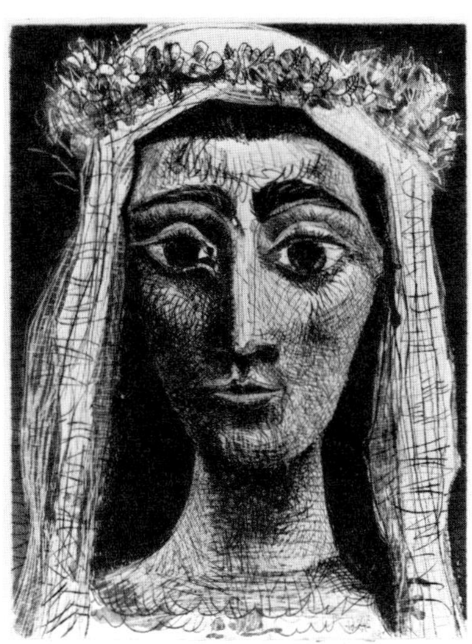
154.

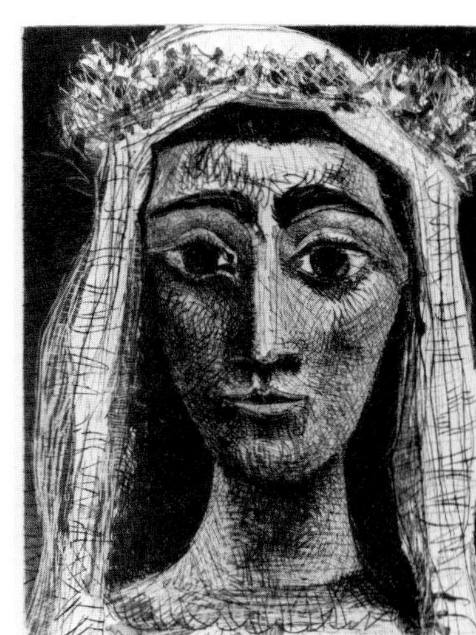
155.

147.
Portrait de Jacqueline en mariée

See no. 144.

4th state: sharp end of the scraper.

Unique proof on handmade Auvergne laid paper.

148.
Portrait de Jacqueline en mariée

See no. 144.

5th state: scraper, drypoint and *vélo* (drypoint with several needles).

Unique proof on handmade Auvergne laid paper.

149.
Portrait de Jacqueline en mariée

See no. 144.

6th state: scraper, drypoint or sharp end of the scraper, burin.

One of four proofs on handmade Auvergne laid paper.

Three more proofs, on old Japan paper, exist.

150.
Portrait de Jacqueline en mariée

See no. 144.

7th state: scraper and drypoint or sharp end of the scraper.

One of four proofs on handmade Auvergne laid paper.

Three more proofs, on old Japan paper, exist.

151.
Portrait de Jacqueline en mariée

See no. 144.

8th state: scraper, drypoint or sharp end of the scraper.

Unique proof on handmade Auvergne laid paper.

152.
Portrait de Jacqueline en mariée

See no. 144.

9th state: drypoint, scraper and sharp end of the scraper.

Unique proof on handmade Auvergne laid paper.

153.
Portrait de Jacqueline en mariée

See no. 144.

10th state: scraper and drypoint.

Unique proof on handmade Auvergne laid paper.

154.
Portrait de Jacqueline en mariée

See no. 144.

11th state: burin and drypoint.

One of five proofs on handmade Auvergne laid paper.

Three more proofs, on old Japan paper, exist.

155.
Portrait de Jacqueline en mariée

See no. 144.

12th state: drypoint

Unique proof on handmade Auvergne laid paper.

156.
Portrait de Jacqueline en mariée

See no. 144.

13th state: scraper.

Unique proof on handmade Auvergne laid paper.

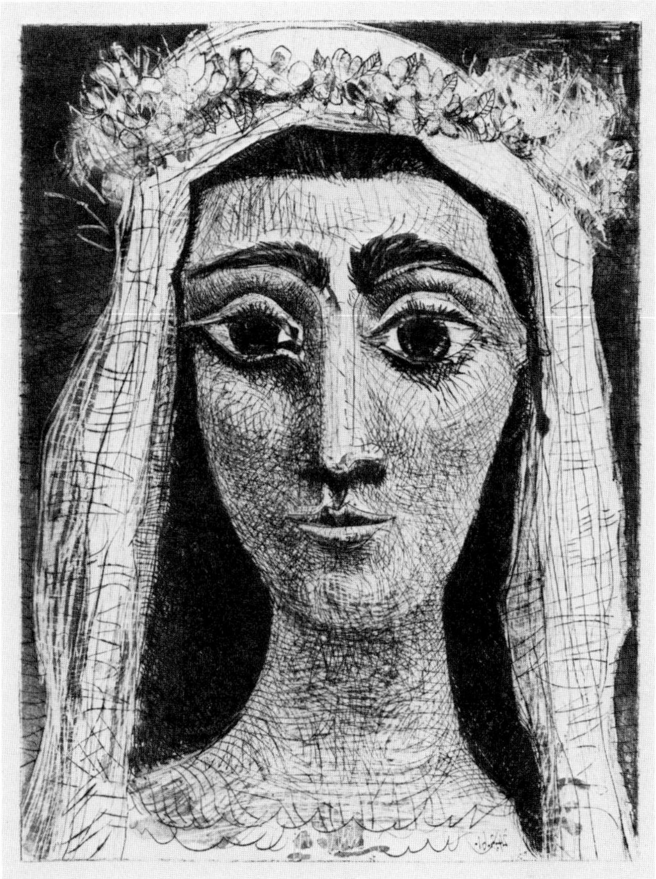

156.

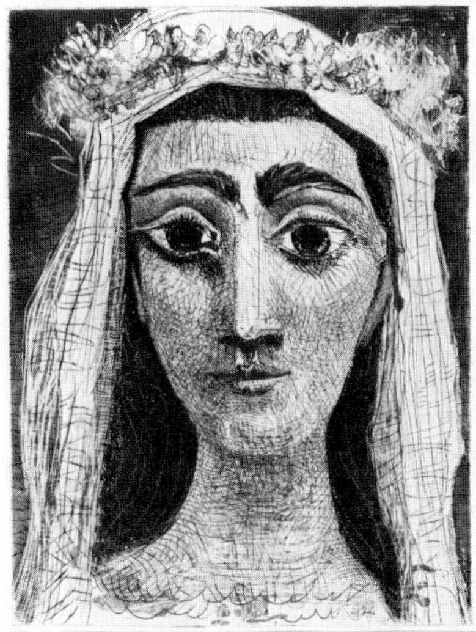
157.

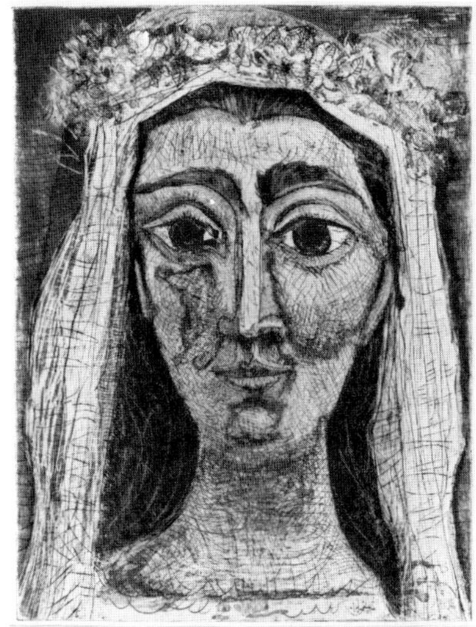
158.

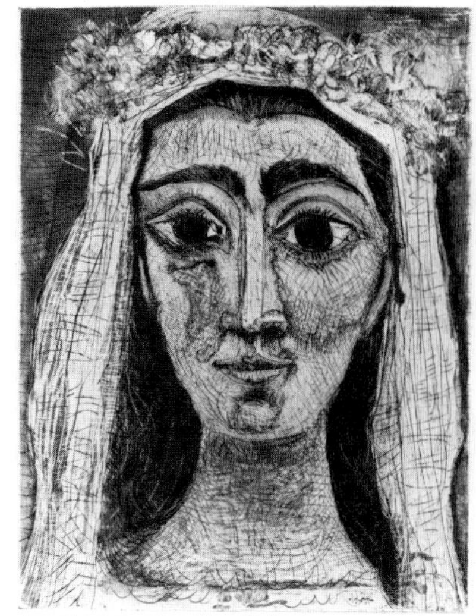
159.

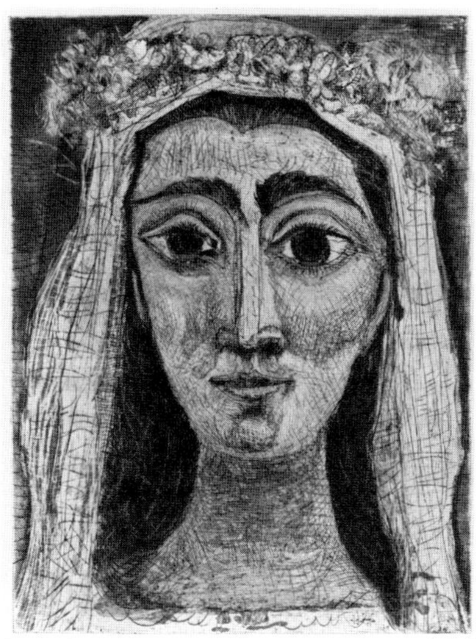
160.

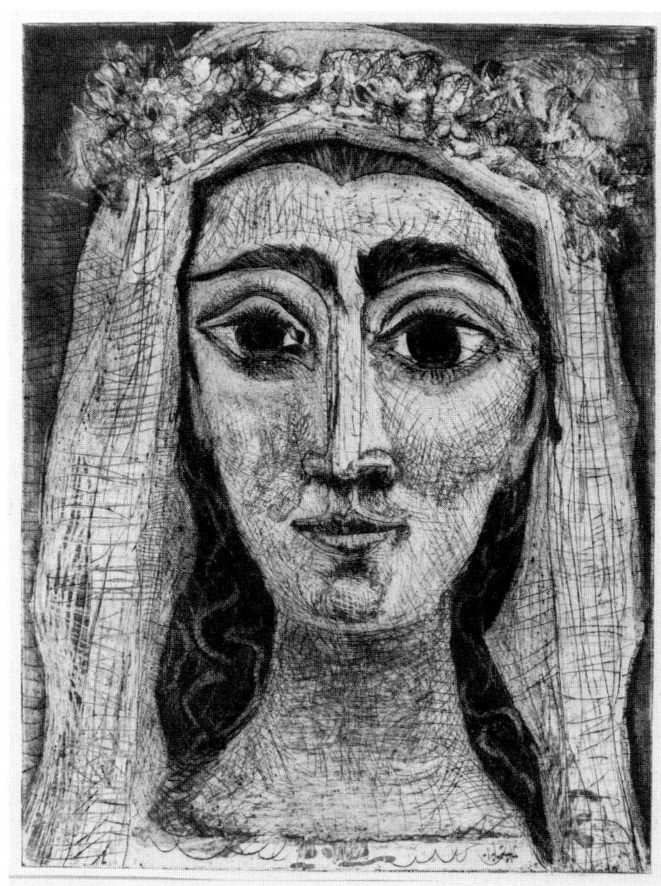
161.

157.
Portrait de Jacqueline en mariée

See no. 144.

14th state: scraper.

One of four proofs on handmade Auvergne laid paper.

Five more proofs, on old Japan paper, exist.

158.
Portrait de Jacqueline en mariée

See no. 144.

15th state: scraper and direct biting with acid and a brush: accident. The plate was deeply ploughed into and the acid ran in an uncontrolled way over the surface.

Proof on handmade Auvergne laid paper.

One more proof exists on Arches wove paper.

159.
Portrait de Jacqueline en mariée

See no. 144.

16th state: scraper (to try to get rid of the accidental blotches) and drypoint.

Unique proof on handmade Auvergne laid paper.

160.
Portrait de Jacqueline en mariée

See no. 144.

17th state: still more polishing with a kind of silver polish called *Blanc d'Espagne* and scraper.

Unique proof on handmade Auvergne laid paper.

161.
Portrait de Jacqueline en mariée

See no. 144.

18th and last state: more polishing and work with the scraper.

Unique proof on handmade Auvergne laid paper.

All the proofs were pulled by Frélaut. The copperplate exists.

The print was never published.

Our choice of this long progression of states has been well considered and is intended to illustrate three major points: the work Picasso was capable of on a single copperplate; his everlasting difficulties when trying to produce a portrait with a real likeness to the model; his progression by ''destruction,'' as he said to Zervos, and the ''metamorphoses'' which allow us a glimpse of ''the likely road which the brain takes in making real its dream.'' (See no. 41.)

Picasso and Jacqueline were married on March the 2nd, 1961, not even three weeks before he began to work on this copperplate. The accident (see no. 158) might have the hidden meaning of an unconscious slip: Picasso had a deep knowledge of the techniques of etching and engraving. He surely knew he was taking an enormous risk in trying to add acid on such a worked-on copperplate. Jacqueline's portrait, in the 14th state, is truly beautiful. The only missing detail, which is very important for the likeness, is her ''widow's peak,'' a sign in France and Spain of classical perfection and good breeding.

162.
Le Déjeuner sur l'herbe, d'après Manet
The ''Déjeuner sur l'herbe,'' after Manet

1961 (July 4)

Linocut in one color on one linoblock

530 x 640 mm.

1st state.

Artist's proof on Arches wove paper, signed.

B.1023, which is (see below) the 1st state.

The linoblock was printed in black and published: edition of 50 signed and numbered impressions, plus approximately 18 artist's proofs.

We can notice that after this date, and this very linocut, that is to say from 1962 onwards, Picasso's artist's proofs were no longer signed.

163. (see color plate)
Le Déjeuner sur l'herbe, d'après Manet

1961 (November 23 and 24)

See no. 162.

3rd state: superimposition of a uniform black background and of the 3rd state of the linoblock of B.1023 (no. 162), printed in creamy white. A very rare and little known state of this linoblock.

Unique proof on Arches wove paper annotated bottom left, in pencil ''3e ETAT.''

Cf.B.1023.

After the 1st state, which was published (no. 162), Picasso resumed working on the linoblock. No proof of the 2nd state seems to exist; the 2nd state corresponds with the date ''23.11'' cut into the linoleum. Our proof can be dated from the second date cut into the block, that is ''24.''

In this state, the linocut was never published. Later, on the 6th of December, Picasso worked on a second linoblock to be printed, in a lighter color, under the 3rd state of the first block. He printed only one proof, in two colors on two linoblocks, and abandoned the blocks. This last proof is in the Musée Picasso, Paris, as well as both the linoblocks.

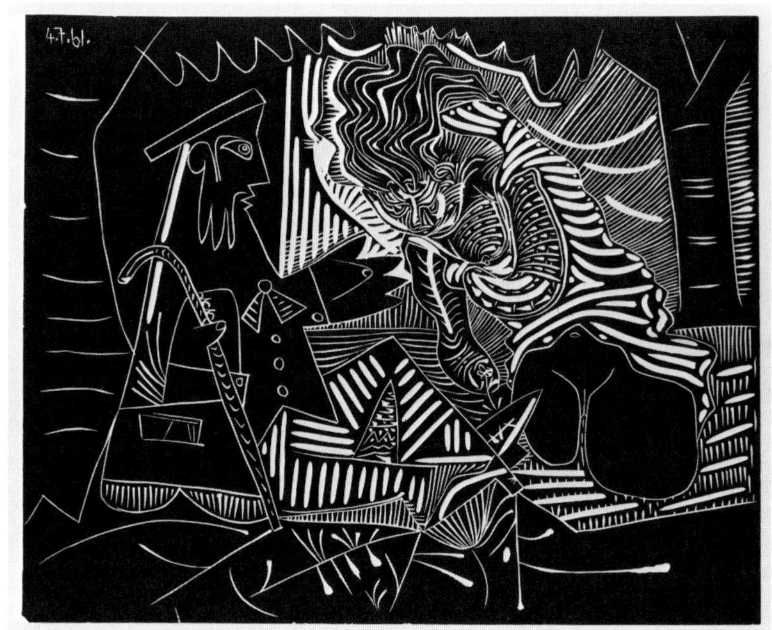

162.

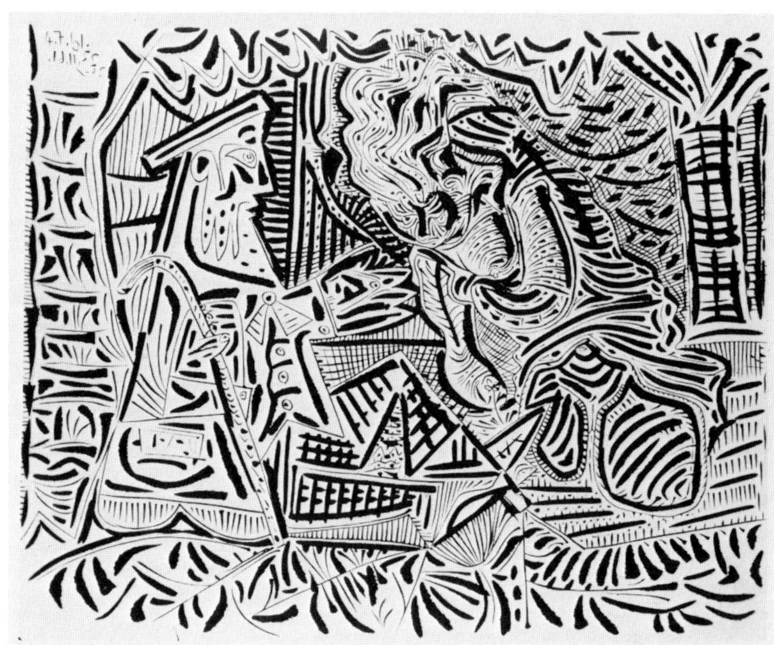

163.

164.
Tête de faune
Head of a Faun

1962 (February 7)

Linocut in two colors, on two linoblocks in the final state.

640 x 528 mm.

1st state: *Head of a Boy*. Linocut on one linoblock, printed in black. Unique proof, on Arches wove paper, annotated bottom left "premier état."

Cf.B.1094.

165.
Tête de faune

See no. 164.

2nd state: *Head of a Faun*. Linocut on one linoblock, printed in black.

Unique proof, on Arches wove paper, annotated bottom left "état IIe."

166.
Tête de faune

See no. 164.

3rd state: linocut on one linoblock, printed in black.

Unique proof, on Arches wove paper, annotated bottom left "3e ETAT."

167.
Tête de faune

See no. 164.

4th state: linocut on one linoblock, printed in black.

Unique proof, on Arches wove paper, annotated bottom left "IVe ETAT."

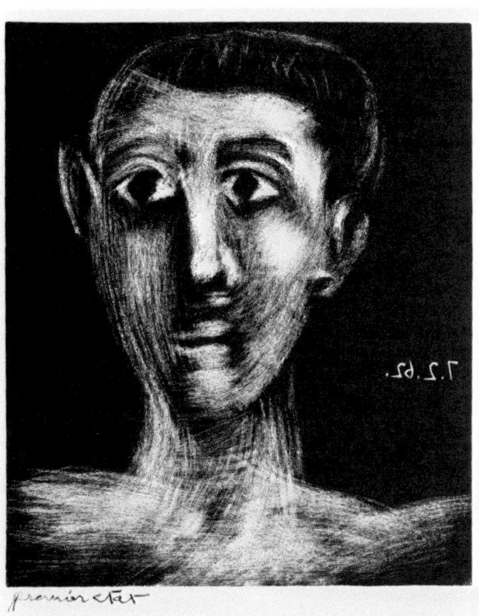

164.

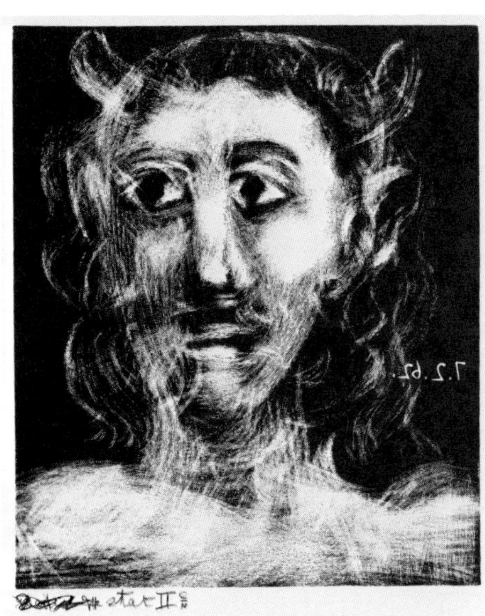

165.

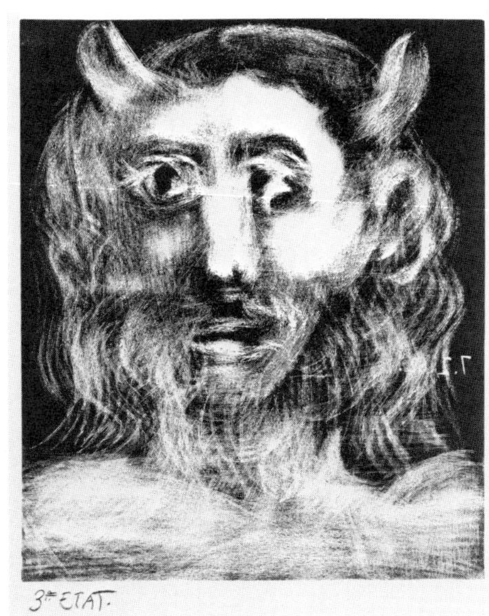

166.

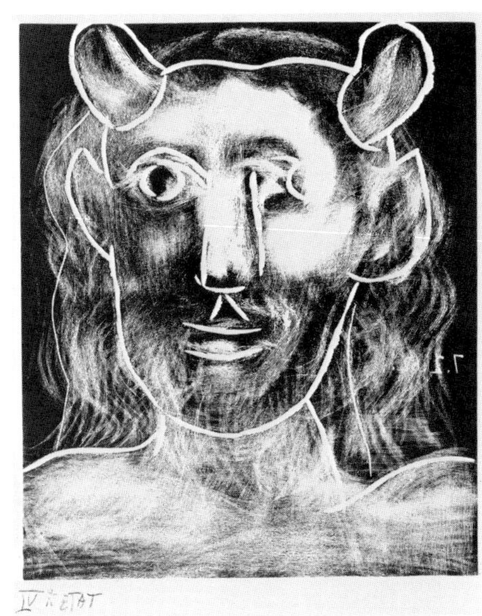

167.

168.
Tête de faune

See no. 164.

5th state: Linocut on one linoblock, printed in black.

Unique proof, on Arches wove paper, annotated bottom left "V ETAT."

At this state, a transfer was made onto a second linoblock; on the surface of the block, only the gouged outline of the head, shoulders and features of the faun from the first linoblock is cut away. One proof exists of the superimposition of the second linoblock printed in caramel color and of the first linoblock (5th state) printed in black.

169. (see cover)
Tête de faune

See no. 164.

Superimposition of the unique state of the second linoblock, printed in caramel color, and of the 6th state of the first linoblock, printed in black: last state.

Artist's proof on Arches wove paper.

The two linoblocks (on exhibition) are not annotated on the back.

B.1094.

In this state the two linoblocks were printed in superimposition and published: 50 signed and numbered impressions plus approximately 15 artist's proofs.

Picasso began by working on one linoblock, using a technique which might be related to the intaglio technique, if the progressive states were printed in negative. In the three first states, he freed his subject from the surface of the linoleum with an instrument which is difficult to identify, as it could have been anything he found at hand. It might have been a combination of steelwool and some kind of graver with several sharp ends, or it could have been a kind of *vélo*. He most certainly added scraping with sandpaper.

Although he went on using this instrument on the first linoblock in the six states, in the 4th state he cut away the outline with a gouge. If one looks closely at the proof of the 5th state, one can see that some scraping was added on the cheek of the faun (left on the proof) before the block was pulled and published in its 6th state.

The second linoblock is cut away only to get a caramel-colored background but with a white outline of the subject.

Notice how the boy, who reminds us, for example, of the boy in cat. no. 51, slowly becomes a faun as the states progress.

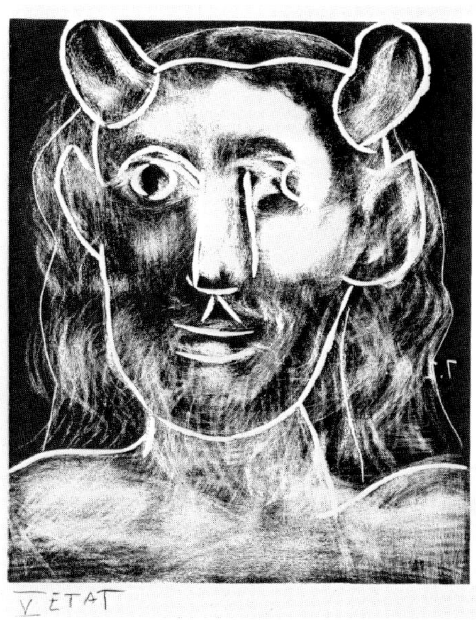

168.

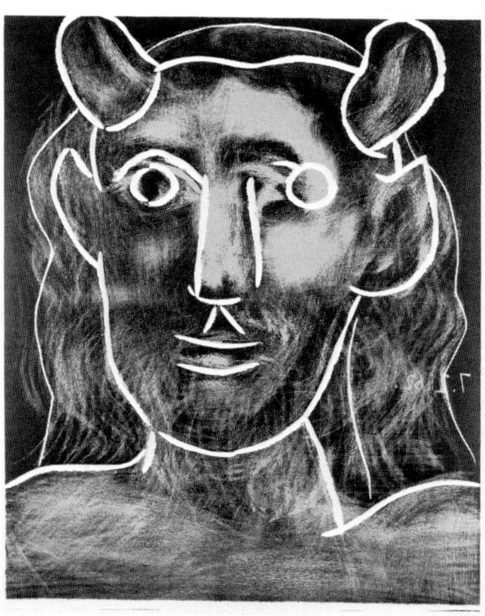

169.

170.
Nature morte à la pastèque
Still Life with Cherries and Watermelon

1962 (February 16)

Linocut in eight colors on three linoblocks

1st to 9th state: 530 x 640 mm.

10th and last state: 593 x 729 mm. approximately

2nd state: the first and unique state of the linoblock of the yellow, then the superimposition of the first state of the linoblock of the brown. This linoblock will be the main one and will be reworked in the following eight states producing seven colors.

Unique proof on Arches wove paper.

Cf.B.1098.

The unique state of the block of the yellow is a cutting away from the surface, which one can notice more clearly in the following state, that is, a uniform background where only the inside parts of the coiled form of the light of the electric bulb are cut away. Notice that there is no yellow under the brown in that area. The first state of the main linoblock is the cutting away of the lines which remain yellow on our proof. As the work progresses, it should be understood that the areas which, on each state's proof, are still visible in the color they had in the previous state, were cut away from the surface of the main linoblock. The third linoblock will be used in the 10th and last state, only to frame the composition.

171.
Nature morte à la pastèque

See no. 170.

3rd state: superimposition of the linoblock of the yellow and of the 2nd state of the main block, printed in brown.

Unique proof on Arches wove paper.

The only work done is the cutting away from the surface of the block which gives shape to the electric bulb.

172.
Nature morte à la pastèque

See no. 170.

4th state: superimposition of the linoblock of the yellow, then of the 2nd state of the main block, printed in brown, then of the 3rd state of this block, printed in pale blue.

Unique proof on Arches wove paper.

In a 5th state, more scraping around the lamp; same superimposition, same colors; it is the main block's 4th state (one proof, which did not show enough changes to justify its inclusion in the exhibition).

173. (see color plate)
Nature morte à la pastèque

See no. 170.

6th state: superimposition of the linoblock of the yellow, then of the 2nd state of the main block, printed in brown, then of the 4th state of this block, printed in pale blue, then of the 5th state, printed in bright pink.

Unique proof on Arches wove paper.

Cf.B.1098.

174.
Nature morte à la pastèque

See no. 170.

7th state: as above, with a 6th state of main block printed in green.

Unique proof on Arches wove paper.

175.
Nature morte à la pastèque

See no. 170.

8th state: as above, with a 7th state of main block printed in dark blue.

Unique proof on Arches wove paper.

In the 9th state, all the areas which were not to be printed in black on the top of the previous superimposition were cut away, and then, over the superimposition of the 8th state of the composition, the 8th state of the main linoblock was printed in black. Picasso reworked his trial proof with ink-wash, in order to prepare the shape of the grey frame.

176. (see color plate)
Nature morte à la pastèque

See no. 170.

593 x 729 mm.

10th state: superimposition of the seven colors, and the addition of a third linoblock, the inner surface of which was cut away entirely in order to be printed as a frame for our composition.

Last state.

Unique trial proof on Arches wove paper.

B.1098.

On the main linoblock (on exhibition) one can see that the only remaining areas correspond to the parts of the proof which are printed in black. The two other blocks are lost. In this state, the linocut was printed and published: 50 signed and numbered impressions plus approximately 15 artist's proofs.

Notice that in the process of obtaining a linocut such as no. 176, the image is built up at the same time as the linoblock diminishes towards its final destruction, bringing us once again to Picasso's quote about the creativity of destructiveness cited in nos. 18, 41, and 161.

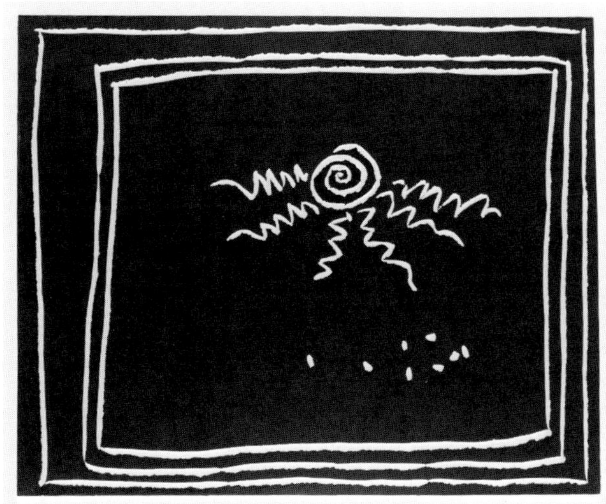

170.

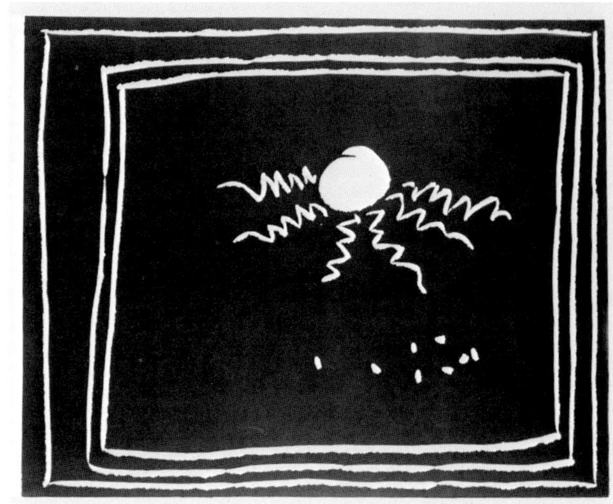

171.

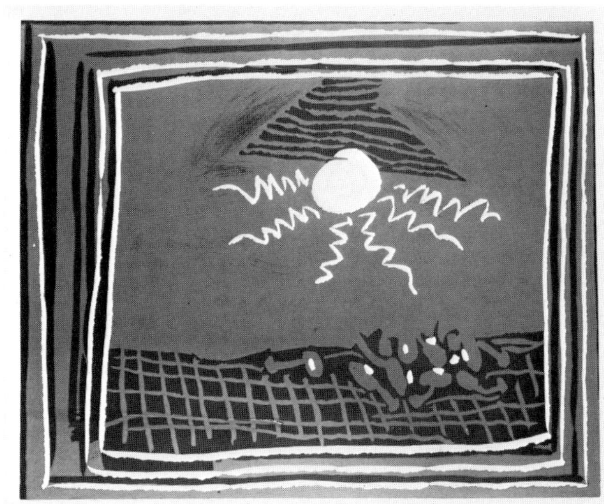

172.

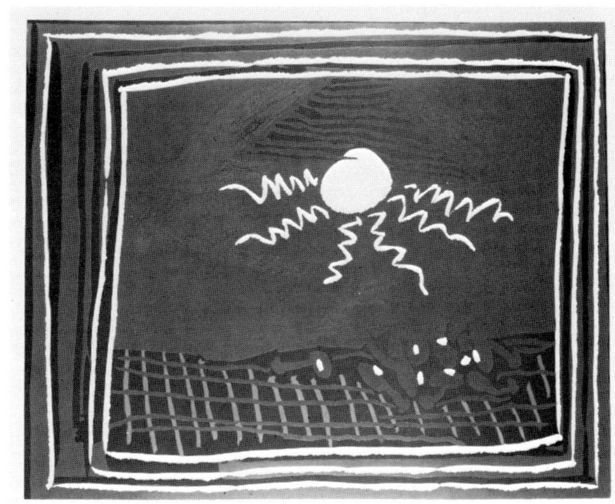

173.

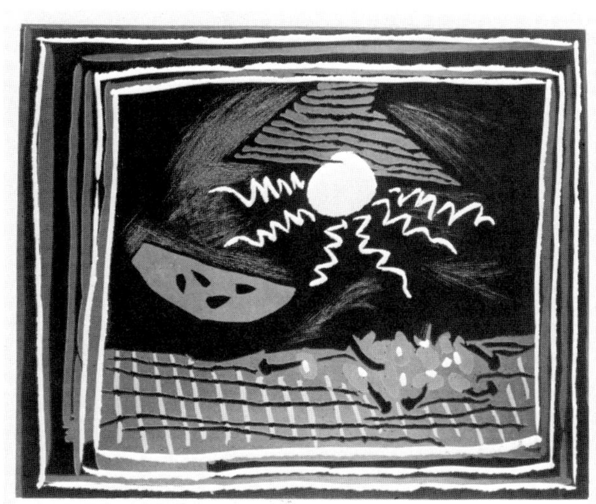

174.

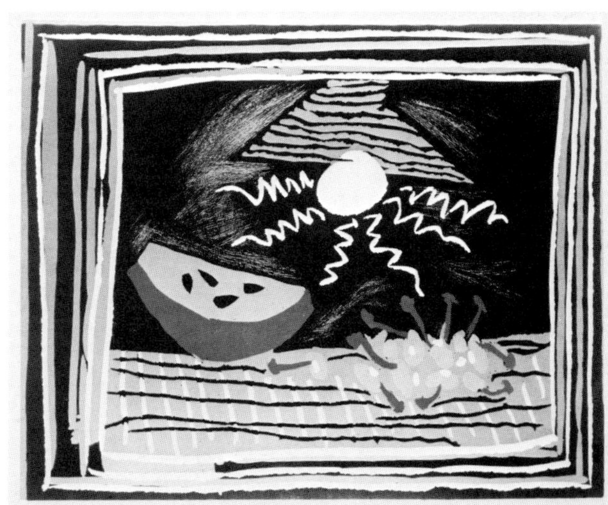

175.

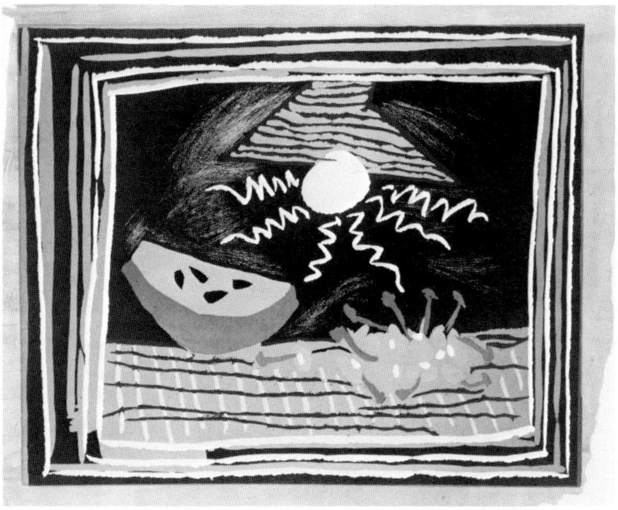

176.

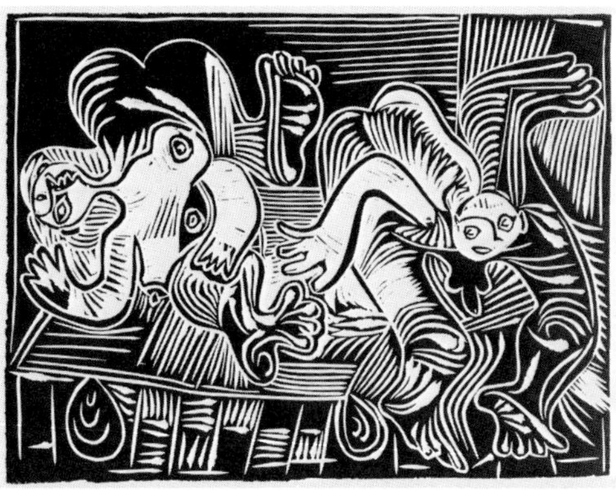

177.

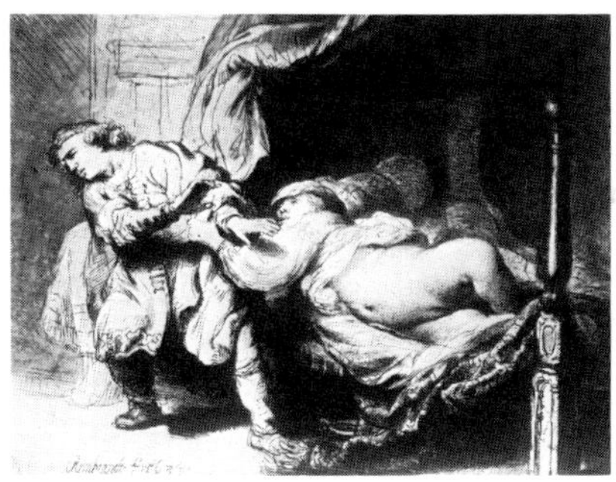

Fig. 8. Rembrandt, *Joseph and Potiphar's Wife*, 1634, etching (Bartsch, 39) (photo: Roger-Viollet, Paris).

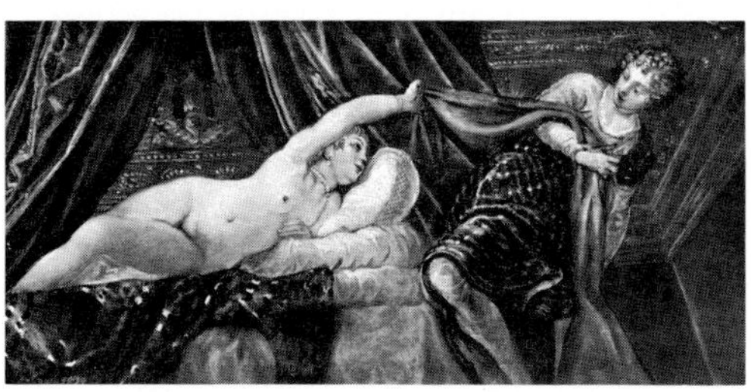

Fig. 9. Tintoretto, *The Chastity of Joseph*, oil on canvas, Prado Museum (photo: Roger-Viollet, Paris).

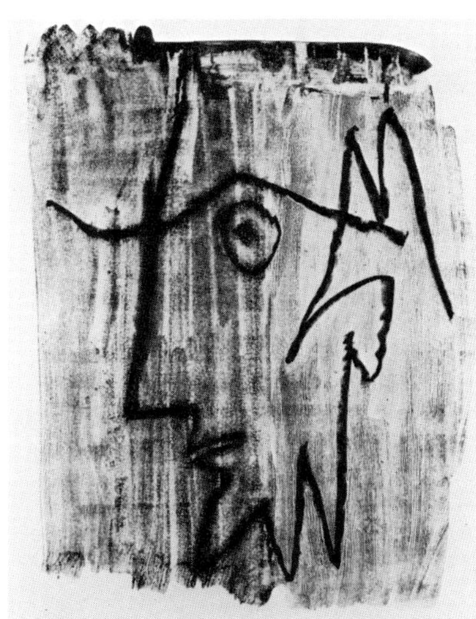

178.

177.
Joseph et la femme de Potiphar
Joseph and Potiphar's Wife

1962 (July 12 and 29)

Linocut in one color on one linoblock

274 x 350 mm.

2nd and last state: July 29

Unique proof on Arches wove paper, printed in black.

There is a unique proof of the 1st state, printed in caramel brown on a uniform black background; it is dated: ''12.7.62'' (Musée Picasso, Paris).

The linoblock exists.

Although he never confirmed it, Picasso surely took his composition from Rembrandt's etching of the same subject (fig. 8) or from the Tintoretto in the Prado (fig. 9). As usual, he surely did not ''copy'' either of them but, as he had a photographic eye, he had at least some reminiscences of both and managed to produce a play upon them. Both earlier works show the same scene: Joseph is tearing himself out of the arms of Potiphar's wife. Picasso made the subject cruder. Joseph is running away from the bed but also from the opened legs of the excited woman. Picasso's sometimes irreverent attitude toward the old master tradition comes through clearly in this small but intense visual joke.

178.
Tête d'homme, de profil
Man's Head, in Profile

1963 (November)

Lithograph on zinc: litho-ink wash and lithographic crayon

600 x 450 mm.

One of ten trial proofs on Arches wove paper.

M.397.

The zincplates of the group of nine lithographs (M.389-397) Picasso made in November 1963 have been lost. We chose to show this one because it is the last true lithograph Picasso ever made, at least by working directly on either stone or zincplate.

XII.

The Crommelynck Brothers

In 1963, the Crommelynck brothers, Aldo and Piero, established themselves at Mougins, where Picasso had been living for two years. They had begun their apprenticeship about 1950 with Lacourière, the best possible teacher at the time. In his workshop, they were principally engaged in color reproductions and became extremely competent technically. By 1963, however, Lacourière was getting on in years, and although Madeleine Lacourière was still very active, Frélaut had taken over the day-to-day running of the atelier. The Crommelynck brothers saw their opportunity. They thought that if they were on the spot, it would make life easier for Picasso and that they would become his ''official'' printers, so they left the Rue Foyatier, taking with them two assistants who had also been part of the workshop family, and set up house and their shop in the village of Mougins. As we might expect, Picasso let them dangle for a time, but intaglio printing was one of his addictions and, as in the case of Mourlot, we have seen that he liked a certain degree of practical comfort. Frélaut's visits were too infrequent. Linocuts began to bore him. The Crommelyncks were literally on his doorstep and he began to take advantage of the situation. The first print in which they participated, pulling the states and the trial proofs, is B.1110 of October 14, 1963. The artist worked with them until his death, and it was they who eventually printed the editions of the ''156'' and the ''60,'' which the Leiris Gallery put on the market after the artist's death, and which had not been completely printed by the end of 1974.

Other artists and publishers followed suit and left Lacourière-Frélaut for the Crommelyncks. Iliazd, however, who was obsessional about the quality both of the paper used and of the actual impressions, stayed faithfully with Lacourière. Gili set up his own printing workshop in Barcelona.

Picasso made a few more linocuts, two of which were

published in an edition of 50, each impression having been "rinsed" by the artist and Jacqueline (B.1150 and 1151, dated October 15, 1963). He made others which were never published (see nos. 179, 180, and 183) or, were put on sale only after his death (B. 1851 and 1852). His passion was intaglio, and he had willing collaborators close at hand who could pull the trial proofs and, several times a day, carry the copperplates back and forth from the press to the house. The Crommelynck brothers became almost part of the household and devoted themselves to Picasso's prints.

For approximately three years, as we have seen, Picasso's major themes were rape, the painter and his model, the painter and his canvas. However, in 1966, Picasso executed a group of intaglio prints with a more complex iconography for *Le Cocu magnifique*, a play written by the father of the Crommelynck brothers. For this, he made approximately 24 prints, all with the same dimensions. As only 12 illustrations were used when the play was printed, Picasso gave the other 12 to Gustav Gili as illustrations for *El entierro del Conde de Orgaz*, which was published in Barcelona in 1969. In addition, he gave Gili three aquatints, also dating from 1966, for inclusion in the suites of the luxury edition (e.g. no.184), as well as the 1939 copperplate, *Trozo de Almibar* (see above, chapter 9).

Between 1963 and 1966, although Picasso went on using traditional etching and drypoint, he also continually employed three other distinctive techniques which need further explanation. As usual, he sometimes used all three on the same copperplate, combining them with etching, drypoint, etc.

First, he employed aquatint with *réserves au vernis* (see no.52), where he used liquid varnish to draw his subject, which then appears in white on the proof; he usually bit the resin-grained copperplate by hand with a brush in order to obtain variant tones of blacks and greys. Further, he would often add drypoint or etching to the areas covered with varnish. The procedure varied, however, and on some occasions he would begin working on a copperplate already grained with resin, or else would draw with varnish on a clean copperplate and have it grained afterwards (see no.182).

Secondly, he employed a technique which is extremely difficult to control, one in which he bit directly into a resin-grained copperplate. Examples of this are B.1163 and B.1176, which are two of the illustrations for *Sables mouvants* (no.181), a poem by Reverdy published by Broder, and also B.1226.

Thirdly, he discovered a trick which allowed him to obtain relatively easily what might be called a negative aquatint. This technique was used for the first time on March 14, 1965 (B.1223). It consists of drawing with a special kind of crayon whose "lead" is made out of solidified varnish. One can either use the point as an ordinary pencil, or, holding it horizontally, shade areas with light wide strokes. This crayon has to be used on resin-grained copperplates which then will be bitten. Thus the subject is rendered in negative on a black background of aquatint. In order to make this technique clear to the visitor, we exhibit one aquatint worked on with this crayon alone (no.184), but Picasso would also combine this technique with etching, drypoint and the usual *réserves* made with liquid varnish. Later, he discovered yet another new technique. He worked on resin-grained areas with an architect's pen loaded with *encre de Chine* in order to draw his subject in negative. By "negative," we mean that on the proof the lines are white against the black aquatint background. Picasso had realized that *encre de Chine* would be acid-resistant like varnish. The only problem with this novel technique occurred when the acid was contaminated with water, as the water would dissolve the ink. For an example of this process, see B.1862 (L.7). The small copperplate of this print was mislaid and so was never published. Hence, it is missing from the group of the edition of the *156 Prints*, reducing their actual number to 155.

Before we leave the period of 1963-1966 we must add that the series known as the *60* from 1966 and 1968, depicting Piero Crommelynck and his family, was published after the artist's death. The edition is stamped with a cachet imitating the artist's signature.

1968 was a very productive year for Picasso's graphics. In a little more than six months, from March 16 to October 5, Picasso made the 347 prints which were published together by the Leiris Gallery and which are now known as the *347 Suite*. If Jacqueline is nearly always the model in most of the prints from 1963 to 1966, she now becomes implicated in very disparate types of iconography. As we remarked above, the major themes of this series are the circus, subjects based in Ingres and, above all, *La Célestine*.

Picasso wanted to illustrate *La Célestine* and made a group of very small prints which were first included in the *347 Suite* but were then reprinted as illustrations for a book edition of *La Célestine* published by the Crommelyncks. Even afterwards, this theme continued to occupy a large place in the graphic work of 1968. Many plates, sometimes of a very large format, depict for us episodes from Spanish picaresque novels: abductions, gypsy camps, travelling actors, scenes from the circus or the theatre, or seduction scenes between a *hidalgo* and a girl. The old procuress and go-between, Célestine, is nearly always present.

In the play by Fernando de Rojas, *Célestine. The Tragi-comedy of Calixtus and Melibea*, the old hag helps Calixtus to meet the girl he is in love with, inspires Melibea with passion, and organizes their elopement, but her only purpose is to make money in order to look after her own daughter and her daughter's lover as well her own affairs. The other pastime of this threesome is to trick respectable people and deceive the townsfolk in general. The play, which is extremely rich psychologically, falls squarely in the picaresque tradition with its array of plots and sub-plots. Célestine and her family lie to everyone and perpetrate the most awful deceits even on their so-called protégés, the barely adolescent Calixtus and Melibea, who end up dying without ever having passed a night together. The many-layered complexity of the story and the author's gleefully precise descriptions clearly caught Picasso's fancy, as he elaborated with obvious delight on its intrigues and nefarious characters.

In the *347 Suite*, every type of traditional technique is used, but we would like to draw attention to the particular brilliance with which Picasso employed sugar-lift aquatint. If grease is left or intentionally smeared on the copperplate, this produces random patterns of small droplets of tinting rather than the uninterrupted ink surface which we are accustomed to. In our opinion, with the exception of the first print of the series (B.1481), the most successful plates of the *347 Suite* are the aquatints with a rather small format treated in this manner. For example, consider the Célestine scene (B.1594), the *Gypsy Camp* (B.1641), the *Abduction* (B.1761), the composition on the river bank with echoes of Corot and Maupassant (B.1827), as well as the three prints which we exhibit here as cat. nos. 190, 191, and 192. An entire book should be consecrated to the techniques and the iconography of the *347 Suite*.

As far as technique is concerned, notice how cleverly the artist uses steelwool to ''draw'' the three figures in the varnish in B.1585 or B.1704. Another example of his remarkable control of the medium is B.1565, where he began by varnishing the areas which were not intended to be grained and bitten in aquatint. Then he decided not to have the plate grained at all and made use of the areas covered by the varnish to etch a moonlight elopement scene, full of mysterious strangeness, the areas not covered by the varnish producing, when bitten, a kind of greyish-white tonality. Notice also how, by rubbing the grained copperplate with sandpaper or steelwool, he evokes a ghostly atmosphere in another elopement or abduction scene (B.1703).

As for the iconography, unhappily we are unable to exhibit here the masterpiece of the *347 Suite*, B.1481, containing a self-portrait of Picasso in a composition which reminds us of the *Minotauromachie*. On the left stands a very small Picasso; behind him, there is a figure of clown/wizard with the head of Jean Cocteau. On the right, a circus strongman carries the Minotaur's bundle. In the center foreground, there is a reclining figure of a woman daydreaming, and behind her, a circus filled with hundreds of spectators who, on this occasion, are not gazing at a woman/torera but a beautiful bareback rider. Once again through mirrored or duplicated identities, here in the eyes and the daydream of the reclining woman, the problem is posed of one's proper identity and of one's relationship with the other. Is it Jacqueline the wife, or Jacqueline as the bareback rider, majestic on her horse? Is it Picasso as himself, or as a Cocteauesque prankster,or as a Minotaur which here is transformed (grandeur and decline) into a pathetic circus strongman with the face of the ''sculptor?''

As we remarked above, the theme of voyeurism was an often repeated one at this time. This is true not only of the compositions inspired by the *Raphael and the Fornarina* and the *Paolo and Francesca* of Ingres, but also over and over again in the *Suite 156* with the figure of Degas in *La Maison Tellier* series. We should not forget that we are in the year 1968 and Picasso is 87.

At this stage, we have chosen to include two big and mysterious prints in the exhibition. Gert Schiff has drawn parallels between our first print, cat. no. 185 (B.1604), and the *Meninas* of Velasquez as well as Picasso's *Demoiselles d'Avignon* (see his short essay in *Picasso in Perspective*, Englewood Cliffs, New Jersey, 1976). Even a casual glance at our print shows that the setting is rather odd. The center of the composition is dominated by what seems to be a scene from a theatrical play. Separated completely from the other actors, three courtesans have been positioned on a luxurious raised platform which is draped in velvet or in some other heavy rich fabric. Once again we have the theme of ''women together.'' This platform is situated on the ground floor, or even in the basement perhaps, of an old house, which reminds us of Spain both by its construction and by those areas covered in bright sunlight. The house is very precisely delineated in the sense that it is clearly not just any old house but a specific building in the artist's memory. Perhaps there had been such a luxurious brothel which played a role in Picasso's adolescence in Barcelona, and Schiff is right to refer to the *Demoiselles d'Avignon*.

Three personages are lost in dreamy memories before this central scene. Not one of them is looking directly in its direction, which only goes to prove that it is a dream or a memory that is depicted. The three personages consist of a young man, handsome and crowned with a wreath of leaves like a Greek god, a painter dressed in 17th-century Spanish costume, and an old man lying on his stomach like a baby, bald, plump, and somewhat grotesque.

May we recognize in these three figures three images of the artist? All three are drawn in sugar-lift aquatint with a mixture of grease, which gives them great presence but a presence hazy in outline; only the central scene has a more definite and defined construction, being drawn in pure sugar-lift aquatint. Beyond any reasonable doubt, the old man is the key figure in the composition. It is he who conjures up the memories while thinking about the other two men. In a combination of reminiscence and daydream, he casts his mind back to the time when he sowed his wild oats (the brothels in Barcelona), when he was young and had, as the saying goes, all his life before him full of hope (hence the god-like aspect of the young man) such a long time ago in Barcelona. But also he evokes another image of himself as the painter. The painter is clearly connected to the central scene since it is he who created the *Demoiselles d'Avignon*. He is dressed as Velasquez might have been but with that negligence so typical of Picasso, his shirt open down to the waist showing his chest and navel. (So many photographs of Picasso show him dressed in shorts, wearing a tee-shirt or bare-chested or with an unbuttoned shirt open down to his waist.) May we interpret the old man as the vehicle of these memories, as what is left behind? A man like him without the hope of youth, stripped, at least in his mind, of all his fame and celebrity as a painter who is asking himself not only all sorts of questions about this subject, but also, who is questioning his very self, old and tired? The posture of the old man, seen as a naked baby, tends to push us in that direction.

The second print, of which we exhibit four successive states here (cat. no. 185-189) is even more mysterious than its predecessor, with an iconography so complex that it defies full interpretation. The composition was virtually complete as early as the 1st state. Only certain details were changed here and there: the costume of the circus giant is reworked and the squares on his trousers made more clear; the trapeze artist in the top right corner becomes more defined; the little man, whom one sees standing behind the neck of the wooden horse in the 3rd state, is suddenly wearing one of Picasso's favorite sailor shirts; the audience on the right becomes more real; and the motion of the flying trapezes is indicated by strokes on the background. The only personage who is heavily worked over is the naked woman at whose feet sits the infant/old man, entirely delineated in the 1st state, and who represents the artist. The naked woman resembles Jacqueline.

One could easily entitle this composition "Picasso's Circus." The acrobats who succeed in forming a human pyramid as high as the tent, the flying trapeze artists performing their somersaults in midair, the strongman dressed as Hercules, the public, all have associations in Picasso's life and work. We are presented, it would seem, with a vision by the artist of his world, as he sits dreaming at the feet of the woman (Jacqueline), pondering over this and his life. All this is not too difficult to comprehend, until we arrive at the figure on the left. He is a carnival or circus giant, a personage that children know well, his long trousers hiding the enormous stilts. But he has a very odd face, like the face of a wizard, a special face which gives us the impression that it could be a portrait. But whose portrait?

The giant is taller than the top of the human pyramid, higher than the most daring leap of the trapeze artist. All this has a meaning, especially when combined with his strange features. In Spain, children are kept in order by frightening them with the vision of *El Gigante*, who will come and punish them. *El Gigante* is at one and the same time the burlesque creature they see in the streets during a fair and whom they can laugh at and also the eerie and terrifying magician who will come after them if they are disobedient. What is he doing here as Picasso in his old age conjures up his life and early childhood? Even though there is no actual resemblance, could he not be an image of that father whom the artist always put on a pedestal, hence his scale - the "magician" who taught him how to draw, of whom he was frightened and whom he could never rival (in his art), despite his somersaults, his flying jumps on the trapeze, and his human pyramids? It is a touching and also frightening vision, in which each of us can find his own meaning.

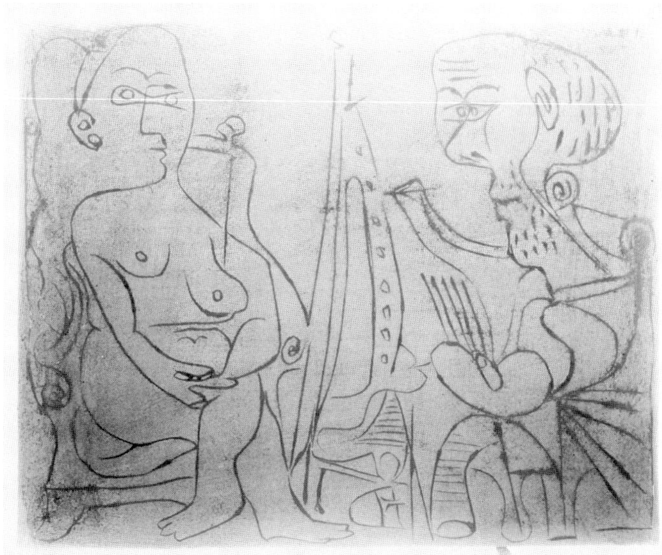

179.

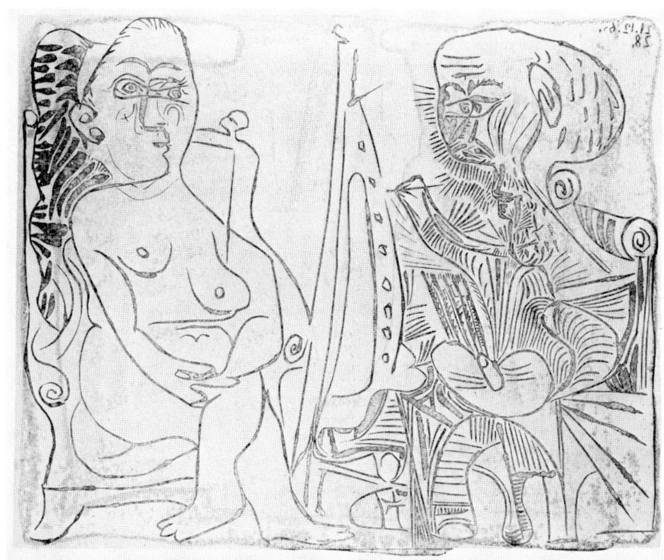

180.

179.
Le peintre et son modèle
The Painter and his Model

1963 (December 21 and 28)

Linocut in one color on one linoblock

540 x 630 mm.

1st state of the linoblock: December 21, 1963.

Proof on Arches wove paper, printed in light chocolate brown, and ''rinsed'' by the artist.

Three more ''rinsed'' proofs are known to exist; two of them are printed in cream white, and signed. One is ''rinsed'' in several colors. One proof was printed in black and signed.

180.
Le peintre et son modèle

See no. 179.

2nd state of the linoblock: December 28, 1963.

Proof on Arches wove paper, printed in caramel brown and ''rinsed'' by the artist.

Two more ''rinsed'' proofs are known to exist; one, printed in cream white, is signed. The linoblock exists. This linocut was never published.

Notice the return to a traditional technique, as well as to a subject which would dominate the intaglio prints from the autumn of 1963 until the end of 1966.

181.
Nu debout
Standing Nude

1965 (February 25)

Aquatint: direct biting on resin-grained copper

382 x 276 mm.

Proof with large margins, on handmade Auvergne laid paper watermarked "PABLO PICASSO," signed and numbered 45/50.

B.1190.

This proof was selected from one of the suites with large margins published by Broder, as an addition to his edition of Reverdy's *Sables mouvants*. It is always difficult to know exactly how many copies, or extra suites Broder made. The colophon states that there are 60 suites with large margins, numbered 1/50 to 50/50 and I/X to X/X, on Auvergne laid paper, plus 20 on old Japan paper, with large margins, numbered I/XX to XX/XX. In the editions Broder made, however, the real figures are always higher.

We decided to put this proof in the exhibition because of its special technique. The artist "paints" on the grained copperplate, using a brush and acid; it is very difficult to judge the lapse of time during which the acid must stay on the plate to get the desired tone of black, and just as in pottery decoration, one does not see the results immediately.

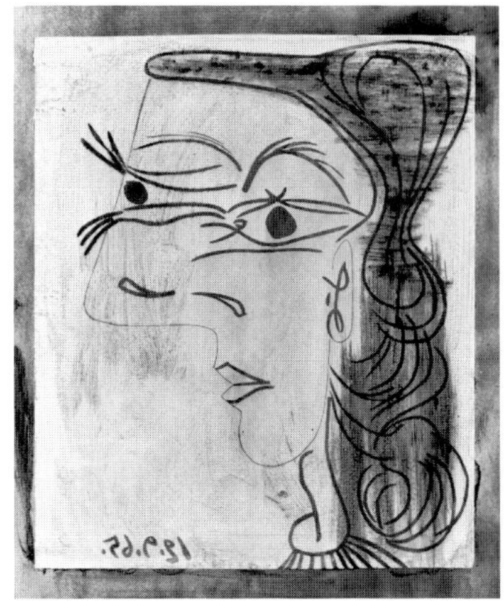

183.

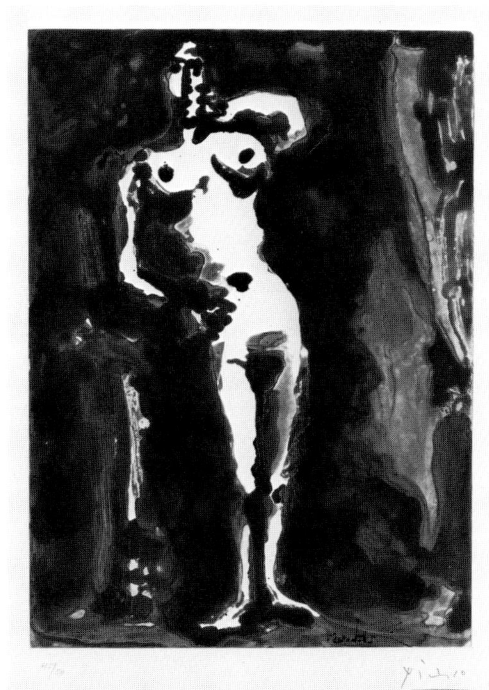

181.

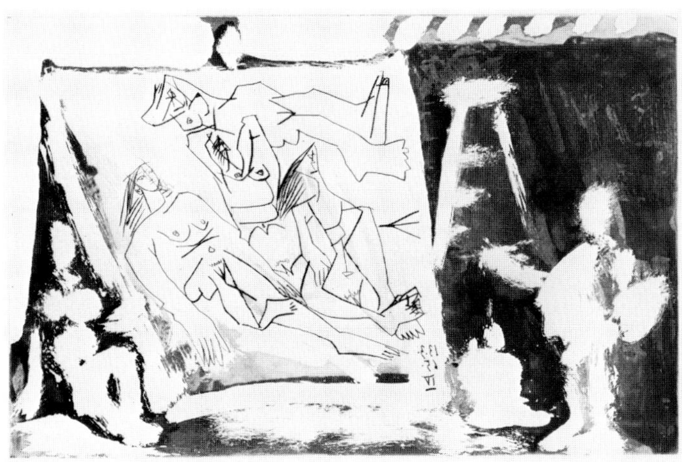

182a.

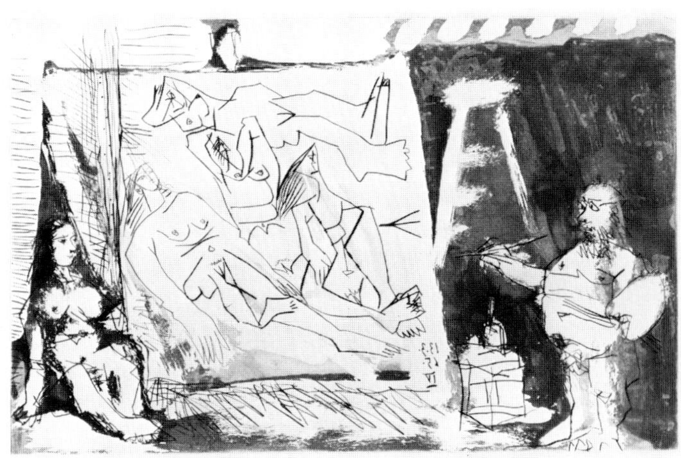

182b.

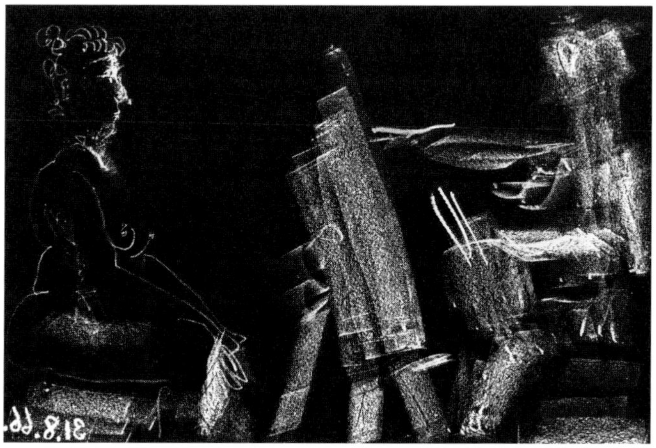

184.

182a&b.
Peintre et sa toile, avec un modèle assis
The Painter with his Canvas and a Seated Model

1965 (March 13)

Aquatint, with *réserves au vernis* and hand-biting, plus drypoint on copper

248 x 376 mm.

a. 1st state: unique proof on Rives wove paper, annotated bottom left, in pencil ''premier Etat/1 épreuve.''

b. 2nd state: one of three trial proofs, on Rives wove paper, pulled before the plate was steelfaced and bevelled.

B.1221.

After steelfacing of the plate: edition of 50 impressions on Auvergne Richard de Bas wove paper, plus 15 artist's proofs. The cancelled copperplate exists. Annotated on the back ''IV.''

It is difficult to know whether Picasso began by drawing with a drypoint the four women depicted on the canvas, then covered the surface of the projected painting with varnish when he ''sketched'' with this medium the painter, the model, the ladder, or whether he used his drypoint after the copperplate had been bitten and the varnish cleaned off. In the 2nd state, details are added. Notice the packing case on which the can of paint, brushes and other instruments are set: Picasso would always use packing cases as chairs, tables, etc. Notice also how precisely sketched the two figures are in the 1st state, yet with only a few brushstrokes.

183.
Profil de femme
Head of a Woman, in Profile

1965 (September 12)

Linocut in one color on one linoblock

640 x 530 mm.

Proof on Arches wove paper, printed in cream white and ''rinsed'' by the artist.

Another proof was printed in black on Arches wove paper. The linoblock exists.

One of the last linocuts by Picasso. He would make only six more in 1966 and 1967, mostly very small ones. This linocut was never published.

184.
Le peintre et son modèle
The Painter and his Model

1966 (August 31)

Aquatint worked with solid varnish on copper

221 x 322 mm.

One of three trial proofs, pulled on Rives wove paper before the plate was bevelled and steelfaced.

B.1478.

After the plate was bevelled and steelfaced, 30 impressions were made as suites for the 30 first copies of *El entierro del Conde de Orgaz*, Barcelona, 1969.

This aquatint was worked only with the solid varnish that we mentioned above. The medium was used on a resin-grained copperplate: notice the grainy-textured surfaces. This type of varnish does not uniformly cover the areas on which it is used, and the resulting effect is completely different from that obtained with normal liquid varnish.

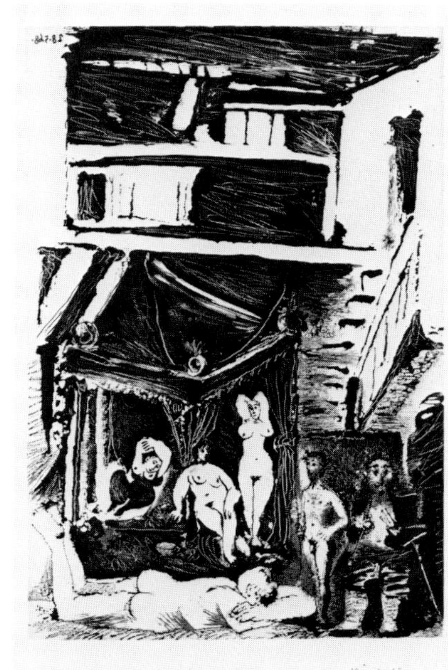

185.

185.
Rêves et souvenirs
Dreams and Remembrances
[our title]

1968 (May 28)

Aquatint on copper

488 x 335 mm.

Artist's proof on Rives wove paper, signed.

B.1604.

As a rule, after the Crommelynck brothers began printing the impressions which were to be signed and numbered 1/50 to 50/50, there would always be a further 15 artist's proofs: two for the Bibliothèque Nationale, Paris; seven for Picasso; two for the Crommelyncks; one for the Museo Picasso in Barcelona in Sabartés's memory; three for the Louise Leiris Galerie.

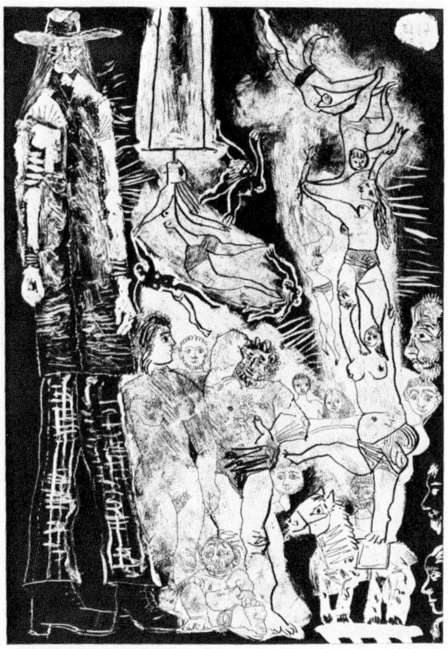

186.

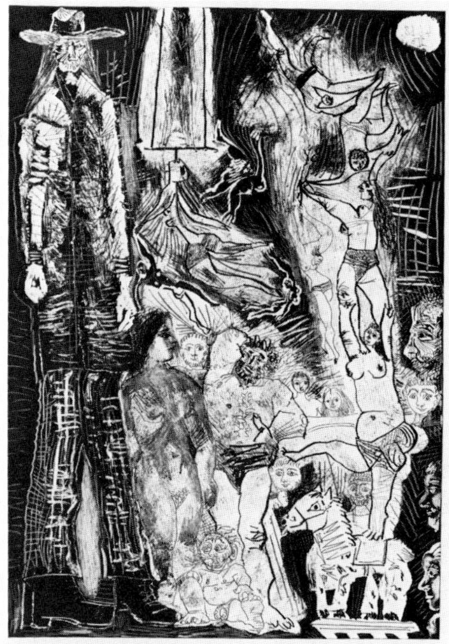

187.

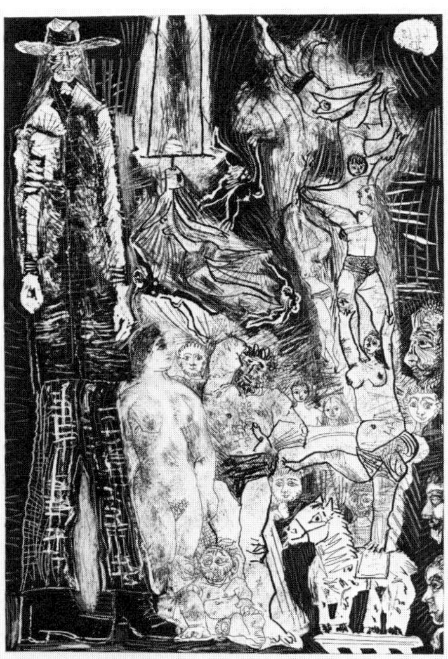

188.

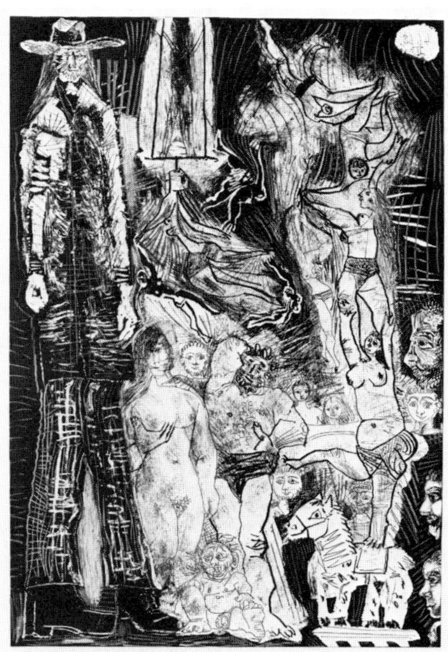

189.

186.
Le Cirque de Picasso
Picasso's Circus
[our title]

1968 (June 4)

Aquatint, with *réserves au vernis*, etching, scraper used as if it were a drypoint, and drypoint on copper

488 x 337 mm.

1st state: aquatint with *réserves au vernis*, etching; the lines are drawn with a scraper and with a needle.

One of two proofs on Rives wove paper.

Cf.B.1622.

187.
Le Cirque de Picasso

See no. 186.

2nd state: scraper and drypoint.

One of two proofs on Rives wove paper.

188.
Le Cirque de Picasso

See no. 186.

3rd state: scraper and drypoint.

One of two proofs on Rives wove paper.

Notice that the naked body of the woman is becoming whiter and more beautiful; the small man one can see behind the neck of the horse now wears a checkered sailor's shirt.

189.
Le Cirque de Picasso

See no. 186.

4th and last state: drypoint.

One of three trial proofs, pulled on Rives wove paper, before the plate was steelfaced and bevelled.

B.1622.

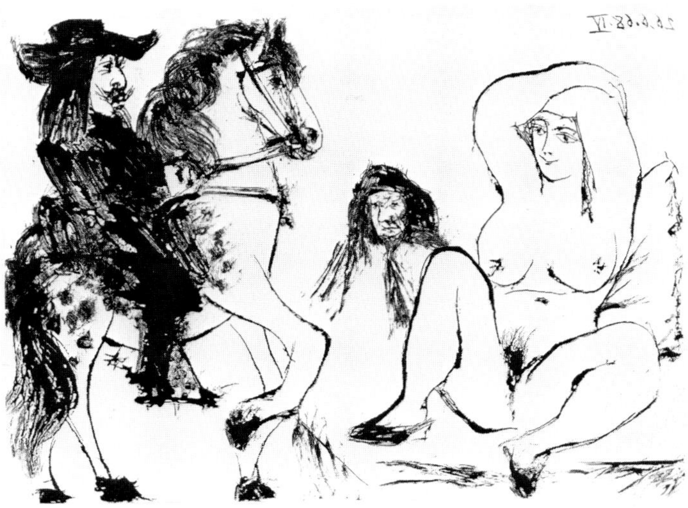

190a.

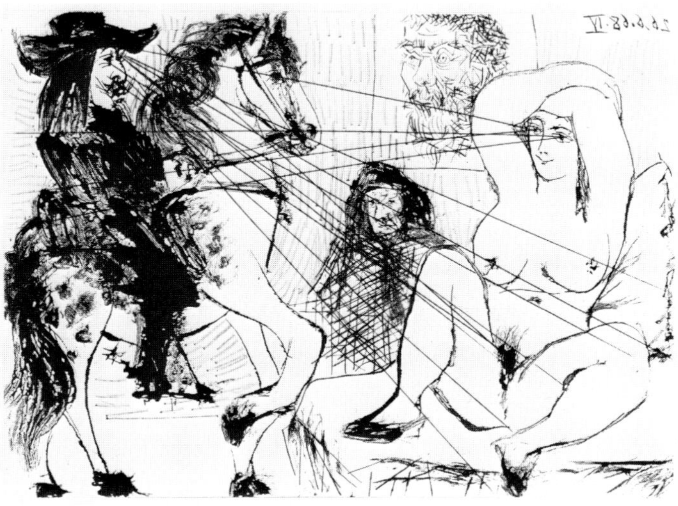

190b.

190a&b.
Cavalier, jeune femme et duègne
A Cavalier, a Young Woman and her Dueña

1968 (June 26)

Sugar-lift aquatint, scraper used like a drypoint, and drypoint on copper

148 x 205 mm.

a. 1st state: sugar-lift aquatint (with grease on the copperplate). One of two proofs on Rives wove paper, annotated bottom left "1er ETAT 2/2."

b. 2nd state: scraper used like a drypoint, and drypoint. One of three trial proofs on Rives wove paper, pulled before the plate was bevelled and steelfaced.

The copperplate (on exhibition) was cancelled in 1979. Annotated on the back "IV."

B.1671.

After the plate was bevelled and steelfaced: edition of 50 impressions plus 15 artist's proofs.

In the 1st state, the scene is straightforward and realistic: the cavalier arrives and sees the beautiful young lady; obviously the *dueña* arranged the meeting. Although the *dueñas* were guardians of the young girls' virtue, they would often overlook that task, at least in picaresque novels.

In the 2nd state, the moment the drypoint of the old husband is hung on the wall, everything becomes more complex. The man, depicted on the canvas, who is both jealous and a voyeur, *sees* precisely the way that the two protagonists stare at one another. To underline the point, drypoint strokes fix (just as in early Italian paintings) exactly the spots of the young girl's body at which the cavalier is leering and vice-versa. The old man painted on the canvas is the exact replica of the sculptor's bust in nos. 38-41.

In a group of drawings in *encre de Chine* and colored crayons, dating from 1954, Picasso used the same device in order to show exactly where his characters are looking at each other's bodies.

191.
Cauchemar
Nightmare
[our title]

1968 (August 5)

Sugar-lift aquatint and scraper used like a drypoint on copper

195 x 325 mm.

One of three trial proofs on Rives wove paper, pulled before the plate was bevelled and steelfaced.

The copperplate (on exhibition) was cancelled in 1979. Annotated on the back "V."

B.1730.

After the plate was bevelled and steelfaced: edition of 50 impressions, plus 15 artist's proofs.

If the technique is fascinating, the subject is so mysterious that the onlooker can only guess at its meaning. The suddenly aroused young lady is drawn with light scraper strokes; although the only real character in the scene, she nearly disappears, with the exception of her dishevelled hair. On the left appears a delightful musketeer; on the right a phantom-like vision, ghastly enough not even to have a shape. Of course, the two sides of her dream are linked to one another. Love and death? Man and monster? Notice the way the phantom is "conjured:" simply strokes of sugar-lift aquatint on a greasy copperplate done with the end of the brush.

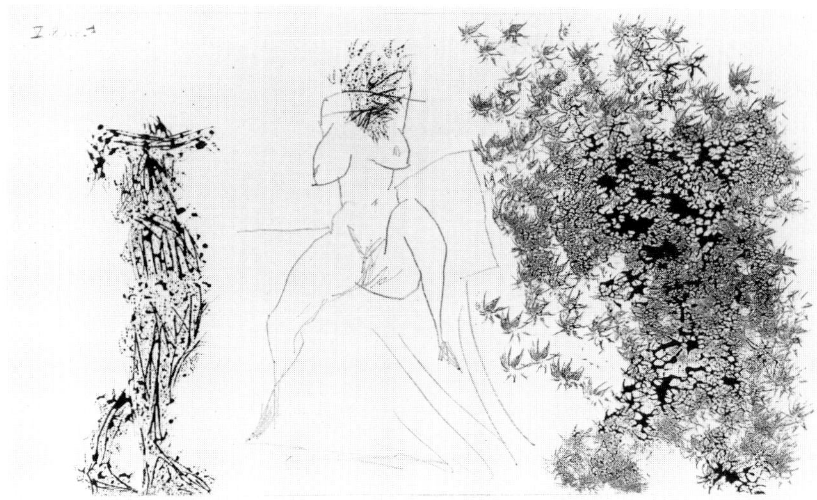

191.

192.
Déjeuner sur l'herbe, d'après Manet
Déjeuner sur l'herbe," after Manet

1968 (September 21)

Sugar-lift aquatint with grease on copper

207 x 265 mm.

Artist's proof on Rives wove paper, signed.

B.1808.

The plate is annotated on the back "I."

This is only an evocation of Manet. In more general terms, the handling is actually closer to Monet than Manet. However, it is true to say that we also have the impression of a reference to Corot and even, via Corot, to the entire tradition of Venetian Renaissance painting exemplified by Giorgione and Campagnola.

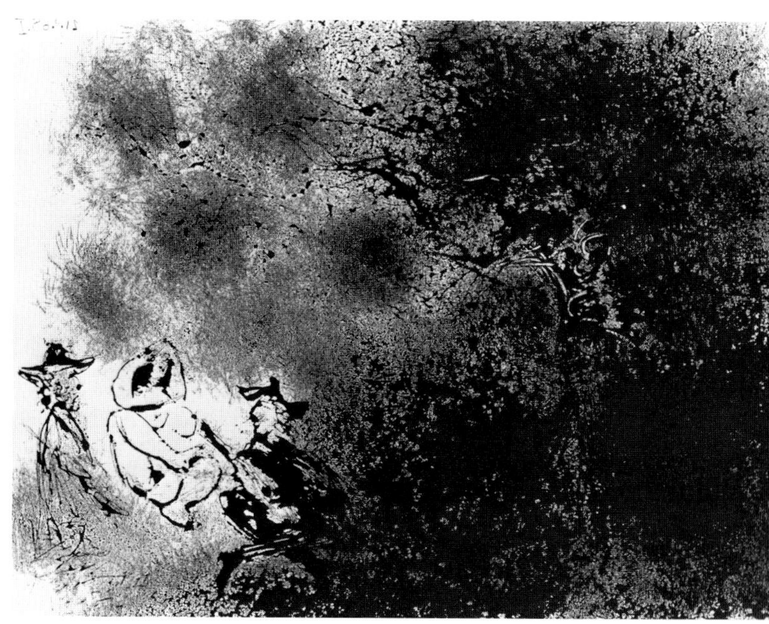

192.

It should be noted again that all the linocuts were printed by Arnéra, and that all the intaglio prints were pulled by Crommelynck.

XIII.

The Last Works

On the 24th of October, 1968, Picasso put to one side an etching which he only took up again in February of 1970. This print depicts Piero Crommelynck with his wife and little daughter. It is the very first print of the *156 Suite* which, in fact, only comprises 155 impressions as the plate of the small aquatint (B.1862; L.7) had been mislaid and could not be included in the published suite. The Leiris Gallery published together with this series two prints which had been executed some time previously, namely *Venus and Cupid* (cat. no. 112) and the *Portrait of Miss Angela Rosengart*, dating from 1966 (B.1844). Picasso signed the impressions of four of the plates in this series before his death (B.1881, 1929, 1935, and 1938). All the others were not printed in time to be signed by him and were stamped later with a cachet imitating the artist's signature. Picasso gave the *bons à tirer* in 1972.

All the impressions were printed by Crommelynck: 50 numbered impressions, plus 15 artist's proofs numbered ''E.A. I/XV'' to ''E.A. XV/XV.'' The artist's proofs of the four plates of the series, cited above, are not numbered but they were signed by the artist.

The second etching in the series, the only one made in 1969, is dated June/July. Picasso began to work in this medium again in June 1970, and all 154 prints were made between this date and March 25, 1972.

In the framework of an exhibition such as ours, it is practically impossible to make an abbreviated and satisfactory selection from this group. It is more than tempting to put on exhibition, if not the group in its entirety, at least the majority of the prints which comprises it, not simply because of their intrinsic beauty, but also because they have a particularly rich and arcane iconography which is fascinating to study in depth.

We have chosen several artist's proofs, using as criteria

not their rarity but their aesthetic and iconographic content (cat. nos. 193, 200, 201, 203, 204 and 205). Two other prints (nos. 194-198 and 199) have been included not only for the above reasons, but also because we were in a position to exhibit all the states and the copperplates as well. No. 202, although it does not comprise any state proofs, was worked on by Picasso in such a special way that we considered it important to include in the exhibition. It is also one of the most amusing plates in the series.

If anyone takes the time and trouble to flip through the Bloch catalogue from no. 1857 to 2011, and if an even more curious person goes through the catalogue published by the Leiris Gallery in 1973, where all the states of the proofs of the suite are published, he cannot help asking certain questions. To invoke Picasso's famous quote again, it might be better to try and understand birdsong instead. But what we can do is try to get nearer their essence, while resigning ourselves to the fact that we will never understand them completely. We can look and then let the waves of our own associations sweep in, without ever losing sight of the realization that Picasso's sense of humor insinuates itself into the smallest of gaps. As Piero Crommelynck remarked: "He always had a good time." Of course, Picasso's sleight of hand and humor are not just trickery, but we must avoid falling into the trap, so cleverly prepared for us by him, of taking everything too seriously. On the other hand, Picasso realized that the success of a work of art depends largely on translating personal fantasies and imagery into a universal language comprehensible to the viewer, and that aesthetic pleasure allows us to approach certain of our own fantasies which are sometimes so hidden that they cannot materialize except through the mirror of images created by another.

Picasso was 88 years old in 1970. It seems more than likely that in this series of prints he made a more or less conscious decision to abandon all logical reasoning in his work and let himself be carried along by a type of logic which is even more rigorous, although very hidden: that of dreams and memories, where one image leads to another which is attached to it not by a conjunction but by parataxis. We can draw a comparison between the *156 Suite* and the *Temps retrouvé* of Marcel Proust. The "language" is similar even though time had passed between 1922 and 1970 and though Picasso takes even more liberties with the normal processes of logic and imagery. For if Proust provides us with relatively clear indications of how his images are linked together, Picasso could not care less, and each image, or at least a good 30 of them in the series, seems to the interested onlooker more like the riddle of the Sphinx.

Among the prints we have selected, some have a simple referential iconography which encourages us in our quest for meaning. Let us examine cat.no. 203, for example. The subject is The Madame's Party, described in a short story by Maupassant which Vollard had published in 1934 with illustrations of monotypes by Degas. Picasso had bought 11 of the original monotypes, nine of which depict women in a brothel. It seems that the monotype entitled *La Fête de la patronne* had particularly struck the artist. This novella is one of Maupassant's best-known works and, with *Boule de suif*, is one of his most tender and nostalgic ones. It tells the story of a small *maison close*[1] in the Norman countryside which we discover on the very day it has been closed down, to the intense fury of the proper gentlemen of the small town who go there every evening to meet in its "family" atmosphere. The madame and her "girls" have gone off into the country to attend a First Communion. Maupassant describes in detail this holiday, the church, the ceremony, finally ending in a joyous party back at the "house" with the gentlemen overjoyed to get back to their usual routine. On this occasion the madame only charges six francs for a bottle of champagne and the novella ends with the following phrase: ''Every day cannot be a *holy/day* (*sic*).'' This work created a huge scandal at the time, and it only appeared in 1881 in a collection of short stories, published under the collective title of our tale. The Degas monotype, which Picasso owned, shows *la patronne* flustered with emotion and surrounded by her ''girls'' (Lemoisne, 549). Degas chose a particularly daring way to insert his composition on the sheet of paper. At the top right, three round light globes, cut by the edge of the print, illuminate the scene.

Even in prints with an entirely different subject, Picasso often reused the three light globes of Degas. In no. 203 he does not include them, although the scene is closely modelled on the monotype referred to above. Madame is not such a nice person, and her claw-like hands are disturbing. There are neither the bunches of flowers nor the three light globes, but, on the right, sliced in two like the young sailor in compositons with the blind Minotaur, Picasso has sketched Degas in the rather strange position which he habitually assumes in those prints of the series where he appears. He is standing with his arms behind his back, his right hand clasping his left, in a position of impotence or a self-inflicted taboo forbidding any physical contact or participation. Rumor had it that Degas was impotent; in any case, we do not know of any dalliance or love affair in which he was implicated.

The schema is a simple one. It deals with impotence and voyeurism, here situated in a context of ''women together.'' We have seen in cat.nos. 38-41, for example, how this subject seems always to have perturbed the artist. Here the setting is a whorehouse, which is sufficiently explicit in itself and has obvious sexual overtones. Impotence, personified by Degas, is counterbalanced by the terrifying hands of the madame, who is somewhat of an ogress, an element which, as we have seen, is completely alien to the gentle family atmosphere which permeates the Degas monotype. Of course, Picasso wanted to amuse himself and caricatured the madame, but the real meaning has literally jumped out of his hand.

In reference to the Minotaur, we have briefly touched on that destructive rage which, in infants, is linked to the state of dependence and impotence in which they are forcibly ''incarcerated'' at that age. Picasso himself describes for us these destructive and voracious demons in the story of the Minotaur. We find the theme of impotence in the literal sense, though here the direct result of old age, added to those earlier fantasies of dependence/impotence. One need not search for recondite theories to understand that we have here a penetrating study of an adult's reaction to this condition. In *Armance*, Stendhal had already insisted on the profound commotion caused in an adult by this ''disgrace.'' In his notes, the writer compares it with the misshapen physique of Richard the Third and goes further when he writes, ''The protagonist (Octave) is perturbed, *enraged*, because he feels impotent.'' (Our italics). Such fury is normally projected onto others who, in turn, become the persecutors and destructive; hence, the horrific hands of the madame.

It therefore seems logical that in the following print we should return to the theme of Salome (no. 204): unsatisfied passion which turns into pure destruction, and clearly an image of woman as castrator. As we know, Picasso had already treated this theme in a magisterial fashion with Salome dancing before Herod, in front of the head of St. John the Baptist on the ritual tray. He made this print in 1905 (G.17; B.14), and perhaps he was influenced in his choice of the theme by the suicide of his great friend, Casagemas, which had a powerful effect on him and which, rumor has it, made him very suspicious and wary of women for a long time. In a fit of jealous rage, Casagemas had decided to kill his mistress, Germaine, and in the belief that he had succeeded, shot himself. Josep Palau i Fabre, whose detailed research into the early years of Picasso's life is well-known, states categorically (oral communication to the author) that at the time everybody in Barcelona gossiped about the impotence of Casagemas.

The theme of Salome unites the voyeurism of old Herod (doubtless impotent) and the refusal of St. John the Baptist (an attitude which can also be linked to impotence) with the fantasy of the ''enraged'' woman, to use Stendahl's expression, who dances for Herod, the voyeur, but in front of the head of St. John the Baptist, the mirror of Herod, the impotent. She herself is the projected image of the fury of an impotent man, and for him she has turned into a bloodthirsty monster, so justifying his fears and his impotence. All this is clear.

However, on the left, above the head of the aging Herod, there are the three globes of light from *La Maison Tellier*, signifying that Picasso somehow associates the old man, some thirty years earlier responsible for the *Massacre of the Innocents*, with Degas. In a clear allusion to the habitual posture of Degas, Herod has his hands thrust deeply into the pockets of his overcoat. On the right, there is an image of feminine voyeurism which mirrors that of Herod: two women one of whom has her arms crossed over her head just as have two of the women in the *Bain turc*. When we recall that Ingres was 82 years old when he painted that canvas, everything seems to fit together in a series of interlocking references. And yet certain details make the iconography more complicated. The superb Salome, with the profile, the large eyes and the hairstyle of Jacqueline, is not dancing for Herod but has her gaze firmly fixed on the head of St. John the Baptist, which, although posed on the ritual platter, is a total caricature. Clearly once again Picasso has allowed his iconoclasm free rein, but not without motivation. In this pathetic servered head, everything is agape, the flared nostrils, the mouth full of teeth which forms a counter-point to the sex of Salome (a hackneyed but clear allusion to the *vagina dentata*), and finally the left eye, which even in death stares wide-open at Salome, betraying a final spasm of fascinated desire for the woman that the saint had rejected in keeping faith. Here once again, Picassoesque mystification is certainly present. But the freshly decapitated head has just been carried in by a servant, or perhaps the executioner himself, a sort of faun stretched out at the feet of the odalisque. His torso and legs are visible although the rest of his body still slumps in the pit which served as St. John the Baptist's prison. This is another doubling of the artist, just as we saw in the theme of the Minotaur who later turned into a faun. Here the faun is not present as a voyeur; he gazes far away into the distance, perhaps into the past.

Lastly, an added reference places the entire composition in context. In the background, the small door from the *Meninas* of Velasquez opens on the room of the palace, which thus becomes the Retiro Palace and reminds us of the theme of the mirror, of duplications and doublings, of the problem of the status of the painter and his art in society. So the aged Herod is simultaneously Degas, Ingres, Velasquez and Picasso, thus endowed with a certain potency. It is he who has the ''keys.'' It is he who ''knows.'' In the mirror images of *Las Meninas*, there is a doubling of the painter with the figure who leaves the room by the small door. As Jonathan Brown has shown, the man who is leaving is José de Nieto, the *aposentador*, the man charged with the responsibility and the honor of guarding the keys of the Queen's quarter. (See his *Images and Ideas in Seventeenth Century Spanish Paintings*, Princeton, 1978, pp. 97-110.) However, in our print, it is not a man who plays this role but a young woman, and she is not leaving the room but coming in instead. Are the ''keys'' then to be found in this personage of a woman? Is she the explanation? If so, she is only an enigmatic explanation. In Picasso's work, it is evident that it is women who possess the keys of inspiration, and he depicts them sufficiently often opening a door with a key. Complicating the entire issue again, however, are questions regarding the relationship between man and woman.

As we next approach the other prints on exhibition, everything seems to become more and more complex. All the personages of Picasso, remembrances of all the periods of his work seem to be present, just as in the *Temps retrouvé*, and the disorder in all this is underlined by Picasso himself in a print which he made early in the series between January 25 and February 15, 1970.

Before he made up his mind to use his self-portrait as a frontispiece for the *Caprichos*, Goya had intended, as is shown by the drawing in the Prado (G.W.537), to start with *Capricho* no.43, ''El sueño de la razon produce monstruos.'' We must not forget that ''sueño'' has two meanings: ''sleep'' and ''dream.'' The ''monsters'' are bats and owl-like creatures (Picasso was very fond of owls), with human heads. But in fact, Goya had made two preliminary drawings, one of which deserves our special attention. The drawing which we show here,(fig. 10; G.W.538), depicts, in addition to the bats, the feet and head of a donkey which reappears again in *Caprichos* nos. 37 to 42, and a group of heads, some jeering, some with serious expressions, which haunt the dream-sleep of the artist, sprawled across his worktable in exhaustion. Among them there is a superb, serious head which is apparently a self-portrait of the artist as a young man, duplicated elsewhere in the same drawing. The title is meant to explain to us that the *Caprichos* were born, sired by sleeping reason which allows all of our inner dreams and compulsions, freed from all restraint, to come to the surface. Now Picasso himself alludes to this plate in the *Caprichos* in our cat. no. 193. On the right, a strange kind of semipigeon, semibat flies off into the air. Just as in the Goya drawing, the images produced by sleeping reason are not monsters in the strict sense of the word, but magic evocations.

There is also a clear doubling of the artist himself. On the right, he appears as an old man/monkey/infant, an image of himself which is already present in various disguises in the *347 Suite* (see nos. 186-189), as well as in the form of a painter/musketeer. On the left, he is there as a circus Hercules or strongman, the final metamorphosis of the one who pointed to the Minotaur in the print which begins the *347 Suite* (B.1481). This Hercules has grown older, is much fatter and vaguely reminds us of the Hercules dressed up and painted like a woman, when he was hiding at Omphale's palace. Behind him there is an old gentleman, bearded and forbidding, the perfect image of a teacher, who also looks like Don José, the artist's father. This man scrutinizes his rejected offspring pitilessly. The ''father'' only appears in the 2nd state. (It is well-known that Picasso, who often depicted painters as bearded, was always tempted to paint the portraits of any bearded men in his circle. This idiosyncrasy produced an epidemic of beard-growing among his male friends. Picasso never hid the fact that the attraction existed because of his father.)

There is another onlooker, a beautiful, dignified, wise woman, a symbol of she who can be sublimated, put on a pedestal and loved.

What scene has been conjured up by the imagination of the old man on the right? As if it were a present, a porter brings on a rather caricatured odalisque seated on a cushion (see no. 20), the whole group being posed on a table. Does it represent a sculpture? A woman one pays for as a present to oneself? Is it a creation of the painter? Doubtless, it represents all three at the same time. In the background, there is one of the women ''borrowed'' from the *Bain turc*, the one who is dancing next to the negress with the tambourine on the edge of the pool. Then follows a very enigmatic figure. This is the barebreasted woman in the long skirt, so Minoan in appearance, but who also looks like one of those automata on old-fashioned music boxes. She tries to hold back or catch the pigeon/bat, whose multiform aspect reminds us simultaneously of the Dove of Peace (actually a pigeon) and also of a bat, a creature which haunts nightmares and cemeteries. In French, the word ''oiseau'' — bird — is also a reference to the penis, as the expression ''I'm going to make my bird sing for you'' is frequently used in an exclusively sexual context. Here, the bird which the ''primal'' woman-automat, this connotation underlined by her Cretan aspect, wants to catch or hold back also symbolizes the duality of life and death.

So we have three images of womanhood: first, the woman as a seductress (the dancer from the *Bain turc*); woman offered as a gift (the somewhat sagging odalisque, who is also the artist's creation); lastly, the woman who does not want to abandon her desire for the bird, even if it is linked with death, as if by some automatic system lost in the darkness of ages.

It is clearly a *caprice* but also a theater image. Picasso, as the expression goes, shows us his colors, and, via the reference to Goya, tells us to abandon reason in order to let ourselves be carried along by his dream-sleep. With this in mind, we feel justified in this chapter in leaving aside the real chronology.

We find our bird again in the five states of the small etching which we next exhibit as no. 199. Certain elements here are familiar. In the 1st state, we have the three light globes, one of which encircles a kneeling woman who looks like a girl in one of the Degas monotypes owned by Picasso. This is the one reproduced by Vollard in his edition of *La Maison Tellier*, facing page 58 (see Eugenia Parry Janis, *Degas Monotypes*, Fogg Art Museum, Harvard University, 1968, no. 83). However, Picasso has sketched her in the posture of another prostitute taken from a second monotype in his collection (Janis, no. 82).

In the 2nd state, the globes of light are replaced by two dancing odalisques, more or less in the positon of the dancer from the *Bain turc*, cited above in no.193.

We also again find the sculpture of the small odalisque, here fast asleep in front of the man with the bird. The latter has the clasical features of the ''painter'' in the so-called Avignon period and, as if to lend substance to our theory, from the 4th state onwards, he wears the striped sailor shirt which reminds us of the sailors of 1939 (see Z. IX.320, 321, and 323-330). The sailor holds hieratically to his chest a large bird which begins by looking like a hunting hawk but which, especially in the 5th state, is clearly transformed into a fat pigeon.

Finally, there is the problem of the circular female face, dark and nocturnal, which after having been distinctly outlined on the equally somber background in the 2nd state, gradually is blotted out in the 3rd, to disappear completely in the 4th. It seems to be the face of the moon, and its proximity to the painter's head refers perhaps to his solar character. We must not forget that it will vanish completely, giving way to the total darkness of night just at the moment that the naked painter puts on his sailor shirt.

In order to attempt a possible interpretation of this image, let us begin with the right side of the composition. It is very striking that the woman, the painter and the sculptured small odalisque are all posed on a sort of dais. By association we cannot help but think of those life-size terracotta sarcophagi on the lids of which the Etruscans depicted a portrait of the dead couple, semirecumbent side by side. This visual reference is further complicated by the figure of the sleeping sculptured woman who reminds us irresistibly of those hounds, heraldic animals, etc., which we find crouched at the feet of the gisant figures in medieval funerary sculpture. This connotation is reinforced by the fact that the painter/sculptor/sailor holds in his left hand a hawk/pigeon, a further visual reminder of Egyptian mortuary practices where a hawk is often used to symbolize the departed spirit. This allegory of the soul was transformed in the late Renaissance into the attributes which we see on funeral monuments where the master and mistress of the house are depicted holding the symbols of their function when alive. For example, often in Neapolitan and Spanish churches the life-size marble portraits depict the man holding, as a sign of his dignity, a sword or a ship's tiller, whereas the woman is shown with the keys or the purse which underline her role as mistress of the house. We must nevertheless not overlook that the naked man looking like ''the painter'' begins by holding the somewhat traditional hawk, and, as he is transformed into a sailor, his hawk is transformed into a pigeon (''Dove'' of Peace, the most famous attribute of Picasso, at least after the Second World War).

On the left side of the composition, the two dancing figures fit well into Picasso's former preoccupations with classical mythology. Parenthetically, there is a further visual reference to this with the two leaping maenads reminding us of the Cretan frescoes of dancing women with profiles dominated by enormous oriental eyes and the strict geomety of their eyebrows.

If the right side of the composition is a prefiguration of death, then these maenads are dancing the ritual celebration of the death of Pentheus who is delineated by Euripides as a figure of abstinence and rigidity (see Euripides' *Bacchantes*). Hence, we cannot escape the feeling that this print is somehow an allegory of the crepuscular (moon then darkness) evening of the artist's existence during which, already fixed as a dead effigy, he ruminates on the meaning of life.

The retrospective and thoughtful atmosphere of this print, with its classical overtones, in which Picasso seems to be reflecting on his long creative life, is repeated in a more direct fashion in the etching which follows (cat. no. 200). A detailed description of the personages is necessary before trying to solve the riddle of the composition. The image is divided into two very definite compartments: on the left, a group of spectators look at a theatrical presentation on the right. To begin with the spectators, in the extreme left foreground there is the usual infant/old man holding a staff surmounted by a human head in a kind of egg-shaped mandala. Between this head and the baby/old man, there are two disembodied hands, one holding the infant's bottom, the other wrapped round the staff. Next to this group on the right is a voluptuous circus lady, naked except for a short diaphanous costume, who is pointing out the spectacle to her companion. Next to her follows a small figure of a tired, boyish Cupid holding three arrows in one hand and an unstrung bow in the other. This figure is halfway between the light and the dark division of the composition and is going from one to the other.

The dark side of the composition, on the right, is dominated by a giant figure of a female Hercules, holding an enormous club in her right hand and a stone in her left. Above her head appears a man and a woman. The man's right hand rests on the Cupid's head; the woman's left arm is bent at the elbow, and the back of her hand supports her chin in the exact attitude we saw in the woman of the *Repas frugal*, although here the couple seems to look at one another. In the top right corner, a maenad dances with her head thrown back in ecstasy. In the bottom right corner, a naked woman reclines, her face heavily made up, with an elaborate hair style and with a ''Spanish'' kiss-curl.

In our opinion, the main idea of the composition is a tragi-comical meditation by the aging artist on the theme of the role which women have played in his life — in short, a picture of the various aspects of womanhood, as seen by him. During our attempt at an explanation we must not forget that the left side is in the light and the right side in darkness, which helps imply a further distinction of attributes: comedy on the left, tragedy on the right. The circus lady who points out the spectacle on the right with an ambiguous ''Latin'' gesture is frankly ridiculous but also highly important, as she is the ringmaster in this circus. Even though her over-blown charms are heavily caricatured, she is treated by the artist with humorous affection. However, it is not without significance that Picasso has chosen a comic figure, a rather snub-nosed, vulgar circus lady, rather than an Olympian goddess, to play so prominent a role and to point out ''the moral of the story.'' For the artist has chosen to show himself in three guises. First, he is there as a rather ridiculous infant/old man, sitting in a fetal crouch with staring eyes. Then comes his second persona where he shows himself as a conflation of his most insistent personifications: the jester's head on top of the jester's staff (there is a well-known convention, above all in 16th-century literature, where the king's jester uses a mini-portrait of himself either as ventriloquist's dummy or to divert the regal wrath inspired by his overly caustic wit), which ties in with the recurring theme of the mirror, a mirror of oneself and the ''other.'' If we look back in Picasso's iconography to the time of the Minotaur, for example, we recall how he used the allusion to the polished mirror-shield given to Perseus in order to allow him to face the horror of the Medusa and her two sisters, which now are transformed into an unpleasant vision of the three faces of womanhood. Even though the three women in our composition have a somewhat terrifying side, they also have a ridiculous aspect which makes Picasso's choice of a circus lady to stand in for the virgin Athena more understandable.

The third persona of the artist provides at one and the same time the connection between the two ''worlds'' as well as giving a useful pointer for solving his riddle. This is Cupid. For poor Cupid not only looks totally exhausted, but he goes off reluctantly like the proverbial lamb being led to the slaughter. Here, there is a very important detail. Cupid clutches rather desperately his bunch of three arrows in one hand, while in the other he holds an unstrung and therefore useless bow, which here only serves as a walking-stick. He is entering the world of darkness.

What vision greets him? Three different aspects of womanhood, and what aspects! The first is the giant female Hercules. Not only has she usurped the club of Hercules (here blown-up into gigantic proportions), but she holds an enormous rock in her other hand, ready to execute by stoning rather than suffer the fate of her unfortunate sisters who perished by lapidation because of their adulteries. At her side lies the enormous figure of a prostitute, but not just any prostitute. Not only is she truly a ''painted lady'' with her eyelashes drawn on her cheeks, but also she wears a typically Spanish hairstyle and is ready to go and walk the pavement with her fringe and her kiss-curl. Above her dances the ecstatic maenad. She is beautiful and is literally mad with excitement. Her dismembered limbs underline the impression of total abandonment, as the memory of the *Femme au tambourin* is forcibly impressed upon us.

Finally, behind the female Hercules, spectators of their own reflected fears, come the man and woman. In spite of the vision of ''primal'' femininity displayed before their very eyes, they are sufficiently adult and distanced from the spectacle to be able to assume the possiblity of the existence of a couple, that is, a man and woman together. In one sense, they strike the only optimistic note in the hellish darkness of their side of the composition (compare the astounding ''success'' of the exemplary couple Theseus/Oberon and Hippolita/Titania at the end of *A Midsummer Night's Dream*. Another stage within a stage!). The man's humanity is emphasized by the fact that he places his right hand on the Cupid's head in a gesture of helpful encouragement.

As for the infant on the left side of the compostion, he needs more than one helping masculine hand. He is reliant on both of the disembodied hands of his mother which encircle him in a gesture of loving protection. They are vital for his existence if he is going to withstand the vision which is a projection of her very motherhood. Not only does one of her hands reassure him by holding him, the other helps him keep his jester's staff upright which serves as a protection and allows him to laugh at his infantile vision. Picasso used to insist on the importance of the ''first step'' in anybody's life and used to keep in his pocket a photograph of Maya's first attempt to walk alone. Cupid is less dependant, as he is at least able to walk.

The last prints in the exhibition carry on, in this same way, the highly reflective and synthetic approach we have been tracing. Each one invites an analysis of Picasso's self-analysis, admittedly sometimes facetious, that is much deeper than we are able to give in the present context.

The print we have entitled *The Magus and the Women* (cat.no. 201), for example, tells a theatrical story in which, again, the theme of the couple is of vital importance. This story is, in some ways, parallel to the one in cat. no. 200, with the stage on the right and the creator's personae on the left. Here the only spectators are the small couple, in the center of the composition, who hardly change during the four states: the man has the features of Picasso's self-portraits of 1964-65 and the woman those of Jacqueline. They seem to applaud the spectacle enacted. They are the only ''real'' people, even though depicted as very small, the action on the stage as well as the author on the left being blown up by their imagination.

On the right, the scene is similar to that in the previous print but the female Hercules has been transformed into a gentle androgynous figure who begins life (1st state) as a young man and becomes a woman without entirely losing its masculine attributes.

On the left side, we have the creator: depicted as a large head with a beard and looking like the painter in the prints of 1963-1966 (e.g. B.1138), he holds a hand out toward the vision of femininity on the right and is seen furthermore as a kind of black, wizard-like visitor who brings with him the darkness of night. Who is he? He wears the 17th century Spanish costume of Velasquez and seems to be supporting a floating object which is simultaneously the mirror/shield of Perseus and a jester's puppet. In brief, he is a conflation of the creator as the painter, as a monster-slaying hero (the allusion, again, to Perseus), and finally as an illusionist who maliciously pokes fun at our preconception of reality.

The scene as rapidly described seems to be coherent, but there is one further detail which at least should be pointed out. This is the large disembodied arm which is shown offering to all these women a jewel. We have emphasized above the jester's side of Picasso's nature. Here we have to deal with a rather scurrilous visual pun: in France, as in America, male genitalia are sometimes referred to as ''the family jewels.'' The women on the right seem uninterested, while only the small ''real'' woman stretches both her hands as if prepared to accept the gift. Along with Picasso's fascination with the mysteries of femininity, the themes of creation and of the artist's persona and vision are clearly once again at work.

The conceit of a staged spectacle is even more apparent in *La Fête de la patronne* (cat. no. 202). Here

Picasso mixes up people from the depraved, gay café-society of the 60s, who congregated each summer in the south of France, with proper bourgeois characters formally dressed in costumes of the period who refer to the men Maupassant describes in *La Maison Tellier*.

The only action, if one can call it that, takes place between the effete Cocteauesque homosexual, seated at the right, and a whore who fully displays to him her ''charms,'' while the other characters simply stare. This central woman wears the elaborate hairstyle and numerous bracelets which were fashionable in the 60s, so in spite of her gesture, she is the archetypal jet-set woman of Cannes and Saint Tropez.

At the left, we find the romantically bearded painter who simultaneously observes our spectacle and paints with watercolor a portrait of Jacqueline in his sketchbook. Other spectators include a naked and attractively feminine woman lying back on the Napoleon III sofa and a young nymphette who has the looks of Cathy, Jacqueline's daughter. In spite of the light globes of *La Maison Tellier*, the whole scene seems to take place in a luxurious southern hotel rather than the small Normandy townhouse of the Maupassant novella. Nevertheless, the madame is present, with an expression both whimsical and stoic. No wonder! The madame is old, as is Picasso. She knows a lot about life, as does Picasso. ''In their time,'' the world was more clearly differentiated, with brothels, for example, on one side and decent ladies on the other, and with men on one side and women on the other. Nowadays (and this is why the character of the madame, identifiable with Picasso, is the center of a story that the artist lavished so much time and technical skill on) everything is topsy-turvy; society women invade the territory of prostitutes, obliging whores to preserve what is left of true femininity.

If we now take a step backwards chronologically to nos. 194-198, we can see how Picasso established a precedent early in this series with a literal depiction of a stage. The composition in its final state is divided horizontally into two sections. The upper part is occupied by a staged spectacle with an audience looking downward, and the bottom section is comprised of numerous actors from Picasso's world.

Nothing could be clearer than the source of Picasso's inspiration. It is the large etching by Rembrandt of the *Ecce Homo* (1655; Bartsch, 76), which we reproduce in two states, the 4th and the 8th and last (figs. 11 & 12). Picasso not only borrowed the actual composition from Rembrandt but also made use of his iconography. Now, it is not Christ who is presented to us but the artist himself. Interestingly enough, Picasso adopted in exactly reverse order Rembrandt's *modus operandi*. Whereas the Dutch artist began by filling the lower half of the plate with a multitude of jeering spectators (1st to 5th states) and then suddenly suppressed them, uncovering the podium supported by two blank arches symbolizing Christ's solitude, Picasso began by leaving the bottom half of his plate practically empty (1st and 2nd states), only later to fill it suddenly with a host of characters central to his existence. He too did not overlook the symbolic quality of these blank arches which he copied faithfully on his plate from the 1st state onwards. Furthermore, it is interesting to note that just as the central stage did not show any major alterations in Rembrandt's etching throughout its eight states, so Picasso did not touch the stage, so central to his composition, during the five states of *his* print.

There is a further direct borrowing from Rembrandt on the right side of the central part of the composition where we find a large female ''caryatid'' wearing an oriental turban. She not only refers to the *Femmes d'Alger* but also reminds us of the large female Hercules in print no. 200. In Rembrandt's etching, a similar figure is placed on the entablature of the right side, symbolizing prudence and liberty in the guise of an amazon. In Picasso's print she makes a sudden appearance in the 5th state but is not fully scraped clear until the 6th and final state. Directly opposite, on the other side of the plate, is a man dressed with a turban and oriental gown who is stepping onto the stage. He is directly lifted from Rembrandt's etching, where he is found in the last state, the only surviving spectator, standing at the foot of the podium as if he too were entering onto the stage. He is an important actor in the scene, for not only does he have a real and distinct presence but also he appears to be looking compassionately at the figure of Christ, who is separated from the jeering crowd. Picasso reuses this figure to stand in for Rembrandt. Just behind the oriental man is another borrowed figure, the naked, curtseying woman who, in Velasquez's *Las Meninas*, appears fully clothed as the personal maid of honor of the Infanta. Thus, these three figures comprise a brief hommage by Picasso to his mentors.

We turn now to the stage, clearly the focal point of the composition, and find on it the multiple personae of the artist seen in various guises and mixed in with characters from Rembrandt's *Ecce Homo*. From left to right, we can identify the following personages. The naked baby and the equally naked standing man are evidently two facets of the artist's own person. Here the child is literally re-enacting the meaning of the title *Ecce Homo* by pointing to the bearded man. Then follows the figure of Pilate, sitting on his throne with his wife standing beside him. Pilate evidently is another persona of the artist himself. Is Picasso, like the Roman, symbolically washing his hands not only of his past, but also perhaps of the present and even the future, washing his hands of all the rest of the world? Next to the throne there is the figure of a naked amazon on horseback (in French, the word *amazone* is widely used to describe a lady rider sitting sidesaddle). Here there is a reference to Rembrandt's caryatid/amazon, symbol of freedom, as well as to Picasso's own multiple versions of circus bareback riders. Just below her is an amusing depiction of a naked blond girl squatting in a bathtub which is clearly shaped like a boat. This is a possible reference to Picasso's own never-ending bathers and perhaps also to Marie-Thérèse. Next to her follow one after the other a standing jester, a seated jester, a standing clown, and, behind them, a standing figure holding a halberd, who is borrowed from Rembrandt's *The Procurator*, as well as a bearded figure leaning on a stick, who also appears in the bottom right corner of Rembrandt's *Ecce Homo*.

Crowded together and leering down over the stage, just as if they were the audience in the balcony of a theater or perhaps a group of stagehands responsible for moving the scenery and lighting the play, appears a group of disembodied heads which are all self-portraits of the artist. Almost half of them, if not actually asleep and dreaming, have their eyes lowered in respectful silence.

The lower half of the composition is populated with larger figures who, on the contrary, show no interest whatsoever in the curtain call taking place over their heads. It is almost as if they were going backstage to congratulate the actors after their performances. Among the personages sandwiched between self-portraits of the artist who we can identify with some certainty are, from left to right, Dora Maar and Françoise Gilot, seen in profile, Marie-Thérèse Walter, leaning with her back half turned as she looks down out of the scene, and finally, standing on the extreme right, an important representation of a naked Jacqueline. Two more enigmatic images complete this group. In the middle, directly under the star which centers and illuminates this dark foreground, is a multiple head with three or four profiles superimposed one on top of the other, and which is perhaps a combined reference to those women who played a part in the early years of Picasso's life. Opposite, there is couple exchanging a kiss. This theme is never absent from the artist's work. We have only to think of the splendid canvas of 1925 (Z.V.460), of the ferocious ''surrealist'' images of this act in 1929-1931 (e.g. Z.VII.323, one of the more beautiful and strange examples), and of the last versions dating from 1969 (e.g. Z.XXXI.484).

Before attempting a summary conclusion of the probable signification of this print, two further details deserve comment. In the 1st state, Picasso placed in the lower archways two women who are extremely reminiscent of figures in *Guernica*. Secondly, on the extreme right, there stood a scarecrow-like ''Don Quixote'' figure. This man lifts his hands in horror as he gazes upwards and at the same time an enormous jet of semen spurts from his erect penis. Is this a clue to help us to unlock the image's meaning? In addition, in the 3rd state, before the artist transformed him into the kissing woman, there is an upturned head of a bearded man who seems to be wailing with open-eyed terror at what is taking place above his head. Another clue?

All of Picasso's women are present. All his world is but a stage. However, Picasso's reaction as he looks back over his shoulder at this cortège which has passed through his life seems to be a mixture of tearful lamentation and whimsical ecstasy.

The last print in the exhibition (cat. no. 205) was not the last that the artist made. On March 25 he etched a relatively cheerful composition of a woman with a mirror. In our print, however, if one is permitted a certain interpretive latitude, the atmosphere of death in some inexplicable way is strongly present.

In this instance, if we stand a chance of entering into Picasso's world we are obliged to look back at the six previous states of the composition. In the 1st state, there are two women and a dog. The women wear the black stockings of the ''girls'' who appear in the Degas monotypes as well as several of Picasso's drawings from 1902. One of these women, the one on the right, remains unchanged until the 7th and last state. She is very strange: angular as a metal cutout sculpture, she is smelling the perfume of a bizarre flower which has the form of a handkerchief. The flower for Picasso is always a direct reference to the female sex and also to relationships of ''women together;'' the handkerchief might refer to the *Weeping Woman* and hence to the artist's mother. This woman is wearing the costume of the circus lady in cat. no. 200, but here, impassive and distant through all seven states, it is she who represents the image, the idea, the vision.

The second woman, who one can see in the last state as the monumental head and bust on the left of the composition, was in the 1st state a full-length figure reminding us of the sphinx in Ingres's painting of *Oedipus and the Sphinx* (Musée du Louvre) but seemingly terrified by our angular lady on the right. One curious thing about the large head into which she is finally transformed, is the vertical line of eyes drawn on her cheek. There are seven of these eyes, which is the exact number of women who played an important role in Picasso's life before Jacqueline, who can be identified as the head itself.

The third character in the 1st state is a huge male dog which also bristles with enraged fright in front of the angular lady on the right, as dogs do in the face of death. He disappears in the 2nd state, progressively turning into a strange head which reminds us of the later self-portraits (Z.XXXIII.435-437) but still more of a large sculpture dating from 1948 (Spies, 337) which is a kind of muzzle-like head of a bull/Minotaur. In our last state, the terrifying central head takes on more the aspect of the gigantic sculpture which is now in the Civic Center of Chicago (Spies, 653) and which also is perhaps a reminder of Picasso's personal iconography of the sphinx. This head sits in the center exactly like the bust of the sculptor as a voyeur, as seen in cat. nos. 38-41, but also recalls for us an African mask which was in Picasso's sculpture studio in Mougins (see David Duncan's *L'Atelier silencieux*, Paris, 1976, page 76). The three parallel ritual scars of this mask are repeated under the bottom eye of the woman's head on the left.

It is not by chance that this strange mask-like head occupies the center of the image, as it stands for the artist himself. But what do the two women represent? The woman on the left could be a shorthand reference for all the women in the artist's life, superimposed one on top of the other, under the guise of Jacqueline. As for the woman on the right, is she not a compilation of all the abstract fixations which Picasso surely had about womanhood and which we all share? She would thus mingle sensuality, deceit, mourning, motherhood, hence Mother Earth and Death, which explains in the 1st state the horror of the woman who is offering herself up to her own mirror image, and the terror of the dog.

The aggressive dog itself is transformed into an image of the artist, reminding us of the bestial quality of the voracious Minotaur, which Picasso himself linked with the myth of the sphinx. In turn the sphinx asks the question of the eternal ambiguity of masculinity and femininity, which both loom out of the voyeuristic monster's gimlet eyes.

To this concentration of many of the themes and recurrent images of the artist's work, something is added, that atmosphere of approaching death which is so palpable in this print, as if Picasso, by using his own multiple personae, was allowing us to share in that moment of premonition when we glimpse a second image of ourself on the very day of our death.

With these examples in mind, it need hardly be stressed how moving and at the same time challenging these late works are. They impress us as a dense compendium of Picasso's themes, obsessions and wide-ranging ruminations on his life and work, and they astonish us by the virtuosity (Picasso at the time was 90 years old!) with which these themes are woven together visually. His love affair with the copperplate continued until his very last days. The copperplate was his toy, his confidant, his only true interlocutor, the one which understands and shares pain, anxiety, pride, and humor as well as reflections on the vanity of life. Moreover, it is the one which could give back all of this to the public - the public which was so vital for Picasso, hence the recurrent themes of theater, circus, etc. — in the form of masterpieces. This affinity, understanding and love, which lasted between Picasso and the copperplate for more than 70 years, led to something truly timeless: Picasso, no doubt, will remain until the end of the world *the* great printmaker of our century.

Note: All titles in this chapter are our titles. There are no titles whatsoever for the last prints of Picasso.

193.
''Los Caprichos'' de Picasso
Picasso's ''Caprichos''

1970 (January 25, February 15)

Etching and scraper on copper

228 x 328 mm.

4th and last state.

Artist's proof on Rives wove paper, numbered ''E.A. IX/XV'' and stamped with a cachet imitating Picasso's signature.

L.5; B.1860.

The old man on the left of the proof only appears in the 2nd state.

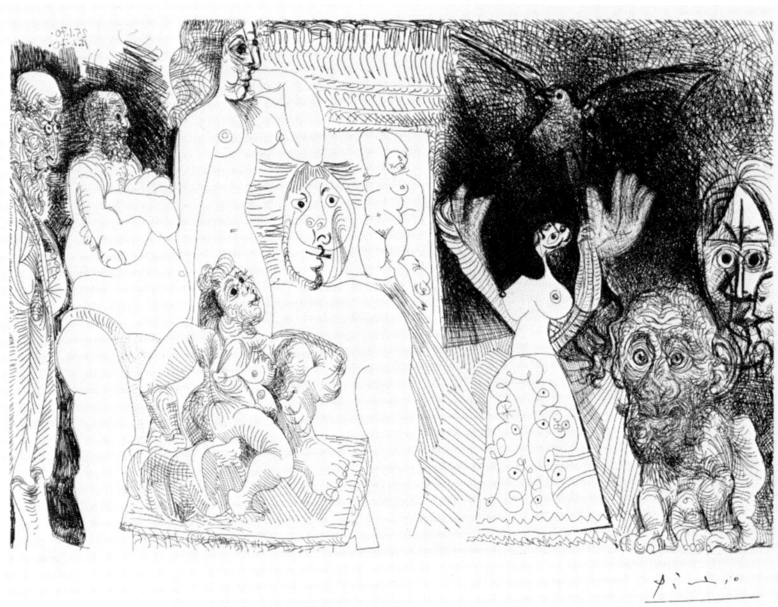

193.

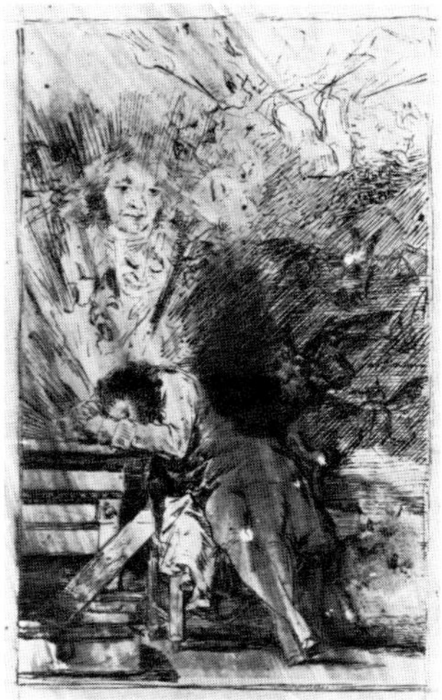

Fig. 10. Goya, *The Sleep of Reason Produces Monsters*, pen and ink on paper, Prado Museum, inv. no. 470 (courtesy of the Prado Museum).

194.
''Ecce Homo'': le théâtre de Picasso
''Ecce Home'': Picasso's Theater

1970 (February 3, March 5 and 6)

Etching, aquatint with *réserves au vernis*, scraper used traditionally and also like a drypoint on copper.

488 x 416 mm.

1st state: etching, aquatint (*réserves au vernis* and *réserves à l'encre de Chine*) and scraper on the resin-grained plate, before biting. Plate is dated February 3 and annotated ''V.''

One of three proofs on Rives wove paper, annotated bottom right, in pencil by the printer ''Etat I.''

L.10.a; cf. B.1865.

Picasso would always do everything on a copperplate by himself. In this case, he asked Piero Crommelynck to cover a rectangular surface with varnish, and told him to put it not right in the middle of the plate but slightly higher, and slightly displaced on the left side of the plate (right side on the proof). Perhaps he wanted the placement to be made somewhat by chance, as he had in mind Rembrandt's *Ecce Homo*. Then he asked him to grain the remaining areas of the plate with resin and began to work on it with liquid varnish, etching needle and the architect's pen and *encre de Chine*, mentioned above.

The visitor can see the use of the architect's pen on the characters at the left side of the central rectangular area as well as on the head of the boy who leans over the stage in the upper left side, it produces white lines on the aquatinted areas. Picasso went on drawing with this pen on the varnish-covered rectangle but, as the varnish was dry, he doubled his lines with a traditional etching needle, at the same time as he drew the ''Ecce Homo'' scene which is the spectacle shown on the stage. If attentive enough, one can also notice the very faintly drawn characters in the varnish covered areas (white areas on the proof) under the stage: these figures seem to be drawn with very light drypoint strokes. In fact, they were drawn into the freshly layed varnish which, not being dry enough, recovered the thin *encre de Chine* lines made with the architect's pen. As this kind of pen is very sharp and thin, the copperplate itself is always somewhat scratched, as can be seen under a magnifying glass, in the middle of the white lines mentioned above.

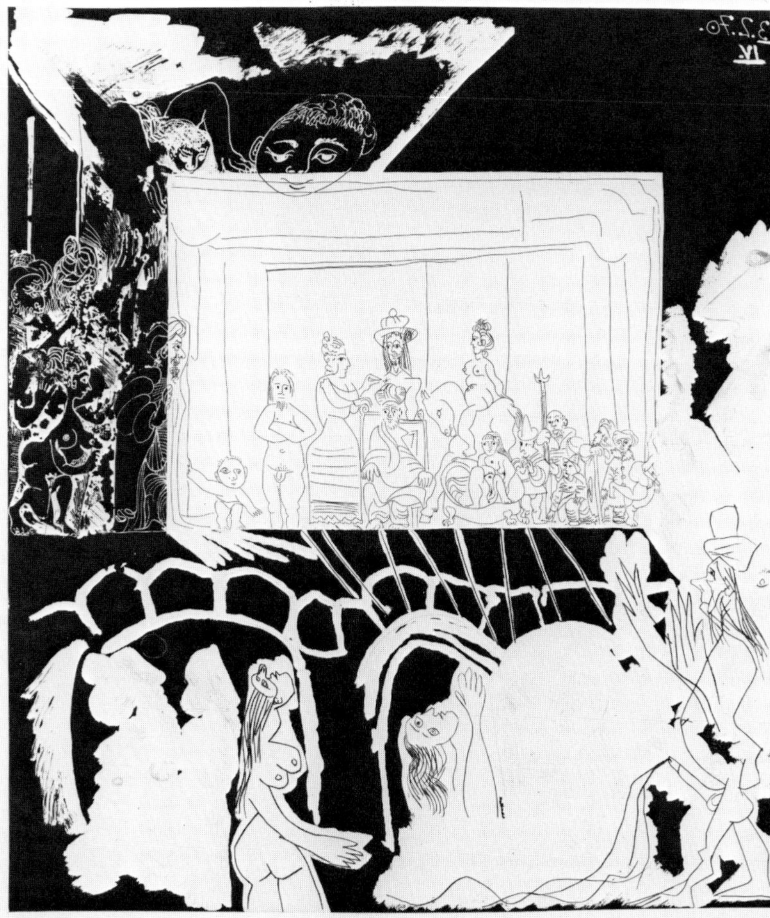

194.

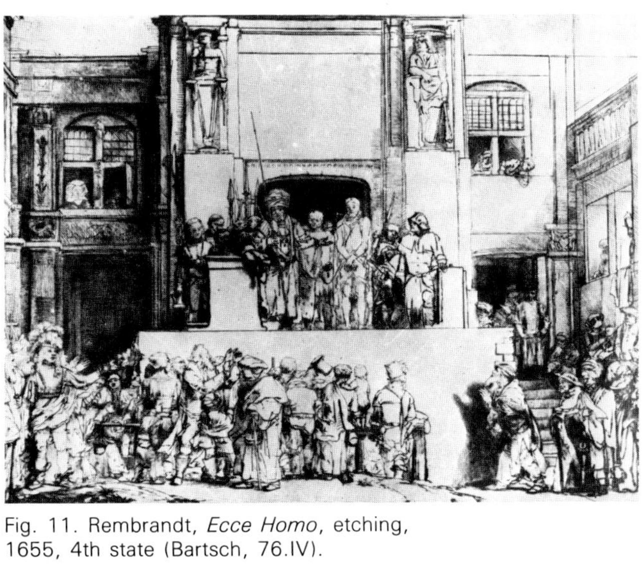

Fig. 11. Rembrandt, *Ecce Homo*, etching, 1655, 4th state (Bartsch, 76.IV).

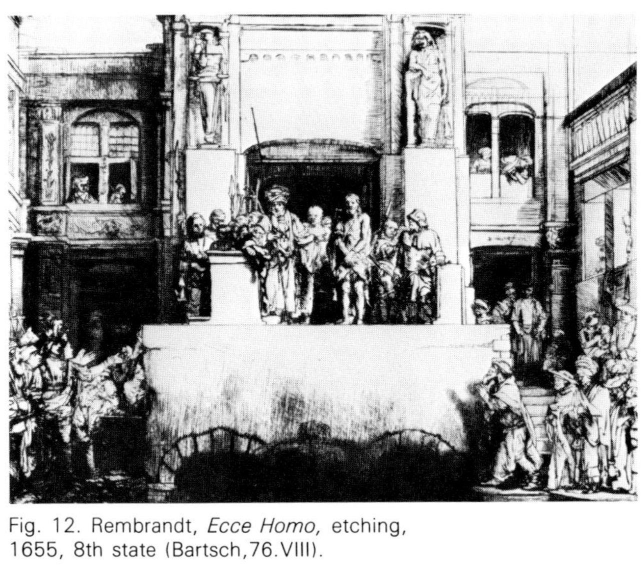

Fig. 12. Rembrandt, *Ecce Homo,* etching, 1655, 8th state (Bartsch,76.VIII).

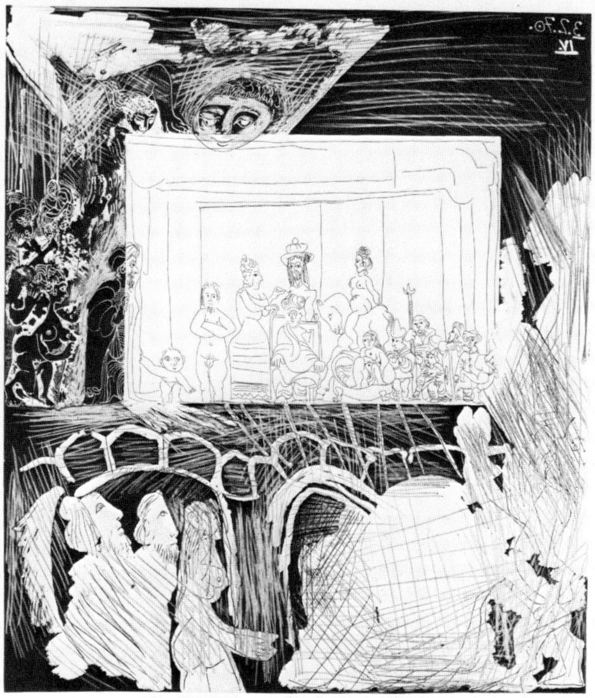

195.

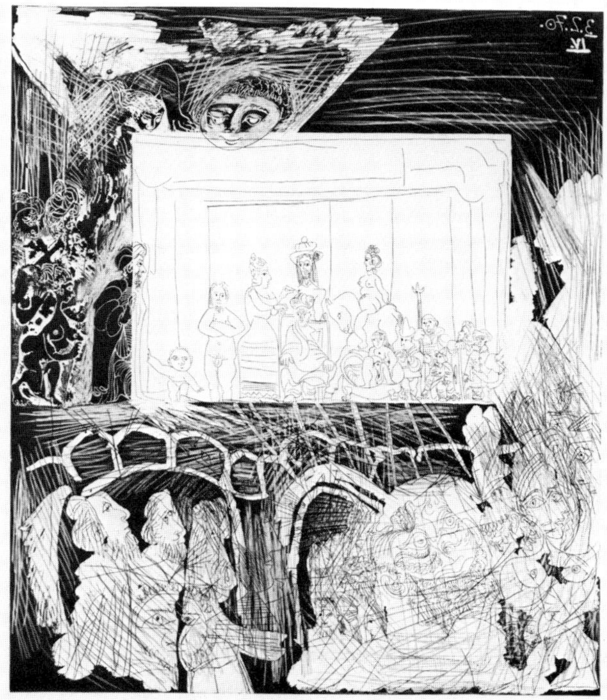

196.

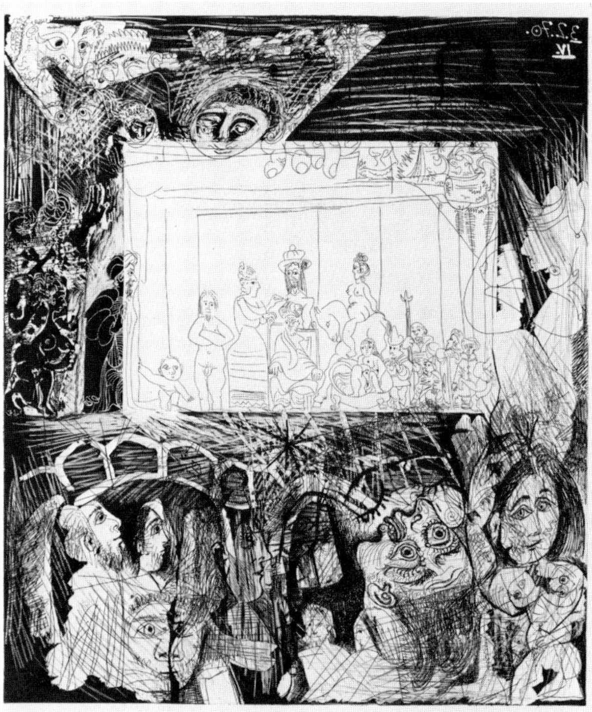

197.

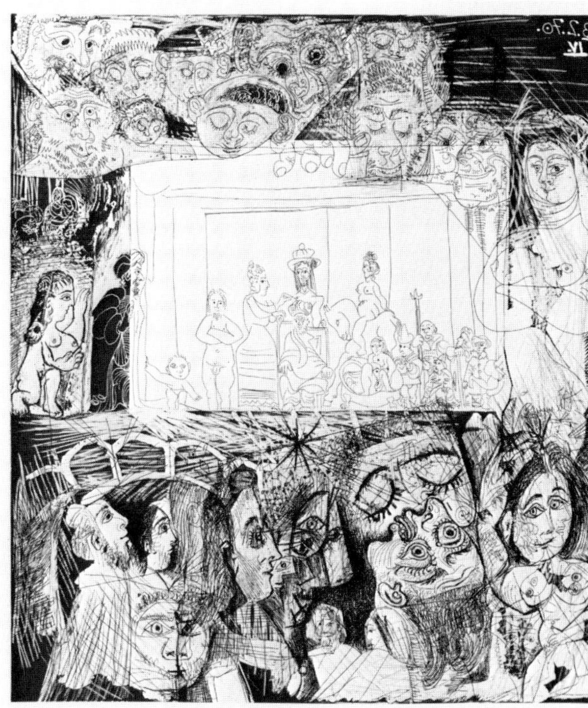

198.

195.
''Ecce Homo'': le théâtre de Picasso

See no. 194.

2nd state: scraper, used traditionally, and also used as a drypoint. The plate is dated February 3.

One of three proofs on Rives wove paper, annotated bottom right, in pencil by the printer ''Etat II.''

L.10.b; cf. B.1865.

196.
''Ecce Homo'': le théâtre de Picasso

See no. 194.

3rd state: etching. Plate dated February 3.

One of three proofs on Rives wove paper, annotated bottom right, in pencil by the printer ''Etat III.''

L.10.c; cf. B.1865.

New characters begin to appear under the stage; among them the naked woman on the right and a praying man whose head is thrown backwards in supplication.

197.
''Ecce Homo'': le théâtre de Picasso

See no. 194.

4th state: etching. Plate dated March 5 and 6.

One of three proofs on Rives wove paper, annotated bottom right, in pencil by the printer ''Etat IV.''

L.10.d; cf. B.1865.

All the characters who will appear in the 5th and last state were drawn with the etching needle in this state although they are difficult to perceive on the aquatint covered areas. The praying man mentioned above becomes a woman who is kissing a man leaning over her with his eyes closed. The *Femme d'Alger* on the right, as well as the jester and all the onlooking faces above the stage are already crawling about, and the small kneeling woman on the left already replaces the somewhat vulgar young lady who had been curtseying there since the 1st state.

198.
''Ecce Homo'': le théâtre de Picasso

See no. 194.

5th and last state: scraper. Plate dated March 6.

One of three trial proofs on Rives wove paper, pulled before the plate was bevelled and steelfaced, annotated bottom right, in pencil by the printer ''Etat V.''

The copperplate (on exhibition) was cancelled in 1979.

L.10; B.1865.

All the characters mentioned above appear in the scraped aquatint background; the jester's bonnet is not completely scraped clear and only one of his horns is visible.

199a-e.
Marin tenant un pigeon, sculpture et femmes
Sailor with a Pigeon, Sculpture and Women

1970 (February 4, 13 and 14)

Etching and scraper on copper

148 x 205 mm.

a. 1st state: etching. February 4.
One of three proofs on Rives wove paper, annotated bottom right in pencil by the printer ''Etat I.''

b. 2nd state: etching. February 13 and 14.
One of three proofs on Rives wove paper, annotated bottom right in pencil by the printer ''Etat II.''

c. 3rd state: etching. The dates are no longer visible. One of three proofs on Rives wove paper, annotated bottom right in pencil by the printer ''Etat III.''

d. 4th state: etching and scraper.
One of three proofs on Rives wove paper, annotated bottom right in pencil by the printer ''Etat IV.''

e. 5th and last state: scraper.
One of three trial proofs on Rives wove paper, pulled before the plate was bevelled and steelfaced, annotated bottom right in pencil by the printer ''Etat V.''

The copperplate (on exhibition) was cancelled in 1979.

L.12.a,b,c,d and definitive state; B.1867.

In the 1st state, one can see the three globes of light which are the symbol of *La Maison Tellier*; then the Ingresque odalisque-like dancers enter the scene. In the 4th state, the naked man with the pigeon wears a sailor shirt. Notice the moonlike head which shows out of the background near the man's head in the 2nd state: it will be completely blotted out in the 3rd and 4th states.

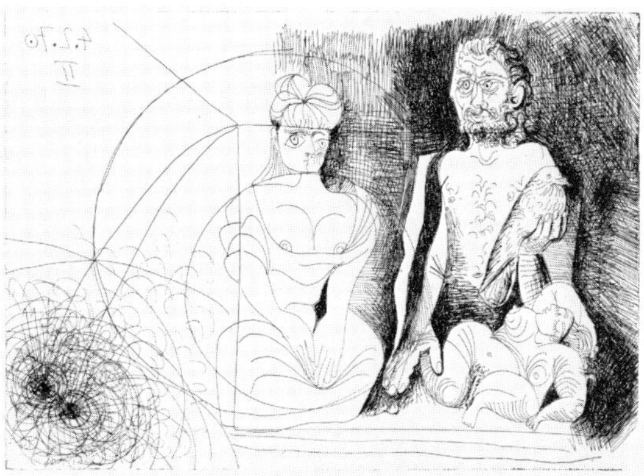

199a.

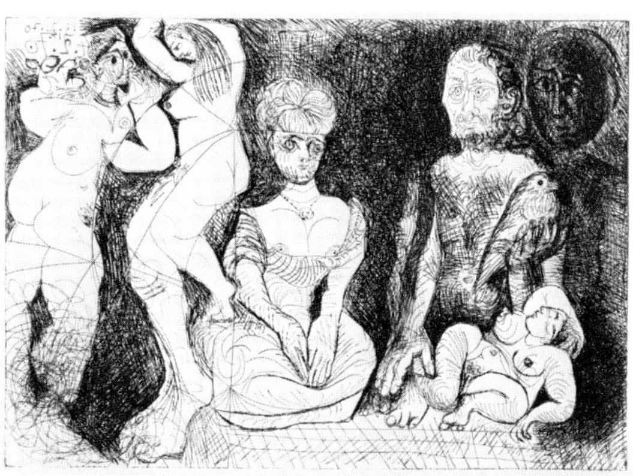

199b.

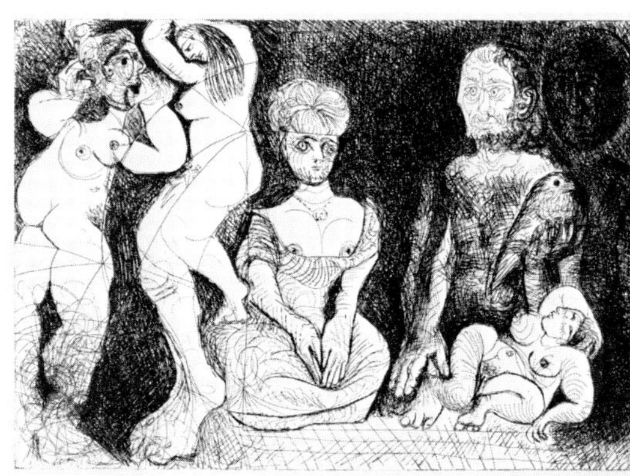

199c.

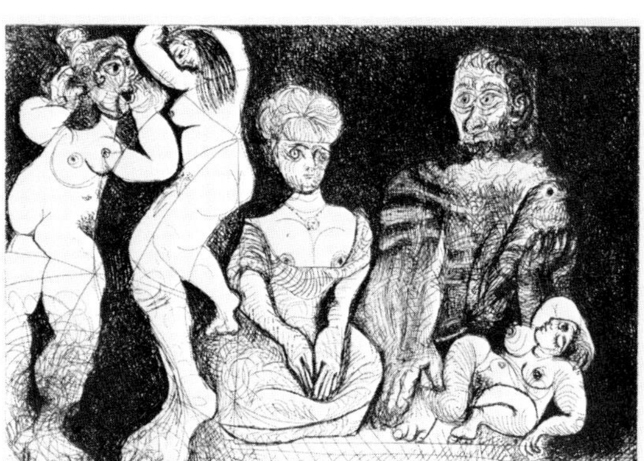

199d.

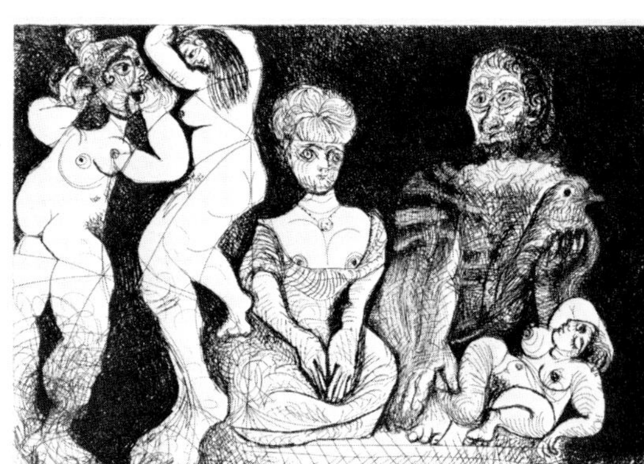

199e.

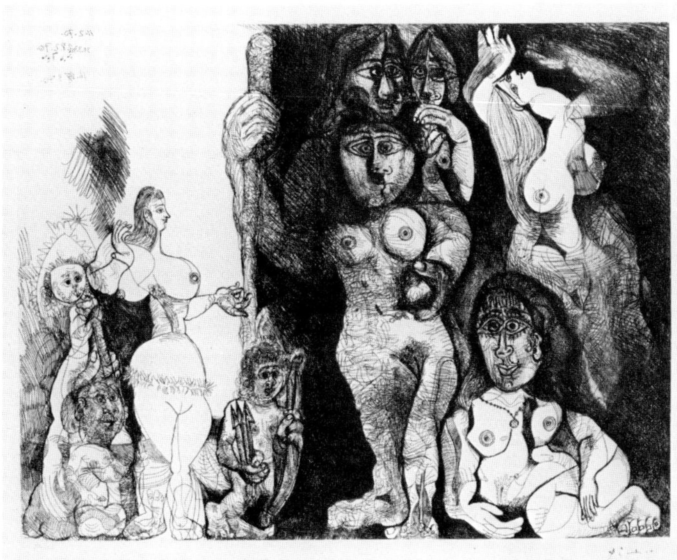

200.

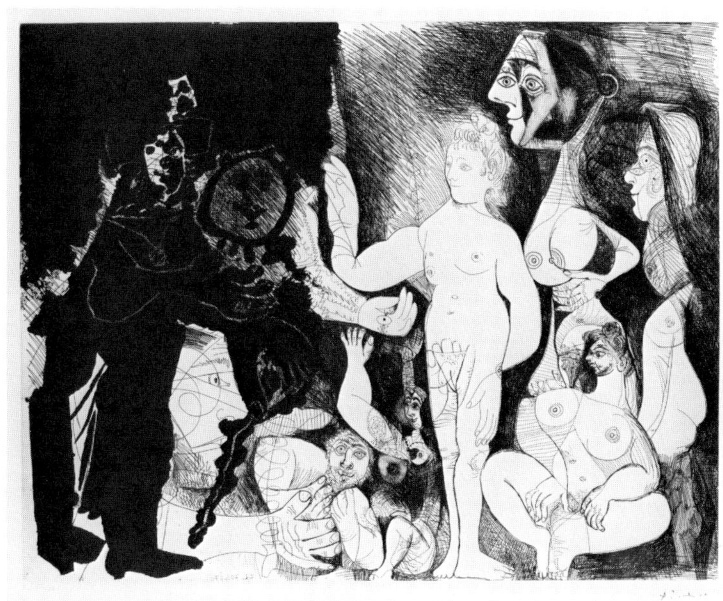

201.

200.
Le Théâtre de Picasso: Eros et les Femmes
Picasso's Theater: Eros and Women

1970 (February 11 and 28, March 3, 6, 30)

Etching and scraper on copper

500 x 635 mm.

9th and last state.

Artist's proof on Rives wove paper, numbered "E.A. VIII/XV" and stamped with a cachet imitating Picasso's signature.

L.13; B.1868.

201.
Le théâtre de Picasso: le prestidigitateur et les femmes
Picasso's Theater: the Magus and the Women

1970 (February 16, March 2 and 4)

Etching, drypoint, scraper and sugar-lift aquatint on copper

500 x 635 mm.

4th and last state.

Artist's proof on Rives wove paper, numbered "E.A. IX/XV" and stamped with a cachet imitating Picasso's signature.

L.15; B.1870.

202.

La Maison Tellier: la fête de la patronne
''La Maison Tellier'': The Madame's Party

1970 (February 19 onwards)

Etching on copper

498 x 632 mm.

Unique state.

One of three trial proofs on Rives wove paper, pulled before the plate was bevelled and steelfaced, annotated bottom right in pencil by the printer ''19.2.70'' and ''Etat I.''

The copperplate (on exhibition) was cancelled in 1979.

L.16; B.1871.

Picasso worked for several days on this astounding etching, without wishing to observe the progression of his endeavours. He told Piero Crommelynck that he wanted no state proofs to be pulled. He went on working, allowing himself no possibility of ''*repentirs*,'' never using his scraper until the plate began to show areas which were worked over so often that he could foretell the effect they would produce on the proof after the biting of the plate: those clear areas, for instance on one of the three globes of light. The only *repentirs* he could permit himself were the ones which are visible on the proof, for instance, the superimposed two brushes in the painter's hand. Piero Crommelynck said that ''he (Picasso) had great fun with this plate.'' It is as if Picasso was attempting to break the world high jump record, having himself put the bar at an impossible height.

203.

La Maison Tellier: la fête de la patronne
''La Maison Tellier'': The Madame's Party

1971 (May 1-4)

Drypoint and scraper on copper

365 x 495 mm.

2nd and last state.

Artist's proof on Rives wove paper, numbered ''E.A. IX/XV'' and stamped with a cachet imitating Picasso's signature.

L.117; B.1972.

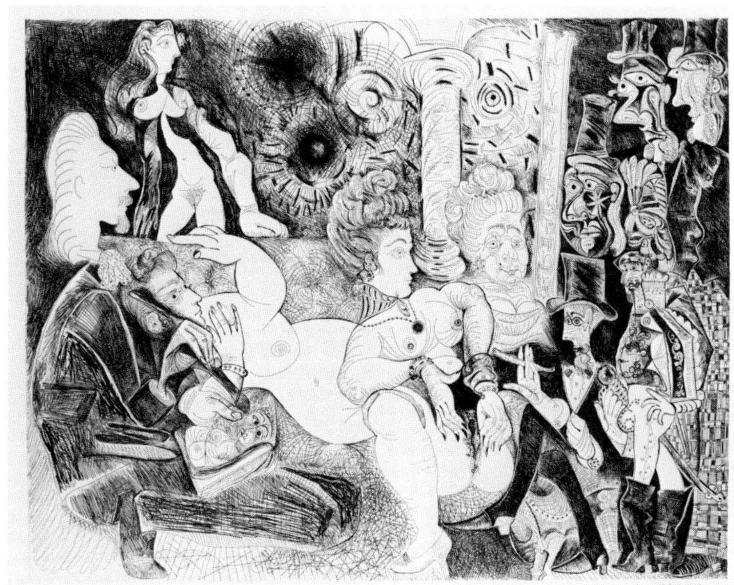

202.

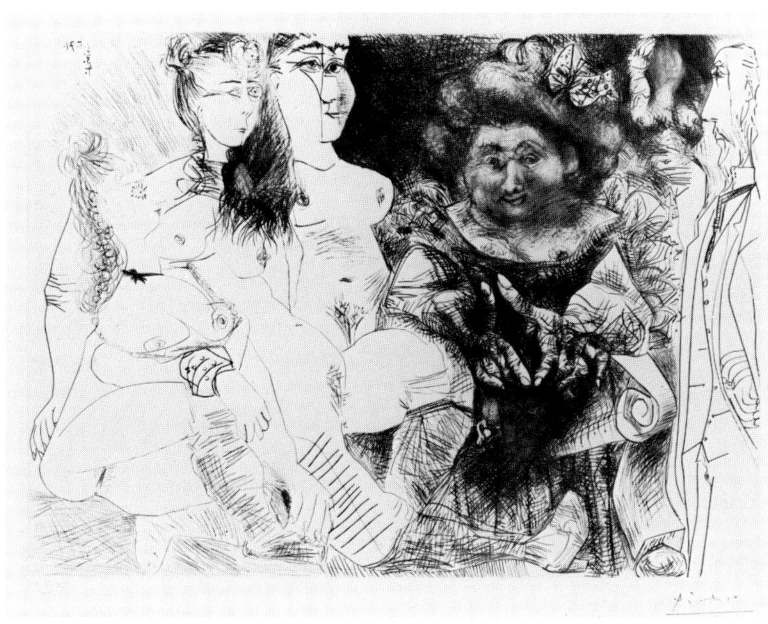

203.

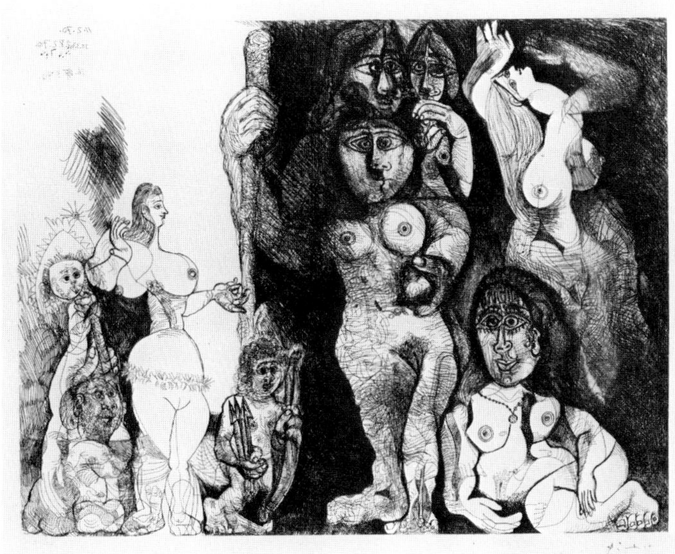

200.

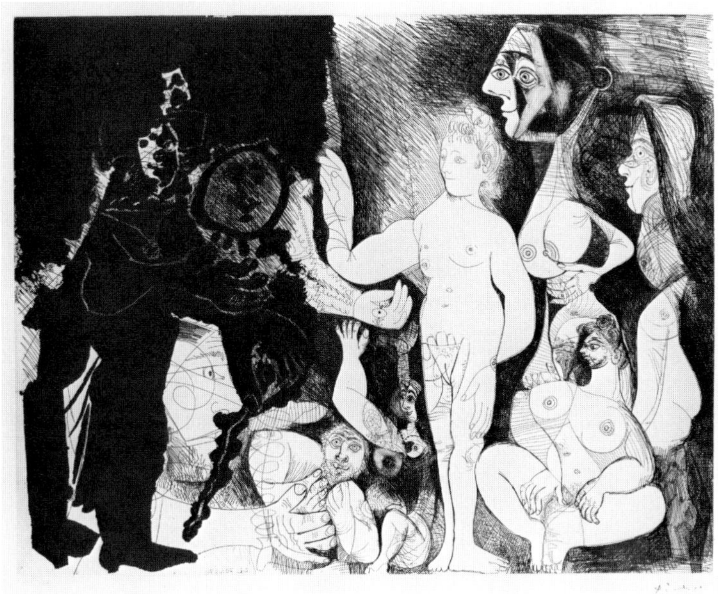

201.

200.
Le Théâtre de Picasso: Eros et les Femmes
Picasso's Theater: Eros and Women

1970 (February 11 and 28, March 3, 6, 30)

Etching and scraper on copper

500 x 635 mm.

9th and last state.

Artist's proof on Rives wove paper, numbered "E.A. VIII/XV" and stamped with a cachet imitating Picasso's signature.

L.13; B.1868.

201.
Le théâtre de Picasso: le prestidigitateur et les femmes
Picasso's Theater: the Magus and the Women

1970 (February 16, March 2 and 4)

Etching, drypoint, scraper and sugar-lift aquatint on copper

500 x 635 mm.

4th and last state.

Artist's proof on Rives wove paper, numbered "E.A. IX/XV" and stamped with a cachet imitating Picasso's signature.

L.15; B.1870.

202.

La Maison Tellier: la fête de la patronne
"La Maison Tellier": The Madame's Party

1970 (February 19 onwards)

Etching on copper

498 x 632 mm.

Unique state.

One of three trial proofs on Rives wove paper, pulled before the plate was bevelled and steelfaced, annotated bottom right in pencil by the printer "19.2.70" and "Etat I."

The copperplate (on exhibition) was cancelled in 1979.

L.16; B.1871.

Picasso worked for several days on this astounding etching, without wishing to observe the progression of his endeavours. He told Piero Crommelynck that he wanted no state proofs to be pulled. He went on working, allowing himself no possibility of "*repentirs*," never using his scraper until the plate began to show areas which were worked over so often that he could foretell the effect they would produce on the proof after the biting of the plate: those clear areas, for instance on one of the three globes of light. The only *repentirs* he could permit himself were the ones which are visible on the proof, for instance, the superimposed two brushes in the painter's hand. Piero Crommelynck said that "he (Picasso) had great fun with this plate." It is as if Picasso was attempting to break the world high jump record, having himself put the bar at an impossible height.

203.

La Maison Tellier: la fête de la patronne
"La Maison Tellier": The Madame's Party

1971 (May 1-4)

Drypoint and scraper on copper

365 x 495 mm.

2nd and last state.

Artist's proof on Rives wove paper, numbered "E.A. IX/XV" and stamped with a cachet imitating Picasso's signature.

L.117; B.1972.

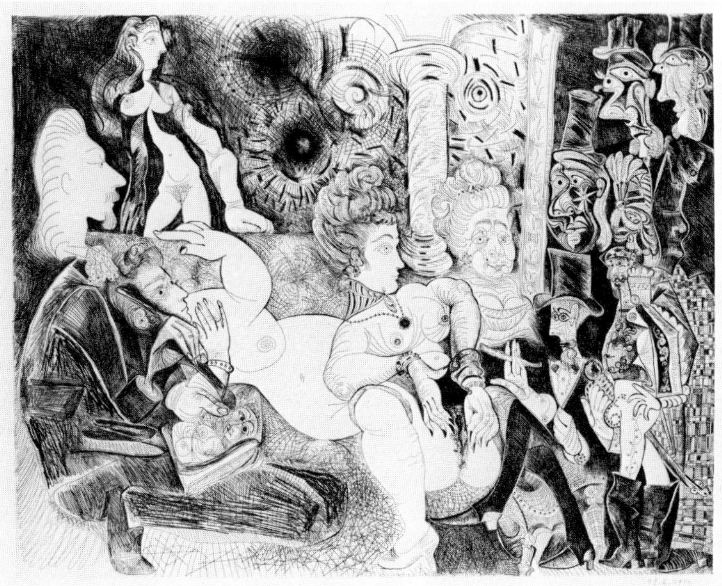

202.

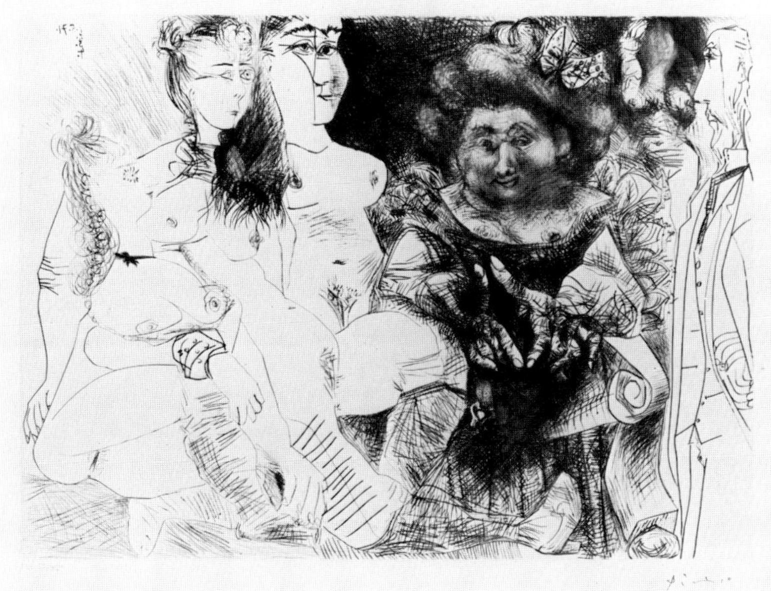

203.

204.
La Danse de Salomé
Salome Dancing Before Herod

1971 (June 6)

Etching on copper

365 x 495 mm.

Unique state.

Artist's proof on Rives wove paper, numbered "E.A. VIII/XV" and stamped with a cachet imitating Picasso's signature.

L.146; B.2000.

205.
Deux femmes et un masque
Two Women and a Mask

1972 (March 1 and 5)

Etching, drypoint, scraper and sugar-lift aquatint on copper

365 x 495 mm.

7th and last state.

Artist's proof on Rives wove paper, numbered "E.A. IX/XV" and stamped with a cachet imitating Picasso's signature.

L.155; B.2010.

Note
[1]*Maison close*: the institution, as institution it is, is a totally French phenomenon. It describes relatively precisely a house, which was not open to the public but only to regular clients and their guests, where men could gather in the atmosphere of an English gentleman's Club, surrounded by the "loving" care of the Madame of the House and her "girls." In English, the nearest equivalent is "whorehouse."

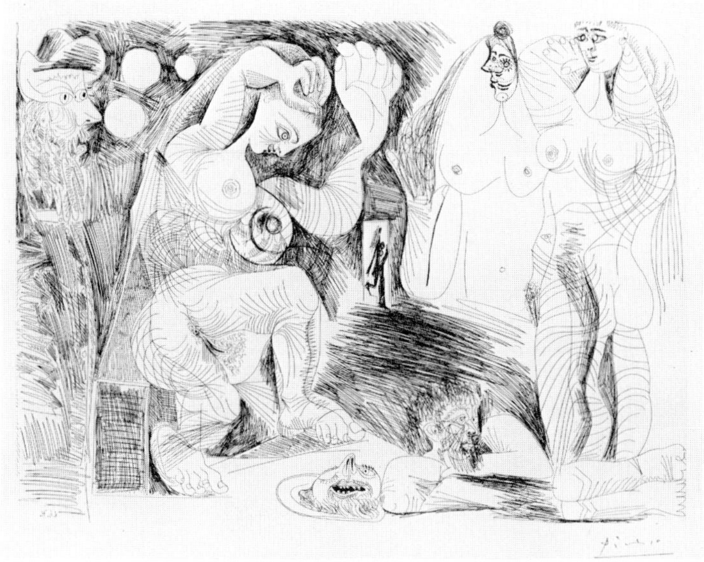

204.

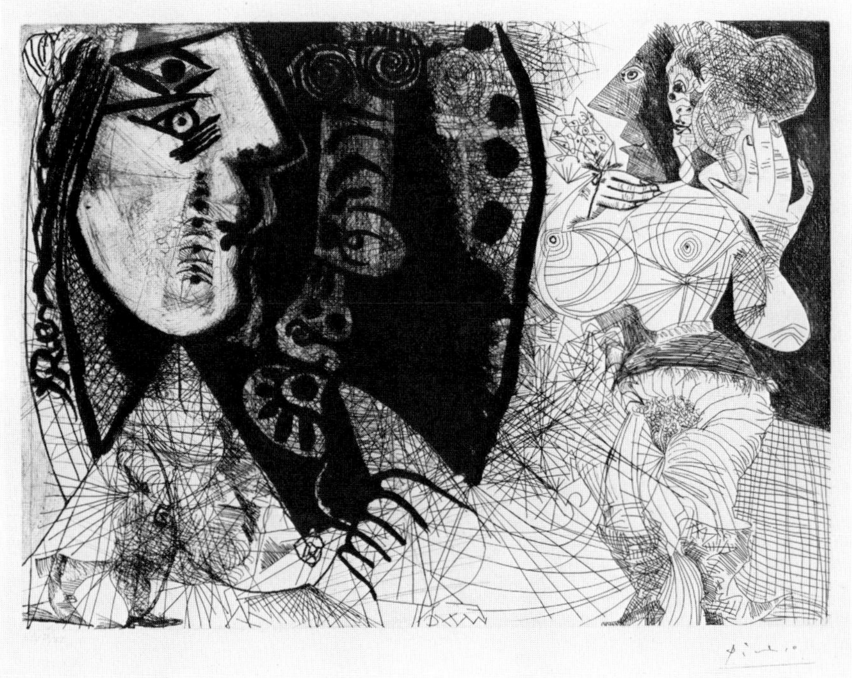

205.

Concordance of variant dates

Catalogue nos.	Geiser nos. and dates	Baer dates
3	10 : 1905	1906, spring
6	33 : 1912	1911, autumn
8	37 : 1914	1913
9	41 : 1914	1913, autumn
12	43 : 1914/1915	1915
13	45 : 1914/1915	1915
15	34 : 1912	1915
16b.	67 : 1922	1923
18	68 : 1922	1924
24	281 : 1932, December	1932, November 29
25	283 : 1932, December	1932, December 7
	Bloch nos. and dates	
	N.B.: For the lithographs: see Mourlot.	
54	288 : 1935	1935, March 23
55	291 : 1936	1936, October 21
57	343 : 1942	1936
59	298 : 1937, January 8	1937, January 8 and 9, June 7
60 - 64	1333 : 1937, July 2	1937, July 1
75	327 : 1940	1940, April 5
77	374 : 1945	1945, January 9
121	695 : 1952	1952, May 17
122	697 : 1952	1952, June 16
137	880 : 1959	beginning 1958
138 - 141	940 : 1959	1959, August 26
142 - 143	936 : 1959	1959, November 18
164 - 169	1094 : 1962	1962, February 7
170 - 176	1098 : 1962	1962, February 16
181	1190 : 1965	1965, February 25

I have only included the variant dates which are relevant to the present exhibition. For a complete table of all variant dates, see my forthcoming volumes and supplements to Geiser's catalogue raisonné.

Chronological Map

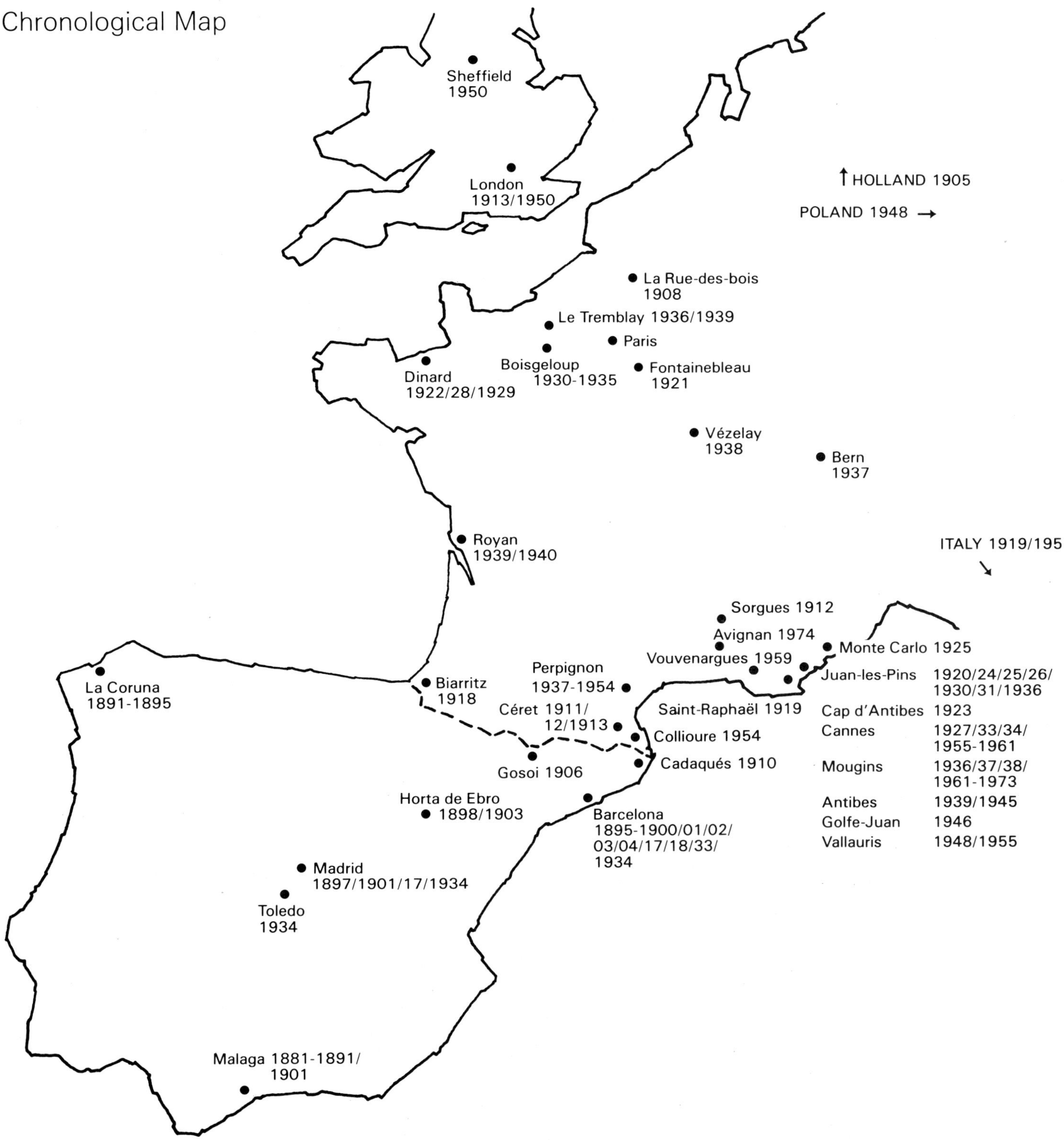

Chronology

Biography	Prints
1881 Born on October 25 in Malaga, Spain. His father, a painter, teaches drawing and is curator of the local museum.	
1891 Family moves to La Coruña. Studies painting and drawing under his father.	
1895 Family moves to Barcelona. Becomes student at the School of Fine Arts.	
1897 Paints *Science et charité,* second large academic work. Admitted to the Royal Academy of San Fernando in Madrid. This is the first time he is on his own. Leaves the Academy during the winter.	
1898 First visit to Horta de Ebro.	
1899 Begins to frequent the café, Els Quatre Gats, where he comes into contact with the Barcelona intelligentsia.	First etching: *El Zurdo.*
1900 Exhibition at Els Quatre Gats. First trip to Paris; stays for two months. Returns to Madrid.	
1901 February, the suicide of Casagemas in Paris. Picasso goes to Barcelona at the end of April, and in May, is in Paris, 130 ter, boulevard de Clichy, Casagemas' former studio. June; exhibition at Galeries Vollard. Meets the writer and poet Max Jacob.	
1902-1903 Returns to Barcelona. Back to Paris in October 1902, where he shares a room with Max Jacob. In Barcelona, in 1903, he creates the most important works of his ''Blue period'': *La Vie, La Celestine, The Blind Man's Meal.*	
1904 In the spring, leaves Catalonia indefinitely. In Paris, moves into the ''Bateau-Lavoir,'' 13, rue Ravignan. Meets Fernande Olivier, who becomes his mistress in 1905, probably after his summer trip to Holland.	September: *Le Repas frugal,* 30 impressions pulled by Auguste Delâtre.

Biography	Prints
1905 Exhibition at Galeries Serrurier in February, includes three etchings. Meets Gertrude and Leo Stein in Paris. Beginning of the ''Rose period.'' The Salon d'Automne of this year includes paintings by Cézanne, *Le Bain turc* by Ingres and gives rise to the ''scandal'' of the Fauves.	Makes 15 etchings and drypoints: only a few impressions are pulled. 13 of them, added to *Le Repas Frugal* will be used to make up *Les Saltimbanques* in 1913.
1906 Meets Henri Matisse who exhibits *La joie de vivre.* Meets André Derain. Spends summer with Fernande in Gosol, in the Spanish Pyrenees. Death of Cézanne. Works on *Chevaux au bain,* paints *Portrait of Gertrude Stein, Two Nudes, Seated Female Nude with Crossed Legs.*	Beginning of the year: *L'Abreuvoir,* drypoint to be included in *Les Saltimbanques.* First woodcut.
1907 In April-July, works on the painting *Les Demoiselles d'Avignon.* Begins to become closely interested in African sculpture. Meets the art dealer Daniel-Henri Kahnweiler during the summer. Meets Georges Braque through his friend Apollinaire in the autumn.	Picasso buys a small printing press. Death of the printer Auguste Delâtre.
1908 With Braque, first experimentations with Cubism. In November, banquet honoring Henri Rousseau at the Bateau-Lavoir. Paints *Three Women, The Dryad, Friendship.*	
1909 Spends spring and summer with Fernande in Spain at Horta de Ebro. First analytic cubist paintings. Moves to 11, boulevard de Clichy in the autumn. Sculpts pre-cubist bust of Fernande: *Head of a Woman.* Paintings include: *Bread and Fruit Dish on a Table, The Reservoir, Horta de Ebro.*	Makes two small engravings on celluloid and two copperplate drypoints.
1910 Spends summer in Cadaqués with Fernande and the Derains. In September, exhibits with Braque at the Galerie Thannhauser in Munich. Paintings: *Girl with a Mandolin, Portrait of Ambroise Vollard, Portrait of Wilhelm Uhde, Portrait of Daniel-Henri Kahnweiler.*	Cadaqués and Paris: illustrations for *Saint Matorel,* by Max Jacob, published by Kahnweiler in 1911.
1911 First American exhibition at Stieglitz's ''291.'' In Céret, spends last summer with Fernande. In the autumn meets Eva Gouel at the Steins. Paintings: *The Accordionist, Mandolin Player.*	Autumn: important drypoint: *Still Life with a Bottle of Marc,* published by Kahnweiler in 1912.

Biography	Prints
1912 Works exhibited in Moscow, Munich, Barcelona, London, Berlin and Cologne. National reputation established. Spends summer in Céret, Avignon and Sorgues with Eva and later with the Braques. Transition to synthetic cubism. First cubist collages with Braque. In October, moves to 242, boulevard Raspail with Eva. Sculpture: *Guitar.* Paintings: *Ma Jolie, Still Life with Chair Caning, The Aficionado.*	
1913 First major retrospective at Galerie Thannhauser, Munich. Eight works included in the "International Exhibition of Modern Art" at 69th Regiment Armory, New York. Spends almost the whole year in Céret; Juan Gris visits him there. New studio, 5bis, rue Schoelcher. May: death of his father in Barcelona. Paints in the autumn: *Femme aux seins dorés.*	Cubist prints. Vollard buys etchings and drypoints from 1904/05 and 1906 and publishes them in *Les Saltimbanques;* printer: Louis Fort. End of 1913 — beginning of 1914: illustrations for *Le siège de Jérusalem,* by Max Jacob.
1914-1915 War declared on August 2, 1914. Spends summer in Avignon with Eva. Spring 1915, Eva's health deteriorates. December: death of Eva. Sculpture: constructions and *The Glass of Absinth.*	Cubist prints. Autumn 1914: the naturalistic *Les Pommes.* 1915: more cubist prints. First aquatint.
1916 Beginning of Dada movement in Zurich. Contact with Diaghilev's *Ballets Russes.* Agrees to design decor and costumes for *Parade* (scenario by Cocteau, music by Satie). Moves to Montrouge in summer.	
1917 With Cocteau and the *Ballets Russes* in Rome. Meets Stravinsky and Bakst as well as his future wife, the dancer, Olga Koklova. Works on decor and costumes for *Parade.* Paints *Portrait of Olga in an Armchair.*	Engraves *Harlequin.*
1918-1919 In July, marries Olga Koklova. They honeymoon in Biarritz. His friend Apollinaire dies two days before the signing of the Armistice on November 11, 1918. Moves to 23, rue la Boétie. May-July 1919 in London with the *Ballets Russes.* Designs *Le tricorne.* Exhibits in October at the Galerie Paul Rosenberg in Paris. Works on *Pulcinella* (music by Stravinsky). 1919-1922: *Femmes géantes.*	Etches *Pierrot* for Max Jacob's *Le Phanérogame.* Drypoint portrait of Olga. First two lithographs.
1920 Kahnweiler returns to Paris after six years of exile in Switzerland. First performance of *Pulcinella.* Olga is pregnant. Spends summer in Juan-les-Pins.	

Biography	Prints
1921 Birth of his son Paulo in February. Summers in his villa in Fontainebleau with the family. Sale of Wilhelm Uhde's collection in May meets with success.	Series of lithographs and drypoints. *La Source.*
1922 Jacques Doucet purchases *Les Demoiselles d'Avignon.* Spends summer in Dinard with Olga and Paulo. Paints the Walter-Guillaume *Large Bather.*	Naturalistic drypoints. Etched illustrations for Pierre Reverdy's *Cravates de chanvre.*
1923-1924 Spends summer in Cap d'Antibes. Meets surrealist André Breton. Costumes and decor for *Mercure* (music by Satie, choreography by Massine. Contact with the surrealists. Spends summer of 1924, 1925 and 1926 in Juan-les-Pins. Paintings: *The Pipes of Pan, Portrait of Olga, Harlequins.*	**1923** Big drypoint of Olga. **1923-1925** Group of experimental prints. Explores theme of *Les Trois Grâces.*
1925 Visits Monte Carlo with Olga and Paulo. Death of Erik Satie. First important surrealist exhibition in Paris includes cubist works by Picasso. Paintings: *La danse, Le baiser.*	
1926 First issue of *Cahiers d'art,* begun by Christian Zervos, who becomes a lifelong friend. Twenty year retrospective at Galerie Paul Rosenberg. Collages: Two large *Guitars* (Musée Picasso, Paris). Paintings: *Painter and Model, The Milliner's Workshop.*	
1927 Meets Marie-Thérèse Walter. Spends summer in Cannes with Olga and Paulo.	Illustrations for *Le Chef-d'oeuvre inconnu* by Balzac (Louis Fort, printer). Begins to work with Louis Fort.
1928-1929 First appearance of the Minotaur in his painting. Works with the sculptor Julio Gonzalez. Spends both summers in Dinard. "Dinard period" *Bathers* in sculpture, drawings and paintings. Sculpture: metal constructions, *Woman in a Garden.* Paintings: *Nude in an Armchair, Bust of a Woman with Self-Portrait.*	Begins the illustrations for *La Tauromaquia* by Pepe Illo.
1930-1931 Several exhibitions in America. Spends both summers in Juan-les-Pins. In April 1931, major retrospective in London. Acquires the Château of Boisgeloup in 1930. Converts the stables into a studio. At Boisgeloup, he paints *The Lamp, Figures by the Sea.*	Marie-Thérèse becomes omnipresent in the intaglio prints. September 13, 1930: first etching. It will be among the prints later chosen by Picasso and given to Vollard for what becomes the *Suite Vollard* (100 prints, 1930-1937). September 1930-spring 1931: illustrations for Ovid's *Metamorphoses. Ovid* and *Le Chef-d'oeuvre inconnu* are published in autumn 1931.

Biography	Prints
1932 Almost the whole year in his Château de Boisgeloup. His major retrospective at Galerie George Petit, Paris, goes to Zurich Kunsthaus. Zervos publishes the first volume of his *Catalogue raisonné de Picasso.* 34 volumes will appear by 1978. Paintings: *Girl Before a Mirror, Woman with a Flower, The Dream, Bather with a Beach Ball.* 1931-1932: sculpts the monumental Boisgeloup heads of Marie-Thérèse.	In painting, sculpture and then in prints, theme of *Large* and *Small Bathers.*
1933 Summer holiday in Cannes and Barcelona with Olga and Paulo. Sculpts *Woman with a Vase,* eventually one of the bronze casts on his tomb at Vauvenargues.	Works extensively on intaglio prints. Between March and November makes 60 of the plates which will be chosen to be part of the *Suite Vollard* and also produces prints based on the Boisgeloup heads of Marie-Thérèse. In the beginning of the year, executes nearly 100 monotypes. Resumes work on the "sculptor and his model" series and the "rapes." In April, the Minotaur appears in his prints. It reappears in May and will remain until March 23, 1955. Works with Lacourière in the beginning of the year. Continues proofing his plates himself. Makes collage for the first issue of *Minotaure,* published by Tériade and Skira: four of the first Minotaur etchings reproduced.
1934 Summer: travels with Olga and Paulo in Spain. December 24: Marie-Thérèse finds out that she is pregnant and tells Picasso.	More etchings that will be part of the *Suite Vollard.* The Minotaur returns again in drawings and prints, and the theme of Marie-Thérèse as a woman bullfighter begins. First sugar-lift aquatint. Autumn: begins work in Lacourière's workshop. Produces the *Blind Minotaur.*
1935 June, Olga and Paulo leave Picasso and settle in Cannes. Picasso and Olga remain married, although divorce proceedings are begun. Rosenberg prepares an inventory of Picasso's works. September 5: birth of María de la Concepcíon, later called Maya. November: Sabartés comes back to Paris and begins to live in Picasso's apartment, Rue la Boétie. Picasso types his manuscripts. Describes end of the year as "the worst period of my life." Paints group of *Muses.*	*The Minotauromachia* (March 23) is printed at the end of the year: approximately 55 impressions are pulled. Never published as an edition.

Biography	Prints
1936 Meets the writer Paul Eluard; beginning of a long friendship. Has 32 works, dating from 1907-1929, included in the exhibition "Cubism and Abstract Art," Museum of Modern Art, New York, organized by Alfred Barr, Jr. Spends the month of April at Juan-les-Pins with Marie-Thérèse and Maya. Spanish Civil War breaks out in July. Because of his anti-Franco stance, the Republicans name him Director of the Prado Museum, Madrid. Summer in Mougins with several friends; once again meets photographer Dora Maar.	Makes 32 sugar-lift aquatints to illustrate Buffon's *Histoire naturelle.* In June, produces *Faune dévoilant une femme,* the most important print of the *Suite Vollard.* Provides illustrations for Paul Eluard's *La Barre d'appui* and *Les Yeux fertiles. The Minotauromachie* is reproduced in *Les Cahiers d'art.*
1937 With Dora Maar's help, finds new studio 7, rue des Grands Augustins. The Spanish Republican government invites Picasso to create a mural for the Spanish Pavilion in the Paris World's Fair. April 26: Germans bomb Guernica. Picasso chooses the bombing of this Basque village as the theme of his painting. Spanish Pavilion opened in July. Spends summer with Dora Maar in Mougins.	January: begins two etchings on the *Sueño y mentira de Franco.* Finishes the second in June. March: the three portraits of Vollard bring the number of prints in the *Suite Vollard* to 100. These 100 were printed by Lacourière before Vollard's death. July 1: *La Femme qui pleure.*
1938 Summer in Mougins with Dora Maar and the Eluards. Visits Zervos in Vézelay.	Makes the famous aquatint *Woman with a Tambourine.* Begins to work with Iliazd: illustrations for *Afat.* Works on other book illustrations as well.
1939 Death of Picasso's mother. The famous mural painting *Guernica* is exhibited in America, where it remains until its return to Spain in 1981. Death of editor Ambroise Vollard in July. Summers in Antibes with Dora Maar. August 1939: *Night Fishing in Antibes.* Second World War breaks out in September. 1939-1940 — travels between Royan and Paris.	Beginning of the year: spends three full months in Lacourière's workshop. Makes the seven portraits of Dora Maar, each in four or five colors on four or five copperplates. Begins project of a book of his manuscripts and color prints, which never was completed. First linocut in spring.
1940-1944 During the war in Royan and Paris. Writes a farcical play *Le Désir attrapé par la queue.* Works in his sculpture studio, Rue des Grands Augustins, Paris. Spring 1943: meets the painter Françoise Gilot. March 5, 1944: death of Max Jacob at Drancy. August 25, 1944: liberation of Paris. Sculptures: *Dora Maar's Head* (1941); *Man with a Sheep* (1944). Paintings: *The Charnel House* (1944-45).	Little graphic work in this period. First idea for *L'Homme au mouton* appears in unpublished print dated July 14, 1942. In 1942, Lacourière prints a copy of old plates on paper leftover from the *Suite Vollard.* He also prints *Le Femme au tambourin* and the seven color aquatints of Dora Maar.
1945-1946 May 7, 1945: Germany surrenders. Spends summer with Dora Maar in Antibes. In autumn, begins to live with Françoise Gilot. 1946: summers in Antibes and lives in Louis Fort's house in Golfe-Juan. Françoise is pregnant. Paints the mural *La Joie de vivre* for the Musée d'Antibes. July 27: death of Gertrude Stein.	Autumn: makes a few etchings in Antibes; Louis Fort pulls the proofs in Golfe-Juan. November 1945: begins to work in Mourlot's lithography workshop.

Biography	Prints
1947 Birth of Claude in May. June in Golfe-Juan with Françoise and Claude. Makes about 200 ceramics in Vallauris.	Continues working in Mourlot's workshop: *David and Bathsheba.* Illustrations for *Pismo, Dos Contes, Gongora.*
1948 Moves to Vallauris with Françoise. Attends Congress of Intellectuals for Peace in Wroclaw, Poland with Eluard. Exhibition of 149 ceramics at Maison de la Pensée Française in Paris.	Group of superb lithographs depicting Françoise wearing the Polish coat he brought back for her from Warsaw. 1948-49: illustrations for *Carmen, Corps perdu.*
1949 Birth of Paloma, Françoise's second child. Summer in Vallauria: works on ceramics. In autumn, more sculpture including *Pregnant Woman*.	May: *Venus and Cupid, after Cranach.* More lithographs including *La colombe de la paix* (poster for Peace Congress; reproduction of a drawing).
1950-1951 Lives in Vallauris almost continuously until autumn 1951. Short stay in Sheffield to attend the Second World Peace Congress. Receives the Lenin Peace Prize. Summer, 1951, takes apartment 7, rue Gay Lussac in Paris. Returns to Paris in autumn with family. February 1950, paints *Les Demoiselles des bords de la Seine, d'après Courbet.* Sculpture: the *She Goat, Girl Jumping Rope, Woman with Baby Carriage, Baboon and Young.*	Lithographs : *Colombes en vol.* Illustration for Iliazd: *La Maigre* by Adrian de Montluc.
1952 Transforms the old chapel in Vallauris into a temple of peace. Summer in Vallauris. Makes sculpture *The Crane.* Death of Eluard. Spends winter in Vallauris.	May 1952: *La Femme à la fenêtre* and in June, other large aquatints in Lacourière's workshop.
1953 Last Summer in Vallauris with Françoise. She leaves with the children in September. Meets his future wife Jacqueline Roque. Spends winter in Vallauris.	In Lacourière's workshop: *Crane de chèvre sur la table* (January). May 11: *Torse de femme.* Portraits of Françoise with Claude and Paloma in lithographs and etchings.
1954 Many drawings during the winter of 1953-54. Death of Matisse. Spends summer in Vallauris and Perpignan. In autumn, begins to live with Jacqueline. Portraits of Sylvette.	
1955 Death of Olga in February in Cannes. Lives in Vallauris until summer. Buys the villa La Californie in Cannes. Film ''Le Mystère Picasso'' by Clouzot. Retrospective at Musée des Arts Décoratifs, Paris.	*Les femmes d'Alger, d'après Delacroix. Portrait of Jacqueline.* Group of prints in September. Illustrations for Iliazd: *Chevaux de minuits*, by Roch Grey (1955-56). Begins to work on linocuts with Arnéra.

Biography	Prints
1956 Spends entire year in Cannes. Celebrates his 75th birthday. Protests against the Russian intervention in Hungary. From 1956 until his death creates numerous portraits of Jacqueline.	
1957 Paints the many versions of *Las Meninas, after Velasquez*, which will be given to the Muséo Picasso in Barcelona.	Louis Fort's press is set up in La Californie. Picasso makes the sugar-lift aquatints for *La Tauromaquia* by Pepe Illo.
1958 Stays in Cannes; buys the Château of Vauvenargues near Aix-en-Provence.	First published linocut: *Buste de femme, d'après Cranach le jeune* in five colors. Works for Iliazd: *Le Frère mendiant.*
1959-60 In Cannes and Vauvenargues both years. 1960: retrospective at the Tate Gallery, London. Begins work on sheet metal sculptures.	Linocuts: new technique. 1960: Frélaut pulls the trial proofs of a large group of plates which were brought back from Paris.
1961 Marries Jacqueline Roque in March. Moves into his new villa Notre-Dame-de-Vie in Mougins. Stays here until the end of his life.	Frèlaut pulls the impressions of the group of prints known as *La Caisse à remords* (edited 1981). Makes a few unpublished prints. Portrait of *Jacqueline as a Bride.*
1962 Exhibition: *Picasso, an American Tribute.*	Important linocuts: *Déjeuner sur l'herbe, d'après Manet*, heads of Jacqueline, *The Lamp.*
1963 Deaths of Braque and Cocteau.	The Crommelynck brothers settle in Mougins. Set up a fully equipped printmaking workshop. In autumn, Picasso once again begins to work on intaglio prints. Produces more than 100 versions of *The Painter and his Model* between 1963 and 1966.
1964 Numerous exhibitions: Toronto, Tokyo, etc.	Dabber-inked aquatints: *The Smokers.* "Rinsed" linocuts.
1965 In November, undergoes an operation in Paris, which was his last trip to Paris.	More works on the theme of the painter and his model. Discovered "solid varnish" to apply on aquatint-grained copperplates.
1966 Exhibition *Hommage à Picasso* held in Grand Palais and Petit Palais, Paris. Death of Breton.	Illustrations for *Le Cocu Magnifique* and for *El entierro del Conde de Orgaz.* Group of important intaglio prints. Death of Roger Lacourière.

Biography	Prints
1967 Evicted from his studio on the Rue des Grands Augustins. Exhibition of sculpture and ceramics at the Tate Gallery, London.	
1968 Death of Sabartés in February.	Makes the *Suite 347* which is exhibited at the end of the year at the Galerie Louise Leiris.
1969 Paints about 170 works during the year. His book *El entierro del Conde de Orgaz* is published.	
1970 Exhibition in the Palais des Papes, Avignon. Death of his friends Christian and Yvonne Zervos. 1970-1972: paintings from what is now called his ''Avignon period.''	Intensive work in 1970-71 and beginning of 1972 leads to the *Suite 156* published after his death; published at the same time: *Venus and Cupid* (1949) and *Portrait of Miss Angela Rosengart* (1966). All but four of the prints will be marked with a stamp reproducing Picasso's signature.
1971 His 90th birthday.	
1972 Exhibition *Picasso in the Collection of the Museum of Modern Art.* Exhibition of 172 recent drawings at Galerie Louise Leiris.	Makes his last two etchings.
1973 Following a brief illness, dies on April 8 in Mougins. Buried on the grounds of the Château of Vauvenargues. Exhibition in Palais des Papes, Avignon.	Exhibition of the last group of the *Suite 156* (with all the states) at the Galerie Louise Leiris, Paris.

Selected Bibliography

1. See list of abbreviations.

2. Graphic work

Geiser, Bernhard and Hans Bolliger, *L'Oeuvre gravé de Picasso,* 2 volumes, Lausanne, 1955 and 1966 (English ed., B. Geiser and H. Bolliger, *Picasso: Fifty-five Years of his Graphic Work,* New York, 1955; and Kurt Leonhard and H. Bolliger, *Pablo Picasso: Recent Etchings, Lithographs, and Linoleum Cuts,* New York, 1966).

Rau, Bernd, ed., *Pablo Picasso: Das Graphische Werk,* Stuttgart, 1974.

Horodisch, Abraham, *Pablo Picasso als Buchkünstler,* Frankfurt, 1957 (English ed., 1962).

Boeck, Wilhelm, *Picasso Linolschnitte,* Stuttgart, 1962 (English ed., *Picasso Linoleum Cuts,* New York, 1963).

Goeppert, Sebastian and Herma and Patrick Cramer, *Pablo Picasso. Catalogue raisonné des livres illustrés,* Genève, 1983.

Czwiklitzer, Christoph, *290 affiches de Pablo Picasso,* Paris, 1968 and 1970.

3. Other books

Sabartés, Jamie, *Picasso. Portraits et souvenirs,* Paris, 1946.

Blunt, Sir Anthony, *Picasso's Guernica,* New York and Toronto, 1969.

Schiff, Gert, ed., *Picasso in Perspective,* Englewood Cliffs, New Jersey, 1976.

Johnson, Una E., *Ambroise Vollard, éditeur,* New York, 1977.

Castleman, Riva, *Prints from Blocks, Gauguin to Now,* New York, 1983.

Cahiers d'Art, Paris. See esp.: v. X, no. 7-10, ''L'Oeuvre de Picasso de 1930-1935;'' v. XII, no. 6-7, ''Picasso photographe.''

Selected Exhibitions and Auctions

1932

1. Cambridge. Harvard Society for Contemporary Art, *Metamorphoses of P. Ovidius Naso: Drawings, Copper Plates, Etchings, Artist's Proofs by Pablo Ruiz Picasso.*
2. Zurich. Kunsthaus, *Picasso.*

1948

3. Amsterdam. Stedelijk Museum, *Picasso, 43 lithographieën 1945-1947.*
4. Hannover. Kestner-Gesellschaft, *Pablo Picasso. 52 Lithographien aus den Jahren 1945-1947.*

1949

5. Berlin. Haus am Waldsee, *Picasso. 52 Lithographien aus den Jahren 1945-1947.*

1952

6. *Pablo Picasso. Radierungen und Lithographien, 1905-1951* (traveled to Basel, Berlin, Essen, Freiburg, Hamburg, Munich, Nuremberg, and Stuttgart).

1953

7. Milan. Palazzo Reale, *Pablo Picasso.*

1954

8. Liège. Musée des Beaux-Arts, *Picasso. l'oeuvre graphique.*
9. Zurich. Kunsthaus, *Pablo Picasso. Das graphische Werk.*

1955

10. Geneva. Musée Rath, *L'oeuvre gravé de Pablo Picasso.*
11. Paris. Bibliothèque Nationale, *Picasso. L'oeuvre gravé.*

1956

12. Cannes. Galerie 65, *Picasso. Peintures, dessins, gravures rares.*
13. Cologne. Eigelsteintorburg, *Pablo Picasso. Suite Vollard. 100 Radierungen, 1930-1937* (traveled to Kunsthalle, Hamburg).
14. London. The Arts Council Gallery, *Picasso: Fifty Years of Graphic Art.*
15. Malmö. Museum, *Hommage à Picasso. Collection Bergengren.*
16. Oslo. Kunstnerns Hus, *Picasso. Malerier, Tegninger, Grafikk, Skulptur, Keramik.*

1957

17. Berlin. Kupferstichkabinett, *Picasso. Das graphische Werk.*
18. Japan. Exposition itinérante, *Picasso. L'oeuvre gravé, 1930-1956.*
19. Copenhagen. Frederiksberg Radhus, *Picasso. Collection Bergengren.*

1958

20. Aukland, New Zealand. City Art Gallery, *Picasso: An Exhibition of Lithographs and Aquatints, 1945-1957.*
21. Philadelphia. Museum of Art, *Picasso: A Loan Exhibition of his Paintings, Drawings, Sculpture, Ceramics, Prints and Illustrated Books.*

1959

22. Cincinnati. Art Museum, *Picasso: Lithographs since 1945.*
23. Paris. Galerie Louise Leiris, *50 ans d'Edition de D. H. Kahnweiler, 1909-1959.*

1960

24. London. Redfern Gallery, *Picasso.*
25. Malmö. Museum, *Picasso. Ny grafik.*
26. Mulhouse. Musée des Beaux-Arts, *Picasso. Oeuvre gravé.*
27. Nice. Bibliothèque municipale, *Picasso. Oeuvre gravé.*
28. Wien. Albertina, *Pablo Picasso. Linolschnitte.*

1961

29. Boston. Museum of Fine Arts, *The Artist and the Book, 1860-1960, in Western Europe and the United States.*
30. Bremen. Kunsthalle, *Picasso.*
31. Haifa. Musée d'Art Moderne, *L'oeuvre gravé de Picasso.*
32. Madrid. Museo Arte Contemporaneo, *Picasso.*
33. Mexico City. Universidad Nacional, *Picasso grabador.*
34. Tokyo. Musée national d'Art occidental, *Picasso. L'oeuvre gravé.*

1961/1962

35. Berkeley. University, *Picasso: Graphics from the Mr. and Mrs. Fred Grunwald Collection.*

1962

36. Lyon. Musée des Beaux-Arts, *Picasso. Gravures, céramiques.*
37. Milan. Palazzo di Brera, *Picasso. Incisioni su linoleum e ''Tauromaquia.''*

1963

38. Bern. Kornfield & Klipstein, *La Tauromaquia, Francisco de Goya, 1815 - Picasso, 1959, und verandte Stierkamfdarstellungen beider Künstler.*
39. Geneva. Musée de l'Athénée, *Picasso.*

1964

40. Auckland, New Zealand. City Art Gallery, *Picasso: 102 Linocuts.*
41. Berlin. Galerie Nierendorf, *Picasso. Graphik.*
42. Bern. Kornfeld & Klipstein, *Picasso. Graphik und illustrierte Bücher, Sammlung Oscar Stern,* Auktion 113, 30 Mai 1964.
43. Frankfurt a.M., Frankfurter Kunstverein, *Stierkampf: Francisco de Goya, Pablo Picasso, August Puig.*
44. Karlsruhe. Badischer Kunstverein, *Pablo Picasso. Radierungen und Lithographien — Henri Laurens. Skulpturen, Radierungen, Lithographien.*
45. Paris. Galerie Heinz Berggruen, *Picasso. 60 ans de gravures.*
46. Paris. Galerie Louise Leiris, *Picasso. 45 gravures sur linoléum 1958-1960.*
47. Saint-Etiennen-du-Rouvray, *''L'Itinéraire de Picasso'' et l'oeuvre gravé 1924-1964.*

1965

48. Bern. Gutekunst & Klipstein. *Picasso. Eaux-fortes — Lithographies 1905-1947.*
49. Prague. Galerie Vincence Kramaere, *Picasso.*
50. St. Gall. Kunstmuseum, *Picsaso. Graphik. 1904-1965.*

1966

51. Dresden. Kupferstichkabinett, *Picasso. Graphik.*
52. Los Angeles. County Museum of Art, *Picasso: Sixty Years of Graphic Works.*
53. Paris. Bibliothèque Nationale, *Pablo Picasso. Gravures.*
54. Tel-Aviv. Musée d'Art, Pavillon Helena Rubinstein, *Picasso.*

1966/1967

55. Bremen. Kunsthalle, *Pablo Picasso. Druckgraphik aus dem besitz der Kunsthalle Bremen.*

1968/1969

56. Augsburg. Holbeinhaus, *Picasso — Graphik.*
57. Paris. Galerie Louise Leiris, *Picasso. 347 gravures 16.3 - 5.10.1968.*

1969

58. Berlin. Akademie der Künste, *Pablo Picasso. 347 Graphische Blätter aus dem Jahr 1968.*
59. Bern. Kornfeld & Klipstein, *Graphik von Pablo Picasso,* Auktion 133, 13 Juni 1969.

1970

60. Munich. Haus der Kunst, *Picasso. Graphik von 1904 bis 1968.*
61. New York. Museum of Modern Art, *Picasso: Master Printmaker.*
62. Stuttgart. Wurttembergischer Kunstverein, *347 x Picasso. Graphische Blätter aus dem Jahr 1968.*

1971

63. Paris. Galerie Berggruen, *Hommage à Picasso, 90 gravures.*

1972

64. Bern. Gottfried-Keller-Stiftung, *Pablo Picasso. Druckgraphik.*

1973

65. Bern. Kornfeld & Klipstein, *Graphik von Pablo Picasso,* Auktion 148, 21 Juni 1973.

66. Paris. Galerie Louise Leiris, *Picasso. 156 gravures récentes.*

1976

67. Paris. Musée d'Art Moderne de la Ville de Paris, *La Rencontré Iliazd — Picasso.*

1978

68. Barcelona. Galerie Sala Gaspar, *Els 156 darrers gravats originals.*

1979

69. Paris. Musée d'Art Moderne de la Ville de Paris, *L'atelier Lacourière — Frélaut 1929-1974.*

1979/1980

70. Paris. Grand Palais, *Picasso. Oeuvres reçues en paiement des droits de succession.*

1980

71. Madrid. Centro de promocion de las artes plasticas e investigacion de nuevas formas expresivas, *Picasso. Obra Grafica Original 1930-1971.*

72. New York. Museum of Modern Art, *Pablo Picasso: A Retrospective.*

1981

73. Arles. Exposition de *linogravures de Picasso.*

74. Basel. Kunstmuseum, Gottfried-Keller-Stiftung, *Schenkung Georges Bloch.*

75. Ingelheim am Rhein, *Pablo Picasso. Peintre, graveur, sculpteur, ceramiste, poète.*

76. London. Arts Council of Great Britain, *Picasso Graphics.*

77. Santa Barbara. University Art Museum, University of California, *The Cubist Print* (traveled to the National Gallery of Art, Washington D.C. and the Toledo Museum of Art).

78. Tokyo. Musée des Arts d'Isetan, *Picasso. 1881-1973.*

1982

79. Bern. Galerie Kornfeld, *Pablo Picasso. Graphische Werke 1904-1972.*

80. Paris. Centre culturel du Marais, *Picasso. La pièce à Musique de Mougins.*

81. Paris. Palais de Tokyo, *L'atelier du sculpteur* (préfiguration Musée Picasso, Paris).

1983

82. London. The Tate Gallery, *The Essential Cubism: Braque, Picasso and their Friends.*

83. Paris. La Bouguinerie de l'Institut, *Pablo Picasso. Estampes diverses.*